Seeing Things as They Are

VERITAS
Series Introduction

"... the truth will set you free" (John 8:32)

In much contemporary discourse, Pilate's question has been taken to mark the absolute boundary of human thought. Beyond this boundary, it is often suggested, is an intellectual hinterland into which we must not venture. This terrain is an agnosticism of thought: because truth cannot be possessed, it must not be spoken. Thus, it is argued that the defenders of "truth" in our day are often traffickers in ideology, merchants of counterfeits, or anti-liberal. They are, because it is somewhat taken for granted that Nietzsche's word is final: truth is the domain of tyranny.

Is this indeed the case, or might another vision of truth offer itself? The ancient Greeks named the love of wisdom as *philia*, or friendship. The one who would become wise, they argued, would be a "friend of truth." For both philosophy and theology might be conceived as schools in the friendship of truth, as a kind of relation. For like friendship, truth is as much discovered as it is made. If truth is then so elusive, if its domain is *terra incognita*, perhaps this is because it arrives to us—unannounced—as gift, as a person, and not some thing.

The aim of the Veritas book series is to publish incisive and original current scholarly work that inhabits "the between" and "the beyond" of theology and philosophy. These volumes will all share a common aspiration to transcend the institutional divorce in which these two disciplines often find themselves, and to engage questions of pressing concern to both philosophers and theologians in such a way as to reinvigorate both disciplines with a kind of interdisciplinary desire, often so absent in contemporary academe. In a word, these volumes represent collective efforts in the befriending of truth, doing so beyond the simulacra of pretend tolerance, the violent, yet insipid reasoning of liberalism that asks with Pilate, "What is truth?"—expecting a consensus of non-commitment; one that encourages the commodification of the mind, now sedated by the civil service of career, ministered by the frightened patrons of position.

The series will therefore consist of two "wings": (1) original monographs; and (2) essay collections on a range of topics in theology and philosophy. The latter will principally be the products of the annual conferences of the Centre of Theology and Philosophy (www.theologyphilosophycentre .co.uk).

Conor Cunningham and Eric Austin Lee, *Series editors*

Seeing Things as They Are

G. K. Chesterton and the Drama of Meaning

DUNCAN REYBURN

CASCADE *Books* · Eugene, Oregon

SEEING THINGS AS THEY ARE
G. K. Chesterton and the Drama of Meaning

Veritas 18

Cascade Books
An Imprint of Wipf and Stock Publishers
199 W. 8th Ave., Suite 3
Eugene, OR 97401

www.wipfandstock.com

PAPERBACK ISBN: 978-1-4982-3188-6
HARDCOVER ISBN: 978-1-4982-3190-9
EBOOK ISBN: 978-1-4982-3189-3

Cataloguing-in-Publication data:

Names: Reyburn, Duncan.

Title: Seeing things as they are : G. K. Chesterton and the drama of meaning / Duncan Reyburn.

Description: Eugene, OR: Cascade Books, 2016 | Series: Veritas 18 | Includes bibliographical references and index.

Identifiers: ISBN 978-1-4982-3188-6 (paperback) | ISBN 978-1-4982-3190-9 (hardcover) | ISBN 978-1-4982-3189-3 (ebook)

Subjects: LCSH: 1. Chesterton, G. K. (Gilbert Keith), 1874–1936—Religion. 2. Hermeneutics. I. Series. II. Title.

Classification: PR4453.C4 R29 2016 (print) | PR4453.C4 (ebook)

Manufactured in the U.S.A.   AUGUST 17, 2016

For Linda and Isla

"For now we see through a glass, darkly; but then face to face: now I know in part; but then shall I know even as also I am known."

—1 Corinthians 13:12, KJV

"We shall not cease from exploration
And the end of all our exploring
Will be to arrive where we started
And know the place for the first time"

—T. S. Eliot, *Little Gidding*

"Now, there is a law written in the darkest of the Books of Life, and it is this: If you look at a thing nine hundred and ninety-nine times, you are perfectly safe; if you look at it the thousandth time, you are in frightful danger of seeing it for the first time."

—Gilbert Keith Chesterton, *The Napoleon of Nottinghill*

Contents

Preface and Acknowledgements

IN THIS BOOK, I set up an unexpected marriage between the work of G. K. Chesterton and philosophical hermeneutics to answer this question: *What can we learn from Chesterton about navigating and participating in the conditions and coordinates of interpretive understanding?* Put more succinctly: *What, in Chesterton's view, is required for us to perceive things clearly, as they are?*

The following answer to this question is certainly not the first word on Chesterton and it will not be the last. Chesterton himself suggests that "[i]t may, perhaps, be wondered whether one could possibly say a worse thing of anybody than that he had said 'the last word' on a subject. A man who says the last word on a subject ought to be killed. He is a murderer; he has slain a topic."[1] Maybe "one crime that cannot be forgiven among free men" is the crime of "[saying] the last word."[2] Against any tendency to end dialogue, "[t]he best kind of critic" instead "draws attention not to the finality of a thing, but to its infinity. Instead of closing a question, he opens a hundred."[3] This is the aim of all philosophical hermeneutics, which finds that meaning is superabundant, excessive, and generative.

This surplus of meaning is evidenced in great deal of Chesterton scholarship. A range of biographies see intersections between Chesterton's life and his writings. Particularly worthy of mention are those by W. R. Titterton (1936), Maisie Ward (1945, 1952), Alzina Stone Dale (1982), Michael Ffinch (1986), Joseph Pearce (1996), Ian Ker (2010), and Denis J. Conlon (2015). Moreover, a number of other contributions are worthy of a mention for focusing more on Chesterton's philosophy and theology than on his life. They are (in chronological order): *The Laughing Prophet: The Seven Virtues of G. K. Chesterton* (1937) by Emile Cammaerts, *G. K. Chesterton* (1938) by Maurice Evans, *The Wild Knight of Battersea: G. K. Chesterton* (1945) by

1. Ward, *Return to Chesterton*, 2.

2. Chesterton, *Illustrated London News,* March 11, 1911.

3. Ward, *Return to Chesterton*, 2.

F. A. Lea, *Paradox in Chesterton* (1947) by Hugh Kenner, *The Mind of Chesterton* (1970) by Christopher Hollis, *The Novels of G. K. Chesterton* (1975) by Ian Boyd, *G. K. Chesterton: Radical Populist* (1977) by Margaret Canovan, *Chesterton and the Edwardian Cultural Crisis* (1984) by John D. Coates, *Chesterton: Seer of Science* (1986) by Stanley Jaki, *G. K.'s Weekly: An Appraisal* (1990) by Brocard Sewel, *Thinkers of Our Time: G. K. Chesterton* (1991) by Ian Crowther, *G. K. Chesterton: Philosopher without Portfolio* (1988) by Quentin Lauer, *The Size of Chesterton's Catholicism* (1998) by David Fagerberg, *Chesterton and Evil* (2004) by Mark Knight, *G. K. Chesterton: Thinking Backward, Looking Forward* (2006) by Stephen R. L. Clark, *The Romance of Orthodoxy: The Making of G. K. C, 1874–1908* (2006) by William Oddie, *The Historical Imagination of G. K. Chesterton: Locality, Patriotism, and Nationalism* (2009) by Joseph McCleary, *Chesterton and Tolkien as Theologians* (2009) by Alison Milbank, *Chesterton, Theologian* (2009) by Aidan Nichols, *Christianity, Patriotism and Nationhood: The England of G. K. Chesterton* (2009) by Julia Stapleton (whose edited editions of Chesterton's *Daily News* articles (2012) are also invaluable), *G. K. Chesterton: A Biography* by Ian Ker (2010), *The Rhetoric of Redemption: Chesterton, Ethical Criticism, and the Common Man* (2012) by Alan Blackstock, and *Chesterton and the Jews* (2015) by Ann Farmer. Denis J. Conlon's two edited collections of critical writings on Chesterton are also invaluable.

Many of the above studies are brilliant and important contributions to Chesterton scholarship, and yet the central question of the uniqueness of Chesterton's hermeneutic—a question that seems to me to be an implicit and vital subtext in every study on Chesterton to date—has hitherto not been directly and comprehensively addressed. Like every difficult "question . . . worth asking," this question leaves "room for reasonable error and human diversity."[4] And, given the volume of Chesterton's output, whatever is included must necessarily imply what has been excluded.

However, this does not mean that boundaries are absent from this engagement with Chesterton. "Narrowness" is always essential to human perception and discovery.[5] Limits are the essence of freedom. Recognizing with Chesterton the value of restrictions, my goal here is to take what is hidden, implied, and fundamental in Chesterton's writings regarding the way we ought to apprehend the world, and make it as plain as I can. Like a philosophical detective, I investigate as many angles as possible to uncover and understand the multifaceted horizon that grounds Chesterton's remarkable interpretive awareness.

4. Chesterton, *Illustrated London News*, January 5, 1907.
5. Chesterton, *Collected Works, Volume 4*, 178.

This investigation is outlined in the seven chapters of this book, each of which builds on the one before it to gradually form a picture of Chesterton's commitment to what I have called the *drama of meaning*. After a detailed introduction to the subject at hand, every chapter traverses an important facet of his hermeneutic, beginning with historical and contextual considerations, before moving onto the foundation, task, and tools of his hermeneutic, as well as a discussion of the hermeneutic event in his work. The book concludes with an account of the gift of Chestertonian mediation, which touches on a number of the themes covered in the book.

Throughout my time researching Chesterton, I have found myself amidst some remarkable people who have stood alongside me, encouraged me, offered critique, and even, often with good reason, distracted me from time to time. You know who you are. In particular, though, I want to acknowledge the following people. Thank you, Amanda du Preez, Danie Goosen, Alison Milbank, Christopher Ben Simpson, Roberto Sirvent, Jeanne van Eeden, and Stella Viljoen—all of you, in different ways, cleared the way to make the present book possible. I am also grateful to the University of Pretoria for financially supporting this project, and to my colleagues and students for allowing me the space I needed to write. Fr. Jerome Bertram and the volunteers at the Chesterton Library in the Oxford Oratory—thank you for your hospitality and help. Thank you, too, Louise Mabille, for going through the original draft and for offering helpful critique and encouragement. Thank you, Lindsay Reyburn, for help with proofreading. And thank you, Robin Parry and the team at Wipf & Stock, for believing in this and in me, and for making the invisible visible.

Then, many thanks are owed to my family and extended family for unfailing support. I especially want to thank my parents, Lindsay and Yvonne, for more things than I can possibly name, but mostly for being the first people to love me and for modeling for me a sense of holy wonder. And, finally, immeasurable thanks to my wife Linda and my daughter Isla, who teach me every day to see the world anew, and who remind me that redemption is a sacrament experienced through the extraordinariness of an ordinary life.

1

Introduction

Although G. K. Chesterton (1874–1936) died many years ago, many people still consider him a spokesman for sanity wherever fads, fickleness, and unreason abound. And he remains an advocate for wholeness in a mysterious world of philosophical fragments and linguistic slippages. Amidst an overwhelming deluge of opinions, a consistent call may still be discerned in his work: it is an exuberant, urgent call for the reader to wake up from a world enveloped in sleep, custom, and nightmare.[1] As a participant in the democracy of the dead, he haunts the world, not with dread or fear, but with analogies, paradoxes, humor, and stories. It is by his decisive commitment to joy rather than anxiety or radical indecision that he disturbs our slumber of habit.

In Chesterton's view, whatever sacred spectacles we choose to look through, we need to be and stay alert.[2] We should refuse to "let the eye [of our understanding] rest."[3] Instead, we must "exercise the eye until it learns to see the startling facts that run across the landscape as plain as a painted fence"; we need to take up the call to "be ocular athletes."[4] As the metaphor implies, such ocular athleticism would seem to require at least some training. The idea of taking anything at face value must be radically called into question.

---

1. Chesterton, *A Miscellany of Men,* 29; Ward, *Gilbert Keith Chesterton,* 137.
2. Chesterton, *Tremendous Trifles,* 5.
3. Ibid., v-vi.
4. Ibid.

Chesterton persistently encourages us to find a clear view of things.[5] This is so important because the world is almost always "in a permanent danger of being misjudged" or overlooked by us given the specific limitations of our perceptual awareness.[6] We are all prone to "not seeing things as they are."[7] Still, as straightforward as it may seem that we should endeavor to have a clearer perception of things, a few important questions must be asked: How is it possible to achieve what Chesterton would regard as a suitable level of perceptual perspicacity? What, in his mind, is required for us to be competent ocular athletes? What does it even mean to "see things as they are"?[8] Is such a thing even possible? Such questions are at the heart of this book, which aims to outline what Chesterton can teach us about reading, interpreting, and participating in the drama of meaning as it unfolds before us in words and in the world.

As the above already implies, I plan here to consider Chesterton's work in the light of philosophical hermeneutics, which is the intellectual discipline that seeks to interrogate and appreciate the conditions and coordinates of (the possibility of) interpretive understanding. I plan to do this while keeping in mind the basic hermeneutic assumption that being—our being as ourselves, our being with other beings, and our being as participating in Being—is always mediated by language, which is a sacrament of this participation. To be is to be unequivocally immersed in language and a world of presences and absences, revelations and concealments, realities and resemblances. Finding meaning—understanding and interpreting—must therefore involve reflecting back on that immersion without assuming any sort of naïvely oblivious "hermeneutics of immediacy."[9]

Philosophical hermeneutics is particularly associated with the ideas introduced by Hans-Georg Gadamer (1900–2002) in his masterwork *Truth and Method,* which deals with the elements of a philosophical hermeneutics. Broadly speaking, philosophical hermeneutics has a threefold aim: firstly, it seeks to understand what any given text means or could mean, and thus considers the philosophical rather than purely methodological parameters of the interpretive experience; secondly, it contemplates the relationships between author, text, reader, and world, and especially tries to navigate how each one of these can or should be emphasized or downplayed in the process of interpretation; then, thirdly, it aims to further question the integration

5. Milbank, *Chesterton and Tolkien as Theologians,* xiii.

6. Chesterton, *The Defendant,* 4–5.

7. Chesterton, *Collected Works, Volume 1,* 68.

8. Chesterton, *Selected Works,* 974; Milbank, *Chesterton and Tolkien as Theologians,* 47.

9. Smith, *The Fall of Interpretation,* 4.

of an interpreted text into life. It builds upon the existential assumption that we are all perpetually in a process of reading and translating the world around us into personal, relatable terms, as well as negotiating its meanings; we are always considering not just what things mean in general, but what they mean for us. Thus, philosophical hermeneutics considers factors such as the hermeneutic circle, whereby meaning is always understood through a dynamic dance between part and whole—also expressed sometimes as the idea that understanding is preceded by an anticipatory structure and confronted via various conscious and unconscious presuppositions. It also incorporates the notion of the hermeneutic spiral, which sees thought turn back to look at itself in the process of deepening experiential understanding.

Hermeneutics takes into account the part played by dialectic in developing our outlooks, as well as the ways in which dialectic (as the mediation of otherness into the same) may fail us when adopted as a strict adherence to the principle of creating a synthesis from antithetical components. Other factors are also important, such as our current horizons of understanding and our attitudes, which are guided by such things as authority and tradition.[10] However, these aforementioned hermeneutic considerations are rooted in a very particular tradition of Continental Philosophy that, it is quite safe to say, had nothing to do with the development of Chesterton's thinking. Chesterton was simply unaware of the developments in hermeneutic philosophy of thinkers like Friedrich Schleiermacher (1768–1834) and Wilhelm Dilthey (1833–1911), and also had no knowledge of the work of his distant contemporary Martin Heidegger (1889–1976). Gadamer was thirty-six when Chesterton died, and still twenty-four years away from seeing *Truth and Method* completed. Most obviously, the hermeneutic tradition before Chesterton's time was distinctly German and Chesterton felt no real compulsion to explore that nation's discourses at length.

Nevertheless, if philosophical hermeneutics encourages us, as Terry Eagleton contends, "to be suspicious of the glaringly self-evident,"[11] then perhaps it is fair to suggest that Chesterton may be considered something of a hermeneutic philosopher, albeit one whose suspicion of the self-evident included a strong trend towards a positive astonishment at the non-self-evident existence of everything. Chesterton unremittingly defied and redefined the supposed limits of the apparently obvious. He sought meaning as a multifaceted jewel to be admired from every angle.[12] And his writings consistently demonstrate a profound interpretive awareness in its

10. See Gadamer, *Truth and Method*.

11. Eagleton, *After Theory*, 53.

12. Lauer, *G. K. Chesterton*, 13.

circumambulation of both interpretation and application in the pursuit of understanding. This is true regarding his approach to his own work, as well as his reading of the work of others. Thus, inasmuch as he is thought of as a writer, it is reasonable to also regard him as a reader in the hermeneutic sense of the word: he demonstrates a constant and self-critical process of engaging with and elucidating texts. In fact, I think that understanding him as a reader in this way allows for better understanding him as a writer and communicator.

Reading was often as much a physical act as it was an intellectual one for Chesterton—a fact that is explored much more fully in the pages that follow. Digby d'Avigdor recalls Chesterton as a boy at St. Paul's: "I always have a vision of him wandering around the corridors with one of his disreputable books. His Greek primer all dog-eared, tattered, covered with drawings of goblins, all over the text as well as in the margins. The masters would say, 'Chesterton, Chesterton, have you *no* care for books?'"[13] Of the books that Chesterton covered with his drawings, perhaps none is more famous than his copy of T. K. Arnold's *A Practical Introduction to Latin Prose, Part II*, which is housed at the Chesterton Library at the Oxford Oratory today. That book is described in Maisie Ward's biography as having been "withdrawn from him . . . because it was drawn all over with devils."[14] This is not precisely true, though; while the book is certainly covered with drawings, not a single one is of a devil. There are many swords and swordsmen, horses, faces, and animals—bats, dragons, a dog, and a fish—but no devils. Chesterton reserved his drawings of devils for other pages, such as those of his *Half-Hours in Hades: An Elementary Handbook of Demonology*.[15]

Father John O'Connor, the man after whom Chesterton modeled his beloved Father Brown, remarked that after Chesterton had read a book, that book would be beyond useful to anyone else: "Most of his books, as and when he read, had gone through every indignity a book may suffer and live. He turned it inside out, dog-eared it, pencilled it, sat on it, took it to bed and rolled on it, and got up again and spilled tea on it—if he were sufficiently interested."[16] Father O'Connor said that when Chesterton was done reading, the object of his attention would have a "refuted look" about it.[17] There is certainly some truth in this. What remains of Chesterton's personal library certainly contains books that he maltreated, including the book he

13. Ward, *Return to Chesterton*, 13.
14. Ward, *Gilbert Keith Chesterton*, 107.
15. Chesterton, *The Coloured Lands*, 66–83.
16. Ward, *Gilbert Keith Chesterton*, 219.
17. Ibid.

was reading when he died—a very badly damaged 1936 Penguin paperback reprint of Ernest Bramah's *The Wallet of Kai Lung* (1900), which was found in one of his pockets.[18]

If we consider Father O'Connor's comments symbolically, rather than purely literally, they take on new meaning: Chesterton, whether he destroyed books or not, was a highly engaged reader. Whether books prompted him to doodle over the text or write remarks in the margins or jot down an idea for a poem on the endsheet, he was always awake to the adventure of words on a page and the world they disclosed. Even if he let his mind wander, as is indicated by so many scribbles inside his books, he was nonetheless still very involved in the process of reading. Reading, for him, was a kind of communion as much as it was a communication, a dwelling with the text rather than a mere looking at the text. It was, like so many aspects of the created order, a sacramental activity that was perpetually reminding him of the real presence of God in the world.[19]

Chesterton's role as a reader is further emblematized by one of his tasks at Fisher-Unwin, the publishing house that he worked at before becoming a fulltime journalist. There he had to duplicate the publicity blurbs that he had written by using a cyclostyle—a messy machine that was not well suited to his lack of coordination. He always finished the job covered in ink, his untidy attire rendered even untidier.[20] This mess left his colleagues roaring with laughter, and it leaves us with a beautiful symbol. A truly Chestertonian way of reading presupposes that reading is an immersive experience and not a dispassionate exercise. Reading may imply stepping out of and away from the world, but for Chesterton it is about stepping into it. It is a matter of participating with earthly realities through reason and imagination. It is not an act whereby we subject the world to our gaze, but a *conversation*; it is, as the etymology of that word implies, a *turning with* or *living intimately among others*. Through this conversation and even through amicable controversy, we may find ourselves in humble submission to the realities beyond us and more aware of the space around us.

This same passionate engagement is mirrored in Chesterton's approach to writing: he wrote or drew on any scrap of paper he could find, or any physical surface that seemed to welcome his scrawls and jottings.[21] He wrote *about* the world he was living in, but also sometimes quite literally wrote *on*

---

18. See Chesterton, *Tremendous Trifles,* 74–78.

19. See Wild, *The Tumbler of* God, 173.

20. Ker, *G. K. Chesterton,* 42; Ward, *Return to Chesterton,* 29.

21. Titterton, *G. K. Chesterton,* 13, 16, 80.

it. His sketches and words were always a direct response to the experience of having the truths of the world etched into his being.

Nevertheless, Chesterton did not ever formally or systematically discuss the framework of his interpretive awareness and his approach to discerning the drama of meaning. As a man of more commonplace and proximate philosophical interests, it was never his concern to tackle such an abstract question. And yet the question of his unique perception remains, if only implicitly, the central fascination of all Chesterton scholarship. We can still undoubtedly gain a great deal from properly understanding the horizon of his interpretive vision. Therefore, my goal here is to offer careful readings and also a kind of reverse-engineering of his writings to provide a clearer sense of the hermeneutic assumptions and recommendations that are implicit in his work. Such a task is not an easy one. To be honest, and to borrow Chesterton's words from a different context, it is a task "for which I feel myself wholly incompetent."[22] Nevertheless, I find it comforting to recognize that it is a task that no one could do perfectly. Thankfully, there will always be more to explore and more to say. Still, my hope is that what I offer here is at least a step in the right direction.

The primary difficulty of unpacking a Chestertonian hermeneutic is found in the inevitable fact that the lines between the reader's subjectivity, the horizon of the text, and the discernible concerns of the author will always be somewhat fuzzy. This is particularly evident in the way that Chesterton relays what he has read. It is well known that he committed large portions of what he read to memory because, as he claims, "that is what literature is for; it ought to be part of a man."[23] As a consequence of relying on memory alone, however, he frequently misquotes the authors that he was referring to. When we read his *Robert Browning* (1903), for instance, we find his own words intermingled with the texts that he quotes by heart. It is only when we compare these texts with Browning's originals that we discover discrepancies. Examining the archived printer's proofs for *Browning* shows that a few more errors would probably have slipped through had an editor not had the courage to write in the margins, "Is this version right?" or simply make corrections—to six poems in total—where inaccuracies were perceived.[24]

Nevertheless, even in the case of his *Robert Browning* we learn something of Chesterton's interpretive practice. We find that for him reading cannot be thought of as a clinical exercise akin to dissecting a corpse on the autopsy table; instead, it is a process of breathing new life into the text.

---

22. Chesterton, *The Victorian Age in Literature*, 10.

23. Dale, *The Outline of Sanity*, 88.

24. Chesterton, *Robert Browning, Draft and Printer's Proofs.*

Even the solid edges of black words on white pages reveal the bleeding of thoughts into one another, the ricocheting of thoughts off one another, and the intimate companionship of words and their assorted denotations and connotations with one another. One could say that reading those lines (and between those lines) becomes an act of finding new life in the self as well. It becomes a contemplative, spiritual practice. Chesterton's way of reading also involves far more than merely reporting on what has been seen and done. Instead, he reads almost as an excuse to revisit his own thoughts.[25] He certainly ventriloquizes from time to time, speaking in the name of other authors instead of letting them speak for themselves. And yet, his ventriloquizing is not without boundaries. In his *Autobiography* (1936), Chesterton admits the following concerning his book on Browning:

> I will not say I wrote a book about Browning; but I wrote a book about love, liberty, poetry, my own views on God and religion (highly underdeveloped), and various theories of my own about optimism and pessimism and the hope of the world; a book in which the name of Browning was introduced from time to time, I might almost say with considerable art, or at any rate with some decent appearance of regularity.[26]

While Chesterton may be accused of having incorrectly remembered a few portions of the texts he is quoting, he can hardly be accused, at least in any simplistic sense, of hermeneutic infidelity or hermeneutic violence. In any case, hermeneutic violence is only possible if we assume the myth of pure, unmediated presence that underpins the illusion of a hermeneutics of immediacy. Perhaps we may say, then, that Chesterton's errors are the result of his ardent fidelity.

Chesterton's preference, however much we may criticize him for it, is always for insight over accuracy. He continuously focuses on the interplay of the text with his own imaginings. Thus, he aims to unambiguously present the world as he sees it rather than merely reproduce a carbon copy of the world as Browning might have seen it. Again, we may criticize Chesterton for his imprecision, but we can hardly criticize him for infidelity. Sadly, though, he observed that his own brand of fidelity—this multifaceted, occasionally inaccurate, but always immersive, personal wrestling match with the text—was becoming increasingly endangered in a culture of haste. Thus, we find him writing the following in 1928:

25. Ahlquist, *Common Sense* 101, 78; Ker, *G. K. Chesterton,* 40.
26. Chesterton, *Autobiography,* 103.

> I wonder how much there is to-day of the secret avoidance of reading. We hear of the men who went into crypts and caverns to conceal the fact that they were reading the Missal or the Bible. I wonder how many people there are now, locked up in studies and libraries, and concealing the fact that they are not reading the newspaper. It is now assumed that we all read, as it was once perhaps assumed that many of us could not read. But I suspect that in both cases there were secrets and surprises. I suspect that there is many an intelligent man to-day walking about the streets who has never read the newspaper for days, or even weeks, but who contrives to keep up a general air of knowledge founded entirely on hearsay.[27]

In the above paragraph, which may be more suggestive today than when it was originally written, we find that when Chesterton refers to reading he is not referring simply to the importance of getting one's facts right, although facts are not entirely unimportant to him. Rather, he is referring to what texts illuminate about our embodied experience. Reading seems to be related in Chesterton's mind to the question of what it means to live intentionally, with a balanced combination of discernment and openness. As much as reading Chesterton as a reader may include examining his approach to literary criticism, therefore, it is primarily about grappling with the way that he considers the act of reading to be the mirror of living.

If, as Dale Ahlquist suggests, "looking at Chesterton is not as important as looking at the whole world through his eyes,"[28] then perhaps it is worth exploring at length and in some depth what it could mean to look through his eyes. What particulars—absolutes, ideals, hermeneutic considerations, principles, and restrictions—guide a uniquely Chestertonian perspective? How might these particulars contribute to our own exploration of meaning and truth in the world? We can certainly learn a lot from what Chesterton gets right, and perhaps just as much from his occasional missteps.

To guide my enquiry, I have adopted a number of preliminary hermeneutic principles of my own, each of which relates directly to principles that seem to underlie Chesterton's approach to reading. Far from supporting any illusion of naïve, epistemic objectivity, such principles are helpful for foregrounding Chesterton's, as well as my own, interpretive biases. The first principle is found in my refusal to attempt what is known in hermeneutic theory as psychologism, which refers to the Diltheyan belief in the possibility of reconstructing the author's persona through hermeneutic analysis.

27. Chesterton, *Illustrated London News*, December 8, 1928.

28. Ahlquist, *Common Sense 101*, 9.

Today, our awareness of the more hidden aspects of human thought have lead to a reasonable skepticism against understanding something like the author's intention. Of course, we may still *imagine* what the author was thinking, and thus gain at least some sense of authorial intention, but our imagining will always go wanting simply because it belongs to us and not the author. It will still be our own interpretation rather than a perfect rendition of the author's intention.

I am following Chesterton's lead in this regard. When writing on Shakespeare, for instance, he notes that it would be somewhat pointless and perhaps even dishonest to try to understand an author "outside . . . the reading of his literary works."[29] In an early draft of his *Robert Louis Stevenson,* in a passage that does not appear in the final draft, Chesterton explains that he aims to "put *The Child's Garden of Verses*, with all that Stevenson really thought about childhood, before any examples from his own childhood" and also strives to situate "*Dr. Jeckyl and Mr. Hyde*, with all its feeling about vice and virtue and temptation before the mere details of his own disturbed and erratic youth."[30] And, as if this were not clear enough, when reviewing Hugh Kingsmill's *The Sentimental Journey: A Life of Charles Dickens* (1934), Chesterton warns his reader concerning the so-called modern tendency to forget the distinction, albeit a blurry one, between the inside of a person and his outside: "in all psychology there is this double and rather confusing quality: that the thing which is being studied is also the thing which is studying it."[31] One's own point of view is always bound to affect the picture one is analyzing. This eventuality is at the heart of all hermeneutic investigation. Subjectivity results not from a lapse in judgment, but from simply being present to something that is being interpreted.

Bearing the above in mind, there can still be no doubt that Chesterton speculates a great deal concerning the thoughts of those he writes about. He is nevertheless careful to recognize the place of his own subjectivity. He knows that we must often acknowledge, especially in the case of those deceased, that we only have access to the author's work, not to the author himself. This is to say that whenever we consider the writings of another, it is helpful to acknowledge a certain intimate distance between the actual man and his work. It is nonetheless convenient to keep Chesterton's life and writings together simply because so many who have written about him to date have done the same. However, while biographical detail is occasionally used below to support my argument, my focus is predominantly on what

29. Chesterton, *In Defense of Sanity,* 149.

30. Chesterton, *Robert Louis Stevenson, Draft and Printer's Proofs.*

31. Chesterton, *Illustrated London News,* December 8, 1934.

can be ascertained from Chesterton's writings. Even biographical details are interpreted through his writings, not the other way around.

The second hermeneutic principle for the following exploration is to assume that Chesterton's words ought to have priority above my own opinions, as well as the opinions of others. This is not done for the sake of presenting Chesterton as absolutely without fault, as so many admirers of his work may be tempted to do. Chesterton may or may not have been a saint, but he was always certainly a human being, with very human struggles, failures, and successes. Instead, my intention is simply to ensure that, whatever we may conclude, at least we know with as much certainty as possible what Chesterton's opinions about an issue, subject, or action actually are. I also think that generosity, something so essential to Chesterton's interpretive approach, ought to be at the center of any reading of him. In my view, unduly harsh critique is often offered as a means to tame the work of especially those writers who, like Chesterton, tend towards the radical. Any attempt to tame Chesterton would, I feel, be out of keeping with his monstrous output.

Thirdly, I have made use of a principle to treat Chesterton's corpus as a unified whole. It is safe to say that despite occasional modifications to his ideas, it is not inaccurate to think of him as a remarkably consistent thinker. His good friend W. R. Titterton suggests that "[h]e changed his opinions, but not his beliefs."[32] There is always a remarkable consistency in his work.[33] Therefore, I have not kept rigidly to chronology. In his *The Victorian Age in Literature* (1913), Chesterton suggests that a chronological approach can often be "as arbitrary as alphabetical order."[34] Therefore, I have chosen a thematic approach, again following the lead of my chief subject, grouping Chesterton's ideas according to topic in the hope of getting a better sense of his stance on specific things.

The fourth hermeneutic principle adopted here relates to Chesterton's context, about which I will say more in the following chapter. One of the errors of hermeneutic psychologism, and one of the errors of the contemporary disease of strict literalism, is the myopic assumption that the ideas of an author can simply be taken as is and thereafter transplanted into a later era or otherwise simply read in light of another historical milieu. Chesterton has far too often been decontextualized by both his admirers and critics and has thus been divorced from the world he actually lived in and wrote for.[35]

---

32. Titterton, *G. K. Chesterton*, 10.

33. Ker, *G. K. Chesterton*, xii; Schall, *Schall on* Chesterton, xiv.

34. Chesterton, *The Victorian Age in Literature*, 8.

35. Stapleton, *Christianity, Patriotism, and Nationhood*, 3; Oddie, *Chesterton and the Romance of Orthodoxy*, 9.

While this may not always be detrimental to our judgments concerning his work, since Chesterton's hope was always to present a kind of commonsense philosophy, it is safe to say that some of what he said has dated.[36]

With Chesterton, I concede that the "[i]mmortal writer is he who does something universal in a special manner";[37] I believe, though, that the *special* is, as the word's etymology suggests, *specific*, and I thereby reject the tendency to take automatically as universal what Chesterton was clearly speaking about in particular terms. Even if abstract ideas can be extrapolated, this should not be at the expense of specificity. A brief example is instructive: Chesterton wrote quite emphatically and very critically of the suffragist movement and is thus often taken today by certain contemporary Chestertonians to be virulently against all possible feminist discourses, including the more subtle discourses that arose long after he had died. However, apart from indulging in a kind of unruly ignorance, the feminism of the suffragettes cannot reasonably be taken to be synonymous with every complex and nuanced branch of feminism that has existed since Chesterton's death. We cannot convincingly speculate that Chesterton would have necessarily and absolutely resisted every feminist theory simply because he resisted this one type of feminism. In fact, there are ways he idealized women that may in fact lead us to believe that he was a kind of feminist himself—a dedicated defender of womanhood. Therefore, when we read Chesterton on feminism we need to understand precisely what *kind* of feminism he was referring to and precisely what it was that he rejected in it. This should apply to any other idea that Chesterton addressed.

Following the principle of the hermeneutic circle, the part—that is, the reader and/or the details of the text—should be affirmed and not negated by the whole—that is, the larger context within which the part is located; and this needs to be done in keeping with the recognition that the precise point at which the part merges into the whole may be impossible to locate. Although I will be extracting and abstracting certain hermeneutic coordinates from his writings, I maintain that Chesterton was a man of his time, albeit a man often at war with his time—a conversationalist and a controversialist. Reading him now either is or is fast becoming an exercise in anachronism, and continuing to read him faithfully and benevolently in the future necessitates making proper allowances for his own historically affected horizon of understanding. It is therefore helpful to realize that Chesterton's many critiques of the problems of his own era can be taken as hermeneutic issues: his concern is persistently with reading the world accurately. His philosophy

36. Lauer, *G. K. Chesterton*, 3.
37. Chesterton, *In Defense of Sanity*, xvii.

repeatedly highlights what is wrong or right in his own age not merely in terms of dogmas, but in terms of approach and attitude.

Of course, I do not presume to be able to capture every nuance regarding what it meant to live in Chesterton's place and time, given that I live in neither and am not in possession of a workable time machine. But the principle of keeping in mind Chesterton's situatedness within an exact historical horizon serves to encourage humility in the reader regarding any judgments or speculations made on the basis of what cannot necessarily be accurately delineated. We would do well in any exercise of theoretical enquiry to avoid the problem of ultracrepidarianism; that is, the practice of speaking outside of our knowledge and experience.

Taking Chesterton's context into account also means grappling as much as possible with his complexity, which happens to be the fifth hermeneutic principle adopted here. While even today Chesterton remains "one of the most quoted writers in the English language,"[38] it is also possible that, like Shakespeare, he is more quoted than read.[39] And the more he is quoted without being read, the more likely we are to misunderstand him. Chesterton's writings are vivid and clear, because he is a skillful communicator, but they are not necessarily simple in the sense of being reducible. The nuances of his perspective, which are specifically evident in the way that he plays with language, need to be noted and extrapolated, perhaps with even more care than even Chesterton allowed in his readings of others.

This, then, is the only point on which my own hermeneutic approach differs from Chesterton's: I have endeavoured, to the best of my ability, to render his opinions with as much detail, accuracy, and fidelty to context as possible. I make it my business not to misquote him as he did others. And to keep me from straying off course I have also allowed my own understanding to be guided by those dedicated Chesterton scholars who have preceded me, especially those within mainstream critical scholarship. The views of populist Chestertonians are kept in mind as being valuable in their own way, but are not dwelt upon at length. Where I quote a writer, though, it should be assumed that I am only dealing with what that writer happened to say at that particular point. I may, for instance, agree with a writer on a particular point, but—this should go without saying—that does not mean that I agree with everything that he or she says.

In addition to the initial hermeneutic principles outlined above, two metaphors can guide our understanding of Chesterton as a reader, namely *sight* and *drama*. I have already used both, but some clarification may help

---

38. Schall, *Schall on Chesterton*, vii.
39. Chesterton, *The Soul of Wit*, 13; Dale, *The Outline of Sanity*, xv.

to explain their appropriateness. The first metaphor is perhaps nowhere better presented than in Chesterton's *The Coloured Lands*—the title story of a collection of his fairytales, poetry, and drawings that was compiled and edited by Maisie Ward in 1938. It tells us about a lonely boy named Tommy and his encounter with a strange-looking, blue-bespectacled young man who claims to be his "long lost brother."[40] The young man, recognizing that he has an opportunity to do something about Tommy's unhappiness, takes off his blue spectacles and hands them to the boy, who is curious enough to try them on. In an instant, the whole world is transformed. As he is looking at a landscape of black roses and bottle-green grass, the young man addresses him: "Looks like a new world, doesn't it?"[41] Tommy is then given rose-colored spectacles, yellow spectacles, and green spectacles to look through, and ends up thinking that he has been "looking at four totally different landscapes."[42]

The strange young man then tells Tommy a story about an opportunity once given to him by a wizard to travel to a land where everything was quite literally blue—with blue flowers, blue skies, blue sea, blue jays, blue kingfishers, blue baboons, and blue books. On finding the Blue Country uninspiring, he had decided to leave. After wandering through a Green Country, where all the people of the land were greengrocers, and thereafter through a Yellow Country, with its yellow fever, yellow flowers, and Yellow Press, he had ended up in a Red Country where he discovered that "in a rose-red city you cannot really see any roses. Everything is a great deal too red. Your eyes are tired until it might just as well all be brown."[43] The young man explains that after he had decided what a terrible mistake these monochromatic worlds were, the wizard who had instigated this excursion reappeared to him and told him to paint a world for himself—a world that he actually liked.

Once he had finished dipping into the paint box of creation and dabbing paint all over the place, he discovered that the world that had once caused him such dissatisfaction was in fact the very same world that he had created. The best of all impossible worlds was the very one he had always been living in. It is a world filled to the brim and overflowing with a wild assortment of different colors and events. It is through this short exchange and this imaginative journey through colored lands that Tommy is given new eyes—spectacle-free. This removal of spectacles does not refer to the

40. Chesterton, *The Coloured Lands*, 20.
41. Ibid.
42. Ibid.
43. Ibid., 24.

removal of mediation, but rather to the transformation of perception after and through mediation.

For those who read and love his work, it is not a stretch to contend that Chesterton, in a way, is our long lost older brother; he is really the strange young man in the story. He strives always to give his readers new eyes, and so his rhetoric is strikingly visual. However, he is also deeply aware of the invisible dimensions of our engagements with the world, and his use of visual metaphors—as we find in *The Coloured Lands*—points to much deeper, hidden impulses in the human spirit. This tension between the visible (the apparent, being, and the world of becoming) and the invisible (the ultimately real, Being) is therefore something that I aim to explore in far more detail in this book.

The second metaphor that guides our understanding of Chesterton as a reader is that of drama. This metaphor is both overt and implied in Chesterton's work. Chesterton suggests that creation, even with its abundance of poetry and metaphor, is still more like a play than a poem.[44] The centrality of drama to Chesterton's perception is also found in his narration of "the very first thing" he remembered "seeing with [his] own eyes"—an image of "a young man walking across a bridge" in his Father's home-made toy theatre.[45] We also discover his eye for drama in the fact that he wrote, acted in, and attended dramas throughout his life and career. "[H]is gift," as Dorothy Sayers notes in her commentary on Chesterton's marvelous posthumously published play *The Surprise* (1952), "was naturally dramatic."[46] His fiction is also obviously dramatic, but the metaphor of drama helps us to understand his non-fiction as well. It is a metaphor that extends into the realm of reason, where our apprehension of the world, via an observable sequence of events in the midst of other acts, scenes, and agents, follows a process of discovery that is unmistakably dramatic. D. C. Schindler contends that "traditional epistemologies are constitutionally undramatic."[47] And while evidence for this fact abounds, Chesterton's approach is most definitely not an extension of such epistemologies. For him, life itself is a drama, which has been "written by somebody else" and much of which has been "settled for us without our permission."[48] It has "a story behind it, not merely intellect which is

44. Chesterton, *Collected Works, Volume 1*, 282.

45. Chesterton, *Autobiography*, 40.

46. Sayers, "Introduction," 9.

47. Schindler, *The Catholicity of Reason*, 51.

48. Chesterton, *Collected Works, Volume 1*, 144.

partly mechanical, but will, which is divine."[49] It is precisely by being in this drama that we find and negotiate meaning.[50]

The drama of meaning is that which considers the metareferential, intermediated interplay of text (as otherness) and reader (as the familiar). This is what Chesterton's work demonstrates: we always interpret "from the inside,"[51] as co-participants in a larger drama that we can never really see from the outside, and yet are still capable of imagining, if only partially, as if from the outside. We see even those things we do not fully comprehend as props, entities, storylines, and characters that are companions to our embeddedness within the perichoretic performance that is reality. And there can be no doubt that Chesterton openly invites us to join in the exploration of what it all means. Even today, he still invites us to join in the play.

49. Ibid.
50. Ibid., 362.
51. Ibid., 141.

2

The Context of Chesterton's Hermeneutic

Reading as a Palimpsest

FOR THE SAKE OF presenting and understanding Chesterton as a reader of the drama of meaning and to avoid displacing him from the world in which he lived and wrote, this chapter aims to grapple with his place within his context. It is in sketching a picture of the multifaceted horizon within which he operated, as well as his dominant responses to his historical milieu, that we discover some important implications for understanding Chesterton's inimitable dramatic perception. "There is always," he notes, "something fanciful about the conjunction of the world that the poet sees and the place he lives in."[1] In fact, there is always something not only fanciful, but *indispensible* to seeing the poet and the place he lives in concurrently, albeit only through an imaginative historical reconstruction. To see one without the other is to fail to see at all. What follows, for obvious reasons, is not a comprehensive historical reconstruction, but a narrow pathway into the specific contextual factors that have a bearing on Chesterton's hermeneutic.

It is not readily admitted in Chesterton scholarship, but it needs to be said: Chesterton was not utterly immune to the philosophical trends of his own time. He is often depicted as a towering and heroic figure, somewhat blithely unaffected by the philosophies of his contemporaries, but this is simply untrue. In an interview with his friend W. R. Titterton towards the end of his life, he admitted that especially "as a young man, superficially at least, [he was] altogether of [his] epoch."[2] He was undoubtedly a product of

1. Chesterton, *Autobiography*, 139.
2. Titterton, *G. K. Chesterton*, 43.

his own time, even though he ultimately contradicted so many of the trends of his time. It is therefore unsurprising that he can be found borrowing the symbolic arsenal, metaphysical presuppositions, and coded narratives of those philosophical and societal structures that first gave him words before moving on to find better ways of expressing his experiences. As it is with all of us, Chesterton was spoken before he learned how to speak.

As a young adult, Chesterton tended to first side with certain perspectives that happened to be fashionable when he first encountered them, and would only later refine or redefine his position in relation to those very same fashionable views. But there was something always stirring in him that caused him on more than one occasion to revolt against the status quo. It seems that only after absorbing the predilections of his age did he discover the courage to rebel. For example, Chesterton, as was typical of a middle-Victorian youth, once thought of himself as a Unitarian like others in his own family; but this "Unitarianism did not long content [him]. For his world was a rollicking world aglow with colour; and the Unitarian world was a sedate world in black and white."[3] The young Chesterton, again following the prejudices of those around him, at one time did not consider miracles to be a genuine possibility even when he was completely convinced that the world was still to be marveled at.[4] He would later overturn his verdict against miracles with great philosophical clarity and force.

As he entered his adolescent years, he started to consider himself an agnostic, but later discovered to his own lasting astonishment that his agnosticism had vanished.[5] He would, at another time, think of himself as a Socialist, but would later, especially under the influence of Hilaire Belloc, recognize the inadequacies of that outlook, despite its seemingly noble impetus.[6] Later, we find him observing that the "ordinary artistic Socialist throws out signals to his own kind, and naturally gravitates to his own environment" even though he "does not in the least know what Socialism is."[7] Certain "sociological conjectures" will bring an individual to align himself with a particular group of people before he has had time to figure out whether such conjectures are any good.[8] Very early in his career, Chesterton would also present himself an optimist, but would subsequently add

3. Ibid., 15.

4. Ibid.

5. Ibid., 30.

6. Chesterton, *Collected Works, Volume 3*, 113; Ward, *Gilbert Keith Chesterton*, 115.

7. Chesterton, *Illustrated London News*, December 23, 1911.

8. Ibid.

several caveats to that label to distinguish his optimism from the optimism of his age.[9]

It seems from all this that the young Chesterton, being a deeply intuitive thinker and desiring to find language to articulate his actual experience of the world, was given to adopting a particular label a little too quickly because of what he thought it meant. Later reflection and scrutiny would then bring him to realize that the label or any specific way of articulating his intuitions had been wrong. In this sense, Titterton may be right: Chesterton changed his opinions rather than his beliefs. Chesterton would test the terms against his experience of the truth. He would, to use his own idea, correct one thought by other thoughts.[10] This process of checking one's thoughts would require one to have a solid sense of what is right against which one can test what may be wrong. Misty notions alone would not suffice for such a project. This is why Chesterton preferred the definite and the concrete to the purely theoretical. His metaphysical convictions always arose out of an experience, albeit one that glimpsed what transcended that experience.[11]

Chesterton understood this process of checking one's thoughts against solid ideas and realities very well because it mirrored his writing process. In fact, properly understanding Chesterton as a reader requires a sense that he was foremost a reader of his own work. Based on years of experience, he points out that a "writer knows he has plenty of elbow room, that he will have almost endless space for explanation and correction," and "may easily hope to convey by repetition what he is not lucid enough to convey by assertion."[12] It has sometimes been assumed that Chesterton wrote hastily and with such ease that he would hardly ever need to return to his manuscripts to make corrections, but this is not quite accurate.

Chesterton always took extensive notes before beginning a book; and the manuscripts that we have access to today are comprised of multiple drafts, with several corrections made to each draft in pen, pencil, or colored pencil. These were then compiled by Frances Chesterton or, later, Dorothy Collins. It is also clear from these manuscripts that whole sections have had new pages inserted and old pages discarded. Even the final printers' proofs of Chesterton's books contain examples of places where he would revisit what he had written and make endless deletions, revisions, and additions. This is a writer who understood the notion of "elbow room" very well indeed.[13]

9. Chesterton, *The Defendant*, 4.

10. Chesterton, *Illustrated London News*, December 23, 1911.

11. Chesterton, *The Everlasting Man*, 132; Wood, *Chesterton*, 4.

12. Chesterton, *Illustrated London News*, November 2, 1935.

13. Ibid.

Recognizing Chesterton's writing process as a constant interplay of re-reading and re-writing is not only a key to understanding Chesterton's dramatic perception, but also to understanding the nature of hermeneutics itself. The visual metaphor of a palimpsest is instructive here. Palimpsest— from the Greek *palin (again)* and *psao (I scrape clean)*—refers to parchments or tablets from which writings have been erased to make room for later writings, even while traces of the previous writings remain partially intact. Although these palimpsests were typical of ancient cultures, they are not only an ancient phenomenon. In my view, Chesterton can be said to have a palimpsestic approach to reading and writing, because of his habit of constantly writing or drawing over existing texts, whether his own or those of others. His tendency to reassess familiar ideas through new imagery and wordplay can be seen as palimpsestic.

The metaphor of the palimpsest suggests three kinds of hermeneutic disclosure, each of which is implied by the way that Chesterton interacts with his own texts. The first is found in the perception that something has been withheld and will always remain withheld. This is the disclosure of the invisible as invisible. It is the disclosure that brings to our awareness the fact that, despite our efforts to uncover what has been hidden from view (such as the intention or agenda of the author, perhaps, or any other text that influenced the creation of the present text), there are certain things that will simply remain concealed. We know, for instance, that things like historical conditions, contextual factors, thought processes and personal experiences have guided the creation of the text before us. But many of those things remain largely inaccessible, no matter how many traces of their presence may be discerned. This type of hermeneutic disclosure indicates the necessity of modesty in the hermeneutic enterprise, but also the importance of openness to endless curiosity and even, where appropriate, guesswork.

Chesterton offers the metaphor of the "tumbling of the trees and the secret energy of the wind as typical of the visible world moving under the violence of the invisible."[14] "The wind is the spirit which bloweth where it listeth; the trees are the material things of this world which are blown where the spirit lists. The wind is philosophy, religion, revolution; the trees are cities and civilisations."[15] Even a group of people would be like the "forest" and their "souls" would be like the wind.[16] In hermeneutics, the text is akin to the trees and the wind is akin to the influence of the author. The fact that the invisible is disclosed as invisible should not lead us to believe that it is

14. Chesterton, *Tremendous Trifles*, 69.

15. Ibid., 60.

16. Ibid., 69.

irrelevant. Rather, it is indicative of its exceptional importance, even if we are unable to properly access it. It intimates that there is more in the text than what we can be sure of, but also more in the text that is there to be investigated.

Meanings can therefore be things we bet on, depending on the texts, contexts, and hermeneutic freedoms that we possess; and the "ethical theory in favour of betting" is rooted in the simple idea that "I have the right to bet what I have the right to lose"—and that would include previous understandings and interpretations.[17] This is not about being careless, but about being calculated in the gamble that one is taking. "I have often thought," Chesterton writes, "there might be a place for intelligent guesswork which admits that it is guesswork."[18] This very guesswork may lead to new insights into what one is reading:

> There might be a place for a fanciful theory, if it was avowedly fanciful. I confess I have suffered many things from the sort of man who has a theory that Bacon wrote Shakespeare, when he does really believe it. But I had great fun in working out a theory that Shakespeare wrote Bacon, because I did not in the least believe it. In the course of turning it into a sketch, which was not more than a skit, I found myself discovering much more than I had known before of the real truth about the Elizabethan and Jacobean epoch.[19]

Chesterton goes so far as to say that reading with a modest view of what may be possible leads to the creation of "a new type of literature, between the solemn stolidity of the academics and the solemn lunacy of the cranks."[20] "[S]omething might come out of [our guessing]," Chesterton suggests, provided it owns up to its theoretical and speculative nature.[21] In his mind, something is disclosed even in the absence of disclosure. Appropriately, he connects his philosophy of guessing with the idea of play, which I address below.

A second kind of disclosure suggested by the metaphor of the palimpsest—after this disclosure of the invisible as invisible—is the disclosure of the withheld or hidden as being partially recoverable. This does not necessarily mean that what is recoverable may be assumed as a subtext, or even that the invisible has necessarily become entirely visible. Nevertheless, what

17. Chesterton, *Illustrated London News*, July 2, 1932.
18. Ibid.
19. Ibid.
20. Ibid.
21. Ibid.

is recoverable may still be of some hermeneutic significance. An example of this is found in many of the corrections that Chesterton made to his own manuscripts, where what has been crossed out is still decipherable and therefore comparable with what it has been replaced by. Every text implies the scenography—the dramatic context, historical horizon, or even the *Zeitgeist*—against which it was written, but such scenography will always remain only partially accessible through a particular frame or window. We should recognize, as Emile Cammaerts does, that "there is a scale in our affections which corresponds no doubt to our own limitations, in size, in memory, in perception."[22] "We admire great things, such as the sea, bright sunsets, mountain scenery, but we cherish small things, children, flowers, brooks, and birds."[23] No game, not even the game of trying to see things as they are, can exist without rules, borders, and subjective interferences.

Finally, implicit in this second type of disclosure is a third type of palimpsestic revelation, which may be called a disclosure of preference, whereby the text written over the original text or texts is given priority. About this final kind of disclosure, it is certainly possible to argue that the priority of the later addition could be arbitrary, or based merely on the passage of time, and yet as I have come to understand from studying Chesterton's writings and corrections, a number of obvious criteria seem to have guided his editing process. To begin with, changes are predominantly made in favor of better form (especially regarding grammar, flow, and punctuation), clearer communication (pertaining especially to the choice of words, having more accurate facts, and reducing the number of overstatements or generalizations), and improved rhetoric (regarding especially making a line more poetic or more humorous, as well as striving to enhance the emotional force of what is being said). Only very occasionally were changes made simply because of subjective preferences that, as an example of the first type of palimpsestic disclosure, would be easier to guess at than accurately decipher. Obviously, one has to allow for the possibility that such changes may have been guided by the perspectives of others, since Chesterton's eyes were not the only ones to have viewed his work before it was published. I have no doubt, for instance, that his editors, his wife, and his secretary could have been of great help to him as he sought to refine what he was trying to say. Still, it is clear from his manuscripts that the final call on what should stay or go, change or keep, was Chesterton's. His was always the hand to alter what had been set down.

22. Cammaerts, *The Laughing Prophet*, 94.
23. Ibid.

The metaphor of the palimpsest implies that the original text has an influence on what comes after it, forming new trails of meaning that would otherwise not have existed. This is to say that writing over other writing sets up different meanings than the act of writing onto a blank page would do. Hermeneutically speaking, though, there is actually no such thing as writing onto a blank page. As the first type of palimpsestic disclosure suggests, the interpretive process always involves forestructures of understanding—pre-judgments or prejudices. Chesterton's understanding of this is evident in his contention that learning, following an aim to "restore simplicity," is primarily about unlearning things.[24] It is never simply an act of writing onto some mythical *tabula rasa*. In particular, what should be unlearned, for Chesterton, is "all the weariness and wickedness of the world" that causes one to lose sight of "that state of exhilaration we all instinctively celebrate" when childlikeness is our primary goal.[25] Even in the "dust heaps of humanity" we should be able to locate "treasure."[26] Perhaps the most obvious thing to Chesterton about reading is that nothing should be taken as obvious. What we deem to be obvious is simply the result of becoming overly accustomed to what is always exceedingly surprising.

Chesterton takes this idea so far as to say that if he were to "examine all examiners," he "would not only ask the teachers how much knowledge they had imparted," but would also ask "how much splendid and scornful ignorance they had erected."[27] He longs for the kind of ignorance that champions "the exquisite intuitions of innocence."[28] It's a wonderful joke, but its point may easily be misunderstood if taken too literally. It is not that one should scrap the possibility of accumulating knowledge at all, for there really is an unhealthy kind of ignorance (and Chesterton uses the word *ignorance* in this negative sense as well). Rather, one ought to see that genuine understanding is impossible without the experience of what is learned as something that is genuinely new, as that which comes from outside of the human subject and as that which presents itself to him or her. The paradox here is that what is experienced as totally new has in fact been written over what existed before. The truly new is really old.

Even repetitions of the same can present the possibility of encountering something new in the old. Repeating the word *dog* "thirty times," for instance, can transform what has been domesticated into something "wild":

24. Chesterton, *All Things Considered*, 40.
25. Ibid., 40–41.
26. Chesterton, *In Defense of Sanity*, 4.
27. Chesterton, *All Things Considered*, 41.
28. Chesterton, *Alarms and Discursions*, 71.

"In the end a dog walks about as startling and undecipherable as Leviathan or Croquemitaine."[29] In Chesterton's mind, we may have been lulled into a dulled perception of things, not because of too much repetition, but because of too little. Perhaps "a man is not startled at the first cat he sees, but jumps into the air with surprise at the seventy-ninth cat. Perhaps he has to pass through thousands of pine trees before he finds the one that is really a pine tree."[30] Chesterton "would insist that people should have so much simplicity as would enable them to see things suddenly and to see things as they are."[31] "Now, there is a law written in the darkest of the Books of Life," he writes elsewhere, "and it is this: If you look at a thing nine hundred and ninety-nine times, you are perfectly safe; if you look at it the thousandth time, you are in frightful danger of seeing it for the first time."[32]

To build on this idea of seeing things "suddenly" through repetition it is helpful to elucidate Chesterton's contention that "[t]he only way of catching a train . . . is to be late for the one before."[33] This may be taken as a hermeneutic maxim, which helps us to better understand the palimpsest of reading. Chesterton suggests that "[t]he true philosopher does not think of coming just in time for his train except as a bet or a joke."[34] We know that Chesterton was typically late for the train he was supposed to have caught, and this allowed him the time to "find in a railway station much of the quietude and consolation of a cathedral."[35] He would extract chocolates, cigarettes, toffees, and any number of other things, even things that he happened not to like, from vending machines, and would even stop to weigh himself—a marvelous inactivity that would produce "sublime results."[36] He would take the trouble to "have no business of any kind"—suspending, as much as possible, his expectations and prejudices—and would thus allow himself the opportunity of simply encountering the train station as it disclosed itself to him.

In continuing to discuss what it means to be late for a train, Chesterton contrasts his experience of the reality of the train station with the unreality of the "educated" mind; he takes issue with those who have learned a great many things, but have not unlearned them: "At worst the uneducated only

29. Chesterton, *All Things Considered*, 7.
30. Ibid.
31. Ibid., 41.
32. Ibid., 13.
33. Chesterton, *Tremendous Trifles*, 173.
34. Ibid.
35. Ibid.
36. Ibid., 175.

wear down old things by sheer walking. But the educated kick them down out of sheer culture."[37] These so-called educated people, in Chesterton's mind, are the ones who refuse to properly look at things as they are because they are too bound up in their own theories about things.[38] They have foggy notions about how things are, but are not paying much attention to the concreteness of the reality before them. Chesterton's point, however, is not to set up a class distinction, as the terms *educated* and *uneducated* can imply, but rather to set up a distinction between looking at the world innocently and academically. The distinction, in other words, is between awareness and a detached world-weariness; between attentiveness and apathy.

We know that Chesterton even "missed his train on his wedding day, because he had insisted on stopping on his way to the station, in order to buy a revolver"—a symbol, for him, not of violence, but of adventure.[39] This love for adventure is essential to his hermeneutic. Apart from this biographical detail, his epiphany about the "only way" to catch a train stresses something more than the purely practical problem of timeliness or kairos; rather, it stresses the paradox that those who try so desperately to be ahead of everything will inevitably be behind everything; those who worship success are doomed to be failures;[40] those who pursue happiness rather than assuming it will never be happy; and those who try so desperately to rise above the masses will always find themselves complicit in the mimetic sway of the crowd. The first will indeed be last. The punctual will be late. The daily paper will never be "up to date."[41] The futurist will forever be behind the times,[42] and it is those who are forever late who are truly ahead of things; in other words, those who humbly acknowledge the fact that they have always arrived late on the scene, even if they have literally arrived on time, will be met with the epiphany or the event of understanding. Chesterton therefore suggests that the commonplace, "'Blessed is he that expecteth nothing, for he shall not be disappointed'" is not only inadequate, but false.[43]

> The truth is "Blessed is he that expecteth nothing, for he shall be gloriously surprised." The man who expects nothing sees redder roses than common men can see, and greener grass, and a more startling sun. Blessed is he that expecteth nothing, for he shall

37. Ibid., 174.

38. Chesterton, *Illustrated London News*, May 28, 1932.

39. Cammaerts, *The Laughing Prophet*, 80.

40. Chesterton, *Illustrated London News*, December 19, 1931.

41. Chesterton, *Illustrated London News*, May 16, 1914.

42. Ibid.

43. Chesterton, *Collected Works, Volume 1*, 69.

possess the cities and the mountains; blessed is the meek, for he shall inherit the earth. Until we realise that things might not be we cannot realise that things are.[44]

More is said below on this idea, for meekness is central to Chesterton's interpretive awareness, but for now I want to touch on an idea that is hinted at in his discussion on the importance of missing a train. It is the idea that one needs to have time to actually play for the sake of the possibility of a true hermeneutic event—an epiphany that reconfigures one's entire field of vision. This is true in both psychology and hermeneutics. While going through Chesterton's books and notebooks, and sifting through his many toy-theatre cut-outs and various other doodles, I find his over-playfulness remarkable; and it seems that this very playfulness was fundamental to his approach to reading and writing: "I for one have never left off playing," he writes in his *Autobiography* (1936), "and I wish there were more time to play. I wish we did not have to fritter away on frivolous things, like lectures and literature, the time we might have given to serious, solid and constructive work like cutting out cardboard figures and pasting coloured tinsel upon them."[45] In *All Things Considered* (1908), Chesterton writes, "It is not only possible to say a great deal in praise of play; it is really possible to say the highest things in praise of it. It might reasonably be maintained that the true object of all human life is play. Earth is a task garden; heaven is a playground."[46] The reason for this elevation of play is found in the fact that it represents a "secure innocence" that is "so good that one can treat everything as a joke."[47] True holiness, for Chesterton, would allow us "to regard the Universe as a lark."[48]

Play is a very important concept in hermeneutics because it provides us with a "clue to [the] ontological."[49] Play, understood as referring to an intense absorption in the constraints of the ordinary, initiates us into a more fundamental mode of being in the world than what is allowed for by the Cartesian prioritization of what is presumably fully disclosed to our conscious minds. We are not simply conscious minds who apprehend and control what we perceive, but beings who actively and co-subjectively

44. Ibid.

45. Chesterton, *Autobiography*, 51.

46. Chesterton, *All things Considered*, 54.

47. Ibid.

48. Ibid.

49. Gadamer, *Truth and Method*, 102.

participate in the play, often in ways that escape our conscious configurations. Play, for Chesterton, is an "institution" that is anything, but childish:[50]

> It differs from all the other arts only in being more serious and direct; it differs from all the other games only in being more varied and poetical. When a grown-up person has an artistic idea he or she scrawls it down in a set of ugly hieroglyphics on a piece of paper and gives it to somebody else to take care of and turn into other and uglier hieroglyphics; or else he takes a stick of burnt wood or a mess of coloured pastes and plasters on to a piece of canvas a laborious and inadequate picture of what he means. A child simply thinks of the idea and performs it. If he thinks of a fight with swords, for example, he does not write and re-write and correct a piece of artificial prose about "ringing parries" and "dazzling thrusts in carte." He does not mix three kinds of white and four kinds of blue in order to imitate the gleam of sunlight on steel. He simply fights with swords. My present contention is not merely that this conduct of the child is more picturesque, more amusing, more poetical, for of this almost all modern writers are fully aware. My contention at present is that it is much more human, much more sensible, much more sane. The conduct of a child who, the moment he thinks of a man in a hat and cloak, puts on a hat and cloak, appears to me preferable to the conduct of the adult artist simply because it is so much more reasonable. If, as one of us walks down the street, it suddenly strikes him how magnificent it would be to lunge and guard with his umbrella like a sword, why should he not lunge and guard with his umbrella? It is a much more serious and creditable proceeding than reading up irrelevant fact in the British Museum in order to write an ephemeral story about someone else lunging and guarding.[51]

Play implies the perception of a thing—an idea, game or performance—in its perfect simplicity. In play, things are appreciated as themselves even as they gain meaning and significance from their surroundings. Chesterton suggests that this is not so in sport, in which "the essential is competition, and the aim victory."[52] Children are particularly adept at playing because they are capable of finding "a certain artistic delight" even in the "fictitious" aspects of play.[53] "They do not play for victory, they play, so far as

50. Chesterton, *The Speaker*, November 16, 1901.

51. Ibid.

52. Chesterton, *The Speaker*, November 30, 1901.

53. Ibid.

their aim can be defined, for self-deception. It is a matter of art for art's sake; they wish to pass into that kind of pictorial trance which we are all seeking when we read books or listen to music."[54]

Play is clearly dramatic. The "impulse most resembling a child's love of play is the impulse which leads us to go to the theatre."[55] Chesterton points out that "the theatre was originally what children's play is, a festival, a strictly ceremonial rejoicing. Children merely reproduce the theatre in a more human, direct, and powerful manner, by being themselves both the spectators and the actors."[56] Their clear perception comes from being both observers and participants. Even in the example of the game "Here we go round the mulberry-bush," there is nothing to the game, but the act of going around in a circle "ritualistically" with a pure sense of "equality and communism."[57] This "happy ritualism" is found in a "hilarious love of order," and "that passion for rules and observances, which is the mark of children and wise men."[58] Even the simple form of a rhyme can become an "elevated poetry" that reconciles the observer-participant to the play. Indeed, for Chesterton, reconciliation is at the center of play.[59]

Nevertheless, even in the innocence of play, there is also something confrontational. Using the metaphor of the train in a different way, Chesterton notes that "[t]he collision between the mind of man and a fact or idea is like the collision between two hurtling trains; it does finally prove which is the stronger."[60] The assumption here is that the two things—the mind and the idea—are on the same track, and are therefore given an opportunity to collide. Seeing clearly—that is, understanding properly—certainly involves what Gadamer calls a "fusion of horizons," but in Chesterton's philosophy a collision of horizons is also possible.[61] Chesterton points out that "all healthy people will agree that you never enjoy a game until you enjoy being beaten at the game."[62] Again, his point is that a game is not about the winning, but about the playing. Even the mere pursuit of the thrill of understanding is not about seeking "what is more and more exciting," but is rather about "the

54. Ibid.
55. Ibid.
56. Ibid.
57. Ibid.
58. Ibid.
59. Ibid.
60. Chesterton, *In Defense of Sanity*, 377.
61. Gadamer, *Truth and Method*, 304.
62. Chesterton, *In Defense of Sanity*, 377.

yet more exciting business of discovering the excitement in things that are called dull."[63] The dull things, too, have something to say to us.

Chesterton's playful attitude is beautifully evidenced in his interactions with Sir Oliver Lodge's book, *The Substance of Faith Allied with Science: A Catechism for Parents and Teachers* (1907). While Chesterton usually drew in his books—and such drawing can also be regarded as profoundly representative of his sense of play—three books have survived from his personal library that include marginalia. The first, G. S. MacQuoid's collection of *Jacobite Songs and Ballads* (1887), given to Chesterton by his school friend E. C. Bentley, includes quite a lot of underlining, some questions ("What on earth does he mean?") and comments ("Good Lord!"), as well as some corrections of the poems in that book. The second, William Allingham's *The Ballad Book* (1864), given to Chesterton by another school friend named Lawrence Solomon, contains drawings and some writing, although far less writing than we find in *Jacobite Songs and Ballads*. Lodge's book, as the third book to contain Chesterton's written comments, is therefore quite significant because it is the only one of Chesterton's personal books remaining from his adult years that contains any direct commentary on the text.

On the inside of the front cover of his copy of Lodge's book, we read the words "G. K. Chesterton, from the author. July 1907." The date of the book may be significant simply because it only just precedes the publishing of Chesterton's spiritual autobiography, *Orthodoxy* (1908). Chesterton actually directly references it in that very same book. While most of the Chesterton's copy of Lodge's book is devoid of his scribblings, towards the end of the book Lodge has asked a series of questions relating to the life of faith and its reconcilability with Darwinism and has then provided a number of answers in summary of the rest of the book's contents. At this point, Chesterton has jotted down his own responses to the questions—responses that reflect both a sense of seriousness, for some of the questions are in fact serious, and a sense of fun, especially where Chesterton seems to tire of the tone of the Lodge's book.

Lodge asks "What are you?" and offers his own response: "I am a being alive and conscious on this earth, a descendent of ancestors who rose by gradual processes from lower forms of animal life, and with struggle and suffering became man."[64] In the margin, Chesterton has jotted down two words in response to the same question: "God knows." When Lodge asks "What, then, may be meant by the Fall of man?" and then answers

63. Ibid., 379.

64. Lodge, *The Substance of Faith Allied with Science*, 129.

how it has something to do with man having lost his "animal innocency,"[65] Chesterton has a different response, which is much more to the point: the fall means "that whatever I am, I am not myself." Lodge, repeating his formula of regarding man as simply a higher and more evolved animal, has in own view of what the "distinctive character of manhood" is, but Chesterton dismisses his suggestion by writing, "Your question conveys nothing to my mind."[66] Lodge asks, "What is the duty of man?"[67] Chesterton responds, "To love God mystically and his neighbor as himself; that is, sanely and without all this fuss." When Lodge asks "What is meant by good and evil?" Chesterton gets more serious, noting that "they are primary ideas." Lodge's own response that good as that which "is akin to health and beauty and happiness," as well as "that which promotes development, and is in harmony with the will of God,"[68] probably would not have alarmed Chesterton, although his assumption that evil is akin to "ugliness" contradicts Chesterton's view that ugliness itself may be a sign of the good in all of its extravagant variety.[69] Chesterton says nothing about this here though.

Further on, Chesterton answers the question "How does man know good from evil?" with another question "How does he do anything?" And Lodge's question "How comes it that evil exists?"[70] is met with Chesterton's answer: "Ah. That's asking." Here, Chesterton shifts the focus away from Lodge's certainty to a kind of helpful mysticism: it is fair to ask how good may be distinguished from evil or how evil happens, but Lodge has forgotten that something far more mysterious underpins any distinction. Here Chesterton reads to get behind what is said; the possibility of properly understanding Lodge, in this case, means understanding what Lodge has neglected to account for in his philosophy. Chesterton seems aware of the palimpsestic process of the author, although the previous ideas and texts before the one that he can see here remain undisclosed.

To continue, the question of what sin is in Lodge's book has Chesterton write that it is "evil, not as a state, but as a desire." Evil, then, is something that disrupts desire or is akin to a desire to disrupt rather than simply being something that undermines the human subject's ontology. Lodge suggests

---

65. Ibid.
66. Ibid., 128.
67. Ibid., 129.
68. Ibid.
69. Chesterton, *The Defendant*, 82–88.
70. Lodge, *The Substance of Faith Allied with Science*, 129.

that sin's root cause is selfishness, which involves "moral suicide";[71] and this certainly fits with Chesterton's own philosophy.

In fact, it seems to me that this book did have some bearing on Chesterton's thinking, albeit minor, as he developed his ideas for *Orthodoxy*, and it is therefore not unreasonable to suggest that this idea of moral suicide lead Chesterton to conceive of what he calls the "suicide of thought."[72] I cannot be absolutely certain of this, of course, but such speculation does not negate the ultimate hermeneutic significance of what we find here: Chesterton, playfully jotting down both serious and frivolous thoughts, is clear on how what he is reading both reflects and differs from his own convictions; nevertheless, reading is not merely an act of determining whether one agrees or disagrees with the views of another. This is not what letting one thought rub against another implies because it is not the hermeneutic collision of horizons that Chesterton is seeking. The very fact that Chesterton lets his words stand side-by-side with Lodge's own answers suggests an interplay between contradictory positions. Thus, reading involves seeing through and beyond the mere contradiction of thoughts and therefore involves testing whether one's own thoughts are as reasonable as one thinks they are. Reading can offer an intellectual duel.

Chesterton, continuing his playful banter with Lodge's writing, agrees with Lodge that there are "beings lower in the scale of existence than man"[73] by retorting, "Has anyone been denying the zoo?" And when Lodge asks, "Are there any beings higher in the scale of existence than man?"[74] Chesterton quips, "I hope so." Lodge offers a materialist guess on what Chesterton expresses as a desire for transcendence: there may be other worlds with other creatures on them, and these aliens may be "far higher in the scale of existence than ourselves."[75] Chesterton's challenge to such thinking, already expressed by this time in his *Heretics* (1905), concerns how what is "higher" is not necessarily better. Where Lodge rests with an almost ridiculous certainty on a theoretical presupposition (regarding what "higher" means) that can neither be disproved nor proved, Chesterton points to hope by noting that Lodge's own presupposing comes from an existential longing that he does not openly acknowledge. Lodge is only conscious of what he is conscious of. Chesterton, in a more playful mode of reading, is able to flit between ideas without ever settling too strongly on any one perspective. He sees what Lodge is saying, but also *through* what Lodge is saying.

71. Ibid., 130.
72. Chesterton, *Collected Works, Volume 1*, 233
73. Lodge, *The Substance of Faith Allied with Science*, 130.
74. Ibid.
75. Ibid.

Lodge tries to dodge the question of "What caused and what maintains existence?"[76] by offering a whirlwind of agnosticism, but Chesterton responds with a clear assertion: "God." When Lodge waxes eloquent on "man's higher faculties,"[77] Chesterton suggests that "as little as possible" ought to be said about man's so-called higher faculties. Other questions are asked, and Chesterton switches easily between levity and gravity, ultimately responding to "Rehearse the prayers taught to us by our Lord" with "With pleasure." He also dismisses Lodge's injunction to "explain the clauses of this prayer" by writing "Leave the room!"[78] Lodge has been too serious, too concerned with appeasing men of science to stay true to more pressing theological concerns. Towards the end of his reading, Chesterton seems to lose interest in Lodge's writings. So, in a bit of space at the end of the chapter, he offers a parody of Lodge's catechism in the form of a "New Scientific-Theological Catechism in 3 Questions":

Q. Why can't pigs fly?

A. I don't know that they can't. They don't. I don't know why.

Q. Under what circumstance would you believe that a pig did fly?

A. If an enormous human tradition said so and certainly saved the world.

Q. Why do scientific men use ten words when one could do?

A. In some cases is it Pride, but more commonly a quite genial sort of mental laziness.

One would not have to go too far into Chesterton's philosophy to find his deeper reasons for responding to Lodge in the way he does, but a few things concerning Chesterton's hermeneutic playfulness are worth noting for now. To begin with, when Chesterton recalls interacting with Lodge's text, he does so by recalling that it was for "amusing" himself.[79] And, moreover, he connects this amusement with joy; that is, with discovering a sense of adventure in reading. This joy embraces the serious and the silly, the profound and the ridiculous, and it leaves room for exploring further insights. It is not merely a negation of what Lodge has said, for Chesterton is against "mere negation" (negation for negation's sake).[80]

---

76. Ibid., 131.

77. Ibid.

78. Ibid., 134.

79. Chesterton, *Collected Works, Volume 1*, 363.

80. Chesterton, *Illustrated London News*, January 30, 1932.

To see things as they are, as we learn from this brief excursion, requires an initial process of simply seeing where things may lead. It must mean leaving space to grow—to revisit, revise, and even reverse what was previously assumed in the palimpsest of thought. This is a process that this Chestertonian playfulness allows for, and it somewhat explains how Chesterton came to revise some of his earlier convictions about, say, Unitarianism, Socialism, or optimism. Nevertheless, the subtle or sometimes more drastic shifts in Chesterton's thinking over the course of his lifetime should not be confused with the advocacy of indecision concerning matters of personal conviction. Chesterton abhorred the sort of thinking that leads a person to accept or reject something only on the basis of a mere whim or fancy, although he maintains that, since some things do change, "truth should be kept reasonably flexible."[81]

A careful reading of the progression of Chesterton's thinking reveals that he possessed, to an extraordinary degree, two qualities that at first may seem terribly antithetical: empathy and combativeness. He was, to put it differently, both deeply compassionate and also profoundly confrontational in his outlook and thus capable of attacking ideas without creating enemies. This unusual combination of qualities was crucial in guiding his thought life and his interpretive process. Some have been quick to point out the latter quality while forgetting the former and thus are guilty of misrepresenting Chesterton as being perpetually hostile in his intellectual attitude. We see this, for instance, in Julius West's unfair contention that Chesterton "would be pugnacious, even when there was nothing to fight."[82] And while there is certainly evidence, as I have noted above, that Chesterton appreciated the collision of thoughts, it would be mistaken to assume that his thinking is entirely dialectical (in the modern, Hegelian sense) and therefore built entirely upon negation.

It is true that Chesterton considered the development of his journalistic philosophy as a result of "having listened rather respectfully and rather bashfully to the very best advice . . . and then going away and doing the [exact] opposite."[83] Because of this, Chesterton may be dismissed as a "reactionary" who is just stubbornly resistant to "spirit of [his] age,"[84] but we should notice that his oppositional stance was always preceded by having listened well, and therefore never consisted only of resisting the perspective of others: "Chesterton," Maisie Ward observes, "was one of the very few

81. Chesterton, *Illustrated London News*, December 30, 1911.

82. West, *G. K. Chesterton*, 23.

83. Chesterton, *Autobiography*, 179; Ward, *Gilbert Keith Chesterton*, 137.

84. McLuhan, "G. K. Chesterton," 456.

conversationalists—perhaps the only one—who would really rather listen than talk."[85] Chesterton contends that "listening, or trying to listen, is the business of everybody."[86] This predilection for listening reveals something about his way of reading that may seem obvious, but is important to highlight nonetheless: Chesterton reads first and responds afterwards. His work presents us with an insistence that seeking to understand, with empathy, ought to precede commentary. His empathy and his desire to understand are mutually inclusive and impossible to disassociate; although, that said, the two qualities, interlocked as they are, should also not be conflated.[87]

Titterton presents a more balanced and I think more accurate view of his friend's fighting spirit than West does: "G. K. C. sprang into the world all armed . . . and his defence of common things was a continual attacking"; he was the "knight errant, with all his heart in the fight, hating the *thing* attacked like the devil, but loving his adversary for the sake of the argument, and roaring with tempestuous laughter as he dealt his slashing blows."[88] Here we get to the core of Chesterton's approach: a magnificent combination of a desire for truth and a heart full of love: truth and grace, together. We find in Titterton's words a sense of what drove Chesterton's pugnacity, namely defense. Chesterton contends that one "cannot fight without something to fight for,"[89] and also "that the main business of a man, however humble, is defence."[90]

Over thirty years after penning those words in *The Defendant* (1902), Chesterton reaffirmed his original impulse in his *Autobiography* (1936): "The name of Defendant is the only thing I cannot defend. . . . The papers were in defence of various other things such as Penny Dreadfuls and Skeletons. But a defendant does not properly mean a person defending other things. It means a person defending himself; and I should be the last to defend anything so indefensible."[91] Chesterton readily empathized with various causes germane to his time, but in the process did not fuss too much with ensuring the preservation of his own reputation. His writings defend many things, therefore, but are often self-effacing. Nevertheless, this simple idea of defense, which seems to have acted as a manifesto for his entire attitude towards life, is stated thus: "things must be loved first and improved

85. Ward, *Gilbert Keith Chesterton*, 136.

86. Chesterton, *Illustrated London News*, January 19, 1929.

87. Ricoeur, *Time and Narrative*, 97, 253.

88. Titterton, *G. K. Chesterton*, 35–36.

89. Chesterton, *Appreciations and Criticisms*, 28.

90. Chesterton, *The Defendant*, 6.

91. Chesterton, *Autobiography*, 121.

afterwards."[92] Allegiance is required before reform is possible.[93] Hospitality must therefore precede and ground all our reasoning, arguing, and reading if we hope to understand anything.

In keeping with this spirit of hospitality, which is the virtue that takes the guest in, warts and all, Chesterton's writings express the need to "fight for everything against nothing, for reality against illusion, for existence against suicide, for waking against nightmare, for sanity against despair."[94] He "defended small nations" when people were "being told to think imperially"; he "defended private property" when socialism was fashionable; he "defended small business" when "chain-stores" were becoming popular, and "home" in the face of anti-home feminists; he also defended marriage when divorce had become perfectly acceptable.[95] Stephen Medcalf writes that "because these were his causes . . . he could reconcile the two poles in himself, that he was at once an usually humble and gentle person, and furiously combative."[96]

I once wondered along the lines of West's critique if Chesterton would not have arrived at other conclusions had he simply had different ideologies and perspectives to fight against, but I have since realized that such speculation makes little sense, for his defenses were never purported for the sake of argument alone. His oppositional impulse, if that is what it was, may have instigated changes in the details of his philosophy, but it was not what grounded his final opinions. In fact, Titterton argues that Chesterton "was not as his best when he was expounding a system. He was at his best in an attack . . . . (When debating he was always best in reply.)"[97] This observation, which again stresses the value of seeking to understand Chesterton as a reader and hermeneut, begs the question of what specific things Chesterton fought for, especially in response to his immediate socio-political environment. This question, as we find in his own writings, is deeply interwoven with the question of how he actually perceived his own world. To get a sense of this, it is helpful to take his approach to criticism into account.

92. Chesterton, *The Defendant*, xii.

93. Chesterton, *Collected Works, Volume 1*, 274.

94. Medcalf, "Introduction," 1.

95. Knox, "G. K. Chesterton," 47.

96. Medcalf, "Introduction," 1.

97. Titterton, *G. K. Chesterton*, 69.

The Art of Criticism

Chesterton observes a problem not often noticed about biographies, namely that they tend to focus on things that the subject would have deemed unimportant.[98] "[Biography] reveals and asserts and insists on exactly those things in a man's life of which the man himself is [typically] wholly unconscious; his exact class in society, the circumstances of his ancestry, the place of his present location. These are things which do not, properly speaking, ever arise before the human vision."[99] Although the present book is not a biography, this point can be kept in mind as we consider Chesterton's interpretive awareness: "The universe, as it really is to us, is an undiscoverable universe; it is a lost universe."[100] The things that most shape a person's perspective tend to be the things that a person is unaware of:

> The fish forgets the sea with the dark irrevocable forgetfulness with which the bird forgets the wood and the daisy forgets the meadow. In other words, he can never know what are his own first thoughts of water. He has got used to it, and in getting used to things is the primitive sin by which Adam fell and by which all creation falls. Just as a fish knows nothing of the sea so we know nothing of the earth. The earth is as far as Atlantis or Asgard. Beyond the last islet of the fantastic archipelago of the sunset lies in immemorial mystery the land which we tread down with our boot soles. And buried under a vast and star-kissing rubbish heap of deductions and generalisations lie our first thoughts, which are best.[101]

Chesterton's frequent use of the word "unconscious" in his writings—not denoting Freud's dark unconscious drives that sabotage our happiness when repressed, but rather simply those facets of thought and experience that elude our awareness—shows just how important this idea is to him. These things may not necessarily arise *before* the human vision, which is to say that these things are not part of our conscious awareness, but they certainly inform the invisible foundation of first thoughts that determines the range of one's view.[102] Hermeneutics is always first a matter of being before it

---

98. Chesterton, *Varied Types*, 3.

99. Ibid.

100. Chesterton, *The Speaker*, May 3, 1902.

101. Ibid.

102. Gadamer, *Truth and Method*, 300–301.

is a matter of knowing.[103] It is a matter of some metaphysical or ontological grounding before it is a matter of epistemology.

This is arguably why in hermeneutic theory we refer to a *horizon* rather than only to a *worldview*. While horizon and worldview both imply contraction and expansion, categorization, varying degrees of clarity and myopia, as well as differing levels of significance, the two terms ought to be subtly differentiated. Steven Cone observes that worldview is "a multifaceted phenomenon that includes, not just understandings of the world, but also [implicit] values."[104] However, "[w]hat horizon brings to the fore is that the most basic understandings and concerns by which we know the world and live in it are not intellectual items that we can inspect" or obvious and explicit terms of reference "but rather the basic constitution of our selves that makes us able to think about things and care about them at all."[105]

An approximation of this hermeneutic understanding of a horizon is captured by Chesterton in his idea of the "symbolism of syntax," which refers to "the way in which the mere construction of a sentence suggests presumptions or prejudices, apart from anything named or defined."[106] It is the idea that "doctrines" and "dogmas" are not just found in the explicit meaning of the words we speak, but also in the "shape of a sentence."[107] Perhaps there is something in this that predicts Jacques Lacan's idea that the "unconscious" is "structured like a language."[108] There is something, in other words, which operates outside of our awareness, which discloses more than we wish to disclose; there is something that speaks through us on our behalf. Chesterton likens this to having a "waste-paper basket" for a head, since it is possible to live out the very ideas that we think we may have discarded.[109] What we think we believe (what we articulate) and what we really believe (as represented by our engagement with words and the world) may even be at odds.

Horizon, as the syntax of being, foregrounds the central aim of hermeneutic philosophy, which is to understand the conditions that make understanding possible. This is analogous to the ending of *The Coloured Lands*, in which the protagonist looks at the world without spectacles, but only after trying on so many other spectacles. He sees anew precisely because

---

103. Ibid., 312.

104. Cone, *An Ocean Vast of Blessing*, 63.

105. Ibid.

106. Chesterton, *Illustrated London News*, April 2, 1932.

107. Ibid.

108. Dor, *Introduction to the Reading of Lacan*, 7.

109. Chesterton, *Illustrated London News*, April 2, 1932; See Chesterton, *Illustrated London News*, July 18, 1914.

of an experience of having his horizon challenged. Horizon is more radical than worldview, since it involves more than our intentional choices of creed and dogma. It implies that what we genuinely care about is not necessarily articulated in the concepts and labels that we use to describe our thoughts. Horizon reveals that, in addition to what a worldview articulates, there are also things that we can know without knowing how to acknowledge them; there are things that we believe and understand—presuppositions and prejudices, for example—without being capable of exposing them.

Horizon indicates that while we cannot always say precisely how our contexts have shaped us, we can be certain they have shaped us nonetheless. Worldview may be easier to unpack, as we find even in the case of Chesterton, because the coordinates of a worldview tend to be fairly easily identifiable in their explicitness. Nevertheless, our understanding of Chesterton's actual horizon is helped by the fact that he was remarkably self-aware and reflective when it came to the intricacies and effects of context. In fact, he consistently stressed, both implicitly and explicitly, the importance of not undervaluing one's own environment.[110] His philosophy looks very carefully and intently at the place and culture that informed his way of seeing. This is significant because an understanding of the drama of meaning depends on its general scenography.

One aspect of Chesterton's scenography is immediately of some significance. He entered into journalism at a time when attitudes were being forged by an pressing topic: the outbreak of the Second Boer War—also known as the Second South African War (1899–1902).[111] Michael Ffinch's contention that "Chesterton made his reputation largely through his writing about the Boer War"[112] is only marginally correct, although there is some truth to the idea that his reputation was helped by his "determined and per-si... opposition to British policy" as Ward records.[113] Rather, early in his ...ecially while he wrote for *The Speaker* and in the early days of his ...*e Daily News,* Chesterton was primarily preoccupied with writ- ...views. Thus, through the "journalism of his earliest years Ches- ...airly quickly established himself as a very considerable critic."[114] ...lackstock notes that Chesterton's criticism has been charged ...er of crimes, including "excessive optimism, slovenly scholar- ...listic theatricality," as well as "inaccuracy, digressiveness, . . .

...rton, *The Defendant,* 3.

...C...rton and the Romance of Orthodoxy, 210.

...ock, *The Rhetoric of Redemption,* ...

moralism, Victorianism, philistinism ('Chesterton *is* the mob!' sneered [Ezra] Pound), impressionism, and romanticism."[115] Chesterton tended to include too much of his own personality in his writing to make it acceptable to scholars. A number of these charges are misplaced, simply because they neglect to take into account Chesterton's audience, which included more than just highly educated, elitist professors. Chesterton always insists that his writing is for the common man. His focus is on men and women and not just ideas.[116]

Because of this, Frank Alfred Lea decides that Chesterton really "excelled" at "literary criticism," which is that "half-way house between art and philosophy."[117] Lea contends that it is precisely this unusual combination of art with philosophy that gives rise to a critical political philosophy, especially because it forces the critic to "make a holocaust at once of conventional prejudice," and "the more intimate bias of his own convictions," especially "if he is to approach it imaginatively, from within outwards."[118] Lea, in examining "Chesterton's studies," contends that he was precisely the kind of critic he had always hoped to be because he allowed his mind to be what John Keats calls a "thoroughfare for all thoughts."[119] He always strived for "direct and individual impressions of primary objects, whether poets or pine trees."[120] This is something already noted in Chesterton's appreciation for the collision of the mind with a fact or idea.

While book reviewers for the *Daily News* were usually not named, the young Chesterton wrote with such profound insights and confidence that, nine months after beginning his work at the newspaper, he was given special credit, his name appearing at the bottom of every article that he wrote.[121] This suited him well, since he despised anonymity.[122] He felt it to be more honest, and more in keeping with an ethic of accountability, to have one's name attached to one's work.[123] It also opened up the possibility of g_____ dialogue with his readers, for he was never afraid to meet the o_____ the public head on.

115. Ibid.

116. Belloc, *On the Place of Gilbert Chesterton,* 27.

117. Lea, *The Wild Knight of Battersea,* 50.

118. Ibid.

119. Ibid.

120. Chesterton, *Illustrated London News,* October 24, 1931.

121. Stapleton, *Christianity, Patriotism, and Nationhood,* 35; Oddie, *the Romance of Orthodoxy,* 203.

122. Chesterton, *Illustrated Lon___ News.* D____

123. Chesterton, *All Thi___*

To understand Chesterton's practice of literary criticism is to gain a few important insights into his hermeneutic. After all, criticism and hermeneutics are very closely related. Criticism always implicitly deals with interpretation. Hermeneutics can also be said to presuppose criticism since criticism is arguably one of the "most accessible hermeneutic models."[124] The history of criticism is long and complex, and a comprehensive survey of its many themes and variations would require a totally different book. My aim here is to briefly cover Chestertonian criticism, which provides a doorway to understanding how this man of letters so naturally became a voice on matters of politics and religion, as well as almost every other subject imaginable.

To begin with, it is helpful to notice that criticism is etymologically linked to two notions that both overlap and diverge, namely the ideas of a court judgment and of a comparison.[125] Chesterton, noting this etymology, takes issue with both ideas as pathways into criticism. To begin with, in a 1902 article from *The Speaker*, he complains that this link with "a criminal judge" may lead us to suppose "that criticism had to do with literary crimes" where "[t]he favourable judgment of the critic has always been, in the ordinary opinion, to acquit a man of a sin, not to convict him of a merit."[126] In Chesterton's mind, a negative view of the role and purpose of criticism ought to be seen as highly problematic: "If criticism were in a sound state it would have discovered some one epithet to express the value of Coleridge instead of a half a hundred epithets to express the uselessness of Marie Corelli."[127]

This contrast of criticism about Coleridge (1772–1834) with criticism about Corelli (1855–1924) demonstrates an elitism that was built into the way that criticism was understood in Chesterton's time: Corelli, a bestselling creator of sentimental melodramas, wrote for the masses and was generally deplored by critics.[128] Coleridge, on the other hand, was generally very well ⟨reg⟩arded by the literati. In mentioning this common distinction between ⟨po⟩pular literature, though, Chesterton has not made his meaning ⟨as⟩ his argument continues:

⟨Opti⟩mism, or the utmost possible praise of all things, ought to ⟨be t⟩he keynote of criticism. It may appear to be an audacious ⟨asse⟩rtion, but it may be tested by one very large and simple

⟨...⟩ & Robinson, *Hermeneutics*, 274.
⟨Sch⟩rmacher, *Hermeneutics and Criticism*, 158.
⟨Chest⟩erton, *The Speaker*, May 3, 1902.
⟨Chest⟩erton, *The Speaker*, May 3, 1902; Chesterton, *The Man Who Was Ortho*-
⟨...⟩ *Marie Corelli*, 30.

process. Compare the reality of a man's criticism when praising anything with its reality when excluding anything, and we
shall all feel how much more often we agree with the former
than with the latter. A man says, for example, "The Yorkshire
moors are incomparably splendid," and we wholly agree. He
goes on, "their superiority to the mere hills of Surrey—" and
we instantly disagree with him. He says, "the Illiad, the highest
expression of man's poetical genius," and all our hearts assent.
He adds, "towering high above all our Hamlets and Macbeths,"
and we flatly deny it. A man may say, "Plato was the greatest
man of antiquity," and we admit it; but if he says, "he was far
greater than Aeschylus," we demur. Briefly, in praising great men
we cheerfully agree to a superlative, but we emphatically decline
a comparative. We come very near to the optimism of that universal superlative which in the morning of the world declared all
things to be very good.[129]

Chesterton's point, connecting with the narrative of Genesis that is
discussed in the following chapter, is not that comparison should be done
away with entirely, for understanding anything is impossible without the
ability to compare things. What is important is that comparison be used
rightly; it should not merely be regarded as a negation of the work that is
being exposed to one's criticism. This idea is demonstrated in Chesterton's
commentary on the way that Robert Louis Stevenson's critics often deferred
to the authority of the "excellent writer" Frank Swinnerton: "I would still
meekly suggest that a man writing on Stevenson should be judged by his
appreciation of Stevenson, and not by his appreciation of Swinnerton."[130]
Moreover, criticism, especially of a writer's whole corpus, seems most reasonable when it takes the author's best work as a context for his worst work,
rather than the other way around.[131]

Chesterton claims that "when a critic is really large-mind
ally sympathetic and comprehensive, and really has a hold of a
enlightening idea, he should still watch with the greatest suspici
limitations and rejections."[132] If a critic has praise to offer, he sho
gladly; but if there is any blame in his offering, such blame "sho
remain to his mind a little dubious."[133]

129. Chesterton, *The Speaker*, May 3, 1902.

130. Chesterton, *Illustrated London News*, October 24, 1931.

131. Ibid.

132. Chesterton, *The Speaker*, May 3, 1902; Chesterton, *The Man Wh
dox*, 173.

133. Ibid.

Chesterton sides with a reasonable hermeneutic when he stresses optimism as a better ground for understanding than pessimism: by jumping too quickly to a negative and exclusionary view of a thing, or a comparative view that places the work of another type above the work being examined, the reader would thereby be subordinating the text to his own egotism, preferences and prejudices; he would not therefore be reading in a way that places himself at odds with the otherness of the text and therefore also at odds with the possibility of genuinely understanding the text. Chesterton coins a word in *Browning*—actually to criticize Browning—that suggests the logical conclusion of such a negative view: "postjudice," which is "not the bias before the fair trial, but the bias that remains afterwards."[134] It is bad enough to judge a thing wrongly before engaging with it; it is positively unforgivable to judge it wrongly afterwards. Thus, as Blackstock suggests, Chesterton's criticism is rooted in a "rhetoric of redemption."[135] He looks for what is salvageable rather than just for what should be discarded.

In the above, Chesterton casts the very notion of criticism into question by shifting the focus from what is read to how it is read. This very idea is taken up by a Chestertonian named C. S. Lewis in his *An Experiment in Criticism* (1961). There we find that while criticism typically deals with "judging books," it may certainly be taken as being very closely related with how we read; that is, with "types of reading."[136] When we examine a few of Chesterton's other ideas on criticism, we discover that it is not only the text that is at stake, but also the reader: "The longer I live the more I am convinced that humanity fails through Pharisaism; or men boasting of washing themselves when they are only whitewashing themselves. It is already antiquated to talk about the Higher Criticism. But there is such a thing as the Highest Criticism; and it is self-criticism."[137] Whatever criticism is, and however it may help us to ground an understanding of Chesterton's perception, it is not an exercise in elitist egotism, which gathers "all the short-sighted people" into a monotonous "city called Myopia."[138] It is more like an exercise in self-reflection. It is not merely a case of separating the sheep from the goats, so to speak, but an exercise in examining how and why we have arrived at our criteria for separating them, or a process of checking whether or not we need to separate them at all.

---

134. Chesterton, *Robert Browning*, 115.

135. See Blackstock, *The Rhetoric of Redemption*.

136. Lewis, *An Experiment in Criticism*, 1.

137. Chesterton, *Illustrated London News*, May 25, 1935.

138. Chesterton, *A Miscellany of Men*, 140.

However, Chesterton is not saying that criticism should avoid being critical. The very fact that the word "test" appears so frequently in Chesterton's vocabulary ought to be proof enough of this. There are too many examples to name—literally thousands—but it is clear from his corpus that Chesterton is unceasingly testing ideas against other ideas, or against history, experience, or even imagination. So, again, he is not in favor of the kind of criticism that avoids being critical. In his mind, criticism concerns seeing what is really there, and that requires a positive sense of what the text is actually disclosing. In reflecting, for instance, on Edith C. Batho's *The Later Wordsworth* (1933), Chesterton concludes that Wordsworth is "hardly a historical person who needs whitewashing" and in fact "appears rather too white,"[139] but Batho, in trying to present Wordsworth only positively, sees only a man who wore "rose-coloured spectacles" and therefore overlooks his lapses into "the blues."[140] Even when one uses the best of an author's work as a context for the worst, one cannot neglect to notice where he has come up short or lost his way.

One of the tests performed the most by Chesterton on those he reads is the simple test of consistency. Is the writer consistent with their aims and intentions as they have articulated them? If Edith Batho is thought of by Chesterton as failing to read Wordsworth, it is because she is claiming to have done that very thing. In an article written in 1929, Chesterton levels this very same criticism against skeptics who claim to have read the Bible, but whose commentary betrays the fact that they have not. They claim that the Bible tell us that "Eve ate an apple" or that "Jonah was swallowed by a whale," which it does not, and then go on to criticize the Bible for opposing rationalism.[141] But the critics, in getting even these small details wrong, betray a larger problem: they essentially create a picture based, not on what they have read in the Bible (exegesis), but on what they have "read into the Bible" (eisegesis).[142] Before one can criticize anything, therefore, one first has to actually see it on its own terms.[143]

With this in mind, the primary test of a book must be the book itself and its context (insofar as it can be understood), rather than the author, the reader, or other books that the reader has read. The terms for criticism are set up by the object of criticism. A further example of this principle is found in Chesterton's "Defence of Ugly Things" where he notes that complaining

139. Chesterton, *In Defense of Sanity*, 396–97.

140. Ibid., 398.

141. Chesterton, *Illustrated London News*, April 20, 1929.

142. Ibid.

143. Chesterton, *Stories, Essays and Poems*, 218.

that a person is ugly because his face does not conform to some convention of beauty, even when his bodily form clearly expresses the man's soul, is "like complaining that a cabbage has not two legs."[144] To compare anything, for Chesterton, is to compare it first with itself: one has to see a thing in its own unique relational particularity rather than only as an extension of its environment or the environment of the reader.

For Chesterton, reading optimistically does not mean reading only through rose-colored spectacles. In fact, it is that very type of optimism that Chesterton is highly critical of, especially since it is so deeply connected to modernist conceptions of "progress" and the "liberation of the human mind."[145] Chestertonian optimism, especially as a hermeneutic coordinate, has three clear implications. Firstly, it allows the critic to see the work before him as a positive thing—a thing with its own unique lines, edges, qualities, and purposes. It is a definite thing apart from the critic and his opinions—a thing existing on and through its own horizon. Secondly, Chestertonian optimism allows the critic to "interpret . . . remarks so as to give them a deeper and often unexpected significance"—something that Cammaerts thinks Chesterton does particularly well.[146] In other words, the deliberate adoption of a positive view allows the critic to look at a work of art or literature in its best possible light. If the work then fails, the critic cannot be accused of just brushing it aside because it was not to his liking.

Then, thirdly, a Chestertonian optimism implies that a person may indeed find the right kind of perspective from which a thing may be understood; it means that what is set before the reader can be understood in accordance with its own integrity, including where it may have taken a turn for the worst. Chesterton is obviously aware of Matthew Arnold's views on criticism, given that, among other references to Arnold, he wrote the "Introduction" for a book of Arnold's criticism in which the essay "On the Function of Criticism at the Present Time" is included. In that essay, Arnold writes, that the "critical endeavour" seeks, "in all branches of knowledge, theology, philosophy, history, art, science, to see the object in itself as really is."[147]

Even when a positive view is foregrounded, however, criticism remains rooted in a confrontation between the reader and the text. Reading is an act of having "one thought rub against another."[148] The necessity remains to be

144. Chesterton, *The Defendant*, 85.

145. Cammaerts, *The Laughing Prophet*, 48.

146. Ibid., 40.

147. Arnold, *Essays, Literary and Critical*, 1.

148. Chesterton, *In Defense of Sanity*, 336.

able to distinguish between ideas, to tell whether one idea is better or worse than another. Chesterton complains that critics who fail to distinguish between ideas are "not . . . stupider than I am; but [rather] . . . stupider than they are."[149] Such critics write without bothering to read honestly and with fidelity to their own intellectual capacities.[150] They have barred themselves from the interpretive experience; they have failed to allow themselves both understanding (of the text) and self-understanding.

This failure to read may be regarded in terms of three traps. In the first place, as I have just intimated, there is the trap of failing to acknowledge the genuine alterity of the text; in the second place, there is the trap of failing to acknowledge the position of the author even if the intention of the author is not completely explicable; and, in the third place, there is the trap that leads to these other traps: the reader's failure to acknowledge his own position. In trying to avoid this vile third trap, Chesterton writes, "I dare say a great deal of the criticism I write is really moved by a mood of self-expression; and certainly it is true enough that there is a satisfaction in self-expression."[151] It is therefore better to own up to one's subjective presence to the text than end up, as Chesterton suggests, "as indifferent as a hen to all noises except her own cackling over her own egg."[152] To fail to acknowledge one's own position is to be in constant danger of having one's opinion completely override what one is reading. In the same way, a failure to acknowledge the role of tradition in hermeneutics is more likely to result in having that tradition dictate and direct interpretation.

In a reflection on Chesterton's *Browning,* James Douglas emphasizes that Chesterton's own practice of criticism does not fall into the traps noted above. He suggests that "[c]riticism is a revelation of the critic as well as of the creator. The better the critic the more subjective the criticism, for criticism is an art of spiritual reverberations as well as an art of spiritual judgments."[153] Douglas argues that "[l]ife and literature, which is life in language, are things too nervously alive to be arranged . . . without passion and without prejudice. The spiritual blow struck by a poet is struck afresh on the soul of every reader, and criticism is the echo of these spiritual blows."[154]

An apparent contradiction seems to be evident, though, when we take this idea together with something mentioned earlier regarding Chesterton's

149. Ibid., 337.

150. Ibid., 338.

151. Chesterton, *Stories, Essays and Poems,* 221.

152. Ibid., 223.

153. Quoted in Oddie, *Chesterton and the Romance of Orthodoxy,* 231.

154. Ibid.

tendency to ventriloquize: in principle, it seems that the critic is somehow both self-effacing and brimming with subjectivity. This is a contradiction that must not be resolved; it is actually the necessary contradiction at the heart of the hermeneutic experience. To resolve it is to assume that there is either (if self-effacement is total) no reader, or (if the reader's opinion is deemed absolute) no text. In practice, though, neither of these positions is tenable. The hermeneutic experience erupts from this clash and fusion of alterities. The reader is subservient to the text; but, paradoxically, the text is not his master. Hermeneutics always operates in this between; it functions intersubjectively.

There is, as every avid reader understands, a resonance that one finds in the text that one is contemplating, but this resonance is only possible in the conversation of two othernesses that come into contact: the hammer and the gong, to use an analogy, or the bow and the string. Each thing is fully itself, and all the more so for its confrontation and conversation with the other. It would not be an exaggeration, in keeping with Chesterton's emphasis on optimism, to assume that criticism is an act of love. "It may be confidently asserted," Lea writes, "that only a great critic [like Chesterton] could have composed his parodies on Tennyson and Walt Whitman."[155] Such parodies, which so perfectly capture the style of the poets in question and yet also so perfectly reflect Chesterton's sense of play and fun, could only have been composed by one willing to see the meeting of the reader and text as a definite and personal thing.

It is Chesterton's ability to step beyond labels typically used by critics—labels like "classical," "romantic," "socialist," and so on—that allows him to appreciate things in their distinctiveness. This is particularly evident in the way that he appraises poetry. Lea notes that by being free from the tyranny of labels, especially like those used so accusatorily against him, Chesterton is "free to acknowledge that there are as many different kinds of poetry as there are poets" and is therefore also free to "enjoy each for its own merits."[156] Terms and labels can certainly be useful, especially as classifications, but Chesterton recognizes how problematic they may become when regarded as judgments. As judgments, they are excuses to assume familiarity, or, worse, to dismiss a thing without properly regarding it as itself.[157] Another hermeneutic paradox is evident here: "Judge not, that ye be not judged"[158] (Matt 7:1) and "Judge not according to the appearance, but judge

155. Lea, *The Wild Knight of Battersea*, 51.
156. Ibid., 5
157. Ibid.
158. Chesterton, *Lunacy and Letters*, 49.

[with] righteous judgment" (John 7:24) function together in Chesterton's work. Regarding criticism, to not judge a thing is to let it be itself as a reality separate from the self, apart from one's thoughts and conclusions about it; to judge with the correct judgment is to judge it as itself, as separate from other things, keeping in mind the unavoidability of the self-mediation of the reader. To see things as clearly as possible, to see things as they are, one must have a perspective that is simultaneously *inside* and *outside*. This is the central hermeneutic principle followed by Chesterton in his *The Everlasting Man* (1925), part of which, as I argue below, can be taken as a case study of Chesterton's approach to criticism.

It is in the interests of so-called objectivity that the critic may be encouraged to maintain a kind of critical distance from the work being examined. This may have its merits, unless that critical distance implies a kind of ruthless and unrelenting agnosticism towards or violence against the text. But critical distance has the potential to hinder perception. It is possible, in Chesterton's mind, to be too far away to be able to see clearly, as is especially true in the case with the "philosopher of the ego."[159] It is often assumed that the clearer vision involves only looking at a thing rather than along it or by it. Lewis describes this as being akin to looking at "a beam of light, with the specks of dust floating in it."[160] This involves "seeing the beam, not seeing things by it."[161] Chesterton's preferable vantage point is the latter. He allows things to be co-participants in their own mediation.

One may learn a great deal about a poem, for instance, when one looks at its syntax, grammar, and rhythm; when one sees the structure and rhetoric of the poem from a place of detachment and reflection. But when one reads it imaginatively and empathically, as if from the inside, it is as if one is looking along the poem and therefore seeing by its light. This indicates that there is a clear difference between *knowing about* a thing and experientially *knowing* it. Distance is suggested by the former and itimacy, as in the archaic use of the word *know*, is suggested in the latter. There is, in other words, a difference between secondary knowledge *about* a thing and primary experiential knowledge *of* a thing. To be a critic, in the Chestertonian sense, an affectionate affinity with the text is of paramount importance. This does not merely require familiarity with the text, which may simply mean that one is too close to a thing to properly see it, but a kind of reflective familiarity, which implies that one can be close enough to a thing to see by its light and yet also far enough away from it to see it clearly.

159. Chesterton, *The Defendant*, 101.
160. Lewis, *Essay Collection*, 199.
161. Ibid.

To describe this hermeneutic experience, Chesterton refers back to his novel *Manalive* (1912) as a story about "two ways of getting home," one of which "is to stay there" and the other of which "is to walk round the whole world till we come back to the same place."[162] Chesterton uses another story to illustrate this same idea, which has a particular relevance to the way that the texts of Christianity are approached:

> I conceived it as a romance of those vast valleys with sloping sides, like those along which the ancient White Horses of Wessex are scrawled along the flanks of the hills. It concerned some boy whose farm or cottage stood on such a slope, and who went on his travels to find something, such as the effigy and grave of some giant; and when he was far enough from home he looked back and saw that his own farm and kitchen-garden, shining flat on the hill-side like the colours and quarterings of a shield, were, but parts of some such gigantic figure, on which he had always lived, but which was too large and too close to be seen. That, I think, is a true picture of the progress of any really independent intelligence today . . . .[163]

Chesterton then offers that "the next best thing to being really inside Christendom is to be really outside it."[164] That, again, means being close enough to experience it personally while also being distant enough to understand the thing's distinctiveness. His criticism of the critics of Christendom, which is a criticism of their way of reading, is that they "are not really outside it" and are therefore not really inside it either.[165] What this means is that their relationship to Christianity is confused; they do not know where its edges are, where it ends and where they begin. Thus, "[t]heir criticism has taken on a curious tone; as of a random and illiterate heckling."[166]

Chesterton tackles the problem with their criticism particularly with regard to the story of the Gospels and their main subject. By addressing the way that some have thought of Christ in the stories, Chesterton starts to imply the importance of approaching reading as a sacramental activity, whereby we become aware of something "human and more than human."[167] Through reading we may discover extraordinary miracles, but also the

---

162. Chesterton, *The Everlasting Man*, 204.
163. Ibid.
164. Ibid.
165. Ibid.
166. Ibid.
167. Ibid.

miracle of the ordinary.[168] While the text in question is undoubtedly part of a spiritual tradition, its implications for reading are not limited to biblical hermeneutics.

Chesterton begins his examination of the Gospels with the assumption that the modern critic, like any human being really, begins his reading of a text with a prejudice. With this in mind, he argues that reading any text should be, among other things, an act of testing that prejudice. That little word "test" appears with dramatic pertinence here; Chesterton is, without doubt, adamant that our ideas ought not to be baseless. "You cannot make a success out of anything," he writes, "even loving, entirely without thinking."[169] Consequently, he tests the bias that "[treats] man merely as an animal" and in the process discovers that man is unique among the animals in too many ways to be accounted for by simply appealing to that reductionist view. Man is too distinct from the animals to be merely classed as indistinct from them. Having shown this, Chesterton then opts to read the Gospels with the assumption that "[treats] Christ merely as a man."[170] If Christ is merely a man, then he should be indistinguishable from any normal man.[171]

By using this logic, Chesterton lets the bias stand out as clearly as it can before approaching the text, especially because he knows that "it is not at all easy to regard the New Testament as a New Testament" or "to realise the good news as new" for "[b]oth for good and evil familiarity fills us with assumptions and associations; and no man of our civilization, whatever he thinks of our religion, can really read the thing as if he had never heard of it before."[172] Here we have a picture of one of the hermeneutic paradoxes mentioned already: Chesterton is highly subjective and yet also self-effacing. He reads the text assuming the position of some "imaginary heathen human being" to demonstrate that the text itself will lead to conclusions that are more aligned with this more orthodox point of view.[173] This is not as simple as conforming to a belief bias that interprets the strength of an argument on the basis of whether it agrees with one's conclusions or not. Rather, it is an attempt to genuinely suspend a prejudice while simultaneously allowing for the possibilities suggested by alternative perspectives. Whatever starting point one begins with, a faithful, honest reading of a text will lead to a

168. Ibid.

169. Chesterton, *Collected Works, Volume 3*, 181.

170. Chesterton, *The Everlasting Man*, 186.

171. Ibid.

172. Ibid.

173. Ibid.

genuine apprehension of what it actually says. This does not mean that there will only be one meaning or one interpretation, or any kind of hermeneutic immediacy, but instead implies that one will find meanings and interpretations that are genuinely congruent with the text, even given the unavoidability of mediation.

Still, no matter one's theoretical commitments, in the end the word will need to become flesh. It will need to point beyond its own symbolic meanings into a deeper sacramental meaning. "Criticism," Chesterton writes, "is only words about words."[174] And, for him, words need to point outside of words. He therefore assumes an imaginary position outside his own tradition, which ultimately leads him to argue that being inside the tradition makes for a more honest hermeneutic. As suggested above, this twofold stance of the reader is simultaneous. He is not either sympathetic or skeptical, but both at the same time.

Chesterton notes that certain critics read the Gospels assuming that Christ should be thought of only as a man; that he "is indeed a most merciful and humane lover of humanity," and that, moreover, the church is at fault for having rendered "this human character in repellent dogmas" and having therefore "stiffened it with ecclesiastical terrors till it has taken on an inhuman character."[175] This, incidentally, is precisely the line of argument taken in Thomas Jefferson's *The Life and Morals of Jesus of Nazareth* (1820) and Leo Tolstoy's *The Gospel in Brief* (1893), and it is also the premise of Philip Pullman's *The Good Man Jesus and the Scoundrel Christ* (2010). Even today, as in history, it is not uncommon to find the Jesus of the New Testament thought of as the noblest of people, whose image has been corrupted by a church that has insisted upon making him into a god. For reasons that are not always clear, the possibility of transcendence is offhandedly resisted.

Chesterton suggests that really paying attention to the texts of the New Testament and looking intently at the church reveals quite the opposite: "The truth is that it is the image of Christ in the churches that is almost entirely mild and merciful."[176] The history of art, which follows the human instinct to seek his words of pity and compassion, is almost excessive in its representations of "Gentle Jesus, meek and mild."[177] If anything, the church is more at fault for humanizing Jesus than for deifying him.

Chesterton suggests that the instinct to seek out and emphasize Christ's theocentric humanism is not inaccurate because the "mass of the poor are

174. Ibid., 209.
175. Ibid., 187.
176. Ibid.
177. Ibid.

broken, and the mass of the people are poor, and for the mass of mankind the main thing is to carry the conviction of the incredible compassion of God."[178] Chesterton is fully aware that there will be exceptions to this rule, but points out that generally the "popular machinery of the Church"—and by this he means the Catholic Church—has sought chiefly to carry "this idea of compassion."[179] Chesterton continues:

> And the point is here that it is very much more specially and exclusively merciful than any impression that could be formed by a man merely reading the New Testament for the first time. A man simply taking the words of the story as they stand would form quite another impression; an impression full of mystery and possibly of inconsistency; but certainly not merely an impression of mildness. It would be intensely interesting; but part of the interest would consist in its leaving a good deal to be guessed at or explained. It is full of sudden gestures evidently significant except that we hardly know what they signify; of enigmatic silences; of ironical replies. The outbreaks of wrath, like storms above our atmosphere, do not seem to break out exactly where we should expect them, but to follow some higher weather-chart of their own.[180]

Here, even at the beginning of his argument, we have Chesterton appealing to those unreasonable critics to properly understand their critical distance as outsiders to help them to see the text as if from the inside. The reality is that the so-called distortions of the image of Jesus as being merely a man are simply less compatible with the text of the New Testament than those critics have allowed. Thus, we find that the critic's claim to have actually read the New Testament is proving difficult to uphold. Chesterton says that he is "simply imagining the effect on a man's mind if he did really do what these critics are always talking about doing; if he did really read the New Testament without reference to orthodoxy and even without reference to doctrine."[181]

A careful, more self-aware interpretation reveals that "if we take [the story of Jesus] as a human story" we have to at least agree that "it is in some ways a very strange story" even apart from "its tremendous and tragic culmination or to any implications involving triumph in that tragedy" or

178. Ibid., 188.
179. Ibi
180. Ibid.
181. Ibid.

even its "miraculous element."[182] In fact, it is often the "unmiraculous" and "inconspicuous" elements of the story that are particularly odd; the unusual things are those things expressed, which have not been of any overt theological use.[183] If the writers of the Gospels were trying to invent something to prove a point, they would not have included such things in the story they were telling. "For instance," Chesterton writes, "there is that long stretch of silence in the life of Christ up to the age of thirty. It is of all silences the most immense and imaginatively impressive."[184] In legends of all kinds about various heroes, the opposite trend can be noticed, where their early years are recounted in great detail.

In the Gospels we also find Jesus quoting the psalm that "the meek shall inherit the earth" (Ps 37:11; Matt 5:5). Its meaning is not at all transparent, and yet no additional clarification is offered.[185] This is a problem in much of the New Testament. The episode of Martha chastising Mary for sitting at the feet of Jesus is another example among many: interpretations of all kinds have been offered precisely because the meaning of the story is not absolutely obvious. It is certainly easier to look at Martha's servanthood and sermonize about the joy of work than to locate a meaning in Mary's apparent laziness. Then, Christ's allusion to "eunuchs of the kingdom of heaven" would be enough to startle even the most well read priest.[186] If the fundamental aim of the Gospel writers had been to persuade others to understand their message, surely a little more clarity could have been included? Biblical scholars and homilists can certainly be grateful that this is not the case: uncertainty is often the mother of invention.

In light of this hermeneutic ambiguity, Chesterton notes, "the Gospel as it stands is almost a book of riddles."[187] The story is rendered surprisingly matter-of-factly, with understatements about even the most extreme of circumstances, and yet the teachings of Jesus are frequently "dark," "dazzling," "defiant or mysterious."[188] If "we *could* read the Gospel reports as things as new as newspaper reports, they would puzzle us and perhaps terrify us *more* than the same things as developed by historical Christianity."[189] Here, Chesterton displays a remarkable awareness concerning the degree to which

182. Ibid., 189.

183. Ibid.

184. Ibid.

185. Ibid., 191.

186. Ibid., 192.

187. Ibid.

188. Ibid.

189. Ibid.

Christianity is a mediated enterprise, which has been and will continue to be filtered through various terministic screens, including those provided by tradition and culture. He assumes, therefore, that there is far more to be uncovered in the text than what is usually assumed, and more to be uncovered in us than is often realized.

Chesterton then turns to the historical context of the Gospels, noting that while the critics tend to regard Jesus only as a man of his time, "there is nothing in the recorded words of Christ that ties him at all to his own time."[190] Chesterton is not referring to the "details of a period, which even a man of the period knows to be passing," but rather to the "fundamentals"—to those ideological edifices that organize our conceptual reality in a predetermined way and are therefore taken to be eternal even when they are not. He uses the example of slavery, which was taken to be natural in the world in which Christ lived, and yet Christ "started a movement that could exist in a world with slavery" that was also "a movement that could exist in a world without slavery."[191]

> [Jesus] never used a phrase that made his philosophy depend even upon the very existence of the social order in which he lived. He spoke as one conscious that everything was ephemeral, including the things that Aristotle thought eternal. By that time the Roman Empire had come to be merely the *orbis terrarum*, another name for the world. But he never made his morality dependent on the existence of the Roman Empire or even on the existence of the world. "Heaven and earth shall pass away, but my words shall not pass away."[192]

Chesterton maintains in the end that "a man reading the New Testament frankly and freshly would not get the impression of what is now often meant by a human Christ."[193] In fact, the reader would only end up realizing that "a merely human Christ is a made-up figure, a piece of artificial selection, like the merely evolutionary man."[194] Rationalists, desperate to maintain this human Christ, concocted a number of theories to explain him, including the theory that he was a divine being who did not exist, or that he was a human being that did not exist, or that he did exist, but was like "Hillel or a hundred other Jews," or even that he was a "madman with a Messianic

---

190. Ibid., 195.
191. Ibid.
192. Ibid.
193. Ibid., 196.
194. Ibid.

delusion."[195] Then, there has been a vast proliferation of other theories about what the ethical nature of his teachings really was; whether he was more Socialist, Pacificist, more aligned with Christian Science, which was an attempt "to expound Christianity without the crucifixion," or simply as a kind of hyperactive apocalypse.[196]

In the end, Chesterton concludes that "[t]here must surely have been something not only mysterious, but many-sided about Christ if so many smaller Christs can be carved out of him."[197] In the end, the critics have not seen the Gospels as they are. What Chesterton does, without overtly defending his own dogmas, is attempt "the rather impossible task of reversing time and the historic method; and in fancy [look] forward to the facts, instead of backward through the memories."[198] Through this process, he allows for the possibility of being genuinely surprised by the text he is reading. He asks, "Would not such a new reader of the New Testament stumble over something that would startle him much more than it startles us?"[199] Reading that allows for the possibility of being startled, for Chesterton, is an indication of being open to the text rather than of imposing one's expectations on it.

This approach to reading is not a surrender to simple-minded credulity or to the myth of hermeneutic immediacy. In fact, "stumbling on that rock of scandal" is only "the first step."[200] For Chesterton, "[s]tark staring incredulity is a far more loyal tribute" to the "truth of the text" than the uncritical adoption of "a modernistic metaphysic" that seeks to make everything credible.[201] One needs to be willing to be confronted by even the most "catastrophic claim" simply because it is a claim that is actually made.[202] When Jesus says, "Before Abraham was, I am," for example, he is not offering room for hermeneutic sidestepping.[203] He is offering, it seems, a very vivid and clear pronouncement about something that is either true or false. And, while there are interpretive issues that are more grey than black and white, conclusions about what appears grey must come from the text itself rather than from one's prejudices and postjudices about the text. All the while, Chesterton does not resort to strictly delimiting the way that Gospels

195. Ibid., 197.
196. Ibid.
197. Ibid.
198. Ibid.
199. Ibid.
200. Ibid., 198.
201. Ibid.
202. Ibid.
203. Ibid.

should be read and what specific meanings one ought to arrive at. What he does do, however, is demonstrate the importance of trying to read the text from the "inside."[204] For Chesterton, the text needs to be imaginatively inhabited.

We find his reading of the life of Christ to have a particular hermeneutic significance, for he is looking for the "Word . . . made flesh" (John 1:14). Moreover, as noted above, he discovers the appropriateness of "incredulity" as a "tribute."[205] It is a testimony to his hermeneutic honesty that the point of engaging in the drama of meaning is not so much about arriving at pure, rational clarity or tidy propositional truth; rather, it seems to involve getting a sense of a more profound mystery. It is not so much about grasping meaning in any totalizing way as it is about recognizing that meaning is sacramentally present in the text prior to the hermeneutic encounter.

This is beautifully represented by a moment in Chesterton's Father Brown story "The Honour of Israel Gow" when the priest exclaims that "every man who sleeps believes in God."[206] The "sacrament" of sleep represents the idea that reality precedes our engagement with it.[207] Even when "the truth makes no sense" it is still true and still discoverable.[208] Truth is a matter of being before it is a matter of believing. For Chesterton, if we allow ourselves the opportunity, we can read the world and discover something sacramental—a sign of real presence—in even the most mundane of subjects:

> A friend of mine has made game of me in a recent book for saying that lamp-posts are poetical; that common things, the boots I wear or the chair I sit on, if they are once understood, can satisfy the most gigantic imagination. I can only adhere with stubborn simplicity to my position. The boots I wear are, I will not say beautiful upon the mountains, but, at least, highly symbolic in the street, being boots of one that bringeth good news. The chair I sit on is really romantic—nay, it is heroic, for it is eternally in danger. The lamp-posts are poetical; not merely from accidental, but from essential causes. It is not merely the softening, sentimental associations that belong to lamp-posts, the beautiful fact that aristocrats were hanged on them, or that intoxicated old gentlemen embrace them: the lamp-post really

204. Ibid., 9.
205. Ibid., 198.
206. Chesterton, *The Annotated Innocence of Father Brown*, 132.
207. Ibid.
208. Chesterton, *Illustrated London News*, July 24, 1909.

has the whole poetry of man, for no other creature can life a
flame so high and guard it so well.[209]

In writing about Matthew Arnold's criticism, Chesterton suggests that
Arnold discovered the essence of intelligence, which also happens to be the
essence of seeing things as they are: "To see things clearly," he said, you must
"get yourself out of the way."[210] Chesterton offers that "oneself is a window. It
can be a coloured window, if you will, but the more thickly you lay on the colours the less of a window it will be. The two things to be done with a window
are to wash it and then forget it. So the truly pious have always said the two
things to do personally are to cleanse and to forget oneself."[211] Others who
read the Gospels as Chesterton suggests they ought to will, no doubt, arrive
at conclusions that differ from his own while remaining equally legitimate.
Nevertheless, they will at least be able to conclude that they have endeavored
to be faithful to the aim of letting the text be the text.

It turns out that this fidelity, this loyalty to the thing itself, is precisely
what fuels Chesterton's engagements with pretty much every other subject
on earth, including his engagement with politics, which has profound hermeneutic significance. Belloc contends that it is Chesterton's very obvious
"national" character that provides a gateway for understanding his contribution to English Letters, and it is certainly helpful for further grappling with
Chesterton's engagement with the drama of meaning.[212]

The Patriotic Idea

Through his many literature reviews and reflections on life itself, Chesterton's opposition of the South African War soon became clear enough. The
finer points of the history of this period are not relevant to the present book's
aims, but Chesterton's critique—like his palimpsestic approach to reading
and writing, and his optimistic approach to criticism—has a clear bearing on
his hermeneutic. What matters most here is that this event helped to sharpen
Chesterton's thinking on the nature of his own patriotism, which was "passionate" to say the least.[213] As he expresses it, "[t]he decay of patriotism in
England . . . is a serious and distressing matter. Only in consequence of such

209. Ibid.

210. Chesterton, "Introduction," ix.

211. Ibid.

212. Belloc, *On the Place of Gilbert Chesterton*, 15.

213. Ward, *Gilbert Keith Chesterton*, 112.

a decay could the . . . lust of territory be confounded with the ancient love of country."[214]

Many examples from Chesterton's work and life can be found of his abiding love for England. The "keynote" and "touchstone" of his whole "social philosophy" begins with a simple sentiment: "Home, home, sweet home."[215] He is decidedly against "dislocation" and "transplantation,"[216] and the sworn enemy of any construction of artificial detachment. However, in keeping with his critical optimism, the loyalty that emanates from this love for his homeland does not mean being blind to his country's faults. As it is with his literary criticism, which begins with an empathy that refuses false idealization, so it is with his patriotism. From his writings, we learn that taking sides does not necessarily imply choosing the path of least resistance. Julia Stapleton observes that "Chesterton maintained that English patriotism—and indeed any patriotism worthy of its name—is best enhanced by consciousness of national weakness and vulnerability rather than strength."[217] Patriotism implies being a servant to the weak. Servility to that which is strong is taken as a contradiction of patriotism.[218]

Chesterton argues that many people criticize this world "as if [they] were house hunting,"[219] but no one is in a fair position to do this. In reality, a "man belongs to this world before he begins to ask if it is nice to belong to it. He has fought for the flag, and often won heroic victories for the flag long before he has ever enlisted. . . . [H]e has loyalty long before he has any admiration."[220] The first thing to understand about Chesterton's views on patriotism is that he finds it "incoherent for an Englishman to claim that his own patriotism [is] based on his love for his own country, but that others" like the Boer patriots during the South African War "[are] not entitled to an equal love" of their own nationality and an "equal right to enjoy an independent national existence."[221] To forget this is to forge a definition of patriotism that places the subjugation of others over the love of one's own country.[222] For Chesterton, a proper understanding of the nature of love is crucial for coming to terms with a proper patriotism.

214. Chesterton, *The Defendant*, 124.

215. Titterton, *G. K. Chesterton*, 33.

216. Belloc, *On the Place of Gilbert Chesterton*, 18.

217. Stapleton, *Christianity, Patriotism, and Nationhood*, 7.

218. Chesterton, *What's Wrong with the World*, 77.

219. Chesterton, *Collected Works, Volume 1*, 269.

220. Ibid., 270.

221. Oddie, *Chesterton and the Romance of Orthodoxy*, 258.

222. Ibid.

In his essay *The Patriotic Idea*, which first appeared in the book *England: A Nation* (1904) edited by his friend Lucian Oldershaw,[223] Chesterton suggests that there are two kinds of love that may drive a person, the first of which focuses exclusively on the way that the object of one's affection meets one's own needs and feeds one's own preferences.[224] This more self-serving love can be entirely consuming; it is a love whereby the other is dialectically mediated into the same and thereby fully subjectivized. The other kind of love, more agapeic in nature, focuses on one's obligations towards the object of one's affection, no matter what the state of that object may be.[225] This first kind of love can be said to revel in the unity of the univocal—the perception of being as "immediate unity" and simple sameness, rather than as a multiplicity of complex, intermediated relationships.[226] The second kind of love, which celebrates "divisions" and differences together with a sense of unity and intermediation, is easily misunderstood, but there can be no doubt that it was the better form of love in Chesterton's mind.[227] Imagine someone who says, "I love this country so much that I dislike its being divided into factions by progressives whilst I love so much the human face divine that I do not wish to see it obscured with soot or greasepaint."[228]

Thus, loving a place like England, or any other homeland, cannot be totally reliant upon one's positive or negative thoughts and feelings towards it. Here we have a further qualifier for what Chesterton means by reading optimistically: one may view a thing positively or negatively without ever once compromising one's loyalty to it. In other words, to capitalize upon another paradox, one can be pessimistic about a thing without ever once ceasing to be optimistic about it.

In the end, Chesterton's patriotism is fundamentally concerned with what is moral. Indeed, his chief issue with imperialism, discussed shortly in more detail, seems to be that it forgets morality. At a more radical level, it forgets its love; for love implies "sensitivity"—a quality that imperialism severely lacks.[229] "Love of one's own kith," as Ralph Wood notes, "is coeval with human life itself"; it is "'deep, continuous and unconquerable,' as Chesterton [has] said."[230] Chesterton famously states, "'My country, right or

223. Oldershaw, *England: A Nation*.

224. Chesterton, *Collected Works, Volume 20*, 598.

225. Ibid.

226. Simpson, *Religion, Metaphysics, and the Postmodern*, 29.

227. Chesterton, *Collected Works, Volume 20*, 596.

228. Ibid.

229. Chesterton, *The Defendant*, 125.

230. Wood, *Chesterton*, 47.

wrong,' is a thing no patriot would think of saying except in a desperate case. It is like saying, 'My mother, drunk or sober.'"[231] His point is that we begin by loving our countries and our mothers apart from any set conditions and should therefore be the very opposite of indifferent when our countries and mothers are less than abstemious. "Kindred loves," Wood points out, are an important source "of the corporate identity and solidarity that become the basis for a common cultural heritage."[232]

The love of a country implies a "transcendental tie" that does not necessarily provide any "earthly reason."[233] This love, like all genuine love, is "not blind," but "bound."[234] It is committed without being naïve about what it is committed to. Chesterton's brand of charity is of the kind that he attributes to Robert Browning: "Charity was his basic philosophy; but it was, as it were, a fierce charity, a charity that went man-hunting. He was a kind of cosmic detective who walked into the foulest thieves' kitchens and accused men of public virtue."[235] Chesterton hunts for goodness, which like meaning is present before being discovered. However, he never does this without also trying to clear away what hinders the discovery and propagation of that goodness.

It is within the bounds of this fierce, agapeic love for England that Chesterton expresses his vehement distaste for two things that pose a threat to patriotism, namely cosmopolitanism and that more extreme category of cosmopolitanism called imperialism.[236] Cosmopolitanism is the enemy of intimacy because it proposes oblivion to what is local. It is the equivalent of seeing things at a distance without seeing them from the inside. "The truth is, of course, that real universality is to be reached rather by convincing ourselves that we are in the best possible relationship with our immediate surroundings. The man who loves his own children is much more universal, is much more fully in the general order, than the man who dandles the infant hippopotamus or puts the young crocodile in a perambulator."[237] Cosmopolitanism, as a failure to appreciate delineations and boundaries, fails to love things individually.

231. Chesterton, *The Defendant*, 125.

232. Wood, *Chesterton*, 47.

233. Chesterton, *Collected Works, Volume 1*, 270.

234. Ibid., 274.

235. Chesterton, *Robert Browning*, 52.

236. Belloc, *On the Place of Gilbert Chesterton*, 19–20.

237. Chesterton, *Collected Works, Volume 20*, 597.

"Cosmopolitanism gives us one country, and it is good" whereas "nationalism gives us a hundred countries, and everyone of them is the best."[238] There is an irony in cosmopolitanism as Chesterton has presented it: it seems initially to be nothing but neighborly and accommodating, but it is a negation of all neighborliness and accommodation. It seems to appreciate the vibrancy and variety of all the colors of the world, but it does so by painting the whole world in a single color. If this view of cosmopolitanism holds, it may even be conceived of as a form of hatred: "To the cosmopolitan . . . who professes to love humanity and hate local preference, we shall reply: 'How can you love humanity and hate anything so human?'"[239] I see this cosmopolitanism as hatred because it is, as an essentially self-serving stance, a stark denial of otherness. It promotes a violent hermeneutic in its negation of the unique alterity of texts. In the end, it is "better occasionally to call some mountains hills, and some hills mountains, than to be in that mental state in which one thinks, because there is no fixed height for a mountain, that there are no mountains in the world."[240]

Chesterton's central premise is that the universal cannot be properly appreciated without a love of the particular.[241] The universal is therefore an extension of the existential rather than a negation of it. Cosmopolitanism—and, as will shortly become clear, imperialism too—is rooted in a blatant rejection of the particular. Perhaps ironically it is this rejection of the particular that undermines the very impetus of the univocal posture towards being that is the driving force behind cosmopolitanism: by embracing the universal only, the various complexities of being that escape this universality are left unaccounted for. Uncertainty, which constitutes a significant portion of the hermeneutic experience, is consequently denied and the indeterminate is determined to be impossible. This stance is not logically consistent with the interpretive experience. Nevertheless, even by allowing the indeterminate, Chesterton's writings tend to reflect a sharp criticism of "ambiguous nonsense," and especially "moral ambiguity."[242] At "the heart" of his pursuit of truth there is a striving for "complete exactitude of definition."[243] "For the mind exists to make . . . distinctions and definitions."[244] "[D]rawing

238. Ibid.

239. Ibid., 600.

240. Ibid.

241. Oddie, *Chesterton and the Romance of Orthodoxy,* 263.

242. Belloc, *On the Place of Gilbert Chesterton,* 30; *Illustrated London News,* February 27, 1932.

243. Belloc, *On the Place of Gilbert Chesterton,* 34.

244. Chesterton, *Illustrated London News,* January 13, 1923.

a line is the beginning of all philosophy, as it is the beginning of all art."[245] Even in the face of the unclear, clarity remains the aim: One can still "search for truth in the reasonable hope of attaining it."[246]

Chesterton's critique of cosmopolitanism remains remarkably potent now in an age in which everything has started to bleed together via electronic media and the culture of globalization, as a Chestertonian admirer named Marshall McLuhan predicted would happen increasingly as time wore on.[247] Through such a pervasive insistence upon mediating reality, the world that we have created seems to be univocally determinate, but remains, in reality, overflowing with mysterious indeterminacies.

Ultimately, for Chesterton, the idea of cosmopolitanism is only partially responsible for the betrayal of patriotism. Imperialism is the main culprit. When he first began his work as a journalist, Chesterton wrote for an audience that, at the culmination of the sixty-four-year reign of Queen Victoria, was unbridled in its self-confidence. Citizens of the nation would often remark that "the sun never set on the British Empire" as if there had never been a greater Empire before it. People "believed in the British empire," Chesterton claims, "precisely because they had nothing else to believe in."[248] The Victorians "were very pleased with themselves. Britain led the world in every way" and would in their minds "always do so."[249] Events that happened outside of Britain's colonial gaze did not receive much or any attention.

Perceptive as ever, Chesterton saw that something was amiss, claiming with a pun on the Latin etymology of the Queen's name that "in the modern sense, Victorian was not at all Victorian. It was a period of increasing strain. It was the very reverse of solid respectability; because its ethics and theology were wearing thin throughout."[250] Maisie Ward recalls how Chesterton complained about the many misguided representations of England concocted in the Victorian era: images of "languishing, fainting females," "tyrannical pious fathers," and "dull conventional lives" suggested a suffusive positivity, despite the fact that social conditions for many were intolerable.[251] The very things Chesterton felt ought to have been at the core of the English nation were being neglected:

245. Ibid.

246. Belloc, *On the Place of Gilbert Chesterton*, 33.

247. See McLuhan, *Understanding Media*.

248. Chesterton, *Autobiography*, 145.

249. Titterton, *G. K. Chesterton*, 18.

250. Chesterton, *Autobiography*, 36.

251. Ward, *Gilbert Keith Chesterton*, 191.

There was much in Victorian ideas that I dislike and much that I respect; but there was nothing whatever about Victorian ideas corresponding to what is now called Victorian. I am actually old enough to remember the Victorian Age; and it was almost a complete contrast to all that is now connoted by that word. It had all the vices that are now called virtues; religious doubt, intellectual unrest, a hungry credulity about new things, a complete lack of equilibrium. It also had all the virtues that are now called vices; a rich sense of romance, a passionate desire to make the love of man and woman once more what it was in Eden, a strong sense of the absolute necessity of some significance in human life. But everything everybody tells me now about the Victorian atmosphere I feel instantly to be false, like a fog, which merely shuts out a vista.[252]

Even after Victoria died and as King Edward VII took the throne, just as Chesterton's career was beginning to take off, England remained assured that the world that it was living in was a world that it had inherited. Various treasures were being discovered in India, gold and diamonds were being mined in South Africa, and England itself possessed bountiful industrial and commercial capital.[253] Peace, certainly a value held in the highest regard by Edwardians (although not always consistently), had lasted so long that any suggestion of an approaching World War would have been met with appall and incredulity.

The idea of leisure, something usually afforded only to the wealthy, had the nation firmly in its grip.[254] New technologies had also increasingly introduced a fresh pace into the rhythms of life.[255] As in the Victorian era, "at the bottom of the Edwardian confidence—of its faith in life and its faith in peace—was the idea of progress."[256] Everyone was "infected" with that idea,[257] which was more-or-less "the belief that man, by the aid of science, can achieve a perfection of living limited only by the imaginative powers of his mind."[258] For many, excitement was brewing at the ongoing prospect—a prospect embraced largely at the expense of historicity—of an even brighter future.

252. Chesterton, *Autobiography,* 141, 144.

253. Chambers, *Ghosts on the* Roof, 224.

254. Ibid., 231.

255. Newsom, *The Victorian World Picture,* 3.

256. Chambers, *Ghosts on the Roof,* 224.

257. Titterton, *G. K. Chesterton,* 21.

258. Chambers, *Ghosts on the Roof,* 224.

This confidence in progress was not without its problems. In Chesterton's words, "[n]ever perhaps since the beginning of the world has there been an age that had less right to use the word 'progress' than we."[259] In his view, progress was particularly problematic because it was "simply a comparative of which we have not settled the superlative."[260] It seemed that any "legitimate meaning" given to the word was totally undermined by a general skepticism towards dogmas and doctrines. And yet ironically the people "least settled" about what progress meant were the "most 'progressive.'"[261] "Progress is a metaphor from merely walking along a road—very likely the wrong road."[262] It amounts not to "changing the world to suit vision," but to "always changing the vision."[263] In short, it implies a general lack of moral clarity. Therefore, when one views it as an optimistic age, one needs to take into account the fact that this optimism was more a fragile hope than something rooted in clear ideas or concrete facts.

This fragile hope was at the root of a great deal of politics in the Edwardian era. While considering this *Zeitgeist*, as well as the British penchant for always seeking to expand its horizons, Chesterton defines imperialism as "an opportunist cosmopolitanism."[264] Where cosmopolitanism seeks to contain a sense of oneness or unity within a large border while destroying all smaller borders, imperialism, with its obsession with growth for growth's sake, seeks to rid itself of all borders whatsoever. The imperialist readily effaces distinctions, pulls down flags, and destroys nationalities.[265]

In Chesterton's world, imperialism is taken to be synonymous with patriotism, but Chesterton refutes this by claiming that the failure to make a distinction between the two ideas is the result of "electioneering bewilderments."[266] True, the "patriotic feeling"—a natural feeling for any human being—can be usurped by imperialists for the sake of their own jingoistic cause,[267] but the result of this is really the negation of patriotism, for "an empire has all the characteristics that render national attachments impossible."[268] In short, the necessity of limitations and boundaries is eas-

259. Chesterton, *Collected Works, Volume 1*, 53.

260. Ibid., 52.

261. Ibid., 53.

262. Ibid., 310.

263. Ibid.

264. Chesterton, *Collected Works, Volume 20*, 601.

265. Ibid.

266. Ibid., 602.

267. Ibid.

268. Ibid., 603.

ily forgotten.[269] In his book *What's Wrong with the World* (1910), written a few years after the South African War had ended, Chesterton continues his tirade against imperialism, regarding it "in the light political sense" as "an illusion of comfort. That an Empire whose heart is failing should be especially proud of the extremities is to me no more sublime a fact than that an old dandy whose brain is gone should still be proud of his legs."[270]

When considering Chesterton's views on the importance of boundaries in maintaining nations, it is possible to conclude that he is a separatist of sorts. That is, one may think him an advocate for the same logic that has bred a great deal of bigotry and racism throughout human history. However, just as his aim in criticism is always praise, his aim in upholding patriotism is always celebration. One cannot appreciate anything without recognizing its uniqueness and personality, as well as its difference from what it is not. Moreover, boundaries are essential for understanding the truth of anything. Even while being "a good thing," civilization "is not a thing like the love of God, by its nature infinite."[271] It is possible to "have too much civilization" just as it is possible to "have too much beer."[272] The "supreme evil of civilization . . . consists in permitting the human achievements to outrun the human imagination."[273] This is why imperialism is ultimately "unreality."[274] It is a failure to appreciate things as they are. This could be observed especially in the contention that while the English thought they could colonize the world, they had still failed, in some sense at least, to colonize England.[275] There was a kind of insanity and hypocrisy evident in seeking to control others when self-control was absent.

It was through England's obvious failings that Chesterton saw a link between the opportunist philosophy of imperialism, which had every indication of being optimistic, with a pessimism that had begun to run rampant in many an Edwardian mind. Somewhat incongruously in such sanguine conditions, pessimism began to permeate this cultural milieu precisely because hope had been placed squarely on the twin fictions of progress and imperialism. Regarding the logic of progress in particular, fulfillment was always deferred to some later date. Achievements could never be properly savored because they were all taken as steps leading to other even greater

269. Ibid.

270. Chesterton, *What's Wrong with the World*, 66.

271. Chesterton, *Collected Works, Volume 20*, 614.

272. Ibid., 614.

273. Ibid.

274. Ibid., 607.

275. Ibid., 618.

achievements. Progress "maintains that we ought to alter the test instead of trying to pass the test."[276] Progress means that everything can be easily attacked, but not easily corrected. Thus the doctrine of progress, which on the surface seems so optimistic, is actually very much akin to pessimism. It is symbolic of a skepticism that Chesterton finds deplorable. It is a skepticism that denies "normal functions of man" such as "effort, protest, judgment, persuasion, and proof";[277] a skepticism that rests on a pessimistic attitude rather than on an attitude of openness to the otherness that praises what is ultimate.

It was this very pessimism that was to be attacked most deliberately in several articles by Chesterton published in *The Speaker* from 1900 to 1902. A large number of these would later be included in *The Defendant* (1902).[278] He argues in that book that while "at first sight it would seem that the pessimist encourages improvement," and thus appears to be complimentary to the aim of contributing to the cult of progress, "in reality it is a singular truth that the era in which pessimism has been cried from the house-tops is also that in which almost all reform has stagnated and fallen into decay."[279] Chesterton's first signed article for *The Daily News,* published on 7 June 1901, deals particularly with this theme of pessimism, especially as it is encountered in the work of Arthur Schopenhauer (1788–1860), as edited and selected by Thomas Bailey Saunders (1860–1928).[280] In Chesterton's article, he expresses his belief that pessimism is, at best, a pseudo-philosophy, masquerading as something with "portentous depths."[281] It seems very profound to begin with, but it is at bottom complete hogwash. Chesterton notices especially where loyalty is missing: "It seems strange that the average man should exhibit so profound a desire to believe that his bread and cheese is valueless and his beer an empty show."[282] As a consequence of a lack of loyalty to the primary experience of things, honesty is compromised; Schopenhauer ends up "tinging [i.e., coloring] all the heavens with his own tremendous mood" and thus resists letting things be what they are.[283] Of course, the mood of the writer will always affect the subject matter. This is as true of Chesterton as it is of Schopenhauer. The question must therefore be:

276. Chesterton, *Collected Works, Volume 1,* 238.

277. Chesterton, *Stories, Essays, and Poems,* 224.

278. Oddie, *Chesterton and the Romance of Orthodoxy,* 207.

279. Chesterton, *The Defendant,* xii.

280. Schopenhauer, *Essays of Arthur Schopenhauer.*

281. Chesterton, *Daily News,* June 7, 1901.

282. Oddie, *Chesterton and the Romance of Orthodoxy,* 208.

283. Ibid., 209.

which mood is most conducive to hermeneutic fidelity and the conditions of the possibility of understanding? For Chesterton, the optimist has the advantage. Nevertheless, it is pessimism, which vacillates from cynicism to nihilism, that is somehow confused with realism.

Truly, though, "of all men whose souls have influenced the world, Schopenhauer"—whose philosophy is taken by Chesterton be to the epitome of pessimism—"appears . . . the most contemptible."[284] Schopenhauer's apparent "photograph of existence" may rightly be viewed as a kind of "nightmare induced by a lack of nerve."[285] It is a stubborn refusal to accept any kind of "good" or "happiness" because such things take actual effort of mind and body to achieve.[286] It resists even the possibility of satisfaction. Schopenhauer's ultimate failure, for Chesterton, was thus, as in the case of imperialism, a failure of imagination: it was a failure to conceive of the obvious fact that being "and all its ages are one divine and dazzling experiment as dramatic as a display of fireworks."[287] The pessimist seems to know what is wrong, but does not have any idea of what is right. And, for Chesterton, genuine improvement is only possible if one has a sense of both. One needs to be, on one hand, fond of the something even when one is dissatisfied with it, but on the other hand also fixated upon an ideal "(real or imaginary)" that can guide any desire to affect a positive change.[288]

Unbridled optimism as opposed to Chesterton's more careful or critical optimism would always be a poor antidote to pessimism, for like cosmopolitanism and imperialism it fails to see things distinctly. If the pessimist sees nothing good, one could conclude that the optimist sees nothing bad, but this would be "meaningless; it is like calling everything right and nothing left."[289] Love remains the primary issue; it is the issue of what an individual chooses to align himself with or attach himself to, without erasing the distinction between the self and the other.

To extend our understanding of Chesterton's conception of love noted above, it is helpful to take heed of his views on the "method" by which our love is made manifest: "One method . . . may roughly be called the teetotal method: that is, that it is better, because of their obvious danger, to do without . . . great historic passions" like patriotism.[290] The other method, the

284. Chesterton, *Daily News*, June 7, 1901.

285. Ibid.

286. Ibid.

287. Ibid.

288. Chesterton, *Collected Works, Volume 1*, 310.

289. Ibid., 269.

290. Chesterton, *Collected Works, Volume 20*, 598.

method adopted by Chesterton, maintains "on the contrary, that the only ultimate and victorious method of getting rid of the danger is thoroughly to understand and experience them."[291]

> We maintain that with every one of the great emotions of life there goes a certain terror, which, when taken with imaginative reality, is the strongest possible opponent of excess; we maintain, that is to say, that the way to be afraid of war is to know something about war; that the way to be afraid of love is to know something about it; that the way to avoid excess in wine is to feel it as a perilous benefit, and that patriotism goes along with these. . . . It is like the Mohammedan [Muslim] and Christian sentiment of temperance. Mohammedanism [Islam] makes wine a poison: Christianity makes it a sacrament.[292]

The fundamentally Christian gesture is the celebration of even what may pose problems to us. Therefore it is no surprise that Chesterton argues that the failure to uphold patriotism, like so many other problems in society, is an interpretive problem with very concrete consequences; it is a problem that he attempts to solve by considering a hermeneutic context: "In order to get to the root of this evil and quite un-English Imperialism we must cast back and begin anew with a more general discussion of the first needs of human intercourse."[293]

To understand where imperialism or anything else is wrong we need to see precisely what it communicates. Already in the example above of how some read the New Testament, Chesterton demonstrates the unfortunate human tendency to create mental caricatures of things; he suggests that imperialism, for one thing, exemplifies a kind of intellectual process. In creating our caricatures or argumentative straw men, which are inevitably impolite and unfriendly, we may miss a simple truth: even caricature must be derived from something subtle.[294] In fact, that seems to be what a caricature is by definition: "It is a complete error to suppose that because a thing is vulgar therefore it is not refined; that is, subtle and hard to define."[295] Chesterton uses two frivolous examples to explain his meaning. The first is the mention of a "song of his youth which began 'In the gloaming, O, my darling.'" While this opening line may be vulgar, it connects two things that

291. Ibid.
292. Ibid.
293. Chesterton, *What's Wrong with the World*, 67.
294. Ibid., 69.
295. Ibid., 68.

are "exquisite" and even "inscrutable": "passion and the twilight."[296] Mother-in-law jokes are another example, since even in their unrefined glory they must almost certainly "arise out of a real human enigma."[297] Imperialism, Chesterton seems to argue, is the result of a particularly nasty vulgarization of patriotism, which by its very nature must always be rooted in a similarly real human enigma.

We learn here that the foundational enigma in Chesterton's mind turns out to be our common bodily existence: "All true friendliness begins with fire and flood and drink and the recognition of rain or frost. Those who will not *begin* at the bodily end of things are already prigs and may soon be Christian scientists. Each human soul has in a sense to enact for itself the gigantic humility of the Incarnation. Every man must descend into the flesh to meet mankind."[298] The various ideological problems that Chesterton encounters and counters are often, it turns out, very clear cases of a refusal of embodied existence. Progress is always too misty to be mystical, and imperialism is always too haughty to be personal; these ideas deal with life at a distance and with people, especially foreigners in the case of imperialism, only as ideas instead of as comrades in the drama of life. Against this, Chesterton proposes that "[t]rue philosophy is concerned with the instant. Will a man take this road or that?—that is the only thing to think about."[299]

"No one has even begun to understand comradeship who does not accept with it a certain hearty eagerness in eating, drinking, or smoking, an uproarious materialism which to many women appears only hoggish."[300] When men are too "theoretical" and "impersonal" they will be prone to certain "disadvantages and dangers."[301] They will start to think of themselves as superior to others whom they have never met and conversed with. They will, as a result of ensuring the distance between themselves and others, forget that all people are equal in value even when they are unequal in other things. Chesterton's interpretive awareness, therefore, can be understood as deeply embodied; it is profoundly embedded within a particular horizon, and ineradicably connected to personal experiences. It is, as I discuss in more detail in the next chapter, built upon a Thomist union and communion of mind and being rather than the Cartesian division of those two things that has had philosophy and culture in its grip for so long. Chester-

296. Ibid.
297. Ibid., 69.
298. Ibid., 69–70.
299. Chesterton, *Orthodoxy*, 198.
300. Chesterton, *What's Wrong with the World*, 70.
301. Ibid., 72.

ton discusses what happens when seeing things merely theoretically and impersonally as follows:

> It is not seeing things as they are to think first of a Briareus with a hundred heads, and then call every man a cripple for having only one. It is not seeing things as they are to start with a vision of Argus with his hundred eyes, and then jeer at every man with two eyes as if he had only one. And it is not seeing things as they are to imagine a demi-god of infinite mental clarity, who may or may not appear in the latter days of this earth, and then to see all men as idiots. . . . When we really see men as they are, we do not criticize, but worship; and very rightly. For a monster with mysterious eyes and miraculous thumbs, with strange dreams in his skull, and a queer tenderness for this place or that baby, is truly a wonderful and unnerving matter.[302]

The symbol of the Briareus represents the opposition of all three elements mentioned above for a realistic and honest hermeneutic—loyalty to things, honesty about things, and idealism concerning things. It represents a laddered, gnostic perspective that removes the bodily reality. It is therefore obvious to Chesterton that when we do descend into the flesh, we will see things more clearly. Only then will we properly understand how we see the world through ourselves.

This clarity brings about the recognition that the primary issue with regard to imperialism as a vulgarized patriotism and as a theoretical world detached from our embodied being—and it turns out that this will be a general problem for seeing things as they are—is the issue of ego. An analogy used by Chesterton is helpful here. He mentions the simple act of "[t]urning a beggar from the door" and points out that after doing such a thing one cannot in the end "[pretend] to know all the stories the beggar might have narrated."[303] In failing to see the humanity of the beggar, the rich man who turns him away also fails to see his own inhumanity and his own capacity for humanity. "[S]elf-assertion" alone, which seems only to revive pessimism, cannot "obtain knowledge."[304] Chesterton points out that "a beetle may or may not be inferior to a man—the matter awaits demonstration; but if he were inferior by ten thousand fathoms, the fact remains that there is probably a beetle view of things of which a man is entirely ignorant. If he wishes to conceive that point of view, he will scarcely reach

---

302. Chesterton, *Collected Works, Volume 1*, 68.

303. Chesterton, *The Defendant*, 100.

304. Ibid., 99, 101.

it by persistently reveling in the fact that he is not a beetle."[305] What is often lacking in our hermeneutics is empathy. This is a problem that Chesterton finds in the pessimism of Schopenhauer's philosophical offspring, Friedrich Nietzsche (1844–1900):

> The most brilliant exponent of the egoistic school, Nietzsche, with deadly and honourable logic, admitted that the philosophy of self-satisfaction led to looking down upon the weak, the cowardly, and the ignorant. Looking down on things may be a delightful experience, only there is nothing, from a mountain to a cabbage, that is really seen when it is seen from a balloon. The philosopher of the ego sees everything, no doubt, from a high and rarified heaven; only he sees everything foreshortened or deformed.[306]

Chesterton describes the opposite perspective, using the same metaphor, as follows:

> It is from a valley that things look large; it is from the level that things look high; I am a child of the level and have no need of that celebrated Alpine guide. I will lift up my eyes to the hills, from whence cometh my help. . . . Everything is in an attitude of mind; and at this moment I am in a comfortable attitude. I will sit still and let the marvels and the adventures settle on me like flies. There are plenty of them, I assure you.[307]

The philosopher of the ego is also rather lonely. Chesterton's entire philosophy, and therefore also his entire approach to reading, points towards an intimate, personal experience of the world. In his view, we cannot possibly understand what is truly good if we are not proximate to the things and people whom we are to respect. We cannot even comprehend our impositions without seeing their effects first hand. We are, as the injunction of Jesus goes, to love our neighbor: "We make our friends; we make our enemies; but God makes our next-door-neighbour" whom we must love simply "because he is there. . . . He is the sample of humanity which is actually given us. Precisely because he may be anybody he is everybody. He is a symbol because he is an accident."[308] It is only in encountering our essential similarities to one another, rather than artificial differences from or artificial similarities to one another, that real love is made possible: "I want to love

---

305. Ibid., 101.
306. Ibid.
307. Chesterton, *Tremendous Trifles*, 7.
308. Chesterton, *Collected Works, Volume 1*, 139–40.

my neighbour not because he is I, but precisely because he is not I."[309] Love begins and is sustained in differences that are only properly recognizable up close. From a distance, the world looks like an extension of the egotistical gaze. Up close, face-to-face, I see that it is a world that I have not made. Solipsism creates distance. Humility connects.

Thus, the above exploration of the patriotic idea already gives us a number of fine insights into Chesterton's unique way of reading and understanding the world. As a reader, a combination of loyalty (loving things despite their present condition), honesty (calling things out as they appear in their present condition), and critical idealism (hoping for things to be improved without setting up impossible fictions) is very much a part of Chesterton's horizon of understanding, and his desire to see things as they are. On what the hermeneutic philosopher Paul Ricoeur regards as central hermeneutic postures—the posture of understanding and the posture of suspicion—we find the latter contextualized by the former in Chesterton's hermeneutic; additionally, the former ought to be characterized by loyalty and idealism. This is the "great lesson of Beauty and the Beast; that a thing must be loved *before* it is loveable."[310]

We learn from Chesterton's interactions with his own culture that it is vital for the writer, who is also the one reading and interpreting the world, to be aware of the way that his own mood may color his experiences wrongly. This is at least part of his point in the story of *The Coloured Lands* referred to in the previous chapter. Chesterton assumes that anyone would be happier if he or she were to let things be themselves. Schopenhauer's philosophy, as Chesterton reads it, seems to be that no one should be happy, no matter what things are. Schopenhauer thus shuts down a whole range of hermeneutic possibilities. By circulating his Teutonic misfortune cookies, he therefore cannot conceive of the option that the abysses of his experience may be clouding his vision rather than heightening it. Chesterton has acknowledged, especially in trumpeting patriotism, that optimism may also potentially cloud one's vision; optimism can even be oppressive, hegemonic, and imperialistic.[311] However, at the bottom of Chesterton's more hopeful outlook is a simple notion: it is precisely when one sees things as they are that one is able to be realistically optimistic or realistically pessimistic. That is what it means to be humble about what one understands about existence: accepting the world that we find ourselves in, before we endeavor to understand it.

---

309. Ibid., 336.
310. Ibid., 253.
311. Chesterton, *What's Wrong with the World*, 55.

Chesterton's humility towards his own world involves his recognition that even modernity contains significant traces of a foundation better than the one offered in many of the philosophies of his day. "Everything . . . in the modern world" with only a few exceptions, he writes, "is of Christian origin, even everything that seems most anti-Christian. The French Revolution is of Christian origin. The newspaper is of Christian origin. The anarchists are of Christian origin. Physical science is of Christian origin."[312] Even "[t]he attack on Christianity is of Christian origin."[313] There is, in other words, a foundation to Chesterton's engagement with the drama of meaning that goes beyond the "obvious" ideals of "modern philosophers."[314] It is the only the "Christian Creed" that has "the audacity to assert that a thing will actually recover its identity because it will recover its form."[315] Any outline of Chesterton's hermeneutic must therefore engage with what this Christian Creed has to say about the cosmos and how it is that we may possibly arrive at an understanding of anything in it.

312. Chesterton, *Collected Works, Volume 1*, 124.

313. Ibid.

314. Chesterton, *Collected Works, Volume 11*, 354.

315. Ibid.

3

The Foundation of
Chesterton's Hermeneutic

Chesterton's Cosmology

IN HIS RELENTLESS PURSUIT of seeing things as they are, Chesterton presents a very strong sense of the connection between the truths of Christianity and his immediate experience of the world. For him, the preoccupation of reading well and interpreting with exactness and clarity presupposes a particular posture encouraged by Catholicism. In fact, Chesterton sees the significance of Catholic Christianity in its posture or attitude towards reality even more than in its doctrines about reality, although the two are obviously interrelated. Catholicism, for Chesterton, is somehow both buoyantly *above* the various twists and turns of human history and philosophy and something that works *with* and *within* it.[1] It works "through wills and not laws."[2] This is fitting for understanding the hermeneutic experience, too, since the reader is outside the text even while he cannot escape it. There may be methodologies and rules at play in hermeneutics, but the experience of understanding is more a matter of will and personal experience than it is a matter of laws. It is a matter, as I have already suggested, of loyalty as loving fidelity to things even when their present condition is less than ideal, as well as being about honesty, as an exercise in being true to things as they are. It also concerns possessing a kind of critical idealism, which is a hope for things to be improvable. These

---

1. Schall, *Schall on Chesterton*, 72.
2. Chesterton, *Collected Works, Volume 3*, 127.

facets of the interpretive experience mirror the primacy of the "virtues of grace"—faith, love, and hope—that St. Paul regards as central to Christian life (1 Cor 13:13), and which Chesterton regards as the central contribution of Christianity to virtue.[3] As I have already intimated, it seems that it was precisely in confronting the realities of his context that Chesterton saw the value of Christian theology for understanding anything. What follows therefore focuses on the way that Chesterton's theology and interpretive awareness are interwoven. The aim here is to demonstrate the implications of Chesterton's faith-based biases for interpretive understanding in general.

Chesterton is clear that any reference to someone's work should emphasize what he values most, and it seems obvious that what he most values is the relationship of his own faith and convictions with the world he encounters. He uses the example of writing a biography of a saint "without God" as being about the same as writing about the Norwegian explorer Fridtjof Nansen (1861–1930) without once mentioning his most important work, namely his expedition to the North Pole.[4]

Chesterton admits that "a great deal of what [he has] written is deliberately propagandist."[5] Even if something is "not in the least propagandist," it will nonetheless still "be full of the implications" and the convictions of the individual's religion "because that is what is meant by having a religion."[6] Today the word *propaganda*, having been hijacked by totalitarian regimes, consumerists, and public relations pundits, has a far more pejorative connotation that it did in Chesterton's day. At that time, it referred predominantly to the dissemination of information in keeping with a particular ideological stance. It therefore did not necessarily presume blind adherence to caricatured facts, although it also did not presume that there is no such thing as bad propaganda. Chesterton, for one, is vehemently against "educational propaganda," which in his opinion amounts to "spiritual kidnapping."[7] Still, on his own use of propaganda, he preempts the anatomizations of his critics by pointing out his aim to examine his own assumptions instead of simply relying on the "ready-made assumptions of the hour."[8] Still, the biases or dogmas of a writer will inevitably find their way into his stories. Dogmatism, for Chesterton, is therefore not a crime because, after all, it concerns

---

3. Chesterton, *Collected Works, Volume 1*, 124–25.
4. Chesterton, *Saint Thomas Aquinas, Saint Francis of Assisi*, 192.
5. Chesterton, *Collected Works, Volume 3*, 225.
6. Ibid.
7. Chesterton, *Illustrated London News*, October 29, 1932.
8. Chesterton, *Collected Works, Volume 3*, 225.

an interest in the truth, "and only in the truth because it is in fact true."[9] The point for Chesterton is not that it is bad or good to use propaganda as promotion, but rather to question how it is used, as well as whether or not the writer is aware of his own use of it.

However, in considering Chesterton's theological stance and its implications on his hermeneutic, as should already be clear, I am not that concerned here with Chesterton's place in history as a theologian among theologians or as a hermeneut among hermeneuts. My focus is on the ideas that he writes about and the implications that these ideas would have on the interpretive experience. Having already considered the context of Chesterton's dramatic perception via his palimpsestic way of reading and writing, his attitude towards criticism and his stance on patriotism, I here want to begin to tackle the conceptual foundations of his dramatic perception.

Three particular facets of Chesterton's philosophy—his cosmology, epistemology, and ontology—are of immediate interest for understanding this foundation. Each of these facets has an interdramatic relationship with the other facets, thus reflecting the way that "mental habits overlap":[10] various moods and movements in the following ideas intertwine and inform each other, thereby revealing, if only partially, Chesterton's horizon of understanding. Even examining each of these facets as distinct demonstrates that they operate in conversation with one another. Each of the facets of Chesterton's philosophy are dramatic within their own narrative and performative structures. His cosmology sees the universe as a drama, his epistemology considers human understanding in relation to this cosmological drama, and his ontology understands being as a drama within a larger drama. To use metaphysical parlance, being (the being of things and ideas) itself has a dramatic, metareferential relationship to Being (God).

This being of beings with and within Being informs the notion of the drama mentioned in the introductory chapter. Chesterton's love for drama is evident in a number of ways in his life and especially in the fact that he attended, acted in, and wrote for theatre.[11] However, it is not only in this literal sense that he is fond of drama, for he sees drama as a metaphor for the whole of life.[12] From his perspective, life is not a random collection of accidents, coincidences, and indecipherable illogicalities, even while contingencies abound. Rather, it is a coherent drama full of meaning. It is something read, interpreted, and responded to. This sense of the ubiquity

9. Lauer, *G. K. Chesterton*, 39.

10. Chesterton, *Collected Works, Volume 3*, 195.

11. Chesterton, *Autobiography*, 276–79; Ker, *G. K. Chesterton*, 342.

12. Chesterton, *What's Wrong with the World*, 129.

and inescapability of meaning as something that precedes our apprehension deeply affects Chesterton's philosophical approach, which I take here to include his theological cosmology, epistemology, and ontology. All of these are interwoven to inform his hermeneutic lens.

Chesterton's conviction that life itself is a drama is rooted in his understanding that everything and everyone is an actor or agent in a theatrical production initiated by the Divine Playwright: "God had written . . . a play; a play he had planned as perfect, but which had necessarily been left to human actors and stage-managers, who had since made a great mess of it."[13] This statement is taken as the premise for Chesterton's posthumously published play *The Surprise* (1952); and, as simple as it may first appear, it coherently presents three key ideas that I take to be foundational to Chesterton's worldview. Below it is therefore my aim to unpack this statement's meaning in relation to a cosmology that Chesterton would regard as a more rational explanation of the nature and state of the universe than any purely materialist doctrine.[14] In doing so I am following Aidan Nichols, who argues that Chesterton's metaphysical realism is directly linked to the doctrine of creation.[15] I consider this very doctrine of creation below under three themes: the Creator, creation and the fall of man, and re-creation. I refer to *The Surprise* quite extensively below because its story also helps to focus a number of ideas regarding Chesterton's epistemology and ontology.

The first theme in Chesterton's dramatic cosmology is that of the Creator. Everything begins with "God."[16] It is as simple and as baffling a start to anything as one could ever ask for. Still, Chesterton writes that no one is able to understand his own Catholic philosophy apart from the recognition that "a fundamental part of it is entirely the praise of Life, the praise of Being, the praise of God as the Creator of the World. Everything else follows a long way after that."[17] Naturally, Chesterton is referring to a very specific "personal God" as encountered and understood through his engagement with the historic Christian tradition and its Scriptures, rather than with an impersonal cosmic force or gnostic demiurge.[18] He recognizes this God as "the highest truth of the cosmos" and thereby implies that truth is directly related to the personality and Being of this God.[19] This means that truth is

13. Chesterton, *Collected Works, Volume 1*, 282.

14. Ibid., 330, 347.

15. Nichols, *Chesterton*, 57.

16. Chesterton, *Collected Works, Volume 1*, 282.

17. Chesterton, *Saint Thomas Aquinas, Saint Francis of Assisi*, 98.

18. Chesterton, *Collected Works, Volume 1*, 347.

19. Ibid., 389.

not primarily bound up in propositions or rationalizations, but is located in the very personhood of God, in a way of relating to God. Of course, the word *God* "is by its nature a name of mystery," although this does not mean that he is entirely inaccessible.[20] God may be understood as the originator and sustainer of all things, although he is first and foremost the Creator. Chesterton insists that "[t]here is no greater thing to be said of God Himself than that He makes things."[21]

At the forefront of Chesterton's thinking is the idea that the Creator God is Goodness Itself, always brimming with generous love towards what he has made. "Unless the background of all things is good"—unless it is Goodness Itself—"it is no substitute to make the foreground better."[22] This God, as the abundant One and source of reality, is certainly not like the vindictive, lightning-bolt hurling, tantrum-throwing Jupiter or Zeus that inhabits some ancient superstitions.[23] He is not merely an authoritarian lawmaker or bureaucratic killjoy.

Having perspective on the nature of God as Goodness Itself, Chesterton presents his readers with a cosmology that places goodness both at the center and the circumference of the created order. In fact, it is precisely the presence of order and unity in creation that points to the goodness of the Creator, for we cannot know the good Creator apart from the order that may be perceived in his creation. Chesterton therefore hears "God, God" in the double-thud of an axe falling on wood, and "God" in the "cry of the rook"; "All things . . . repeat in a thousand languages—God."[24] This God, Goodness Itself, is the enabler of intelligibility and intellection. The discernment of any truth in any thing is a gift given by Being.

The goodness of the Creator is reflected by analogy in the opening of *The Surprise*, which concerns a brief interaction between a Franciscan friar and an unnamed Author. This Author explains to the friar that he is the "Master Puppet-Maker of the World, who has marionettes to move without wires and speak human speech as melodiously as a musical-box."[25] His puppets operate in a world in which all creatures are virtuous and magnanimous, and where "heroic virtue always conquers."[26] The insistence here is that the good, creative mind of the Author is reflected in the goodness

20. Chesterton, *The Everlasting Man*, 24.

21. Chesterton, *Autobiography*, 51.

22. Chesterton, *A Year With G. K. Chesterton*, 187.

23. Chesterton, *The Everlasting Man*, 117.

24. Ward, *Gilbert Keith Chesterton*, 61.

25. Chesterton, *The Surprise*, 13.

26. Ibid.

of his created world. After their brief discussion, the Author and the friar leave the stage so that the play may continue with them hidden behind the curtain. The audience is then left with an awareness of the presence of the Author even in his apparent absence. This confirms Chesterton's idea that the absence of God is not a negation of God, but an affirmation of him in the void—a hiddenness *as* presence. And it is precisely in this void and in the text that the Author's voice is heard.[27] The audience has been enlightened as to the nature of the Author so as to be better informed of the nature of his work; it has been privy to the character of God to better understand the dignity of man.

Chesterton argues that there is a subtle argument embedded in the idea that "God 'looked on all things and saw that they were good.' It is the thesis that there are no bad things, but only bad uses of things."[28] Aquinas puts it simply as follows: "Every being as being is good."[29] Chesterton continues:

> If you will, there are no bad things, but only bad thoughts; and especially bad intentions. Only Calvinists can really believe that hell is paved with good intentions. That is exactly one thing it cannot be paved with. But it is possible to have bad intentions about good things; and good things, like the world and the flesh, have been twisted by a bad intention called the devil. But he cannot make things bad; they remain as on the first day of creation. The work of heaven alone was material; the making of a material world. The work of hell is entirely spiritual.[30]

Chesterton passes judgment on two troublesome theologies here. The first is Calvinism, which in his friend Hillaire Belloc's words "[admits] evil into the Divine nature" and makes God out to be a lot like Moloch "by the permission of but One Will in the universe."[31] It tends also to "dwell" less "on the positive and happy side of its visions" than on "the stern or punitive side."[32] Miracles seem to be rendered unmiraculous and free will is arguably rendered impossible by Calvin's pen. As Chesterton notes, Calvinism ensures the belief that "once a man is born it is too late to damn or save him."[33] By making the terms of salvation absolute and thus insisting that some or

---

27. Chesterton, *The Everlasting Man,* 92.

28. Chesterton, *Saint Thomas Aquinas, Saint Francis of Assisi,* 100.

29. Aquinas, *Selected Philosophical Texts,* 75.

30. Chesterton, *Saint Thomas Aquinas, Saint Francis of Assisi,* 100.

31. Belloc, *The Great Heresies.*

32. Chesterton, *Illustrated London News,* October 1, 1932.

33. Chesterton, *What's Wrong with the World,* 129.

perhaps most people have no chance of salvation at all,[34] Calvinism also makes "[f]ear in itself" essential to the "character of Christianity."[35]

The second troublesome theology noted in the above passage is that of Manicheanism, which effectively contends that it was Satan who created the world rather than God.[36] This latter theological vision divides God from his world and uproots the claim that being as being is good by claiming that being as being is evil. This evil, Chesterton stresses, is really a spiritual problem rather than a problem of materiality.[37] One example of such evil mentioned by Chesterton is his almost Marxian observation that "America has really worshipped money," not because "money is tangible," but "because money is intangible."[38] He contends that it is in its "invisible strength" that it is adored for having a kind of "airy magic," and it is because of this that it is then disregarded for the "actual pleasures that it stands for."[39] It is when money is considered in terms of "shares, trusts, promises, implicit understandings, illegal powers," and in even the mere exercise of adding a zero to the end of a number, that it does the most damage.[40] The primary issue represented here, then, is with how materiality is considered rather than with materiality itself.

Chesterton is adamant that God's goodness should be upheld as an unimpeachable reality. For him, God is not pantheistically or univocally bound to creation; he is not the same thing as creation. And yet, he is discernable through creation precisely because goodness is given to and located in its concrete materiality. As Aquinas puts it, "[t]he perfections of all things are communicated by God; between them and him there is simultaneous likeness and unlikeness."[41] When Chesterton contends that all things remain good even when they have been abused,[42] he implies that God, as the uncaused and necessary cause of creation, is not merely a presence at the beginning of time, but is one who brings creation into existence in every moment of its being. God is not simply a watchmaker deity who sets the thing into motion, but is always the timeless ground of being.

34. Chesterton, *Irish Impressions*, 204.

35. Chesterton, *Illustrated London News*, February 9, 1929.

36. Chesterton, *Saint Thomas Aquinas, Saint Francis of Assisi*, 99.

37. Ibid., 100.

38. Chesterton, *Illustrated London News*, September 17, 1910.

39. Ibid.

40. Ibid.

41. Aquinas, *Selected Philosophical Texts*, 68.

42. Chesterton, *Saint Thomas Aquinas, Saint Francis of Assisi*, 100.

God's creation of the world is not something that happens only once, but something that is happening continuously. "It is possible," Chesterton writes, "that God says every morning, 'Do it again' to the sun; and every evening, 'Do it again' to the moon.[43] It may not be automatic necessity that makes all daisies alike; it may be that God makes every daisy separately, but has never got tired of making them."[44] Perhaps "our little tragedy" is so admired and treasured by divinity that "every human drama" ought to be "called again and again before the curtain."[45] The repetitions in creation seem willful rather than automatic, implying that there is someone to will them; the magic of the world implies a magician; the storied appearance life implies a storyteller; and the meaning felt in the cosmos suggests someone who means it.[46]

For Chesterton, creation always points back to the good Creator in the way that the daylight implies the presence of the sun. Chesterton regards this as an *a priori* truth even when goodness seems difficult to decipher. The consequence of this belief, once again, is that he is not all that concerned about the origin of the universe in purely materialist terms. He assumes that the precise process by which nothing came to be something detracts from the fact that at the center of the story of the universe is the mysterious Being who brings everything into being and sets everything into motion. As the "first efficient cause," this Being is not "identical with its effect."[47] This is to say that "being *qua* determinate" is always ontologically "dependent."[48]

After establishing God as the initiator and sustainer of the drama of creation, Chesterton shifts his focus to creation itself—to the act of creating and to the things created. When Chesterton writes that "God had written . . . a play,"[49] he seems to be paraphrasing the first verse of Genesis: "In the beginning God created the heaven and the earth." The word *play* implies both fun and drama, and also encompasses the entwined homes of God and humanity: heaven and earth.

The act of creating is an act of bringing something out of nothing. This in itself is difficult enough to conceive of. It may even appear absurd. And yet comprehensibility is not a criterion for engagement with or the

43. Chesterton, *Collected Works, Volume 1*, 264.

44. Ibid.

45. Ibid.

46. Ibid., 264, 268.

47. Aquinas, *Selected Philosophical Texts*, 71.

48. Perl, *Theophany*, 19.

49. Chesterton, *Collected Works, Volume 1*, 282.

enjoyment of what is.[50] Incomprehensibility does not render anything automatically false, nor does it rule out the possibility of a thing becoming comprehensible later on.

For Chesterton it is nevertheless still easier and more reasonable to believe that an uncreated Being creates a perceptible reality than it is to believe, as many strict materialistic evolutionists do, that something came out of mere nothing.[51] In fact, a strictly materialistic evolutionist should not be able to make any kind of pronouncement on any kind of cosmology if he wishes to remain unhypocritical, since the minute he makes any claim to know and understand the cosmos, he has already stepped beyond the bounds of pure materiality, into consciousness and the realm of metaphysical speculation. It is impossible, it would seem, to be a pure materialist while retaining the ability to think.

While the Genesis account of creation assumes an "earth" that is "without form, and void" before God announces the birth of light and its separation from darkness, Chesterton nonetheless assumes, in Augustinian fashion, that creation is creation *ex nihilo* rather than out of any kind of primordial substance. Such creation *ex nihilo* suggests that God creates out of his own abundance, not his lack. He creates primarily because he wants to create; he does so for the hell of it (to use a theological phrase) rather than for any clear purpose or end. If Plotinus's thinking may be followed on this point—for Chesterton's thinking does overlap with Plotinus's in ways that he does not quite manage to acknowledge[52]—the idea that God creates out of nothing may be taken quite literally, since God is not any *thing* at all, but is that which is before anything.[53] God can "make something out of nothing" because he creates out of himself. It is left to man "to make something out of anything."[54] Man may be said to possess a power of combination rather than of creation.

As intimated already, Chesterton does not regard the play of the cosmos as something created and then abandoned or disregarded by God.[55] God is anything, but careless. He is abundant and selfless. Creation is given up as a living, breathing, offering to the reader who participates in its being. The play cannot be a play, after all, without an audience; therefore creation

50. Chesterton, *Alarms and Discursions*, 31, 34.

51. Chesterton, *Saint Thomas Aquinas, Saint Francis of Assisi*, 159.

52. Clark, *G. K. Chesterton*, viii.

53. Perl, *Theophany*, 12.

54. Quoted in Ward, *G. K. Chesterton*, 258.

55. Chesterton, *Collected Works, Volume 1*, 173.

is not a solipsistic gesture by God and for God. It is something that is really given to itself, for others.

Chesterton argues that God's good creation "had necessarily been left to human actors and stage-managers . . . ."[56] In *The Surprise,* it is of particular significance that Chesterton begins by casting puppets as the first actors in the Author's drama. On returning to the stage after the first act, the Author notes that what makes his play particularly remarkable is the fact that he wrote it "for a bet," and that he ended up winning the bet:[57]

> I did not incidentally end up with the money; because, to tell the truth, I made the bet with an itinerant artist like myself. He was a showman with a very popular and successful set of puppets; and his plays were infested with villains. They depended entirely on villains. Whenever the heroine was doubtful about the hero, up jumped the most valuable villain, with a tactful taste for poison or a diplomatic dagger; and then she knew that the hero was a hero. It seemed as if all virtue was really produced by villains. Well, he betted me I could not write a play without a villain.[58]

The "itinerant artist" that the Author speaks about, whether intended by Chesterton or not, evokes the dialogue between God and Satan in the opening chapters of the book of Job, a book that Chesterton often refers to and which I discuss at length in chapter 6. Just as Satan challenges God about the legitimacy of his goodness, so the itinerant artist challenges the Author about the possibility of a genuine drama without evil. In both cases, these Authors insist upon the goodness within the dramas that they have scripted. In his work, Chesterton is well aware of the problem and presence of evil in the world, but his understanding of God as Goodness Itself forces him to contemplate the possibility that there is more going on in the drama than is readily apparent to the actors within the drama or even to those who are watching the play.

In *The Surprise,* the Author notes that he created a play not only without a villain, but in which the whole play is comprised not only of "good people, but of good actions."[59] In other words, there is not only no villain, but "no villainy."[60] Perhaps unexpectedly, despite the lack of villainy, there is a great deal of humor and action in the first act of the play. Chesterton's Author succeeds in presenting the possibility that being and virtue are not

56. Ibid., 282.

57. Chesterton, *The Surprise,* 39.

58. Ibid.

59. Ibid., 40.

60. Ibid.

inextricably bound to evil, as well as the possibility that drama, even while still being reliant upon conflict and subtext to move the plot forward, is not necessarily dependent on the negative charge of evil.

The Author then observes that the play's short length is owed to the fact that everyone in the play behaved well; after all, there is no doubt, hesitation, or wrongdoing to hinder their actions. However, he has found a single problem with his characters; they are "everything except alive."[61] His puppets are "intelligent, complex, combative, brilliant, bursting with life and yet they are not alive."[62] It is revealed that the reason that they are not alive is that they are still, in a manner of speaking, in the mind of the Author and thus do not have wills of their own. In this way, the first act of *The Surprise* reflects Augustine's understanding of the first chapter of Genesis as a poetic reflection of creation as it is known in the mind of God before it becomes a reality.[63] This also mirrors Hans Urs von Balthasar's observation that no one can act on a stage if God, the Author, is "all,"[64] as well as Simone Weil's contention that for God to create he would have to hide himself, otherwise "there would be nothing, but himself."[65] There is perhaps also something here of the Kabbalistic symbol of "*Tzimtzum*" or divine contraction: God, to allow relation to emerge, would have needed to recede to create space within which that creation could dwell.[66] The Author in Chesterton's play seems to acknowledge that for there to be any real action, and any possibility of genuine love, human freedom is necessary. Therefore, a "miracle" takes place by which the puppets turn into real people, leaving them free even to reject the ideal play of the Author and make the play their own.[67]

Chesterton therefore cuts the strings that tie the Puppeteer to the puppets. When reflecting on the theodrama of creation, he argues that the creative event is, and in fact must be, an act of "division," "divorce," "rejection," and "separation" whereby the Author sets free what he has created.[68] This is precisely the "miracle" that Chesterton is referring to in *The Surprise*. It would be a mistake, of course, to suggest that this miracle turns Chesterton's God into the god of the deists—a God who sets the created order into mo-

61. Ibid., 43.

62. Ibid.

63. Capon, *Genesis*, 78.

64. von Balthasar, *Theo-Drama, Volume 5*, 17.

65. Weil, *Gravity and Grace*, 38.

66. Koren, *The Mystery of the Earth*, 287.

67. Chesterton, *The Surprise*, 45.

68. Chesterton, *The Everlasting Man*, 236; Chesterton, *Collected Works, Volume 1*, 171, 281; Chesterton, *The Man Who Was Orthodox*, 109.

tion before receding into irrelevance and indifference. For in Chesterton's cosmology, as I have already said, God lovingly perpetually calls all things into being. Even creation *ex nihilo* is a continuous reality and not just a once-off event. And yet even in this there is a sense in which God creates by letting things be instead of forcing them into the embrace of absolute determinism. Freedom is interwoven into the natural order of creation and the result is that rocks are free to be rocks, just as frogs are free to be frogs. In hermeneutic terms, the text is free to be the text.

This has obvious implications for understanding Chesterton's interpretive awareness: he intimates in his view of creation, if only by analogy, that any author is not the sovereign determinant of the meaning of his created text. The play or performance of the text is free to be itself; its meanings are open to interpretations that the author is not necessarily in control of. There is, consequently, a sense of both solidity and flexibility in the act of reading. Chesterton writes that "[i]n everything that bows gracefully there must be an effort at stiffness. . . . Rigidity yielding a little, like justice swayed by mercy, is the whole beauty of the earth. The cosmos is a diagram just bent out of shape. Everything tries to be straight; and everything just fortunately fails."[69] If one takes this as a principle for Chesterton's hermeneutic, the idea is that the text can retain its structure and even its rigidity, but reading and interpreting the text must allow room for movement. Reading can even involve a failure to read. Rigidity without flexibility may be taken as an ungodly construct; it may be an attempt to regard a thing as other than what it is.

The freedom that God gives to the participants in the drama of creation is similar to the freedom that God gives to his human actors: "Man was free, not because there was no God, but because it needed a God to set him free. By authority he was free."[70] Chesterton imagines the "fun" of having actors in a drama suddenly acting "like real people" by having them work in accordance with "what theologians call Free Will."[71] An introduction of such a surprise would turn "genuine art" with all of its predestined drama into "genuine life" with all of its indeterminacies.[72] Surprise is the recognition that "[e]very artistic drama" is bound to a particular end right from the start, because "the last page is written before the first" and yet constraints of form, style and narrative may still be defied. Surprise sees that this tendency of dramas to enclose themselves within their own worlds is

69. Chesterton, *Alarms and Discursions*, 31.

70. Chesterton, *A Miscellany of Men*, 296.

71. Chesterton, *Illustrated London News*, March 16, 1912.

72. Ibid.

"not so in that terrific drama which Heaven has given us to play upon this earth."[73] Life is not an ossification of the will of God, but a persistent resurrection of dead matter. It is a movement from lumbering travail and tragedy to the astonishment of comedy and the surprise of a joke.

If the universe was brought into existence by the free will of God, then the idea of human free will fits with the doctrine that man is made in the image of God (Gen 1:26). On this, Nichols writes that the "defense of free will is central to Chesterton's metaphysical realism inasmuch as the latter includes the recognition of human will as a genuine albeit conditioned choice."[74] Humanity "is entirely free to choose between right and left, or between right and wrong."[75] This "conditioned choice," mentioned by Nichols, highlights the unavoidability of limitations.[76] Freedom is not only concerned with escape or a movement away from confines, but with constriction and a movement towards or within confines. The only kind of freedom that is true is "the freedom that limits itself."[77] Against this, one type of anarchism appeals to an "absolute liberty" that renounces limitations as such.[78] Chesterton regards this as

> incurably futile and childish, because it will not face a fundamental logical fact. This fact is that there is no such thing as a condition of complete emancipation, unless we can speak of a condition of nonentity. What we call emancipation is always and of necessity simply the free choice of the soul between one set of limitations and another. If I have a piece of chalk in my hand, I can make either a circle or a square; that is the sacred thing called liberty. But I cannot make a thing that is both a circle and a square. I cannot make an unlimited square. I cannot draw an emancipated circle. If I wish to make anything at all, I must abide by the limitations and principles of the thing I make. . . . And, of course, in moral matters it is the same; there is no lawlessness, there is only a free choice between limitations.[79]

Emile Cammaerts describes the Chestertonian doctrine of freedom as follows: "Freedom, as such, is meaningless. . . . The highest civilization

---

73. Ibid.

74. Nichols, *Chesterton*, 72.

75. Chesterton, *Collected Works, Volume 20*, 195.

76. Ahlquist, *The Apostle of Common Sense*, 27; Chesterton, *The Man Who Was Orthodox*, 118; Nichols, *Chesterton*, 72.

77. Lauer, *G. K. Chesterton*, 104.

78. Chesterton, *The Man Who Was Orthodox*, 118.

79. Ibid.

allows the citizen a maximum of independence within the widest limits. He is free to choose a wife—and bound by the institution of marriage; he is free to give—but not to take; to follow his own religion and philosophy—but not to prevent others from doing so."[80] It is the delineation of limitations that "gives to life a particular value."[81]

Chesterton's point about the impossibility of doing away with limitations is still worth noting, especially because of its implications for understanding human choice:

> Every act of will is an act of self-limitation. To desire action is to desire limitation. In that sense, every act is an act of self-sacrifice. When you choose anything, you reject everything else. . . . Every act is an irrevocable selection and exclusion. Just as when you marry one woman you give up all the others, so when you take one course of action you give up all the other courses. . . . Art is limitation; the essence of every picture is the frame. If you draw a giraffe, you must draw him with a long neck. If, in you bold creative way, you hold yourself free to draw a giraffe with a short neck, you will really find that you are not free to draw a giraffe. The moment you step into the world of facts, you step into a world of limits. You can free things from alien or accidental laws, but not from the laws of their own nature. You may, if you like, free a tiger from his bars; but do not free him from his stripes. Do not free a camel from the burden of his hump; you may be freeing him from being a camel. Do not go about as a demagogue, encouraging triangles to break out of the prison of their three sides. If a triangle breaks out of its three sides, its life comes to a lamentable end. Somebody wrote a work called "The Loves of the Triangles"; I never read it, but I am sure that if triangles ever were loved, they were loved for being triangular. This is certainly the case with all artistic creation, which is in some ways the most decisive example of pure will. The artist loves his limitations: they constitute the thing he is doing.[82]

Even in the above, Chesterton delineates two kinds of freedom, both of which are primarily positive forms of freedom rather than forms of freedom built entirely upon antithesis. They are freedoms *for* rather than just freedoms *from*. The first is the freedom that things have to be fully themselves. The second is the human freedom involved in choosing how to act towards

---

80. Cammaerts, *The Laughing Prophet*, 94.

81. Ibid.

82. Chesterton, *Collected Works, Volume 1*, 243–44.

the world. It is this second freedom, however, that is the most dangerous, as Chesterton writes on the story in Genesis 2 and 3.

> Whether or no the garden [of Eden] was an allegory, the truth itself can be very well allegorised as a garden. And the point of it is that Man, whatever else he is, is certainly not merely one of the plants of the garden that has plucked its roots out of the soil and walked about with them like legs, or, on the principle of a double dahlia, has grown duplicate eyes and ears. He is something else, something strange and solitary, and more like the statue that was once the god of the garden; but the statue has fallen from its pedestal and lies broken among the plants and weeds.[83]

The separation from God that permits human freedom also allows for the possibility of choosing either good or evil to enter the human drama.[84] The choices made by human beings have a moral weight that has the potential to affect the rest of the natural order even when that natural order remains "perfect according to [its] own plan."[85] This is demonstrated in *The Surprise* when the puppets of the first act are transformed into real actors in the second. What follows is supposed to be a reenactment of the first act, but because of the freedom of the human characters the result is mayhem. This is the upshot of the risk taken by the Author when he gives his characters freedom to be themselves: the risk is that his original intention for his characters may be violated.

Nevertheless, freedom is not the sole purpose of the division built into creation. Division is a prerequisite for love, since love desires personality.[86] God, being in his very nature love, grants separation and freedom to the created order and gives humanity the ability to choose. Like St. Augustine, and unlike Calvin, Chesterton assumes that God's love takes priority over his will. God's will, which is to create this division, follows in the wake of his love. This is what allows man to choose to love the God who had loved him into being. Chesterton suggests that God made man to come into contact with reality.[87] This contact with reality is epitomized in the reciprocation of the love of God rather than in detached rationality. It is a reciprocation that is built into creation, along with a movement from division to union, from disconnection and disintegration to connection and integration, as well as

83. Chesterton, *The Man Who Was Orthodox*, 157.

84. Chesterton, *What's Wrong with the World*, 129.

85. Chesterton, *The Man Who Was Orthodox*, 157.

86. Chesterton, *Collected Works, Volume 1*, 337; Chesterton, *The Man Who Was Orthodox*, 108.

87. Chesterton, *Saint Thomas Aquinas, Saint Francis of Assisi*, 137, 170.

from the absence of understanding to understanding. Love, in the end, is the highest form of understanding. It is the sort of understanding that ensures that the "fairy tale" of reality ends "happily ever after."[88] Indeed, the "prince and princess" in the usual fairy tale symbolize this happiness even when "it is very likely that from time to time they [will throw] the furniture at each other."[89] Even strife is bound to the contingencies of creation, whereas peace is bound to God's necessary goodness.

This fairy tale ending as a movement towards loving reconciliation is reflected in the outcome of the play performed in *The Surprise*: a movement is towards a wedding. And the contradictions of existence are particularly reflected in the fact that humankind, having been given the power to choose, has chosen against God's original design in both real and symbolic ways throughout history, with dire consequences.[90] Division, as the mechanism of freedom, has allowed for further division. Thus, even virtues can be found isolated from each other and wandering alone.[91] Truth can be found removed from pity, for instance, resulting in a pitiless truth or a truthless pity.[92] One insight that arises from this observation is that a lie may not necessarily be simply the absence of truth, but can also be the truth out of place. With regard to hermeneutics, misinterpretation not only implies the absence of understanding, but implies a kind of understanding that fails to adhere to the boundaries suggested by the fusing and clashing of horizons.

In summary of the above, the Creator, like the Author in *The Surprise*, holds his good creation in his mind. His authorial intent remains perfectly intact in his own loving knowledge of that creation. But for his intent to be properly realized, his imagined world has to be set free. It needs to be released to live as text in its own right and thus become a text that can be appropriated, misappropriated, understood, misunderstood, or even regarded with some indifference. In Chesterton's cosmology, human beings serve a dual purpose: they are both the text and an audience to this creation. It is left to them to decide to work with or against God's love and the order that he has instilled into creation.

The doctrine of the fall that Chesterton so often points to argues that human beings have made a great mess of God's good creation.[93] The ac-

---

88. Chesterton, *Appreciations and Criticisms*, 132.

89. Ibid.

90. Chesterton, *Collected Works, Volume 1*, 282.

91. Ibid., 233.

92. Ibid.

93. Chesterton, *Collected Works, Volume 1*, 282; Chesterton, *The Man Who Was Orthodox*, 158.

tors in the play have often chosen, whether consciously or unconsciously, to move against the script of the Author precisely because the script itself has allowed them the freedom to do so. The outcome is a broken creation. This is not to say in any simplistic sense that creation is itself necessarily and absolutely fallen, but rather that it is deeply affected by the fall. Chesterton's vision of the fall includes the intrusion of systemic and relational horrors that negatively affect even the connection of innocent people with what is ultimate and is not just concerned with individual sins. Thus, if there is any hope of redemption it must involve redeeming more than just individuals. The whole world, including all of creation, needs to be put right. The play needs to be brought back into contact with its Author, while keeping the possibility of human freedom intact.

Therefore, as desperate as the situation of the fall may be, Chesterton's fundamental belief in a good Creator remains untouched. This leaves open the way for genuine restoration—a revolutionary movement towards the original good.[94] Once again, *The Surprise* provides a fitting analogy for how this restoration could take place. Just when two of the characters in *The Surprise* are about to engage in an unholy war, the Author's head appears "bursting out through an upper part of the scenery."[95] He calls out in alarm, "And in the devil's name, what do you think you are doing with my play? Drop it! Stop! I am coming down."[96] The "devil's name" may quite easily be taken as a symbol of the itinerant artist that the Author mentions at the start of the play, since the play that has been left to the actors is now clearly following the itinerant artist's original assumption that drama cannot exist without villains or villainy. It also evokes the image of the serpent in the Garden of Eden who instigates the fall of humanity by proclaiming that God is in fact a rival of human desires rather than the originator and perfecter of them. It is likely, though, that Chesterton is merely offering a joke. Where people might use the word *God* in an exclamation, the God-figure is quite within his rights to use the name of the devil instead.

The main point of this surprise at the end of *The Surprise* is not to reinforce the failure of the characters to reflect the intentions of the Author through their actions, but rather to reflect the fact that the Author has been involved all along, albeit in a rather unexpected way. His desire to have the play reflect his original plan—to establish an order within which goodness can run wild[97]—remains. It would be incorrect to read Chesterton as sug-

---

94. Chesterton, *Collected Works, Volume 1*, 315.

95. Chesterton, *The Surprise*, 63.

96. Ibid.

97. Chesterton, *Collected Works, Volume 1*, 300.

gesting a kind of *Deus Ex Machina* God who steps in right at the end of a bungled drama to fix an impossible plot conundrum: Chesterton's Author, like God, is central to the entire plot. The surprise of the incarnation is the recognition of this fact.

So, for Chesterton, the fall does not mean an inevitable movement towards degradation and decay, but rather catalyzes the Author's ongoing desire for the possibility of "reconciliation," "reconstruction," "redemption," "reform," "renewal," "remaking," "restoration," "revision," and "revolution."[98] This trend towards renewal begins in a moment of truth-telling; it begins with the acceptance of all the ways in which one's personal and political position is out of line with the nonrivalrous nature of the divine. It is found even in owning up to the most obvious of facts: the personal sense of original sin.[99] This is articulated, for instance, Chesterton's explanation of Confession:

> Well, when a Catholic comes from Confession, he does truly, by definition, step out again into that dawn of his own beginning and look with new eyes across the world to a Crystal Palace that is really crystal. He believes that in that dim corner, and in that brief ritual, God has really remade him in His own image. He is now a new experiment of the Creator. He is as much a new experiment as he was when he was really only five years old. He stands, as I said, in the white light at the worthy beginning of the life of a man. The accumulations of time can no longer terrify. He may be grey and gouty; but he is only five minutes old.[100]

The central idea here, and in all of Chesterton's thinking, is that of the very real possibility of a return to the original good, which concerns seeing the world with "new eyes" and perceiving it with renewed understanding.[101] It is, in short, re-creation. Chesterton even compares the word *recreation* to the word *resurrection*, which is signified by the Christian Sabbath as the first day of the week.[102] It is a reminder of the Pauline notion of a "new creation" (2 Cor 5:17), which implies that even the myriad ways that humankind and nature have been defaced, defeated, and entangled in inhuman processes can be repaired.

---

98. Chesterton, *Autobiography*, 324; Chesterton, *Collected Works, Volume 1*, 310, 315; Chesterton, *Collected Works, Volume 5*, 426; Chesterton, *The Everlasting Man*, 241;

99. Chesterton, *Collected Works, Volume 1*, 77.

100. Chesterton, *Autobiography*, 325.

101. Ibid.

102. Chesterton, *Collected Works, Volume 5*, 418.

It is clear from the above that Chesterton's cosmology is not a detached scientific speculation regarding any neutral or purely factual description of how the universe began. Rather, it is a picture of what the universe may actually mean. It starts with a theological proposition: the physical universe began with God and is held into being by God. Chesterton then moves on to a moral proposition by claiming that this material world is good since it was made by a Creator who is Goodness Itself. This good creation was left in the charge of human beings, as per the biblical narrative in Genesis, who then "made a mess of things" by losing sight of God's original intent. However, God, being hidden in some ways behind a curtain, is still discernible as being committed to putting right what has gone wrong. In other ways, Chesterton argues that the divine intent is to have human beings participate with him in this very act of re-creation. In all of this, Chesterton emphasizes the importance of the physical world. If God had bothered to make the world in the first place, then it must certainly be meaningful; if he had taken the trouble to compose this play, then it is a play that is there to be viewed, interpreted, and understood.

Chesterton's Epistemology

When one examines Chesterton's cosmology as I have done above, it is clear that he does not work solely in literal, rationalist terms. Sometimes problematically, as Quentin Lauer points out, Chesterton's tendency is "to claim rational justification for moral and religious convictions whose rational foundations [are] not overwhelmingly evident."[103] Nevertheless, the Genesis account that guides Chesterton's cosmology is primarily mythological and poetic. He prioritizes *mythos* over *logos* and thus also prioritizes contextualized meaning over isolated facts. Stories, images, and ideas guide Chesterton's thinking more than any kind of overtly systematic philosophy.[104] As a result, his arguments are bound to an analogical epistemology, which means that his concerns about the nature, scope, and limitations of knowledge are not necessarily easy to delineate in analytic terms. I would therefore maintain that the narratives of Genesis and *The Surprise* may be just as helpful for grappling with his epistemology as they are for outlining his cosmology.

From the sheer scope and depth of Chesterton's work, we find that he has great respect for the human capacity to understand. As I have already noted, he insists on the link between the mind and reality[105]—between in-

103. Lauer, *G. K. Chesterton*, 29.

104. Chesterton, *Autobiography*, 58.

105. Chesterton, *Saint Thomas Aquinas, Saint Francis of Assisi*, 137.

tellection and being—and therefore thinks it possible for the human mind to know and understand what is being perceived. This does not mean that "the intellect always knows the essences of things (in the totality of their properties)" or with respect to their perfect distinctiveness.[106] Human intellect is limited after all. But "intellect is" nonetheless "capable of knowing" things.[107] Even if confusion about things is possible, what is "certain" is that intellect "is capable of apprehending them."[108] By retaining his intellectual humility, Chesterton observes that there is a need for a "working" philosophy that "nearly all philosophies" simply cannot provide; and that there are those who espouse philosophies that simply do not work:[109]

> No sceptics work sceptically; no fatalists work fatalistically; all without exception work on the principle that it is possible to assume what it is not possible to believe. No materialist who thinks his mind was made up for him, by mud and blood and heredity, has any hesitation in making up his mind. No sceptic who believes that truth is subjective has any hesitation about treating it as objective.[110]

Chesterton again argues here for a definite, although by no means absolute link between theory and experience. Therefore, he implies that if we are to understand anything about the world, our philosophy should correspond with reality as we encounter it.[111] It is not necessarily a fault to want to imagine a philosophy that is detached from reality, because such a philosophy could produce a number of interesting provocations and diversions. Nevertheless, Chesterton's concern is with finding a philosophy that one can actually live by. This has definite implications for Chesterton's interpretive approach, especially because it suggests that our understanding cannot be absolutely remote from the author, text, or reader. Rather, understanding results from a dramatic connection between, confrontation with, and overlapping of their respective dramas and horizons. Even if the precise details of this connection cannot be easily articulated, it is clear nonetheless that the connection exists.

The absolute skepticism that Chesterton is so often at war with in his writings reveals only a break in the link between perception and reality. This would especially be true of the nominalist school of thought, which claims

106. Maritan, *Introduction to Philosophy*, 129.

107. Ibid.

108. Ibid.

109. Chesterton, *Saint Thomas Aquinas, Saint Francis of Assisi*, 170.

110. Ibid.

111. Chesterton, *Alarms and Discursions*, 17.

that "universals have no existence except as names or ideas with which nothing in reality corresponds."[112] Chesterton regards this nominalism as a kind of "nonsense":[113]

> [Nominalism] can easily be applied to any other norm as well as the norm of the rationalist. Is there such a thing as a dog? And if there is, what are its essential characteristics? What is there in common between a mastiff and a minute Pekinese, between an Italian greyhound and a bulldog, between a St. Bernard and a dachshund, and so on? In the one sense the difference is indeed very difficult to ignore, and the identity very difficult to define. In practice we can only say two things about it. First, that we know that all the dogs know they are dogs, and act accordingly. And second that a man who ignores the fact may soon be found trying to teach a pig to be a watch-dog, and to hunt a fox with a pack of cats; and may be found soon after that in a madhouse.[114]

Nominalism is what leads some modern thinkers, like H. G. Wells (1866–1946), to claim that "'there is no being, but a universal becoming of individualities,'" or that "'[t]here is no abiding thing in what we know. We change from weaker to stronger lights, and each more powerful light pierces our hitherto opaque foundations and reveals fresh and different opacities below.'"[115] For Chesterton, Wells fails to make "an evident mental distinction."[116]

> It *cannot* be true that there is nothing abiding in what we know. For if that were so we should not know it all and should not call it knowledge. Our mental state may be different from that of somebody else some thousands of years back; but it cannot be entirely different, or else we should not be conscious of a difference. Mr. Wells must realise the first and simplest of the paradoxes that sit by the springs of truth. He must surely see that the fact of two things being different implies that they are similar. The hare and the tortoise may differ in the quality of swiftness, but they must agree in the quality of motion. The swiftest hare cannot be swifter than an isosceles triangle or the idea of pinkness. When we say that the hare moves faster, we say that the tortoise moves. And when we say of a thing that it moves, we

112. Maritan, *Introduction to Philosophy*, 98.

113. Chesterton, *Illustrated London News*, March 24, 1924.

114. Ibid.

115. Chesterton, *Collected Works, Volume 1*, 78.

116. Ibid.

say, without need of other words, that there are things that do
not move. And even in the act of saying that things change, we
say that there is something unchangeable.[117]

Even Wells's own example regarding light is evidence of a sense of the
universal. Light may change as much as it possibly can; it may be stronger or
weaker. "But the quality of light remains the same thing, or else we should
not call it a stronger light or recognise it as such."[118] Nominalism leads to
skepticism, whereas the Platonist sense of universals is right: "Plato turned
his face to truth, but his back on Mr. H. G. Wells, when he turned to his
museum of specified ideals. It is precisely here that Plato saw sense. It is
not true that everything changes; the things that change are all the manifest
and material things. There is something that does not change; and that is
precisely the abstract quality, the invisible idea."[119]

For Chesterton, the rupture between the mind and reality created by
this nominalism needs to be corrected. It therefore makes sense that he
would turn to a theology that articulates the possibility of such correction.
Even if some may disdain his reliance on theology, it must be acknowledged
that one cannot understand the human without including a "testimony to
the spirituality of the human."[120] Chesterton therefore writes of his own
Anglo-Catholic theology, "I have only found one creed that could not be
satisfied with a truth, but only with the Truth, which is made of a million
such truths and yet is one."[121] If the key fits perfectly, Chesterton argues, it is
the right key, especially when the lock is particularly complex.[122]

Chesterton's metaphor of a key is fitting in a few ways: firstly, because
a key has a definite shape and "depends entirely upon keeping its shape";
secondly, because its specificity either works or does not; and, thirdly, because it allows for complexity without necessarily sacrificing clarity.[123] The
metaphor of a key also suggests a dramatic meeting of alterities: a fusion
and collision of horizons. A similar idea is found in another metaphor that
Chesterton offers on the same issue: "When the hammer has hit the right

---

117. Ibid., 78–79.

118. Ibid., 79.

119. Ibid.

120. Lauer, *G. K. Chesterton*, 93.

121. Chesterton, *Autobiography*, 332.

122. Chesterton, *Collected Works, Volume 1*, 287; Chesterton, *The Everlasting Man*,
248.

123. *The Everlasting Man*, 215; Ker, *G. K. Chesterton*, 526.

nail on the head a hundred times, there comes a time when we think it was not altogether by accident."[124]

Chesterton finds that there is a universal sense of the unity and interconnectedness of meaning, no matter how incompletely or disconnectedly we perceive it. The world he lives in is not an impenetrable fog of non-sequiturs, but something decodable and decipherable; it holds the "fragmentary suggestions of a philosophy" that forms a coherent whole even if that whole is not perfectly graspable by the human subject.[125] Chesterton therefore seeks to avoid any view of knowledge that sees the world purely in terms of neat propositions and reductionisms, hence his emphasis on the storied and dramatic configuration of life.[126] This deep-rooted sense of the coherence and dramatic order of the world is rooted in Chesterton's opinions on the character of God. If God is good, and good is that which aligns with the true, then the authority of the senses can be trusted.[127] Chesterton's epistemology, therefore, is directly linked to his cosmology. Each facet of his cosmology—Creator, creation and fall, re-creation—corresponds with a facet of his epistemology—divine knowledge, human knowledge and non-knowledge, and remembering or re-membering.

I have already pointed out that Chesterton is a realist in the sense that he believes that at least some understanding of reality is open to human beings. If one begins with the acceptance of the realness of reality, "further deductions from it will be equally real; they will be things and not words."[128] To begin with the assumption of the real is to assume that the real can be discovered. This is perhaps a convenient metaphysical assumption made possible by the invocation of God, who being the ground of both knowledge and being is therefore the one who guarantees their correspondence. Still, for Chesterton, God "made the world of reason" and is at least somewhat discernable through the meanings located in the text of creation.[129] He is, thus, not just a convenient concept or a mere abstraction. He is not merely a neat presupposition to fuel further presuppositions, but the ultimate personal reality, as well as the source of reality and our real ability to experience it.

Chesterton does not support the idea of a so-called God-of-the-gaps. As is evident throughout his work, he assumes that we know God not by

124. Chesterton, *Collected Works, Volume 3*, 190.

125. Chesterton, *Autobiography*, 41.

126. Williams, *Mere Humanity*, 23.

127. Chesterton, *Saint Thomas Aquinas, Saint Francis of Assisi*, 136.

128. Ibid., 170.

129. Chesterton, *Autobiography*, 165.

simplistically legitimating his existence as an explanation for the things we do not understand, but by recognizing his Being as intimated by the things that we do understand.[130] The fact of our understanding insists on something that guarantees the bridge between the thought and things. Even when we embrace mystery, it is not the unknown that urges the discovery of meaning, but the astonishing and almost overwhelming presence of the known. Nevertheless, sometimes God is experienced or revealed to smash our explanations to smithereens; he is not so much a God who fills the gaps as a God who creates gaps. The hermeneutic event therefore not only involves being initiated into understanding, but also being confronted with what one may never understand.

Chesterton assumes that the Author knows the work before it is separate from his mind. Creation is known before is it even a fact. This is reflected in what the Author says about the guard that he made for his play: "I knew him before he was made."[131] Consequently, knowledge is not something to be reduced to pure empiricism. Empiricism can only really be taken as part of knowledge, not as the whole of it. The empiricist can only "clutch his fragment of fact, almost as the primitive man clutched his fragment of flint."[132] The fact is never enough because, as Chesterton's cosmology suggests, the fact is a fragment of a much larger knowing. The fact can only be understood, because the fact is known into being by an author who means for the fact to be understood in a particular way. Even while he supports the separation of author and text, Chesterton would oppose the gnostic or deist tendency to make the disconnection of text from author absolute. There may be a varying distance between the reader's knowledge of the text and the intention of the author, but this distance is by no means insurmountable. There is no real separation between the sacred and secular orders except one that we construct. Thus, even when the author's pure intention cannot be perfectly known from the text, it must still be assumed that the text originated from his mind.

While Chesterton is committed to the link between mind and reality, he acknowledges that human knowledge has definite and sometimes noticeable constraints. He readily accepts that there is much to reality that we must first assume even before we can understand it:

> All argument begins with an assumption; that is with something
> that you do not doubt. You can, if you like, doubt the assump-
> tion at the beginning of your argument, but in that case you

130. Chesterton, *Collected Works, Volume 1*, 231.

131. Chesterton, *The Surprise*, 12.

132. Chesterton, *The Everlasting Man*, 41.

are beginning a different argument with another assumption at the beginning of it. Every argument begins with an infallible dogma, and that infallible dogma can only be disputed by falling back on some other infallible dogma; you can never prove your first statement or it would not be your first.[133]

It is this very reliance on assumptions and this awareness of one's own dogmas that can prevent a philosophy of absolute skepticism. Chesterton consequently argues that there are four assumptions in the alphabet of philosophy that one has to begin with before one can begin to philosophize. The first is that the world actually exists, since no one can really prove that the whole thing is not just a dream.[134] The second is that the world matters, for even arguments against meaning or truth are founded on some version of meaning or truth.[135] The third assumption is that there is such a thing as a continuous self.[136] Chesterton points out that while the material state of the self is in constant flux, one cannot argue anything coherently without assuming that the self is a constant; if the self were discontinuous, all of reality would be perceived only as fractured, unstable, and unreliable, rendering hermeneutics a time-wasting, hit-and-miss affair, caught in an untamable vortex of equivocities. The fourth and final assumption is that human beings can choose, implying that they have responsibility over their thoughts and actions.[137]

With these four pillars in place—reality, meaning, the continuous self and choice—Chesterton argues that knowledge itself is rooted in faith. All four of these unprovable assumptions are taken on faith; and since any attack on the four pillars of reason mentioned above is ultimately an attack on knowledge, it may be said that faith is essential to Chesterton's epistemology. One cannot prove reality, meaning, the continuous self, or the possibility of choice,[138] for all of reason is a matter of faith.[139] In other words, faith is the fundamental pre-epistemological condition of all understanding. As St. Anselm suggests, following St. Augustine's thinking, *Credo ut intelligam*: one believes to understand.[140] Faith, which is itself a gift given by God, is

133. Chesterton, *The Man Who Was Orthodox*, 91.

134. Chesterton, *Collected Works, Volume 1*, 229; Chesterton, *The Man Who Was Orthodox*, 92.

135. Chesterton, *The Man Who Was Orthodox*, 92.

136. Ibid.

137. Ibid.

138. Ibid.

139. Chesterton, *Collected Works, Volume 1*, 236.

140. Marías, *History of Philosophy*, 144.

fundamental to Chesterton's hermeneutic, but it also seems to be fundamental to all hermeneutics.

Bearing this in mind, it is not much of a logical leap to assume, on
faith, that there is a God whose own thoughts were and remain catalysts for
reality as we know it. It is on faith in the good Creator that Chesterton assumes the possibility of human understanding. If God is the source of both
being and knowing, it is not unreasonable to assume the correspondence
of reality and perception. In other words, there is a definite connection between God's knowledge and the human ability know him:

> You cannot evade the issue of God; whether you talk about
> pigs or binomial theory, you are still talking about Him. Now
> if Christianity be . . . a fragment of metaphysical nonsense in-
> vented by a few people, then, of course, defending it will simply
> mean talking that metaphysical nonsense over and over again.
> But if Christianity should happen to be true—then defending it
> may mean talking about anything and everything. Things can be
> irrelevant to the proposition that Christianity is false, but noth-
> ing can be irrelevant to the proposition that Christianity is true.
> Zulus, gardening, butchers' shops, lunatic asylums, housemaids
> and the French Revolution—all these things not only may have
> something to do with the Christian God, but must have some-
> thing to do with Him if He really lives and reigns.[141]

This passage reinforces what I have already noted, namely that if God
is to be known at all by people he must be known through the text of his
creation, not apart from it. But this in itself is a problem for epistemology:
since creation has been separated and freed from the mind of God and
given a will of its own, it is difficult to decipher the exact will and intention
of the Author through the text. Indeed, the mind of any author remains
hidden insofar as the exact meaning of the text has been left open to multiple interpretations. Chesterton acknowledges this difficulty for interpretive processes when he writes that in ages past "the minority, the sages or
thinkers, had withdrawn apart and had taken up an equally congenial trade.
They were drawing up plans of the world; of the world which all believed to
have a plan. They were trying to set forth the plan seriously and to scale."[142]
They were, in other words, "setting their minds directly to the mind that
had made the mysterious world; considering what sort of a mind it might

---

141. Chesterton, *Daily News*, December 12, 1903; Chesterton, *The Man Who Was
Orthodox*, 89–90.

142. Chesterton, *The Everlasting Man*, 265.

be and what its ultimate purpose might be."[143] Nevertheless, because of the ambiguities that arise in the separation of author from text, "[s]ome of them made that mind much more impersonal than mankind has generally made it; some simplified it almost to a blank; a few, a very few, doubted it altogether."[144] Some even thought that it might be "evil or an enemy" while others, even more confused, "worshipped demons instead of gods."[145] Still, Chesterton notes that monotheism was at the heart of all the views, which is to say that there was an almost unanimous agreement in ancient speculations that there was indeed one Author: "they not only saw a moral plan in nature, but they generally laid down a moral plan for humanity" in what they regarded "more or less" as "holy scriptures."[146]

Throughout human history, people have tried to search the knowledge of God by examining the text of creation. And while Chesterton argues that this natural theology has revealed a great number of likely truths, the mind of God remains largely a mystery even in the afterglow of definite revelation. But mysteries are meant to be inhabited more than they are meant to be understood.[147] Once again, understanding is only possible by what is found beyond the limitations of human comprehension. Reason, which is always of the whole, is "ecstatic" and therefore "always exceeds explicit consciousness."[148] It is always ahead of itself, reaching beyond its own limits, and yet it is also in a perpetual process of catching up with itself.[149] Reason transcends us while being immanent to us; it is within us, pulling us beyond ourselves. It is not of us, but abides with us, calling us from mystery into mystery.

It is in praise of mystery that Chesterton argues that solitary facts are insufficient when it comes to understanding.[150] The interpretive experience takes place within a drama of interconnected truths. Even God knew the truth of the world before the world had become a fact because its truth was in him.[151] He understood the truth of the world in its fullness even before it had any concrete substance. When it comes to understanding Chesterton's

143. Ibid.

144. Ibid.

145. Ibid.

146. Ibid.

147. Chesterton, *Collected Works, Volume 1*, 231.

148. Schindler, *The Catholicity of Reason*, 9.

149. Ibid., 14.

150. Chesterton, *Collected Works, Volume 1*, 231; Chesterton, *Tremendous Trifles*, 32.

151. Capon, *Genesis*, 35; Chesterton, *The Surprise*, 12.

hermeneutic horizon, this particular insight is essential. Chesterton plays with the images in his mind and in his world to point to the connection of the transcendent with the immanent, and also to the link between what is beyond our ability to comprehend and what is as clear as daylight.

Therefore, while he claims to be interested in Zulus, gardening, butchers' shops, and lunatic asylums for what they tell us about themselves, he is more interested in things like these for what they tell us about how we understand the mind of God. For Chesterton, reality is iconic and sacramental; it is something *looked through* and not just *looked at*. He begins with certainties and yet all the while remains aware that the primary limitation of human knowledge is its inability to fully comprehend divine knowledge. However, the knowledge of God stays central to Chesterton's thoughts on how one may understand human knowledge. An ever-present tension between what can be known without being fully understood and what can be understood without being fully known is always present. This is the first hint of the dramatic tension between mystery and revelation in Chesterton's hermeneutic.

Chesterton contends that "[t]hinking means connecting things, and stops if they cannot be connected."[152] The very act of thinking relies upon the awareness that things are separate, as per Chesterton's cosmology, and yet also interconnected. However, mere connection is not the main aim of thinking. If this were the case, one could connect anything to anything else, creating chaos and confusion instead of understanding. Chesterton therefore has a number of checks and balances to ensure that knowledge connects realities in the right way. This is crucial for understanding Chesterton's way of seeing things. Thus, what follows is a brief summary of Chesterton's specific parameters regarding the four, faith-sustained pillars of human knowledge already mentioned.

In the first place, when Chesterton asserts the importance of acknowledging reality as a fact, he assumes the place of human beings in reality and is, in a limited sense, a pragmatist. However, he argues that while he supports the idea that pragmatism may be a "preliminary guide to truth," he is against any kind of extreme pragmatism that results in "an absence of all truth whatever."[153] Extreme pragmatism at its best is akin to utilitarianism and at its worst to solipsism. Utilitarianism is problematically limited because it argues the value of a thing only by its end result, leaving almost everything, including knowledge, devoid of any intrinsic value. On the other hand, solipsism promotes the absence of any kind of objective or theoretical

152. Chesterton, *Collected Works, Volume 1*, 238.

153. Ibid., 239.

measurement of truth or falsehood. Because of this, Chesterton argues that pragmatism "is a matter of human needs; and one of the first human needs is to be something more than a pragmatist."[154] After all, "[e]xtreme pragmatism is just as inhuman as the determinism it so powerfully attacks. The determinist (who, to do him justice, does not pretend to be a human being) makes nonsense of the human sense of actual choice. The pragmatist, who professes to be specially human, makes nonsense of the human sense of the actual fact."[155]

For the sake of understanding, one has to begin with the presence of choice, but without refuting the facts that allow one to choose. One has to be free from anything to be able to choose to understand it and commune with it. One can only arrive at knowledge or understanding if one is thoroughly convinced that the patterns, words, and images in one's own mind are more than just fictions of one's own making.[156]

In the second place, when Chesterton argues that one needs to assume that there is meaning to be found in the world, this meaning needs to be taken as both discernable and reasonable. I have already noted one of Chesterton's responses to skeptics, but that response needs to be put into context since a certain amount of skepticism can be reasonable and even helpful. In fact, Chesterton is just as critical of those who assume that they can navigate the world without a smidgen of doubt as he is of those who doubt everything.[157] Doubt can helpful because it points to mystery and therefore also to faith.[158] Doubt is only problematic when it prevents further thought. It is possible for a thought to stop a person from thinking and Chesterton argues that this is the only kind of thought that should be stopped.[159] As an example, if the only thing that a man can be certain of is his uncertainty, thinking can be of no use to him. Moreover, he will find that life itself is drained of any adventure, joy, and purpose:

> The despair [of a great deal of modern philosophy] is this, that it does not really believe that there is any meaning in the universe; therefore it cannot hope to find any romance; its romances will have no plots. A man cannot expect any adventures in the land of anarchy, but a man can expect any number of adventures if he

---

154. Ibid., 240.

155. Ibid.

156. Chesterton, *Saint Thomas Aquinas, Saint Francis of Assisi*, 136.

157. Chesterton, *Collected Works, Volume 1*, 227.

158. Chesterton, *Alarms and Discursions*, 44; Chesterton, *In Defense of Sanity*, 99.

159. Chesterton, *Collected Works, Volume 1*, 236; Chesterton, *Illustrated London News*, August 6, 1932.

goes traveling in the land of authority. One can find no meanings in a jungle of scepticism; but the man will find more meanings who walks through a forest of doctrine and design. Here
everything has a story tied to its tail, like the tools or pictures in
my father's house; for it is my father's house.[160]

If thinking means connecting things, it also means connecting the self
to things. It means recognizing that even apart from our ability to completely comprehend the world, we are still related to it. The above passage
has Chesterton musing about the connections between things in his father's
house, but it is clear that he is also alluding to the house of God the Father. If
God always holds all things into being, then the connection between things
is primarily found in relation to him. Apart from this anchor in Christian
epistemology, knowledge and understanding inevitably become fragmented
because the fragmented self becomes the only point of connection, thereby
making connection as arbitrary as the fluctuating awareness of the human
subject.[161] With God the Author as the unchanged yet dynamic Trinitarian
Being at the center, epistemology can expect to make stable connections
between one fact and another even within the fluctuations of human experience. With the self at the center, egocentrism rules, and such egocentrism
almost certainly hampers understanding since it promotes movement without a solid foundation.

In the third place, regarding the continuous self, Chesterton opposes the modernist conception of the self as absolutely stable, isolated or
detached *res cogitans*. There is both change and stability in the self, rather
than just one or the other. Chesterton argues that there is a paradox in the
tension between movement and stillness: "it's possible to reach the same
results in reality by treating motion as a fixed point and stability as a form
of motion."[162] By asserting this paradox, Chesterton, by inference, exposes
the inescapability of the continuous self. If one takes the self's discontinuity
as a fact or as something known, this discontinuity becomes a stable point
of reference; thus, even in asserting the discontinuity of the self, the self is
assumed to be continuous. There needs to be some kind of continuity for
knowledge to be accessible. If the self shifts all the time, knowledge becomes
impossible, and yet without movement, knowledge cannot be attained since
there would be no room for change or growth in understanding. However,
once again the paradox of the changing-stable self is that knowledge cannot
rationally be bound to egotism or one's over-assertion of the self: egotism

160. Chesterton, *Collected Works, Volume 1*, 362.

161. Williams, *Mere Humanity*, 67.

162. Chesterton, *Tales of the Long Bow*.

is something denied when one preaches it; for to promote egotism is to practice altruism.[163] Even egotism can imply humility, since it is "impossible without humility to enjoy anything—even pride."[164]

In the fourth place, regarding human choice, Chesterton does not praise the human ability to choose alone. Choice is not an isolated matter, and without a purpose is not choice at all:

> [Many people] say that choice is itself the divine thing. Thus Mr. Bernard Shaw has attacked the old idea that men's acts are to be judged by the standard of the desire of happiness. He says that a man does not act for his happiness, but from his will. He does not say, "Jam will make me happy," but "I want jam." . . . [A]nd the test of will is simply that the test of happiness is a test and the other isn't. You can discuss whether a man's act in jumping over a cliff was directed towards happiness; you cannot discuss whether it was derived from will. Of course it was. You can praise an action by saying that it is calculated to bring pleasure or pain to discover truth or to save the soul. But you cannot praise an action because it shows will; for to say that is merely to say that it is an action. By this praise of will you cannot really choose one course as better than another. And yet choosing one course as better than another is the very definition of the will you are praising. The worship of will is the negation of will. To admire mere choice is to refuse to choose. If Mr. Bernard Shaw comes up to me and says, "Will something," that is tantamount to saying, "I do not mind what you will," and that is tantamount to saying, "I have no will in the matter." You cannot admire will in general, because the essence of will is that it is particular.[165]

Choice as a key to participating in the drama is also the key to understanding. One chooses to accept or reject information, knowledge, and wisdom just as one can choose between good and evil. Thus choice is at the heart of deciding to know things as true, untrue, unknown, or unknowable. At every point in Chesterton's epistemology regarding the acceptance of reality, meaning and the continuous self, choice is of vital importance. To refuse to choose is to live in a permanent state of agnosticism, and such agnosticism is tantamount to choosing to side with the status quo. The less complimentary name for the Greek word *agnostic* is the Latin *ignoramus*. Even if agnosticism is the most natural attitude of human beings, at some

163. Chesterton, *Collected Works, Volume 1*, 241.

164. Ibid., 234.

165. Chesterton, *Collected Works, Volume 1*, 242–43.

point one has to admit that it does not work;[166] for wilful ignorance is really the suppression of reason.[167]

Choice is ultimately an "act of self-limitation" since choosing anything means rejecting other things.[168] Every affirmation implies at least one negation. The very nature of any expression of truth is that, by being inclusive of something, it must exclude other things. The basic law of non-contradiction, which is reliant upon the actual limitations of human thought and the reality of the world, still stands, although it should not be taken as so universal that actual contradictions in reality should be ignored. In affirming the unavoidability of choice, it becomes clear that ignorance is not the absence of knowledge; rather, it is the presence of incorrect knowledge.[169] "There are no uneducated people," Chesterton writes; what we find is that "most people are educated wrong."[170] And so the fight against ignorance, which involves establishing a new kind of ignorance as simplicity is restored,[171] is not a fight against a lack of knowledge; rather, it is a fight against non-knowledge masquerading itself as knowledge, and a fight against untruth masquerading itself as truth.

Consequently, while Chesterton takes great pains to defend the mystery of "Divine Reason," which may be understood as the knowledge that is the root of human reason, so he also strongly defends human reason and knowledge. He observes that the world is frequently at war with reason, first in its rejection of mystery, but also in its unyielding reliance upon skepticism and doubt.[172] Because of this, he aims to recover the sense that we can be certain about some things. He acknowledges that doubt about some spiritual realities may not be completely unreasonable, but insists that generally the human experience of the self or the good can be trusted.[173]

However, Chesterton's faith in the human capacity for understanding is tempered by his view that we live in a broken world, or at least that our perception of the world has been uprooted. For him, then, the story of the fall as a "view of life" in the book of Genesis may be taken a myth that partly concerns the human capacity for misunderstanding—the human tendency

---

166. Ibid., 382.

167. Ibid., 244.

168. Ibid., 243.

169. Chesterton, *Collected Works, Volume 1*, 354; Chesterton, *What's Wrong with the World*, 147.

170. Chesterton, *What's Wrong with the World*, 147.

171. Chesterton, *All Things Considered*, 40.

172. Chesterton, *Collected Works, Volume 1*, 235.

173. Ibid., 355, 357.

to move from knowledge to confusion or non-knowledge.[174] Again, as a myth, it is a story that is perpetually true, since good gets confused with evil and evil with good all the time. Chesterton observes that "when it comes to unfamiliar things"—things we do not yet understand—"we often mistake what is real for what is sham."[175]

The story of the fall begins with the serpent asking the woman in Eden, "Hath God said, Ye shall not eat of every tree of the garden?" (Gen 3:1). This, at its heart, is a question about the woman's knowledge: *what do you really know about any of this?* The significance of knowledge here is found in its relationship to power or the parameters of action. What is known will always guide what is done, although not in a purely deterministic sense. The serpent shifts the focus from God's knowledge, and thus the parameters of his knowing and management of creation, to the woman's knowledge, and thus the parameters according to which she understands and manages her life. After this, the serpent explains that the fruit will not cause her to die and therefore directly supplants God's metaphorical revelation with a brutal literalism. In other words, the serpent explains that the woman's knowledge, which had previously worked in images and experiential realities, is wrong because it does not literally and immediately hold true. And all the while the serpent does not quite lie; he works in misplaced truths and half-truths.[176] The issue here, then, is not the story's historical veracity, but rather what it symbolizes for Chesterton, and how it affects his interpretive lens. He writes that the fall

> is not only the only enlightening, but the only encouraging view of life. It holds, against the only real alternative philosophies, those of the Buddhist or the Pessimist or the Promethean, that we have misused a good world and not merely been entrapped into a bad one. It refers evil back to the wrong use of the will and thus declares that it can eventually be righted by the right use of the will. Every other creed except that one is some form of surrender to fate. A man who holds this view of life will find it giving light on a thousand things on which mere evolutionary ethics have not a word to say. For instance, on the colossal contrast between the completeness of man's machines and the continued corruption of his motives; on the fact that no social progress really seems to leave the self behind; on the fact that first and not the last men of any school or revolution are generally the best and the purest, as William Penn was better than

174. Chesterton, *The Man Who Was Orthodox*, 158.
175. Chesterton, *What's Wrong with the World*, 101.
176. Chesterton, *The Ball and the Cross*, 44.

a Quaker millionaire or Washington better than an American oil magnate; on that proverb which says "The price of liberty is eternal vigilance," which is only what the theologians say of every other virtue and is itself only a way of stating the truth of original sin; on those extremes of good and evil by which man exceeds all the animals by the measure of heaven and hell; on that sublime sense of loss that is in the very sound of all great poetry, and nowhere more than in the poetry of pagans and sceptics—"We look before and after and pine for what is not"; which cries against all prigs and progressives out of the very depths and abysses of the broken heart of man that happiness is not only a hope, but also in some strange manner a memory; and that we are all kings in exile.[177]

Chesterton argues that he likes "to have some intellectual justification for [his] intuitions" and therefore finds it convenient to accept that if man seems to be a fallen creature, he must necessarily conclude that at some point man fell.[178]

When the serpent offers Eve the fruit of the tree, it is significant that he offers it as a means to have her and Adam's eyes opened so that they will see more clearly: ". . . and ye shall be as gods, knowing good and evil" (Gen 3:5). While the fall is often used to symbolize the birth of hermeneutics, thereby effectively regarding hermeneutics (or mediation) as a problem to be overcome, it is easier to regard the fall—this grasping for divine knowledge—as a symbol of whatever supports the belief that perfect, unmediated, and infinite knowledge is possible.[179] The fall symbolizes, not the birth of interpretation, but the *end* of interpretation. Construal and mediation are not things that must be abolished, but are instead fundamental to the human experience. The fall, whereby Eve steps into agreement with the serpent, also suggests siding with the (singular) lie over the (multifarious) truth. Whatever non-knowledge is, as I have discussed it, it is not concerned with hermeneutics per se, but with any bad hermeneutic.

Still, for Chesterton, the fall is in fact an optimistic doctrine, because it argues that whatever human beings are they are not themselves.[180] "It is so easy," he writes, "to turn against what is really yourself for the sake of some accidental resemblance to yourself."[181] This means that the fall is not total. And with regard to ethics and epistemology, it implies that there may be a

177. Chesterton, *The Man Who Was Orthodox*, 158.

178. Chesterton, *Collected Works, Volume 1*, 347.

179. See Smith, *The Fall of Interpretation*.

180. Chesterton, *The Man Who Was Orthodox*, 363.

181. Chesterton, *William Blake*, 197.

way for man to get back to his true nature. In a sense, knowledge may be re-paired in the same way that creation may be restored; non-knowledge may be corrected. Chesterton does not root his epistemology solely upon this simple, mythical narrative construction. Experience is the primary teacher: if we have a sense of what is wrong, then some clarity about what is right must also be possible.

Therefore, just as Chesterton's ethic of restoration and re-creation is at the heart of his cosmology, so his epistemology allows for a process of re-membering and re-cognition; that is, for putting-back-together and therefore correcting knowledge where it goes wrong. Even if this is not something Chesterton speaks of explicitly, it is evident throughout his work. He is forever attacking false certainties, modernist egocentricities, and con-ceptual inaccuracies, thereby demonstrating his belief that knowledge and truth are worth fighting for and reclaiming. In fact, it is precisely his un-derstanding of the fall that leads him to determine that one can be both "at peace with everything" and "at war with everything else."[182] In other words, there is a tension between the acceptance of what is in a state of ruin and the desire to set things right again. This is why the fall, as a dogma about human degeneration, is more hopeful and even optimistic than strictly pessimistic for Chesterton: it is a reminder that we have forgotten who we are and thus suggests the possibility of remembering. In *Orthodoxy* (1908), Chesterton writes:

> We have all read in scientific books, and, indeed, in all romances, the story of the man who has forgotten his name. The man walks about the streets and can see and appreciate everything; only he cannot remember who he is. Well, every man is that man in the story. Every man has forgotten who he is. One may understand the cosmos, but never the ego; the self is more distant than any star. Thou shalt love the Lord thy God; but thou shalt not know thyself. We are all under the same mental calamity; we have all forgotten our names. We have all forgotten what we really are. All that we call common sense and rationality and practicality and positivism only means that for certain dead levels of our life we forget that we have forgotten. All that we call spirit and art and ecstasy only means that for one awful instant we remember that we forget.[183]

It seems to me from this that Chesterton agrees with the notion of *anamnesis* or *reminiscence* that comes out of Plato's *Meno* and *Phaedo,*

182. Chesterton, *Collected Works, Volume 1*, 364.

183. Ibid., 257.

although in saying this I am contesting Quentin Lauer's unsubstantiated suggestion that this is a "myth" that Chesterton really "had little sympathy" for.[184] In fact, anamnesis seems to be a fundamental component of Chesterton's way of reading things. It is an idea proposed by Socrates to overcome the paradox of knowledge.[185] This paradox questions how we can seek to find or anticipate what we do not know. It asks how we can be certain, when we find it, that it was what we were looking for. It is therefore rooted in the question of whether anything genuinely new can be introduced to the soul to take the soul by surprise.[186] Anamnesis answers this paradox by suggesting that we in a sense discover what we already know; we forget our amnesia and thus recover what we had thought to be lost. D. C. Schindler proposes that

> the soul anticipates its object, but because that object is not derivable from the soul itself, its anticipation gets recast in the encounter, so that its anticipation is simultaneously surprised and fulfilled. In this respect, the strangely satisfying upheaval that one experiences in great drama turns out to be—surprise!—not an exception to the normal act of cognition, but in fact simply a particularly intense instance of what occurs in every act of knowing whatever insofar as every act is the soul's grasping, and being grasped by, what is other than the soul itself.[187]

John Milbank suggests that the "Meno problematic" includes the problem of how to find God: "we can only seek God who is beyond all reach if in some strange sense we have already arrived at this destination, because he has always already reached down to us."[188] In keeping with this idea of unforgetting, Chesterton writes that even in pagan antiquity

> men were conscious of the Fall, if they were conscious of nothing else; and the same is true of all heathen humanity. Those who have fallen may remember the fall, even when they forget the height. Some such tantalising blank or break in memory is at the back of all pagan sentiment. There is such a thing as the momentary power to remember that we forget. And the most ignorant of humanity know by the very look of earth that they have forgotten heaven.[189]

184. Lauer, G. K. Chesterton, 63.

185. Allen, "Anamnesis in Plato," 165.

186. Schindler, The Catholicity of Reason, 39.

187. Ibid., 52.

188. Milbank, Beyond Secular Order, 27.

189. Chesterton, The Everlasting Man, 94.

For Chesterton, though, even our remembering can be distorted both by our human limitations and by original sin. He recalls, for instance, how the death of his sister when he was very young somehow got mixed in with a memory of her falling from a rocking horse, which then grew into a sense that she had really been killed after being thrown by a real horse. "This," he says, "is the real difficulty about remembering anything; that we have remembered too much—for we have remembered too often."[190] And yet, despite occasional confusion and misremembering, the possibility of recovering a clear view remains. We can remember that we have misremembered.

From the above, a few details that are central to understanding Chesterton's epistemology can be unpacked. The first is that a loss of a sense of identity deeply affects the way that one knows and understands the world. A loss of self-knowledge becomes a barrier to knowledge itself. Therefore, the key to the recovery of understanding in general is the recovery of self-understanding. In a hermeneutic context, interpretive understanding is hampered by a lack of self-understanding. The second detail, directly linked to this first detail, is that it is in the act of appreciating creation and in creating that one reclaims a sense of self. This is to say that interpretive understanding, inasmuch as it is a means to understand written and visual texts, is also a creative means to engage with one's self-understanding and one's horizon of understanding. An act of imagination or creation, therefore, is a transformative activity for any hermeneut.

Chesterton refers in particular to tales that speak of golden apples that exist "only to refresh the forgotten moment when we found that they were green" and tales that tell of rivers flowing with wine that "make us remember, for one wild moment, that they run with water."[191] Re-membering intimates a kind of twofold movement away from dis-memberment: firstly, it looks back to recall how the pieces of a story have fitted together and, secondly, it looks forward at what the result of the restoration can be. Re-membering, then, is not simply concerned with the past per se, but with the integration of one's knowledge of the past with one's hopes for the future.[192]

This points to the fact that there is a strong eucharistic foundation in Chesterton's epistemology: the Eucharist, from the Greek *eucharista* meaning *thankfulness* or *giving thanks*, is precisely an act of remembering that the body broken and the blood poured out for the healing of the world comes not out of a fallen man, but out of wholeness and goodness itself. Chesterton does not provide any explicit atonement theory, but he seems to hold to

---

190. Chesterton, *Autobiography*, 44.

191. Chesterton, *Collected Works, Volume 1*, 257.

192. Ker, *G. K. Chesterton*, 533.

the incarnation as an event of perpetual reconciliation: God is communicated most completely while walking on legs and speaking through human lips, and his restoration of humanity is most exuberantly demonstrated in the love that is still abundantly clear, or perhaps is even most abundantly clear, when the God-man is mocked and killed. Paradoxically, we know God as love and reconciliation—we see things as they are again—even in this deconstruction of the divine—in this breaking down of our conceptions about God and reality that is known in the cry of dereliction: where "God is forsaken of God" and even "seems like an atheist."[193] On the cross especially, sin as an "arbitrary violence" is shown in all its ugliness against the backdrop of an even more profound, more "infinite generosity."[194] "The theme of the Greek tragedy is the division of God and Man; the theme of the Gospel tragedy is the union of God and man; and its immediate effects are more tragic."[195]

> In every century, in this century, in the next century, the Passion is what it was in the first century, when it occurred; a thing stared at by the crowd. It remains a tragedy of the people; a crime of the people; a consolation of the people; but never merely a thing of the period. And its vitality comes from the very things that its foes find a scandal and a stumbling block; from its dogmatism and from its dreadfulness. It lives, because it involves the staggering story of the Creator truly groaning and travailing with his Creation; and the highest thing thinkable passing through some nadir of the lowest curve of the cosmos. And it lives, because the very blast from this black cloud of death comes upon the world as a wind of everlasting life; by which all things wake and are alive.[196]

Even in this tragedy, Chesterton finds comedy. "[H]ope has never been absent; rather it has been errant, extravagant, excessively fixed upon fugitive chances."[197] And part of this hope is the hope that even our broken understanding may be reconciled with reality. Integration is central to Chesterton's dramatic epistemology. He is particularly critical of any mode of thought that attempts to "split the human head into two."[198] In particular, he addresses the one man's declaration that "a man has two minds,

---

193. Chesterton, *The Everlasting Man,* 212.

194. Milbank, *Theology and Social Theory,* 397.

195. Chesterton, *Collected Works, Volume 3,* 543.

196. Ibid., 549.

197. Chesterton, *The Everlasting Man.* 240.

198. Chesterton, *Saint Thomas Aquinas, Saint Francis of Assisi,* 86.

with one of which he must entirely believe and with the other may utterly disbelieve."[199] He suggests, in keeping with St. Thomas, that it is possible for truth to be approached by different, even seemingly contradictory paths only if one believes that there is one truth: "Because the Faith was the one truth, nothing discovered in nature could ultimately contradict the Faith. Because the Faith was the one truth, nothing really deduced from the Faith could ultimately contradict the facts."[200]

Even if one discovers a contradiction, where opposite sides of the contradiction both seem valid or true, it is possible to take the contradiction as a whole.[201] If such contradictions are irresolvable, then the truth, insofar as the limitations of human reason and perception are concerned, must also be irresolvable. And so, for Chesterton, the supernatural and the natural, heaven and earth, spirit and flesh, science and faith, language and reality, and many other seeming contradictions are all part of one truth. These apparent polarities simply articulate this one truth from different perspectives. Reason and knowledge, too, even when digressing into incessant hair-splitting, ought to be concerned with the real world as it is. It is good and yet fallen, mysterious and yet knowable. In short, reality should be treated as real.[202] This foregrounds the last component of the foundation of Chesterton's hermeneutic to be dealt with in this chapter, namely his ontology.

Chesterton's Ontology

For Chesterton knowledge is concerned with creating connections because the universe is actually connected. Chesterton's philosophy thus follows what John Milbank calls "the ontological priority of peace over conflict."[203] This means that peace, harmony, communion, community, and so on, are the very gifts that God gives us when he gives us reality. The peace of God is "coterminous with all Being whatsoever."[204] Even "[w]hat is wrong" is always preceded by and understood by "what is right."[205] This rightness of being has a dramatic structure that may be appreciated in terms of three

199. Ibid.

200. Ibid.

201. Chesterton, *Collected Works, Volume 1*, 230.

202. Chesterton, *Saint Thomas Aquinas, Saint Francis of Assisi*, 29.

203. Milbank, *Theology and Social Theory*, 390.

204. Ibid., 392.

205. Chesterton, *What's Wrong with the World*, 17.

considerations: the riddle of being, the answer of being, and the romance of being.[206]

To begin with, in Chesterton's work, being is first and foremost viewed as a riddle, which reflects the ultimate riddle that is God. Therefore, he writes:

> We all feel the riddle of the earth without anyone to point it out. The mystery of life is the plainest part of it. The clouds and curtains of darkness, the confounding vapours, these are the daily weather of this world. Whatever else we have grown accustomed to, we have grown accustomed to the unaccountable. Every stone or flower is a hieroglyphic of which we have lost the key; with every step to our lives we enter into the middle of some story which we are certain to misunderstand.[207]

This passage references a number of ideas already discussed: the storied nature of life, the need for a key by which one can understand the story, as well as the inevitability of misunderstanding. But it does something else as well: it points to the centrality of mystery in the Chestertonian canon.

To say that being is a riddle is to say that things that exist—stand out or appear as the Latin *existere* implies—do not exist because of any kind of precise, logical inevitability, and thus do not necessarily presuppose total intelligibility.[208] Inasmuch as it may be comprehended, being remains a mystery. There is a riddle even in the obviousness of the text that has been created: the text does not have to be. This idea is found in Chesterton's interpretation of an episode in Daniel Defoe's *Robinson Crusoe* (1719), which tells of a man who escapes a shipwreck with his life and a few rudimentary possessions:

> The greatest of all poems is an inventory. Every kitchen tool becomes ideal because Crusoe might not have dropped it in the sea. It is a good exercise, in empty or ugly hours of the day, to look at anything, the coal-scuttle or the bookcase, and think how happy one could be to have brought it out of the sinking ship on to the solitary island. But it is a better exercise still to remember how all things have had this hair-breadth escape: everything has been saved from the wreck.[209]

Chesterton takes the shipwreck of Crusoe as a parable for the mysteriousness of all of life. He dares to conceive of a world that has been "saved

---

206. Reyburn, "Chesterton's Ontology," 51.

207. Chesterton, *William Blake*, 131.

208. Ibid., 132; Reyburn, "Chesterton's Ontology," 52.

209. Chesterton, *Collected Works, Volume 1*, 267.

from the wreck" of its own non-existence.[210] This is particularly applicable to his view of human beings. For example, it seems nonsensical to speak of anything like the fallenness of great men of genius without first noticing the very miraculous, surprising presence of such men.[211] Chesterton observes that it is common to view the lives of the fallen as the "Great Might-Have-Been," but that it is far more concrete a realization that "any man in the street is a Great Might-Not-Have-Been."[212] Once again, we find the idea that there is a goodness that precedes the goodness of creation. The miracle of being is built into even the most obvious things. Echoing this observation, Chesterton explains that one of his central concerns is for "the problem of how men could be made to realise the wonder and splendour of being alive, in environments which their own daily criticism treated as dead-alive, and which their imagination had left for dead."[213]

Ontologically and even probabilistically speaking, "nothingness" is more likely than "somethingness" or being. Chesterton allows for the possibility that being might never have been.[214] In hermeneutic terms, this makes even the very presence of the reader to the text remarkable.

It is worth asking, as Gottfried Leibniz does, why there should be anything at all rather than just nothing. Leibniz's argument, put briefly, is that nothing would be far simpler than something. He moves on to make the assumption that just because things do exist that they *must* exist by necessity and must therefore have a reason for existing.[215] This is not the line of reasoning that Chesterton follows. There may still be an answer to the question *why is there something rather than nothing?*—but it remains mysterious. In fact, for Chesterton, contra Leibniz, the "world does not explain itself"; being should therefore not fundamentally be understood as a necessity.[216] There does not have to be something rather than nothing. Being is not something that ought to be, but a gift given without explanation. To parody Leibniz, Chesterton writes that this is not the "best of all possible worlds," but "the best of all impossible worlds."[217] "Its merit is not that it is orderly and explicable," but "that it is wild and utterly unexplained."[218] No human

---

210. Ibid.

211. Ibid.

212. Ibid.

213. Chesterton, *Autobiography*, 134.

214. Schall, *Schall on Chesterton*, 42, 58.

215. Leibniz, *Philosophical Papers and Letters*, 639.

216. Chesterton, *Collected Works, Volume 1*, 268; Chesterton, *Saint Thomas Aquinas, Saint Francis of Assisi*,155.

217. Chesterton, *Charles Dickens*, 290.

218. Ibid.

mind could have thought the world or existence up and therefore everyone is subtly compelled to acknowledge that he is swimming in an ocean of "miracle and unreason."[219] This unreason, however, is not the opposite of reason, but its complement.

Terry Eagleton suggests along these lines that everything is always "overshadowed by the possibility of its own nonexistence."[220] All being is, in philosophical terms, contingent and unnecessary. The idea of being as a riddle needs to be introduced into one's understanding of being to resist making necessity absolute. It is precisely in the riddle of being that human subjects are called to contemplate the possibility of a Being who is responsible for being. While the riddle of being may not necessarily be connected to the belief that there is a God, this is certainly the conclusion that Chesterton draws.[221] For Chesterton, following the logic of Pseudo-Dionysius and St. Thomas, being is derived from the "Pre-existent."[222] Nothing, including the self that perceives, is self-sustained. Even understanding the nature of the structure of being cannot be owed only to the one who understands. The plot of the drama of being cannot merely be framed as a liner movement from purpose to rising action to consequence; instead, it is a fluid toing and froing within the perichoretic theodrama of the Trinitarian Godhead. This movement of Being beyond and through being is an adventure story about discovery and rediscovery. If mystery underpins all of life, then it cannot be worn out. The fatigue of familiarity is an illusion perpetuated by a refusal to engage imaginatively with the world that is there.[223] Mystery cannot be explained away by simplistic plausibilities.

Chesterton describes himself as a "man who with utmost daring discovered what had been discovered before."[224] He comes across the old as if it were new and it is this sense of the new that supports the riddle of being: it is a drama that moves from mystery to mystery and not from commonplace to commonplace. It is this very knowledge of the riddle of being that produces surprise. It considers the riddle of being on the premise that the riddle has already, to some extent, been answered. Or, perhaps, the riddle itself is an answer.

219. Ibid.

220. Eagleton, *Reason, Faith, and Revolution*, 8.

221. Chesterton, *Autobiography*, 150.

222. Aquinas, *Selected Philosophical Texts*, 113, 128; Pseudo-Dionysius, *The Complete Works*, 98.

223. Chesterton, *The Everlasting Man*, 14.

224. Chesterton, *Collected Works, Volume 1*, 214.

Chesterton admits that before he had arrived at a deeper understanding of philosophy, his earliest engagements with the world concluded with the presence of "Anything."[225] Chesterton's *Anything* is not the same as the *aliquid* of Aquinas, which indicates the "thingness" of something: a thing must retain substantial consistency or relative completeness to sustain its own nature.[226] Rather, Chesterton's *Anything* is something that he humorously equates with the *Ens* of Aquinas.[227] On this point, a bridge is formed between the riddle of being and the second consideration of Chesterton's ontology, namely the answer of being. Being, as it is disclosed to itself via language, is a mystery that is endlessly knowable through revelation.

Continuing his idea that creation involves an act of separation and setting free, Chesterton argues that things that exist need to be seen as distinct in their being. Chesterton sides with Aquinas's argument for the individual character of things that would allow him to distinguish "between chalk and cheese, and pigs and pelicans."[228] Robert Farrar Capon builds on Chesterton's reasoning, with reference an example given by Chesterton,[229] by arguing that

> [t]he physical question of what beings are made out of can never be allowed to preempt our proper metaphysical concern with what being is. Our alienation, our boredom, and our estrangement can be cured only by the recovery of the philosophical sanity that will allow us to meet things face to face. An egg is an egg, and must be saluted as such. And china is china, and all *things* are themselves: mushrooms and artichokes, wine and cheese, earth and stars and sky and oceans.[230]

Capon, following Chesterton, argues that there is clearly a dimension of objectivity to reality that is reliant on the separateness of beings. As problematic as the term *objectivity* has become in recent phenomenological discourse, it needs to be recognized as a valid term in Chesterton's philosophy, since he is by no means arguing that subjectivities are irrelevant or that reality is accessible apart from mediation. There is a definite sense of the "subjectivity of objectivity" as well as the "objectivity of subjectivity."[231]

---

225. Chesterton, *Autobiography*, 150.
226. Milbank, "The Double Glory," 133.
227. Chesterton, *Autobiography*, 150.
228. Chesterton, *Saint Thomas Aquinas, Saint Francis of Assisi*, 137.
229. Ibid.
230. Capon, *The Romance of the Word*, 155.
231. Lauer, *G. K. Chesterton*, 69.

Objectivity, for Chesterton, simply represents the externality of truth as an antidote to solipsism and gnostic dualism.[232]

Moreover, to point out that Chesterton adheres to the idea of objectivity is not to say that he sees entities as being completely and utterly unrelated or self-existent. In fact, it is on this point that he departs from the Aristotelian explanation of being as being self-sufficient.[233] Chesterton is not a substance ontologist. He argues that "[l]ooking at [b]eing as it is now, as the baby looks at the grass, we see . . . [that being] looks secondary and dependent. Existence exists; but it is not sufficiently self-existent; and would never become so merely by going on existing."[234] By saying that existence is *secondary*, Chesterton is alluding to the Being that brings and holds all things into being. By saying that existence is *dependent*, he is alluding to two things. Firstly, all things are dependent on the Creator for their being even though they have been divorced from his mind, as is evident in Chesterton's cosmology. And secondly, all things are dependent on each other for their relationship with their own being. It is in their separateness that their interconnectedness may be allowed for. Moreover, Chesterton recognizes that the interconnectedness of being is discovered through phenomenological perception as his reference here to *looking* shows.[235] So, while there is separateness to being, there is also a definite sense that being is reliant on connections and relationships. It is in these relationships that interpretation is made possible. Ultimately, nothing is intelligible in isolation because nothing exists in isolation. Even people are only intelligible as part of an interconnected world.[236]

Chesterton understands perception as the glue that holds together the separateness and interconnectedness of things from the point of view of human beings. One can only determine the nature of being in accordance with one's own perception of being. This is where Chesterton's epistemology and his ontology are deeply interwoven. The recognition of being is already a part of simply being:

> [E]ven those who appreciate the metaphysical depth of Thomism
> in other matters have expressed surprise that he does not deal
> at all with what many now think the main metaphysical ques-
> tion; whether we can prove that the primary act of recognition
> of any reality is real. The answer is that St. Thomas recognised

232. Schwartz, *The Third Spring*, 43.

233. Aristotle, *Metaphysics*, 126.

234. Chesterton, *Saint Thomas Aquinas, Saint Francis of Assisi*, 158.

235. Ibid.

236. Chesterton, *The Victorian Age in Literature*, 10.

instantly what so many modern sceptics have begun to suspect rather laboriously; that a man must either answer that question in the affirmative, or else never answer any question, never ask any question, never even exist intellectually, to answer or to ask. I suppose it is true in a sense that a man can be a fundamental sceptic, but he cannot be anything else; certainly not even a defender of fundamental scepticism. If a man feels that the movements of his own mind are meaningless, then his mind is meaningless and he is meaningless; and it does not mean anything to attempt to discover its meaning.[237]

Chesterton goes on to argue that either "there is no philosophy, no philosophers, no thinkers, no thought, no anything; or else there is a real bridge between the mind and reality."[238] With Aquinas, Chesterton begins with the assumption that reality is there and that it is, at least to some degree, knowable; "God made Man so that he was capable of coming into contact with reality; and those whom God hath joined, let no man put asunder."[239] He argues against the skeptics of his day by pointing out that their "philosophies are not philosophy, but philosophic doubt; that is, doubt about whether there can be any philosophy."[240] In doing so, he speaks as much to postmodern skepticism as to the skepticism of his own era.

If the self is physical, and thus actively capable of engaging with the world instead of insisting upon an erroneously constructed detachment from the world, dogmatic skepticism is a fool's errand. Chesterton argues that skeptical detachment from reality is particularly evident in how thinkers abstract and then divorce concepts from their source. For example, he writes that "[the typical modernist] will not say there is grass, but only growth."[241] Here the concept of *growth* symbolizes transition, change, and flux. Nevertheless, when abstracted or detached from its object, it ceases to be dramatic.[242] This is an essential component of understanding the conceivability of being, as Étienne Gilson suggests: "'Being' is conceivable, 'to be' is not. We cannot possibly conceive an 'is' except as belonging to some thing that is, or exists."[243] However, as Gilson continues, "the reverse is not true. Being is quite conceivable apart from actual existence; so much so that

---

237. Chesterton, *Saint Thomas Aquinas, Saint Francis of Assisi*, 136.

238. Ibid., 137.

239. Ibid., 137, 170.

240. Ibid., 171.

241. Ibid., 163.

242. See Gadamer, *Truth and Method*, 116.

243. Gilson, *Being and Some Philosophers*, 2.

the very first and the most universal of all the distinctions in the realm of being is that which divides it into two classes, that of the real and that of the possible."[244]

One may suggest that at the root of our dramatic engagement with the created text or world is the essential acknowledgement that it exists alongside us. This view of being alongside things is preferable to the view that there is merely an "external world" as familiar language would have us believe.[245] Eagleton asks, "In what sense is a laburnum tree 'outside' me, rather than alongside me? If I see it as 'outside,' then the real me must somehow be squatting inside my own body, like a man operating a crane. And who is operating him?"[246] This echoes Heidegger's contention that to be is to be alongside the world, and that this "being alongside" the world is to be absorbed by the world. The world, as a discernable matrix of interwoven meanings, is a container for the self.[247]

Even before the self is aware of itself—that is, even in a pre-ontological state—the self is aware that "something is something" and that "there *is* an Is."[248] There can be no bridge between the mind and reality if one negates the suggestion of such an *Anything*.[249] With Aquinas, Chesterton's basic assumption is that truth is correspondence or equation of thought and thing: *adequatio intellectus et rei*.[250] While this *adequatio* as adequation or correspondence is often rendered in terms of mere equality in the English translation, the original Latin carries with it the ideas of adaptation, adjustment, and continuation.[251] Thus, the equation of thought and thing is dynamic and not static in Aquinas's thinking.[252] Moreover, this Thomist take on correspondence suggests that when a thing is known in the mind, this thinking about things "actually brings them to their telos" or "fruition."[253] This means that "[i]ntellection . . . is not an indifferent speculation; it is rather a beautiful ratio which is instantiated between things and the mind which leaves neither things nor the mind unchanged."[254] Knowing anything, therefore,

244. Ibid., 3.

245. Eagleton, *Reason, Faith, and Revolution*, 80.

246. Ibid.

247. Heidegger, *Being and Time*, 80.

248. Chesterton, *Saint Thomas Aquinas, Saint Francis of Assisi*, 153.

249. Ibid., 137.

250. Aquinas, *Selected Philosophical Texts*, 13.

251. Milbank and Pickstock, *Truth in Aquinas*, 7.

252. Gilson, *Being and Some Philosophers*, 3.

253. Milbank and Pickstock, *Truth in Aquinas*, 7.

254. Ibid.

is an "act of generosity, or salvific compensation for the exclusivity and discreteness of things."[255] Put otherwise, knowing anything is an extension of and participation in the generosity of Being.

Following this Thomist idea, Thomas Merton's definition of truth highlights it as a dynamic, overabundant dialogue between reality and the self: "Truth, in things, is their reality. In our minds, it is the conformity of our knowledge with the things known. In our words, it is the conformity of our words to what we think. In our conduct, it is the conformity of our acts to what we are supposed to be."[256] This is to say that things become more themselves in our contemplating them, and that we, too, are transformed by thinking about things. Accordingly, understanding truth as correspondence with reality, as William Desmond observes, ought not to imply that "[m]ind is 'in here,' [and that] reality is 'out there.'"[257] Truth is not an "extrinsic relation between two univocally fixed determinacies," but a "community of mind and being."[258] Truth exists in dialogue; it is the correspondence of our whole being with reality as it is. But this correspondence, in keeping with Chesterton's thinking, does not imply that being human in correspondence with reality is somehow the full realization of truth. Being in the drama cannot encompass the fullness of reality, but is encompassed by the fuller reality of the whole drama. There is a dialogue between part (being) and whole (beings participating in Being). Using clumsy phrasing, it may be said that there is Being in being and being in Being, and yet the two remain distinct.

Reality and the recognition of reality are "two agencies at work" within being, and their meeting is "a kind of marriage."[259] Perception and reality are impossible to split even while a gap between them may remain. Chesterton suggests that subjectivism forces the imagination inwards, creating an imaginary split between the subject and the object of his contemplation, but the one who accepts the objectivity of reality has his imagination "forced outwards."[260] The result is that the mind does not merely think about objects as external self-sustained entities, but "actually becomes the object";[261] it

> becomes the object, but does not create the object. In other words, the object is an object; it can and does exist outside the mind, or in the absence of the mind. And *therefore* it enlarges

255. Ibid.

256. Merton, *The Thomas Merton Reader,* 121.

257. Desmond, *Being and the Between,* 467.

258. Ibid., 468.

259. Chesterton, *Saint Thomas Aquinas, Saint Francis of Assisi,* 169.

260. Ibid., 168.

261. Ibid., 169.

the mind of which it becomes a part. The mind conquers a new province like an emperor; but only because the mind has answered the bell like a servant. The mind has opened doors and windows, because it is the natural activity of what is inside the house to find out what is outside the house. If the mind is sufficient to itself, it is insufficient for itself. For this feeding upon fact is itself; as an organ it has an object which is objective; this eating of the strange strong meat of reality.[262]

Thus, while Chesterton uses words like *objectivity* and *subjectivity*, he does so in a very specific way that avoids causing a dichotomy between mind and matter. The mind is not merely receptive so that the human being is conceived of as "wholly servile to his environment," but nor is the mind purely creative "in the sense that it paints pictures on the windows and then mistakes them for a landscape outside."[263] The mind is an active participant in reality. Reading remains subjective because human beings simultaneously act and are acted upon, not only by other people, but also by the material world they live alongside. Once again, Chesterton's epistemology of re-cognition and re-membering is concerned with the reconciliation of the separateness of things without allowing things to lose their distinctness.

All of this fundamentally affects the way that human beings interpret and understand their own being and therefore the being of other beings. Chesterton does not describe the world or any text as remote or removed from human experience, but treats the intricate dialogical dynamism between thought and thing as crucial. For example, a white piece of chalk is not merely an impersonal object, but something "positive and essential"— a symbol of "religious morality."[264] Moreover, colors are alive and filled with exuberant vitality: red is not just red, but red-hot; green calls forth the "live green figure of Robin Hood"; and blue invokes the "blue robes of the Virgin."[265] Interpretation begins before comprehension, in the very moment of apprehension. The world is not made present through conscious understanding, although it can certainly be illuminated by it. It is already readily accessible from the instant of encounter. It is a subjective whole—a cosmos of meaning—before it is perceived in its constituent parts. It is, to use dramatic metaphor, an entire play before it becomes an issue of actors, audience, plot, stage, and experience.

262. Ibid.
263. Ibid., 139.
264. Chesterton, *Tremendous Trifles*, 11.
265. Ibid.

Any hermeneutic begins even before the text has been contemplated. In fact, before the audience has had the chance to analyze or study the constituent parts of the drama, it has been implicated in the text merely by observing the play. The audience is part of the text, already inside the text, in the act of observing. This idea is captured in the opening of the second chapter of Chesterton's *Autobiography* (1937), where he recalls his earliest memory: an image of a "young man walking across a bridge," which turns out to be a scene played out from the stage of a toy theatre made by his father.[266] This becomes a symbol for his love for "edges," "frames and limits," and the "boundary-line that brings one thing sharply against another."[267] He insists that "the largest wilderness looks larger when seen through a window," which is to say that the "perfect drama" is not one of spectacle, but one of smallness and intimacy.[268] "[T]he perfect drama must strive to rise to the higher ecstasy of the peep-show."[269]

This echoes the idea of the distinctness of things already discussed, but adds a phenomenological dimension. Chesterton speaks of the peep show—a sequence of images viewed through a lens or a small hole set into a box. He does this, not to argue for the removal of the spectator, but to demonstrate that the spectator is so involved and enveloped in the drama that his self-importance is diminished. The spectator is usually so enveloped by the objective reality that he has not had the chance to properly contemplate it.[270] Its objective truth does not initially show its affect on his awareness, although this is not to say that it has had no impact.

Therefore, while Chesterton argues for objectivity, he never promotes detachment. And it is precisely by participating in the drama that human beings are able to find themselves in relation to the drama. Again, in this drama of being, there is a sense in which the object of contemplation becomes more itself while being contemplated, and the one who contemplates becomes more himself in contemplating the otherness of something. The answer of being becomes more evident, because the audience is a part of the same riddle of being. In other words, the viewer comes more into his own being when he accepts that he is already lost in the drama, just as the actor becomes more himself when he willingly succumbs to the events of a play.[271]

266. Chesterton, *Autobiography*, 40.

267. Ibid., 41.

268. Ibid.

269. Ibid.

270. Chesterton, *The Everlasting Man*, 9.

271. Gadamer, *Truth and Method*, 103.

The fact that the reader becomes implicated in the text and alive to the experience of reading the drama allows for the possibility of an answer to the riddle of being. And it is the reader's presence that gives birth to the interpretive experience, whereby the riddle of being and the answer of being, in tension, give rise to the romance of being. With only riddles and answers, the interpretive process operates in dichotomies, but, with the added dimension of romance, the interpretive process becomes a dialogue, and a strictly dialectical hermeneutic becomes a paradoxical hermeneutic. This means that the interpretive experience is realized and experienced as a story within a story.

The above—as an extension of Chesterton's idea that "there are two ways of getting home"—touches a major theme in Chesterton's writings, namely that, while the wholeness of meaning is always present, one still has to strive to fully participate in that meaning.[272] Interpretive understanding is already there to be discovered before it has been discovered. It is present even when it is felt to be absent. Or, in other words, even if one *is* at home in the completeness of things, one has to *get* home to the completeness of things. The other way to get home, as I have already noted, involves a journey of indefinite length that covers immeasurable territory, but arrives at the same place.[273] This mirrors Chesterton's introduction to *Orthodoxy*:

> I have often had a fancy for writing a romance about an English yachtsman who slightly miscalculated his course and discovered England under the impression that it was a new island in the South Seas. I always find, however, that I am either too busy or too lazy to write this fine work, so I may as well give it away for the purposes of philosophical illustration. There will probably be a general impression that the man who landed (armed to the teeth and talking by signs) to plant the British flag on that barbaric temple which turned out to be the Pavilion at Brighton, felt rather a fool. I am not here concerned to deny that he looked a fool. But if you imagine that he felt a fool, or at any rate that the sense of folly was his sole or his dominant emotion, then you have not studied with sufficient delicacy the rich romantic nature of the hero of this tale. His mistake was really a most enviable mistake; and he knew it, if he was the man I take him for. What could be more delightful than to have in the same few minutes all the fascinating terrors of going abroad combined with all the humane security of coming home again? What could be better than to have all the fun of discovering South

272. Chesterton, *The Everlasting Man*, 9.
273. Ibid.

Africa without the disgusting necessity of landing there? What could be more glorious than to brace one's self up to discover New South Wales and then realise, with a gush of happy tears, that it was really old South Wales. This at least seems to me the main problem for philosophers[:] . . . How can we contrive to be at once astonished at the world and yet at home in it?[274]

This "main problem" for philosophers—how to bring about a sense of wonder even within the common—is almost certainly the best summary of Chesterton's own philosophical struggle. It is in this *between* that the truth of the human experience is best located and articulated. Further on, Chesterton announces that he is in fact the "fool" that has discovered what already is.[275] He is the man who boldly set out to be some eighteen minutes ahead of the truth, only to find out that he was almost two millennia behind it.[276] Behind the humor of this passage, Chesterton is arguing that one's engagement with the world is not as straightforward as discovering what is known in the sense of arriving without ever needing to depart again. Finding any truth at all is not as certain as simply finding a destination. Rather, it is an experience brought about when one's perception is properly awakened to a reality experienced in the betweens of life.

Being in the drama involves a dialogue between being and becoming, between longing and belonging, or, as Pseudo-Dionysius argues, between yearning (*eros*) and consummated love (*agape*).[277] Life is a drama that is experienced as a kind of homesickness whilst being at home.[278] In all of these elements, the clear line between opposites is both present and absent, since Chesterton operates in accordance with paradoxes rather than antagonisms. For Chesterton, being is fundamentally driven by desire and is thus a romance. If riddles and answers are seen as the substance of being, romance may be seen as its agency; it is the thing that drives the life of being.

While at home in the world, being may involve a sense of longing for home; whilst feeling estranged from the world, being may involve a sense of being at home. In praise of metaphysical realism, Chesterton contends that "we [are] all in exile, and . . . no earthly house [can] cure the holy home-sickness that forbids us rest."[279] There is, in other words, a movement

---

274. Chesterton, *Collected Works, Volume 1*, 212.

275. Ibid., 213.

276. Ibid.

277. Pseudo-Dionysius, *The Complete Works*, 80.

278. Chesterton, *Collected Works, Volume 1*, 284.

279. Chesterton, *Manalive*, 108.

between what is in stasis and what may yet be in stasis.[280] Both are always fully present. This romance or desire is intrinsic to the text of creation. Romance, a word with all "the mystery and ancient meaning of Rome," always contains something "strange" and something "secure." [281] It is concerned with embracing danger to claim health and life.[282] It is a courageous leap towards imagination, joy, delight, reality, and wonderment.[283] It suggests that being itself is always in excess. Everything is itself and yet also more than itself.

Chesterton argues that there are two searches at play in the human psyche: the search for romance (*mythos*) and the search for truth or reason (*logos*). Both of these searches may be found in a mythology that happens to be true.[284] It is Christianity that embodies these searches. It provides the ultimate goal of romance, which is the awareness and worship of the Creator who made all things.[285] Romance is never a perfect or complete state of arrival, but remains an ongoing journey "to the temple"—to the state of being in which one is given room to worship God.[286] This romance is symbolized in *The Surprise* by the movement towards a marriage celebration. And it is precisely this that gets corrupted when the actors violate the script of the Author: what was intended by the Author as a movement towards peace, harmony, and connection gets turned into a discordant, chaotic quarrel.[287] It is not the riddle of being or the answer of being that gets corrupted, but the romance of being: what is thrown out of kilter is not being itself, but rather the way that desire is articulated and performed.

For Chesterton, being is not just a dead, fixed, or concrete thing. It is a movement. This again aligns his ontology directly with his cosmology. Riddles, answers, and romances are in a dance together; they are participants in the ongoing, dynamic drama of being. Chesterton's understanding of the romance or desire at the heart of being, which may be defined as a "vividness of visionary or spiritual experience" that creates a sense of the "glory of all experience,"[288] is directly related to his cosmology of re-creation and his epistemology of re-membering. In short, what Chesterton calls the

280. Chesterton, *Tales of the Long Bow.*

281. Chesterton, *Collected Works, Volume 1,* 212–13.

282. Ibid., 362.

283. Chesterton, *Collected Works, Volume 1,* 305; *The Everlasting Man,* 58, 248.

284. Chesterton, *The Everlasting Man,* 248.

285. Chesterton, *Alarms and Discursions,* ii.

286. Ibid., iii.

287. Chesterton, *The Surprise.*

288. Chesterton, *Illustrated London News,* August 27, 1932.

"romance of orthodoxy" emphasizes the storied character of life; it is a story that is always in pursuit of its own genesis.[289] For this reason, Chesterton is truly an original writer: he always works towards understanding origins. I have thus far tried to trace the outline of Chesterton's philosophical framework within which this pursuit of originality or origins takes place—a framework that sets up the boundaries according to which the drama of understanding is enacted.

It becomes clear here that Chesterton's hermeneutic operates along the lines of metareference or, in dramaturgical terms, metatheatre. Metareference is an event whereby the characters in a work of fiction or the fantasy of the real become aware that they are in a world or drama that is not of their own making. It is the idea that what is present within the drama (being) is given purpose and meaning by what is found both in and beyond the drama (Being). In literature, metareference is used to disrupt the enchantment of the constructed world—the work of cinema, drama, or literature; but this is not quite the nature of metareference in the work of Chesterton. If anything, becoming aware of a transcendent order leads to the re-enchantment of the world. Life is re-encountered as a coherent drama, bursting with surprise. This encounter with surprise is founded, as the following chapter argues, on the wonderfully paradoxical realization that the inside of the hermeneutic circle is larger than the outside even while it is perpetually challenged and informed by what is outside.[290] It is the suggestion that for Chesterton man is not made to serve a philosophy of abstract notions surrounding the nature of the human drama; rather, this philosophy ought to serve the man.

289. Chesterton, *Collected Works, Volume 1*, 329.

290. Chesterton, *Autobiography*, 49; Chesterton, *Saint Thomas Aquinas, Saint Francis of Assisi*, 131.

4

The Task of Chesterton's Hermeneutic

In Defense of Human Dignity

If Chesterton is a difficult writer to pin down, it is probably because, as Dale Ahlquist suggests, his subject is "everything."[1] He deems anything that crosses his path to be something worth contemplating and discussing. He is aware of the richness and complication that is interwoven into the human story, and is therefore reluctant to present too constricted a view of that richness and complication.[2] Nevertheless, it is possible to argue that Chesterton uses a "narrow compass" to "focus a large range of material" towards the "great labor of synthesis and reconstruction."[3] This narrow compass is a particular kind of moral philosophy, which operates from a single point of departure and return. It is the idea of the "dignity of man" or "human dignity," which he regards as the foremost articulation of the goodness that grounds all of reality.[4]

Chesterton declares, "This is an age in which we must defend human dignity."[5] Marshall McLuhan suggests that for Chesterton, "[human] existence has a value utterly . . . superior to any arguments for optimism or

---

1. Ahlquist, G. K. Chesterton, 19.

2. Chesterton, All Things Considered, 107; Maycock, "Introduction," 79.

3. McLuhan, "G. K. Chesterton," 462.

4. Chesterton, Autobiography, 239; Chesterton, Collected Works, Volume 1, 94, 298; Chesterton, The Everlasting Man, 52–53; Chesterton, Saint Thomas Aquinas, Saint Francis of Assisi, 36, 177; Chesterton, What's Wrong with the World, 15–24; Nichols, Chesterton, 121–59; Williams, Mere Humanity, 15–24.

5. Maycock, "Introduction," 74.

pessimism."[6] Therefore, rather than underplaying the wideness of Chesterton's gaze regarding the many causes and subjects that he addresses, this idea stresses the fact that the ultimate focus of his way of reading is not on merely propositional or abstract truth, but on a personal relation to truth. He always endeavors to attain a "freshness of perception" that "dignifies and illuminates" any of the present activities of people.[7] This love of people, which simultaneously expresses love of God, allows for a great deal of exegetical flexibility as in the philosophy of St. Augustine, who allows for any literal and symbolic interpretation even if it is not one intended by an author. For both Chesterton and Augustine, the primary guide for hermeneutics is the rule of love—"the love of God and the love of man."[8]

As a general rule, Chesterton therefore denigrates any notion or action that would compromise human dignity and applauds any notion or action that promotes it. His "creed" or "gospel of wonder" is one example of something that affirms human dignity because"[m]an is more himself, man is more manlike, when joy is the fundamental thing in him, and grief the superficial."[9] Chesterton's lifelong defense of Christian orthodoxy in general and, later on, Catholic orthodoxy in particular, also comes back to an ideal view of humanity that he finds expressed in the person of Jesus of Nazareth.[10] And his "search for the overall [paradoxical] *logic* of Christian belief" is directly bound to the "incarnational paradox" that is represented by this same person.[11] Thus, Chesterton's affirmation of human immanence is simultaneously an affirmation of divine transcendence, and his affirmation of human dignity is ultimately an affirmation of the goodness of God. He contends that the "common conscience of sane people" is something that is simultaneously "the voice of God" and "the voice of Man."[12]

However, while Chesterton certainly implies a paradoxical tension between the transcendent and the immanent, his emphasis remains on the immanent as that which is known through direct experience. He is, in this sense, more on the side of Aristotle than he is on the side of Plato, although it should be clear by now that he takes the work of the latter very seriously.[13]

6. McLuhan, "G. K. Chesterton," 456.

7. Ibid.

8. Chesterton, *Illustrated London News*, October 1, 1932; St. Augustine, *On Christian Doctrine*, 80.

9. Chesterton, *Collected Works, Volume 1*, 364. Ker, *G. K. Chesterton*, 100; McLuhan, "G. K. Chesterton,"455.

10. Chesterton, *The Everlasting Man*, 185.

11. Milbank, "The Double Glory," 117, 177.

12. Chesterton, *The Man Who Was Orthodox*, 120.

13. Chesterton, *Saint Thomas Aquinas, Saint Francis of Assisi*, 29.

He is critical of Plato and the Neo-Platonists only when they tend "to the view that the mind [is] lit entirely from within"; and prefers the Thomist perspective that the mind is "lit by five windows, that we call the windows of the senses."[14] It is this light, discovered in the externality of truth, that needs to "shine on what [is] within."[15] It is through this experience of an external light that man is able to "climb the House of Man, step by step and story by story, until he has come out on the highest tower and beheld the largest vision."[16] As in the work of Hans Urs von Balthasar, his metaphysical realism, as that which relentlessly pursues the transcendent, is never separate from "concrete experience, which is always of the senses."[17]

With this in mind, it may be said that even when Chesterton's subject changes to consider the polyphonic and dramatic character of life, his interpretive gaze remains on affirming human dignity. This naturally raises the question of exactly how Chesterton understands human dignity, and it is the aim of this chapter to address this very question. To achieve this aim, three dimensions of what Chesterton regards as central to human dignity are discussed below, namely the defense of the "old beer-drinking, creed-making, fighting, failing, sensual, respectable" common man, the defense of common sense, and the defense of democracy.[18]

In Defense of the Common Man

With joking-seriousness Chesterton proposes that, "[r]oughly speaking, there are three kinds of people in this world."[19]

> The first kind of people are People; they are the largest and probably the most valuable class. We owe to this class the chairs we sit down on, the clothes we wear, the houses we live in; and, indeed (when we come to think of it), we probably belong to this class of people ourselves. The second class may be called for convenience the Poets; they are often a nuisance to their families, but, generally speaking, a blessing to mankind. The third class is that of the Professors or Intellectuals; sometimes described as the thoughtful people; and these are a blight and a desolation both to their families and also to mankind. Of course, the

14. Ibid., 148–49.

15. Ibid.

16. Ibid.

17. von Balthasar, "Transcendentality and Gestalt," 34.

18. Ahlquist, *Common Sense 101*, 155; Chesterton, *Collected Works, Volume 1*, 70.

19. Chesterton, *Alarms and Discursions*, 70.

classification sometimes overlaps, like all classification. Some
good people are almost poets and some bad poets are almost
professors. But the division follows lines of real psychological
cleavage. I do not offer it lightly. It has been the fruit of more
than eighteen minutes of earnest reflection and research.[20]

Chesterton deepens this playful and overlapping classification by arguing that people are bound by various ethical commonplaces and a grounded
clarity that comes from living in the world without trying to explain too
much of it. He seems here to be particularly wary of those totalizing sche-
mas that certain modernists are so fond of. This clarity celebrates things like
"hilarity," "a regard for helplessness," "sentiment," "pity, dramatic surprise, a
desire for justice, a delight in experiment and the indeterminate."[21] This celebration, which unites the emotional, ethical, and mysterious dimensions of
human experience, underscores the fact that ordinary people live by subtle
ideas even if they fail to convey their ideas with any subtlety.

The second class of people participate in the sentiments of ordinary
people, but find that they are able to express the subtle ideas of people with
genuine subtlety: "The Poets carry the popular sentiments to a keener and
more splendid pitch; but let it always be remembered that they are popular
sentiments that they are carrying. . . . The Poets are those who rise above the
people by understanding them."[22] This is not to say that poets are necessarily
writers or that they necessarily write poetry, but rather that they are simply
the kind of people who engage with life in the world with more imagination
and with a more acute awareness than is ordinarily found among the mob.
Their "[p]oetry is that separation of the soul from some object, whereby we
can regard it with wonder."[23] The third class of people, professors or intellectuals, are those people who tend to be somewhat detached from the sensibilities of the masses. They possess ideals of their own, but their ideals lose
track of the commonplace sensibilities and realities that most other people
have to live with.

One cannot understand Chesterton until one understands that he is
primarily concerned with combating the theories of this educated class of
people, who are really people who have forgotten that they are people. In
fact, Chesterton's worldview is understood largely as the antithesis of the
vague ideologies of many of the intellectuals of his time.[24] For dramatic em-

20. Ibid.
21. Ibid.
22. Ibid., 71.
23. Chesterton, *Collected Works, Volume 20*, 49.
24. Maycock, "Introduction," 29.

phasis, Chesterton uses the blanket terms *heresy* or *lunacy* to describe any number of worldviews that override the interests of the common man, and the terms *heretic, lunatic,* or *maniac* to describe the one who subscribes to and promotes any such worldview. Such labels may seem harsh to one who is unfamiliar with Chesterton's rhetoric, but there is a fair measure of good humor implied in the use of these melodramatic descriptors. In Chesterton's estimation, even the genius of his close friends—Rudyard Kipling (1865–1936), George Bernard Shaw (1856–1950), and H. G. Wells, for instance—is regarded affectionately as a kind of madness.

Chesterton's work constantly unpacks the philosophical consequences of the ideas of these and other authors in such a way as to suggest that the authors themselves are not aware of their own philosophical assumptions.[25] In this regard, he follows Thomas Carlyle (1795–1881), whose ability to expose the assumptions that underpin the reasoning of those around him he holds in particularly high regard even if he does not altogether approve of his brand of hero worship.[26] For Chesterton we should always be looking behind the curtain of reasoning to get a sense of the machinery, faulty or not, of thought.

Against this aim, lunacy occurs when thought processes are straitjacketed in such a way as to render reflective self-awareness unlikely. Lunacy is most easily observable in thinking that refuses to expose any "unconscious dogma."[27] It seems to be that the "special mark of the modern world" is found not in its skepticism, but in its being "dogmatic without knowing it."[28] It mocks "old devotees" for believing "without knowing *why* they believed,"[29] but such "moderns believe without knowing *what* they believe—and without even knowing that they do believe it. Their freedom consists in first freely assuming a creed, and then freely forgetting that they are assuming it. In short, they always have an unconscious dogma; and an unconscious dogma is the definition of a prejudice."[30]

Whatever the limitations of the above classification of people may be, it at least points out that for Chesterton the ideal perspective adopted for preaching and upholding human dignity is the perspective of the poet. His poetic perception, which dwells between the worlds of people and professors, "floats easily in an infinite sea" of subjects and sensibilities, allowing

25. Chesterton, *Twelve Types*, 35; Ker, *G. K. Chesterton*, 104.
26. Ibid.
27. Chesterton, *Illustrated London News*, March 15, 1919.
28. Ibid.
29. Ibid.
30. Ibid.

for understanding without reductionism.[31] However, for Chesterton, it is not the extraordinary things that are truly "poetical," but the "common things."[32] His writings seem to indicate that this poetic perspective is the very ideal that he strives for in his reading of the world. There is one contradiction particularly in McLuhan's assessment of Chesterton that should be highlighted here. In one instance, McLuhan suggests that Chesterton is an "intellectual poet"[33] and in another instance he contends that Chesterton is "not a poet," but a "metaphysical moralist."[34] The second assessment, I believe, is misguided because it creates a dichotomy between Chesterton's philosophical genius and his poetic instinct. Why can he not be *both* a poet *and* a metaphysical moralist? This is an issue that Chesterton addresses in his assessment of Robert Browning when he notes that those who do not like Browning's work tend to say that he was not a poet, but a philosopher, whereas those who do like Browning's work tend to suggest, more reasonably, that he was both a philosopher and a poet.[35] A particular label is adopted simply as a means to dismiss the thinker in question. Chesterton's poetic philosophy, which explores many of the heights of human achievement, is always tied to the concerns of ordinary people. He tries to bring intellectuals back down to earth and he tries to elevate the concerns of common folk to new heights of awareness.[36]

A. L. Maycock observes that "Chesterton has justly been called the poet and the prophet of the man in the street."[37] He often intimates that there is "no such thing as the average man; and scattered throughout his writings there are numerous phrases that express his profound belief in the inalienable dignity of the individual person."[38] He admits that he more easily aligns himself with the "ruck of hard-working people" than with "that special and troublesome literary class" to which he belongs.[39] He therefore prefers the "prejudices of the people who see life on the inside to the clearest demonstrations of [those] who [claim to] see life from the outside."[40] In this, Chesterton reflects an ideal espoused by Rudyard Kipling in his poem

31. Chesterton, *Collected Works, Volume 1*, 220.

32. Ibid., 55.

33. McLuhan, "G. K. Chesterton," 464.

34. McLuhan, "Introduction," xxi.

35. Chesterton, *Robert Browning*, 17.

36. McLuhan, "G. K. Chesterton," 464.

37. Maycock, "Introduction," 29.

38. Ibid.

39. Chesterton, *Collected Works, Volume 1*, 251.

40. Ibid., 252.

"If": Chesterton manages to "walk with Kings" without losing "the common touch," although his general posture is far less stoical than the one proposed by Kipling in the rest of that poem.[41]

From his point of view, enacting the truth of Christianity means recognizing the central, undeniable claim of Christianity: "Whatever else Christianity means or ever meant, it obviously means or meant an interference with the physical sorrows of humanity by the physical appearance of Divinity. If it does not mean that, I cannot conceive what it does mean."[42] In this recognition—in this understanding that the "strong part of religion" is a "story of bodily manhood, bodily valour, and bodily death"[43]—he negates the remote position of the professors by invoking the scripture that explains that "the Word was made flesh, and dwelt among us" (John 1:14), and thereby implies that turning flesh back into mere words is not desirable:

> Whenever you hear of things being unutterable and indefinable and impalpable and unnamable and subtly indescribable, then elevate your aristocratic nose towards heaven and snuff up the smell of decay. It is perfectly true that there is something in all good things that is beyond all speech or figure of speech. But it is also true that there is in all good things a perpetual desire for expression and concrete embodiment; and though the attempt to embody is always inadequate, the attempt is always made. If the idea does not seek to be the word, the chances are that it is an evil idea. If the word is not made flesh it is a bad word.[44]

In harmony with Chesterton's approval of concrete expression, Ahlquist observes that his rhetoric is intensely visual so that his words "become flesh" and "spring to life."[45] This observation aligns with Chesterton's insistence that "[n]o man must be superior to the things that are common to men."[46] The things that are "common to all men" are in fact "more important than the things peculiar to any men."[47] The "sense of the miracle of humanity itself should be always more vivid to us than any marvels of power, intellect, art, or civilization" and the simple image of a "man on two legs . . . should be felt as something more heartbreaking than any music and more startling

41. Kipling, *Gunga Din and Other Favorite Poems*, 60.

42. Chesterton, *Illustrated London News*, February 21, 1914.

43. Ibid.

44. Chesterton, *In Defense of Sanity*, 65.

45. Ahlquist, *Common Sense 101*, 53.

46. Chesterton, *What's Wrong with the World*, 71.

47. Chesterton, *Collected Works, Volume 1*, 249.

than any caricature."[48] Man is elevated here above all other things in the whole of creation, including the products of creative thought. As discussed below, this ideal forms the core of Chesterton's defense of democracy.

Ian Ker observes that Chesterton's defense of the common man distinguishes him from the misguided Nietzschean arrogance that is found in the work of so many of his contemporaries.[49] In particular, Chesterton criticizes Nietzsche's *Übermensch* who exclaims that "[m]an is a thing which needs to be surpassed" because such an injunction implies the end of humanity.[50] It implies throwing the existing man out of the window and asking for a new kind of man instead of finding out if there is a way to improve the existing man.[51] It also rests upon a nominalist error that forgets universals. "[T]he very word 'surpass' implies the existence of a standard common to us and the thing surpassing us."[52] And the standard, for Chesterton, must always be that of the ordinary man who is small enough to possess real courage—a courage enough to defeat giants the way that Jack does in the tale of "Jack the Giant-Killer."[53] This ordinary man is not necessarily "normal," for "[n]obody exactly represents the normal; or even claims to represent the normal."[54] Rather, he is the man that one recognizes as an individual member of humanity living in the midst of humanity.

It is the story of smallness raging against bigness that we find truly compelling. Nothing truly inspiring arises from sheer power or sheer force. In fact, one of the central contributions of Christianity is that it is the "only religion on earth that has felt that omnipotence made God incomplete."[55] Christianity alone felt that God, to be wholly God, must have been a rebel as well as a king and so it "added courage to the virtues of the Creator. For the only courage worth calling courage must necessarily mean that the soul passes a breaking point—and does not break."[56] The truly human and the truly heroic imply an adventure, and adventure implies something to overcome. However, the thing to be overcome or surpassed is not the human, but the inhuman. This is what Nietzsche's *Übermensch* misses and so ends

---

48. Ibid., 250.
49. Ker, *G. K. Chesterton*, 89.
50. Chesterton, *Collected Works, Volume 1*, 80.
51. Ibid., 70, 80.
52. Ibid., 80.
53. Chesterton, *Illustrated London News*, August 13, 1932.
54. Ibid.
55. Chesterton, *Collected Works, Volume 1*, 212.
56. Ibid.

up being "cold and friendless."[57] The *Übermensch*, "being unborn," is really a "dead" thing.[58] He stands in opposition even to the "[s]ensibility" that is "the definition of life."[59] In Chesterton's opinion, this Nietzschean idealism, like the idealism of the professors discussed above, is tantamount to a kind of conceptual blindness because it dulls perception. It is a form of self-hypnosis that lulls its supporters into being bored by everything.[60] It refuses to be challenged by anything in the world of experience.[61] Chesterton therefore points out that the Nietzschean ideal ultimately stands directly in the way of "seeing things as they are."[62]

The climax of the Nietzschean obsession with superiority is an attitude of general contempt towards things that are deemed inferior. And this, Chesterton argues, is what removes the delight of dramatic surprise that is at the heart of his ideal of human dignity.[63] A further critique offered by Chesterton against the ideal of the *Übermensch* is that it is not actually clear what such an ideal really stands for. Nietzsche seems uncertain about what exactly he is aiming at because, especially in *Twilight of the Idols* (1889),[64] he relies too heavily on metaphors of height and distance instead of considering the actual, commonsense consequences of his philosophy. Thus, instead of striving for a higher good, Nietzsche strives to stand somewhere beyond good and evil.[65] And "when he describes his hero, he does not dare to say, 'the purer man,' or 'the happier man,' or 'the sadder man,' for all these are ideas; and ideas are alarming. He says 'the upper man,' or 'over man,' a physical metaphor from acrobats or alpine climbers."[66]

Basically, Chesterton, who unlike Nietzsche is not blinded by his own metaphors, is not looking for an ideal that stands outside of humanity, but for one that is "more human than humanity itself."[67] He does not oppose improvement, which is what writers like Shaw and Wells call for, but insists that any kind of improvement is only possible if it truly celebrates our hu-

---

57. Chesterton, *Illustrated London News*, June 1, 1907.

58. Ibid.

59. Chesterton, *Collected Works, Volume 1*, 81.

60. Chesterton, *A Miscellany of Men*, 22–23.

61. Ibid.

62. Chesterton, *Collected Works, Volume 1*, 68.

63. Ibid., 69; *Alarms and Discursions*, 70.

64. Nietzsche, *Twilight of the Idols*, 19.

65. Chesterton, *Collected Works, Volume 1*, 309.

66. Ibid.

67. Chesterton, *Collected Works, Volume 1*, 82; Chesterton, *The Everlasting Man*, 204.

manity.[68] He is not promoting a more detached, more stoical kind of human being, but a human being who experiences life more acutely and more fully. His point is not that ideals are to be done away with, but that the ideals that one holds need to keep with the ideals that support ordinary people.[69] In the end, a Nietzschean posture towards life and reading the text of life is too aloof to be relevant to human experience, whereas Chesterton's ideal is everywhere in the faces of ordinary people.[70]

For Chesterton, the Nietzschean view is erroneous primarily in its assumption that humanity must be merely an "evolution" and therefore a product of the same chain of material causes and effects that has produced all earthly creatures.[71] This supposed evolution presumes that humanity was something else at one time, an ape of sorts, and will therefore become something else, an *Übermensch* of sorts. However, humanity is not just an evolution, but "a revolution."[72] Humanity is not just a conservative conclusion to a long process, but an insurrection against the established natural order.[73] Humanity represents something "doctrinal" because "it stands to common sense that you cannot upset all existing things, customs, and compromises, unless you believe in something outside them, something positive and divine."[74] Humanity itself, either by fact or potential, is the word made flesh. Humanity is a living thing that goes against the stream, not a dead thing that goes with it.[75]

What Chesterton is getting at is quite simple: man does not quite fit into the expected scheme of nature, which is to say that man is a hermeneutic anomaly. Therefore, the more one tries to see man merely as an animal, the more one must conclude that he is not merely an animal.[76] The "simplest" and most obvious truth about man is that he is too odd to be considered the product of purely natural processes.[77] Man lives and acts in a way that is alien to the life and actions of any other animal.[78] Unlike the animals, his thoughts turn back to think about themselves; his mind is ob-

---

68. Clark, *G. K. Chesterton*, 5.

69. Chesterton, *Collected Works, Volume 1*, 250.

70. Ibid., 68.

71. Chesterton, *The Everlasting Man*, 19, 26.

72. Ibid., 26.

73. Ibid., 320.

74. Chesterton, *Selected Works*, 12.

75. Chesterton, *The Everlasting Man*, 256.

76. Ibid., 17.

77. Ibid, 36.

78. Ibid.

sessed with secrets and the avoidance or transcendence of bodily realities.[79] Man is so unnatural that he may well be supernatural. If anything "man is the ape upside down."[80]

Even the most ordinary man is extraordinary. If man is merely an animal bound to entirely material processes, then there is no reason, either Nietzschean or Darwinian, to see him as being better than any other animal. However, Chesterton does not reject the theory of evolution, which presumes the idea that non-human species survive by a process called natural selection, as long as it is in keeping with Darwin's original thesis.[81] "The point of Darwinism," he explains, "was not that a bird with a longer beak (let us say) thrust it into other birds, and had the advantage of a duellist with a longer sword."

> The point of Darwinism was that the bird with the longer beak could reach worms (let us say) at the bottom of a deeper hole; that the birds who could not do so would die; and he alone would remain to found a race of long-beaked birds. Darwinism suggested that if this happened a vast number of times, in a vast series of ages, it might account for the difference between the beaks of a sparrow and a stork. But the point was that the fittest did not need to struggle against the unfit. The survivor . . . survived because he alone had the features and organs necessary for survival.[82]

What Chesterton rejects, however, is the suggestion that "Darwinism [can] explain the human soul—the distinctively human configuration of consciousness and activity."[83] Man is too different from other animals—he is too dignified—to make the Darwinian position on the human spirit plausible. As a theory, Darwinism may be perfectly logical and even plausible on many fronts, but, when it comes to explaining humanity by referring to such things as the "Missing Link" or gaps in the fossil record, it starts to resemble "being on friendly terms with the gap in a narrative or the hole in an argument."[84] Accordingly, Chesterton contends that the sincere "agnosticism of Darwin" should be taken more seriously by his followers.[85]

79. Ibid.

80. Chesterton, *In Defense of Sanity*, 110.

81. Chesterton, *The Well and the Shallows*, 61; Nichols, *Chesterton*, 127.

82. Chesterton, *The Well and the Shallows*, 61.

83. Chesterton, *The Everlasting Man*, 51; Nichols, *Chesterton*, 128.

84. Chesterton, *The Everlasting Man*, 42.

85. Ibid.

Correspondingly, intellectualism needs a fair dose of humility to resist being blind to its own prejudices.

As an alternative to the Darwinian theory, Chesterton proposes that the idea that best explains the uniqueness of the human creature among animals, and the idea that best supports his ethic of human dignity, is the idea that man is "the image of God."[86] If nature is "always looking for something of the supernatural," the figure of the dignified human being is a good place to start.[87] Obviously, this is not to propose that man is literally identical in physical likeness to the invisible God, but rather that the image of the dignified man is analogous to the nature of God. Chesterton suggests that an image is "outline" and therefore also a "limit."[88] In this particular case, the limitations of human beings have been set by God. They indicate what it is actually possible for a human being to conform to.

Man is the image of God and thus retains a kind of dignity, not because he actually manages to bear that image or stick to its limitations particularly well, but because it is possible for him to work within the outline and limitations evoked by this idea. In particular, man, like God, is limited to being a creator who has a moral nature and the freedom to make his own decisions.[89] As far as Chesterton is concerned, the notion of human dignity is impossible to sustain apart from his creative, virtuous status. Human dignity is directly bound to what people choose and not just to their ability to choose.[90]

Regarding the things that people choose, Chesterton is more interested in the choices of the common man than he is in the usually insane choices of the "Uncommon Man" like the professor or intellectual in the classification discussed above.[91] While the professor may choose to "found a sect" such as "Malthusianism or Eugenics or Sterilisation" or some other elitist club, the common man probably has no interest in founding such a sect and is therefore probably more likely to found a family.[92] And while the professor may choose to "publish a newspaper," the common man would rather "talk about politics in a pothouse or the parlour of an inn" even if he could afford

86. Chesterton, *The Everlasting Man*, 35; Chesterton, *What's Wrong with the World*, 42; Nichols, *Chesterton*, 119.

87. Chesterton, *The Everlasting Man*, 129.

88. Ahlquist, *Common Sense 101*, 36.

89. Chesterton, *The Everlasting Man*, 34.

90. Chesterton, *Collected Works, Volume 1*, 241.

91. Chesterton, *In Defense of Sanity*, 326.

92. Ibid., 321.

to publish a newspaper.[93] The common man would, in all likelihood, rather be in the living room playing games with his one-year-old daughter than in his study writing a book.[94] Perhaps the common man should take a lunch break to do just that before he continues with the next paragraph.

And when he returns to his writing, he would be reminded that Chesterton does not split the pragmatic and the theoretical here. The point he is making is simply that the common man is on the side of developing genuine relationships and connections with the world he lives in and the people he lives with rather than creating barriers between himself and his experience of the world by mere intellectual assent. Moreover, one should not assume that Chesterton is making human experience the measurement of all truth, although it is certainly an important factor in understanding the truth.[95] For him, truth is ultimately larger than what human experience can account for. Human experience allows for depth and complexity in a way that pure rationalism does not. Truth finding and truth telling are therefore more about "making a map of a labyrinth" than about "making a map of a mist," which conceals what is there.[96]

For Chesterton, the complexity of human experience is bound to the notion that the common man is the "heir of all the ages."[97] Man is heir to a heritage, a history, and a tradition, even if he seems to be "the kind of heir who tells the family solicitor to sell the whole damned estate, lock, stock, and barrel, and give him a little ready money to throw away at the races or the night-clubs."[98] By implication, Chesterton suggests that man has a historically-affected consciousness where "forgetting the past" is tantamount to forgetting (and therefore not understanding) both the present and the future.[99] This historically-affected consciousness is bound to four broadly-defined aspects of the "spiritual story of humanity": the "spiritual element" in private human experience, the seasonal and ritualistic aspects of life, the communal religious order given to frame these spiritual and ritualistic aspects of life and, finally, the "controversial classification of the Christian system."[100]

93. Ibid., 322.

94. See Chesterton, *In Defense of Sanity*, 323.

95. Chesterton, *Collected Works, Volume 1*, 201.

96. Chesterton, *Robert Browning*, 3.

97. Chesterton, *In Defense of Sanity*, 242.

98. Ibid., 242.

99. Chesterton, *Illustrated London News*, June 18, 1932; Chesterton, *Illustrated London News*, November 12, 1932.

100. Chesterton, *In Defense of Sanity*, 243–45.

The first aspect is the sense that a "vast and vague supernatural power ... pervades the world."[101] This is a kind of shamanistic spirituality that plays in the territory of mystical non-specificity. The second aspect, still vague despite moving towards specificity, is that pagan sensibility, which proposes that the spiritual and the physical are one thing. Building on this idea, the third aspect of the spiritual story of humanity is the more concrete realization that while the spiritual and physical are intricately connected, and are therefore deeply affected by one another, they are not one and the same thing. This means that human actions ought to be geared towards appeasing the supernatural powers that affect and control the natural world through religious assent. The fourth aspect, embodied in Christian orthodoxy, is the awareness that the "world could not save itself."[102] All human attempts to bridge the gap between themselves and the divine only end up exacerbating the divide. All attempts at forging new forms of redemption via totalizing metanarratives fail in praxis. Even the "strength of the world" is really weakness in this regard, and the "wisdom of the world" is ultimately folly.[103]

Finally, Chesterton contends that a "complete human being ought to have all these [aspects of spiritual awareness] stratified in him" in the correct order so that it brings him to the realization that he is looking at the world "from the pinnacle of a tower built by his fathers."[104] Such a realization, Chesterton hopes, would prevent man from being a "contemptuous cad" who "perpetually [kicks] down the ladders by which he climbed."[105] It is only by understanding his place in history that man is able to see his own existence in the correct light and with reasonable humility. This insistence on the centrality of history to interpretive experience pervades Chesterton's work and becomes an important aspect of understanding the defense of democracy, which is discussed below.

Chesterton pre-empts a possible criticism against his celebration of the common man by pointing out that the common man is often wrongly accused for many of the "appalling blunders" that litter history,[106] but history has shown that an overwhelming number of the strange new ideas that have compromised human dignity have been "founded by merchants or manufactures of the comfortable, and sometimes of the luxurious classes."[107] Such

101. Ibid., 244.

102. Chesterton, *The Everlasting Man*, 210.

103. Ibid.

104. Chesterton, *In Defense of Sanity*, 245.

105. Ibid.

106. Ibid., 326.

107. Ibid., 322.

ideas have often been directed towards maintaining the wellbeing of the aristocracy at the cost of the wellbeing of the "lower classes."[108]

> It is easy enough to argue that the mob makes mistakes; but as a fact it never has a chance even to make mistakes until its superiors have used their superiority to make much worse mistakes. It is easy to weary of democracy and cry out for an intellectual aristocracy, but the trouble is that every intellectual aristocracy seems to have been utterly unintellectual. Anybody might guess beforehand that there would be blunders of the ignorant. What nobody could have guessed, what nobody could have dreamed of in a nightmare, what no morbid mortal imagination could ever have dared to imagine, was the mistakes of the well-informed. It is true, in a sense, to say that the mob has always been led by more educated men. It is much more true, in every sense, to say that it has always been misled by educated men. It is easy enough to say the cultured man should be the crowd's guide, philosopher and friend. Unfortunately, he has nearly always been a misguiding guide, a false friend and a very shallow philosopher. And the actual catastrophes we have suffered, including those we are now suffering, have not in historical fact been due to the prosaic practical people who are supposed to know nothing, but almost invariably to the highly theoretical people who knew that they knew everything. The world may learn by its mistakes; but they are mostly the mistakes of the learned.[109]

The mistakes of the learned "academic priesthood" are many and varied, and Chesterton's writings are overflowing with his critiques of such mistakes.[110] As I have already mentioned, he opposes Nietzsche and Darwin, but he also opposes Freud and Marx.[111] Chesterton caricatures the work of these thinkers, but his caricatures are not entirely off the mark even if they display a rare lack of generosity on his part. The problem with such thinkers is not that they are entirely wrong, but that they build their theories on a "hundredth part of a truth" and then expand that fractional truth to explain "everything."[112] Each of their theories "hangs the whole world on a single hair" until everything becomes a matter of will, biology, sex, or economy.[113] McLuhan suggests that in the particular case of economics, Chesterton ex-

108. Ibid.
109. Ibid.
110. Chesterton, *The Common Man*, 167.
111. Ahlquist, *Common Sense 101*, 108.
112. Quoted in Ahlquist, *Common Sense 101*, 109.
113. Ibid., 110.

poses a "Christless cynicism of [its] supposedly ironclad laws," but I would add that he exposes this same cynicism in other ideologies as well.[114]

Chesterton recognizes the main problem with these new theories: they are all the result of making individual men the measure of things instead of the common man.[115] He does not mean that man is the measure of all things in the sense offered by Protagoras, but rather in the sense that the common man is the one for whom any philosophy needs to work. On the contrary, many of the new theories have taken the exception as the rule rather than taking the exception as something that implies a rule. In this Chesterton foreshadows Allan Bloom's thesis that "the disorder of [the] soul found in . . . society arises primarily through the academy."[116] It is the idea that the intellectual aristocracy has fractured the masses by placing lofty theories above the equality and value of those human beings who make up the mob. In other words, it is precisely when man is not the measure of all things that things start to go wrong. In one instance, Chesterton attacks the philosophy of evolution because it proposes a "prejudice" instead of a "dogma" or "doctrine," and therefore dethrones the idea that man is the measure of all things.

It is by dethroning the common man that abuses become uses: "It will be easy for the scientific plutocrat to maintain that humanity will adapt itself to conditions which we now consider evil."[117] It therefore becomes reasonable that people need not make the effort to alter conditions on the theory that conditions will alter people: "The head can be beaten small enough to fit the hat" and the slave can be knocked instead of knocking "the fetters off the slave."[118] Chesterton argues that this sort of prejudice is the "modern argument for oppression," which sets the "perfect man who isn't there" as the precedent.[119] To counter this, the Catholic religion has proposed that the "ultimate sanity of Man" is discovered in the fact that man should be judged by incarnate, human truth, not by detached or even divine superiority.[120] It is the "Son of Man . . . who shall judge the quick and the dead."[121]

Contrary to the professors and intellectuals, it is the common man who believes in the fundamental unity of things. He stands by his beliefs in

114. McLuhan, "G. K. Chesterton," 457.

115. Chesterton, *The Everlasting Man*, 35.

116. Schall, *Schall on Chesterton*, 118.

117. Chesterton, *What's Wrong with the World*, 26.

118. Ibid.

119. Ibid.

120. Ibid.

121. Ibid.

verbal consistency, in the notion that one's creed should align with truth as it is, in the need for a connection between a promise and actions based upon that promise, in the general sanity of the masses and the occasional insanity of minorities, in human equality and the brotherhood of man, in peace, and in historical traditions.[122] The common man believes that reality is a whole even if it may only be understood in part. In simple terms, it is the common man who trusts in common sense.

Chesterton argues that "[t]he most dangerous assumptions are the ones we don't discuss."[123] For this reason, he makes explicit that which may have been taken as self-evidently true. He especially emphasizes those things that are commonly held to be true by the common man and may therefore rightly be given the title of "Apostle of Common Sense."[124] The question therefore arises: What constitutes Chesterton's philosophy of common sense? It is my aim to unpack an answer to this question in the following section by examining a few of the broad principles that underpin Chesterton's hermeneutical thinking, namely the ideas that attitude and doctrine are inseparable, that reality trumps illusion, that good supersedes evil, and, finally, that the world should be understood as a picture rather than as a pattern.

In Defense of Common Sense

The idea of common sense has a long history, beginning with Aristotle's definition of common sense (or common sensibles), which refers more to inner sensation—that which unifies sensory experience—than to the experience of reality through sensory perception. Chesterton's view of common sense is not entirely Aristotelian in that it has more to do with practical wisdom than it has to do with the way that one receives any particular sensation. Common sense is about the "balance of all the sensibilities."[125] For this reason, "common sense" can often be tied to an "uncommon sensibility."[126] Chesterton, like Aristotle and Aquinas, is nonetheless a great believer in the fact that reason is "fed by [the] senses; that [we] owe a great deal of what

122. Chesterton, *The Everlasting Man,* 38; Chesterton, *A Miscellany of Men,* 108–110.

123. Quoted in Clark, *G. K. Chesterton,* 176.

124. Ahlquist, *G. K. Chesterton,* 14.

125. Chesterton, *Charles Dickens,* 128.

126. Ibid.

[we] think to what [we] see and smell and taste and handle."[127] He is also clear that it is reason that balances our sensory experiences.

Chesterton claims that the most primary "fact of common sense is the common bond of man."[128] Again, in this idea, we find the ontological prioritization of peace. And yet, paradoxically, Chesterton argues that even the French Revolution was a result of this commitment to common sense and common humanity. "The French feeling—the feeling at the back of the Revolution—was that the more sensible a man was, the more you must look for slaughter."[129] No matter how much the French Revolution was gripped by violence and vices, for Chesterton the driving center of it was an aim to preserve values that matter to the ordinary man: *Liberté, égalité, fraternité.* No matter their failings, the "human beings" at the center of the French Revolution "were human; varied, complex and inconsistent."[130] In fact, "in the French affair everybody occupied an individual position. . . . There were not two people, I think, in that most practical crisis who stood in precisely the same attitude towards the situation."[131]

And yet, for all the bloodshed and slaughter, Chesterton sees that good can be found in it. Even the muck of human conflict has some symbolic value for understanding perception and philosophical hermeneutics: "It is when you really perceive the unity of mankind that you really perceive its variety. It is not a flippancy, it is a very sacred truth, to say that when men really understand that they are brothers they instantly begin to fight."[132] It is in the process of recognizing this first fact of common sense that one can see the first act of common sense, which "is to recognise the difference between a cloud and a mountain."[133] That is, common sense begins by seeing similarity and difference, and by seeing unity even in conflict. Indeed, "in real revolutions men discover that no one man can really agree with another man until he has disagreed with him."[134]

Following the first fact of common sense and the first act of common sense, the first principle of Chesterton's philosophy of common sense considers the relationship of attitude to doctrine. Chesterton is clear that "the most practical and important thing about a man is his view of the

---

127. Chesterton, *Saint Thomas Aquinas, Saint Francis of Assisi*, 29.

128. Chesterton, *Collected Works, Volume 20*, 213.

129. Chesterton, *Charles Dickens*, 234.

130. Chesterton, "The French Revolution and the Irish."

131. Ibid.

132. Ibid.

133. Chesterton, *Collected Works, Volume 1*, 41.

134. Ibid.

universe."[135] This view of the universe is not only rooted in particular propositions, but also considers the manner in which various propositions are
held. Therefore, pivotal to his hermeneutic is the idea that one's apprehension of everything perceived is filtered through one's attitude. This implies
that before understanding can occur, one has to become aware of the attitude that would either facilitate or hinder the process of understanding.[136]
For Chesterton, understanding is first dependent on a particular frame of
mind before it is dependent on a particular assertion of doctrinal specifics.
One's "ultimate attitudes" are the "soils for the seeds of doctrine."[137] Discovering and understanding any particular thing is therefore deeply reliant on
one's temper and temperament. The dramatic hermeneutic experience is a
matter of the entire personhood of the reader and not merely a concern of
rational processes alone.

The implication here is that it is not enough to merely defend a particular precept as if any precept can somehow not be a part of one's whole
being; to do so is to divorce meaning from context and theory from action.
For example, when we "thank God for beer and Burgundy by not drinking too much of them" we demonstrate the theory of gratitude by acting
accordingly.[138] This means that Chesterton is just as comfortable with disagreeing with a person's attitude as he is with disagreeing with his ideas;
and he is equally comfortable with defending a particular attitude as he is
with defending a particular idea.[139] In fact, while Chesterton contends that
attitude is an issue of "style," it is nonetheless by style that individuality is
recognized.[140]

Chesterton's marrying of thought and actions mirrors the Aristotelian
word *phronesis*, which embodies an attitude of practical wisdom. By implication, if two people subscribe to the same dogma, but differ in attitude,
the result is a different belief or a different kind of faith. It is arguably for
this reason that Chesterton regards Protestantism as being quite different
from Catholicism, as we discover especially in his arguments in *The Well
and the Shallows* (1935).[141] While the creeds of these two broad streams of
the Christian faith are largely the same, their approaches and attitudes differ
substantially in many ways. Chesterton's orthodoxy—believing in the right

135. Ibid.

136. Chesterton, *Tremendous Trifles*, 7.

137. Chesterton, *Collected Works, Volume 1*, 268.

138. Ibid.

139. Chesterton, *The Well and the Shallows*, 17; Chesterton, *Autobiography*, 161.

140. Chesterton, *The Well and the Shallows*, 17.

141. Ibid., 29–60; Wood, *Chesterton*, 3.

thing—is therefore directly interwoven with orthopraxy—believing in the right way. Orthodoxy cannot exist without orthopraxy. In the same way, we find that ethics is connected to being, and that interpretation itself will be affected by character.

Still, to distinguish between attitude and doctrine is not to say that the difference between them can always be easily delineated, nor does it imply that these two can necessarily be split and understood apart from each other. Instead, this distinction underscores the fact that one's experience and interpretations are bound to specific *a priori* conditions that are often implicit in one's demeanor. Thus, in Chesterton's work, attitude can be taken as pivotal to the hermeneutic horizon. For example, he describes atheism, Buddhism, immanentism, materialism, pantheism, and stoicism as "attitudes," thereby implying that there is a subtle motivating force beneath the facade of ideas that needs to be recognized.[142] Chesterton's attitude towards the world is again summed up in his explanation that the main problem for philosophers is the question of how one may "contrive to be at once astonished at the world and yet at home in it."[143] Chesterton's hermeneutic is caught in this very same tension, in the space between awe and peace, gratitude and humility. It is only in this tension that a richer encounter with the text of reality becomes possible.

It is this tension that introduces the second principle of Chesterton's philosophy of common sense, namely that "so long as a glimmer of it remains, in spite of all journalism and State instruction, it is possible to appreciate what we call a reality."[144] "[W]ith all the facts before it," common sense is able to recognize the sharp distinctions between things and understand that "black is not white,"[145] but common sense is also capable of recognizing that "white" can be "yellow" as in the case of "white wine," or "pale green" as in the case of "white grapes," or "pink" as in the description of the complexion of a "white man."[146]

Common sense sees things better than our labels do. And yet, a person may choose to stick with labels, however imprecise they may be, because common sense reveals that ordering "yellow wine in a restaurant" or "some greenish-yellow grapes" would have any waiter look at him as if he were

142. Chesterton, *Collected Works, Volume 1,* 333; Chesterton, *The Everlasting Man,* 129; Chesterton, *What's Wrong with the World,* 179.

143. Chesterton, *Collected Works, Volume 1,* 212.

144. Chesterton, *Collected Works, Volume 3,* 111.

145. Chesterton, *A Miscellany of Men,* 84.

146. Chesterton, *Collected Works, Volume 1,* 66.

mad.[147] If a "Government official, reporting on the Europeans in Burmah [sic], said, 'There are only two thousand pinkish men here,' he would be accused of cracking jokes, and kicked out of his post."[148] Common sense would also tell us that both a person who orders yellow wine and the person who refers to white men as pinkish "would have come to grief through telling the strict truth."[149]

Chesterton mocks the kind of "large-mindedness [that] is supposed to consist of confusing everything with everything else" and insists, in keeping with the first act of common sense, upon the power of making distinctions between "man and woman," or between irreligion and religion, or "the good and the unnatural."[150] Is it such distinctions "by which man in the true sense becomes distinguished."[151] At the risk of forgetting the genuine ambiguities of life, Chesterton is highly critical of those critics who fail to make such distinctions. He writes that the "modern critic" whose "whole business" is speech, "professes to be entirely inarticulate": "Before Botticelli he is mute. But if there is any good in Botticelli (there is much good, and much evil too) it is emphatically the critic's business to explain it; to translate it from terms of painting into terms of diction."[152] Common sense, as the power of making such distinctions, is therefore Chesterton's primary weapon against what he calls the "age of skepticism."[153]

One example of Chesterton's attack on skepticism is his critique of the "philosophy of Impressionism," which in his estimation is little more than "the philosophy of Illusion."[154] Chesterton contends that there is a "spiritual significance in [the philosophy of] Impressionism" that is connected with the philosophy skepticism:

> I mean that it illustrated scepticism in the sense of subjectivism. Its principal was that if all that could be seen of a cow was a white line and a purple shadow, we should only render the line and the shadow; in a sense we should only believe in the line and the shadow, rather than in the cow. In one sense the Impressionist sceptic contradicted the poet who said he had never seen a purple cow. He tended rather to say that he had only seen a

147. Ibid.
148. Ibid.
149. Ibid.
150. Chesterton, *The Man Who Was Orthodox*, 109.
151. Chesterton, *G. K.'s Weekly*, March 29, 1930.
152. Chesterton, *In Defense of Sanity*, 67.
153. Chesterton, *Autobiography*, 96.
154. Ibid., 97.

purple cow; or rather that he had not seen the cow, but only the purple. Whatever may be the merits of this method of art, there is obviously something highly subjective and sceptical about it as a method of thought. It naturally lends itself to the metaphysical suggestion that things only exist as we perceive them, or that things do not exist at all.[155]

This idea is echoed in Chesterton's assessment of the function of pictures: "Pictures are always meant to catch a certain aspect, at a certain angle, in a certain light; sometimes in light that is almost as brief as lightning. But when the artists became anarchists and began to exhibit the community and the cosmos by these flashes of lightning, the result was not realism, but simply nightmare."[156] As a philosophy, Impressionism turns all that is solid into air. It implies that "everything might be a dream" or "nothing, but thought."[157] As explained by the English artist and critic Roger Fry (1866–1934), to whose essay "The Philosophy of Impressionism"[158] Chesterton is likely referring, "[t]he Impressionist realises above all things the truth that absolute rest and absolute identity are mental abstractions and have no counterpart in external nature."[159] Nothing is fixed and everything becomes a process in flux, suggesting that we "can never know anything about 'things in themselves.'"[160] Still, even when the philosophy of Impressionism is deplorable, the art of the impressionists is redeemable for Chesterton. He writes, "Impressionism is, but Christianity [applied] to a canvas."[161] The "painter gives what the healthy moralist gives—hints."[162] The problem with Impressionism as a philosophy is that it assumes that hints and flashes of lightning are all we have, whereas the actual artwork of the impressionist suggests precisely the opposite. Hints are hints because they hint at something specific. Ultimately, for Chesterton, the philosophy of Impressionism violates common sense because it makes false distinctions.

The skepticism embodied in that philosophy, it turns out, is really more rigid than religiosity: it turns change into the unchanging standard and thereby inadvertently argues that there is something absolute after all. And if everything is a dream of anarchy, inconsistency, instability, and

155. Ibid., 96–97; See Oddie, *Chesterton and the Romance of Orthodoxy*, 142–43.

156. Chesterton, *Collected Works, Volume 3*, 176.

157. Chesterton, *Autobiography*, 97; See Ker, *G. K. Chesterton*, 32.

158. Fry, *A Roger Fry Reader*, 12–20.

159. Ibid., 13.

160. Ibid.

161. Chesterton, *Daily News*, August 1, 1903.

162. Ibid.

fluidity, then everything is really perceived as a nightmare, as Chesterton suggests especially through the narrative of *The Man Who Was Thursday* (1908). It is only when the mask of the nightmare is removed that goodness can be recovered.[163] In other words, as argued in greater detail further on, it is only when skepticism is replaced by a sense of mystery that one can begin to distinguish between illusion and reality.

Chesterton notes that skepticism needs to have limitations to be helpful. Absolute skepticism turns the world into a landscape of negations, which is to say that it somehow manages to celebrate difference without agreeing on similarity. It argues for the affirmation of "No," but not of "Yes."[164] Additionally, it may conflate affirmation and negation into a dialectical synthesis—a "Yo"—so that difference is both affirmed and dissolved instead of held in paradoxical tension with similarity.[165] Again, this skepticism is rooted in what Chesterton observes to be a nominalist error:

> I remember when Mr. H. G. Wells had an alarming fit of Nominalist philosophy; and poured forth book after book to argue that everything is unique and untypical as that a man is so much an individual that he is not even a man. It is a quaint and almost comic fact, that this chaotic negation especially attracts those who are always complaining of social chaos, and who propose to replace it by the most sweeping social regulations. It is the very men who say that nothing can be classified, who say that everything must be codified. Thus Mr. Bernard Shaw said that the only golden rule is that there is no golden rule. He prefers an iron rule; as in Russia.[166]

Nominalism, far from celebrating the uniqueness of things by insisting upon their uniqueness, actually flattens everything. To say, for instance, that no two chairs are alike is to end up denying that there is a thing as marvelous and as useful as a chair.[167] Another consequence of this vehement skepticism is that it does not produce the kind of freedom that upholds the ideal of human dignity. It only offers imprisonment. Instead of being bound by only a few specific boundaries, dogmas, and doctrines, it suggests that one is in fact constrained by everything. Chesterton follows somewhat Lacanian logic here. It turns out that "[i]f there is no God"—no God to legitimate our

163. Ker, *G. K. Chesterton*, 192.

164. Chesterton, *Saint Thomas Aquinas, Saint Francis of Assisi*, 154.

165. Ibid.

166. Ibid., 160.

167. Chesterton, *Collected Works, Volume 1*, 238.

freedom to choose and no God to set up various hierarchies in the order of being—"then everything is prohibited."[168]

Yet another consequence of skepticism is that it results in an uncritical credulity. As Cammaerts notes when reflecting on Chesterton's thinking, "The first effect of not believing in God is to believe in anything."[169] This paraphrases Chesterton's words, "It's the first effect of not believing in God that you lose your common sense."[170] Without any "religious authority" we will be "disposed to have any religious authority."[171] Also, the "man who refuses to have his own philosophy will only have the used-up scraps of somebody else's philosophy."[172] Ultimately, Chesterton contends, the skeptic is too easily fooled.[173] He is not skeptical enough to see that his skepticism must fail to be successfully skeptical. Because the skeptic has no standard, he may easily be taken captive by myriad misguided philosophies.

If everything is illusory, what remains is an ontology of violence that is typified by rigidity and ossification: it is the sort of ontology that leads to hermeneutic violence, where texts are forever deemed subordinate to the reader's prejudices. The absence of a solid, commonsense creed on matters pertaining to reality does not save people from fanaticism, but only leads them deeper into it.[174] Moreover, the location of any kind of interpretive meaning becomes impossible. Chesterton argues that one "can find no meanings in a jungle of scepticism; but the man will find more and more meanings who walks through a forest of doctrine and design."[175] This forest of doctrine and design insists that affirmation calls for the inevitability of "contradiction" or the ability to make "reasonable distinctions."[176] "[R]easonable distinctions" are a remedy for confusion.[177] The ability to create distinctions is really a "triumph of the human mind" against any tendency to "[confuse] everything with everything else, of saying that a man is the same as a woman and religion is the same as irreligion, and the unnatural

168. Žižek and Gunjević, *God in Pain*, 44.

169. Cammaerts, *The Laughing Prophet*, 211; See also: http://www.chesterton.org/ceases-to-worship/.

170. Chesterton, *Selected Works*, 974.

171. Chesterton, *Illustrated London News*, April 26, 1924.

172. Chesterton, *The Common Man*, 173.

173. Chesterton, *Collected Works, Volume 1*, 353.

174. Chesterton, *What's Wrong with the World*, 24.

175. Chesterton, *Collected Works, Volume 1*, 362.

176. Chesterton, *Saint Thomas Aquinas, Saint Francis of Assisi*, 153; *G. K.'s Weekly*, March 29, 1930; Chesterton, *The Man Who Was Orthodox*, 105.

177. Chesterton, *G. K.'s Weekly*, March 29, 1930; Chesterton, *The Man Who Was Orthodox*, 106.

good as the natural and all the rest of it."[178] In fact, it is by "the great power of distinction" that human beings become "in the true sense distinguished."[179] Chesterton writes that even in a dream, the dream retains the "first fact of being," namely "that a thing cannot be and not be."[180] Even a dream is more believable than uncompromising skepticism.

Keeping with the idea that common sense allows for distinctions between black and white and between reality and illusion, there must ultimately be a difference between what is false and what is true.[181] However, the commonsensical preference of reality over illusion does not suggest that there is a clean dichotomy between reality and fiction. Instead, fiction is a sub-reality, rather than any kind of anti-reality, and can therefore inform reality. Fiction is not the opposite of reality, but its complement: "fiction is a necessity" rather than a "luxury."[182] Slavoj Žižek presents a similar view when writing that "as soon as we renounce fiction and illusion, we lose reality itself; *the moment we subtract fictions from reality, reality itself loses its discursive-logical consistency.*"[183]

Fiction, for Chesterton, can be a helpful if not indispensible way for navigating life. "Fiction means the common things as seen by the uncommon people."[184] Paradoxically, it is through the fiction of fiction that reality can cease to be perceived in fictional terms. Again, the residue of Plato's philosophy is found here, which insists upon the "fundamental fact that ideas are realities; that ideas exist just as men exist."[185] Still, Chesterton is quick to add that there is a danger in allowing ideas to supersede the importance of people.[186] In this, he challenges the role of the intellectual by encouraging the view that people ought to be more important than ideas.

This danger of valuing ideas over people is captured in Chesterton's description of Harold March, in *The Man Who Knew Too Much* (1922), who "was the sort of man who knows everything about politics, and nothing about politicians. He also knew a great deal about art, letters, philosophy, and general culture; about almost everything, indeed, except the world he

---

178. Ibid.

179. Ibid.

180. Chesterton, *Saint Thomas Aquinas, Saint Francis of Assisi,* 153.

181. Ibid.

182. Chesterton, *The Defendant,* 10.

183. Žižek, *Tarrying With The Negative,* 88.

184. Chesterton, *Charles Dickens,* 84; Clark, *G. K. Chesterton,* 34.

185. Chesterton, *The Everlasting Man,* 125.

186. Ibid.

was living in."[187] He knew everything except everything. In fact, it is precisely by misunderstanding the human dimension—by knowing about politics, but not about politicians—that March misunderstands and misinterprets the world he is living in. By being "thoroughly worldly" he fails to allow himself the possibility of understanding of the world.[188]

To avoid the trap of letting ideas supersede the importance of people, Chesterton tends towards the "sacramental sanity" of Aristotle, who seeks "to combine the body and the soul of things."[189] He thus understands that ideas, as part of reality, are capable of shaping our perceptions of reality even while they should not be confused with reality. Just as the reality is always preferable to the illusion, so the true is always preferable to the false. This preference is echoed in Chesterton's contention that while some may contend that "a man can believe that he is always in a dream" on grounds that any apparently irrefutable proof that is given to him might be the same "proof" that is offered in a dream, the result is less than livable.[190] In essence, Chesterton assumes that existence requires certainty, and he refers to Aquinas to affirm this position:

> Against all this the philosophy of St. Thomas stands founded on the universal common conviction that eggs are eggs. The Hegelian may say that an egg is really a hen, because it is a part of an endless process of Becoming; the Berkeleian may hold that poached eggs only exist as a dream exists, since it is quite as easy to call the dream the cause of the eggs as the eggs the cause of the dream; the Pragmatist may believe that we get the best out of scrambled eggs by forgetting that they ever were eggs, and only remembering the scramble. But no pupil of St. Thomas needs to addle his brains in order adequately to addle his eggs; to put his head at any peculiar angle in looking at eggs, or squinting at eggs, or winking the other eye in order to see a new simplification of eggs. The Thomist stands in the broad daylight of the brotherhood of men, in their common consciousness that eggs are not hens or dreams or mere practical assumptions; but things attested by the Authority of the Senses, which is from God.[191]

187. Chesterton, *The Man Who Knew Too Much*, 1.

188. Chesterton, *Collected Works, Volume 1*, 216.

189. Chesterton, *The Everlasting Man*, 126.

190. Chesterton, *Collected Works, Volume 1*, 229.

191. Chesterton, *Saint Thomas Aquinas, Saint Francis of Assisi*, 135.

William Desmond argues that to test the validity of doubt as a philosophy for life, one ought to "radicalize" it: "Radical doubt defeats itself because
doubt has *to be*, even in all its negations."[192] This is the very idea adopted
by Chesterton in his reading of the book of Job.[193] Even doubts should be
doubted.[194] Without this radicalization of doubt, Chesterton suggests that
the Cartesian maxim should read: "I am not; therefore I cannot think,"[195]
but through this radicalization of doubt, the maxim *cogito ergo sum* is reversed to become *sum ergo cogito*.[196] In this, dreams and impressions are
recognized as dreams and impressions. They may be very much like the
reality, but to say that something is like something else is not to say that the
two things are exactly the same.[197]

The affirmation of reality over illusion and truth over falsehood both
point to the third principle of Chesterton's common sense, namely his affirmation of good over evil. Chesterton finds that having a false view of reality
can only ever arrive at the "certainty of ill."[198] This can be understood in light
of the allegory of the fall, according to which, in falling once, the human
race gained the knowledge of good and evil; but now, Chesterton writes,
"we have fallen a second time, and only the knowledge of evil remains."[199]
The first fall implies the difficulty of distinguishing between good and evil,
while the second fall implies an inability to recognize that there is any good
at all. A "modern morality" may end up being little more than the ability to
observe "imperfection" without having any "perfection to point to."[200] This
"certainty of ill" without any certainty of the good is what Chesterton calls
the "negative spirit."[201] He writes that this

> is the arresting and dominant fact about modern social discus-
> sion; that the quarrel is not merely about the difficulties, but
> about the aim. We agree about the evil; it is about the good that
> we should tear each other's eyes out. We all admit that a lazy
> aristocracy is a bad thing. We should not by any means all admit

192. Desmond, *Being and the Between*, 22.

193. Chesterton, *In Defense Of Sanity*, xxi.

194. Chesterton, *Collected Works, Volume 1*, 288.

195. Ibid.

196. Desmond, *Being and the Between*, 22.

197. Chesterton, *Collected Works, Volume 1*, 238; Chesterton, *The Everlasting Man*, 114.

198. Chesterton, *Collected Works, Volume 1*, 47.

199. Ibid., 51.

200. Ibid., 47.

201. Ibid.

that an active aristocracy would be a good thing. We all feel
angry with an irreligious priesthood; but some of us would go
mad with disgust at a really religious one. Everyone is indignant
if our army is weak, including the people who would be even
more indignant if it were strong. The social case is exactly the
opposite of the medical case. We do not disagree, like doctors,
about the precise nature of the illness, while agreeing about the
nature of health. On the contrary, we all agree that England is
unhealthy, but half of us would not look at her in what the other
half would call blooming health. . . . I maintain, therefore, that
the common sociological method is quite useless: that of first
dissecting abject poverty or cataloguing prostitution. We all dislike abject poverty; but it might be another business if we began
to discuss independent and dignified poverty. We all disapprove
of prostitution; but we do not all approve of purity. The only way
to discuss the social evil is to get at once to the social ideal. We
can all see the national madness; but what is national sanity?[202]

Every problem that Chesterton encounters in his world may be
summed up in a single statement: "What is wrong [with the world] is that
we do not ask what is right."[203] Without any universal good to interpret,
goodness, like everything else, becomes an entirely arbitrary matter. Thus,
Chesterton argues that when "things will not work" it is essential to find
the thinking person "who has some doctrine about why they work at all."[204]
There is, therefore, a definite need for the idealist whose idealism would
consider things in their "practical essence."[205] This idealism would, for
instance, "consider a poker in reference to poking before" considering "its
suitability for wife-beating."[206]

Ultimately, all understanding is futile without some indication of what
the good is, and Chesterton's hermeneutic, which certainly allows for cutting critique, is concerned with the recovery of ideals in pursuit of what is
good. One may be tempted to overcomplicate the issue of what constitutes
the good, but since Chesterton is concerned primarily with the dignity of
the common man, which is really a desire to hear the voice of the voice-
less, his philosophy of goodness is also a matter of common sense: the aim

202. Chesterton, *What's Wrong with the World*, 17.
203. Ibid., 17.
204. Ibid., 19.
205. Ibid.
206. Ibid.

should always be towards "altering conditions to fit the human soul" instead of "altering the human soul to fit conditions."[207]

The fourth principle of Chesterton's philosophy of common sense—after his focus on attitudes, realities, and goodness—is the idea that faith precedes and grounds facts. Put differently, intuition is a fundamental context for human reason.[208] While it is argued above that Chesterton is opposed to making doubt absolute, he is not opposed to doubt per se, especially considering that doubt is a common human experience. Therefore, he does not posit certainty or epistemological arrogance as opposites of doubt. Rather, he suggests that even doubt ought to be understood in relation to faith. For Chesterton, reason itself is a "matter of faith" and skepticism is a matter of a different kind of faith.[209] This means that any proclamation about reality or truth is only made possible by an underlying faith claim. Chesterton's work suggests a process by which one is constantly engaged in testing and challenging one's own assumptions, as well as the assumptions of others. In short, he recognizes that the familiar is dangerous when it induces unthinking habit—an unacknowledged, hidden faith—whereby one sees without seeing or dreams without recognizing that one is dreaming.[210] He warns that through overfamiliarity, reality is perceived in totally illusory terms.

To address the neglect of faith in a transcendent order and the problem of a widespread, unquestioning faith in facts, Chesterton's sets many of his stories in a world gone mad. Elements of this madness are found, for example, in the anti-revolutionary backdrop of *The Napoleon of Notting Hill* (1904), the nightmarish anarchy in *The Man Who Was Thursday* (1908), the chaotic, lawless courtroom scenario and the strange events of *Manalive* (1912), and the militant teetotalism in *The Flying Inn* (1914). In particular, though, I want to highlight the way that Chesterton illustrates the problem of the lunatic in his first piece of detective fiction, *The Club of Queer Trades* (1905). Early on in this story, the reader is introduced to Basil Grant, a judge who "suddenly went mad on the bench" and "accused criminals" of a whole range of unusual crimes: "monstrous egoism, lack of humour and morbidity deliberately encouraged."[211] In this, Basil Grant lurches past the symptomatic nature of crimes to grip onto deeper attitudinal concerns. For instance, thieving becomes not so much a problem of economics, but a

207. Ibid., 80.
208. Ker, *G. K. Chesterton,* 245.
209. Chesterton, *Collected Works, Volume 1,* 230.
210. Chesterton, *Tremendous Trifles,* 163.
211. Chesterton, *The Club of Queer Trades,* 5.

problem of human dignity and forgiveness; and criminal activity becomes a consequence of pride.

After Basil Grant tells a man to "[g]et a new soul" because his is "not fit for a dog," he decides to "[retire] from public life" to take up a new occupation alongside his brother Rupert Grant as a private detective.[212] What follows this is series of stories centered around some very odd happenings: a respected Major receives a series of outlandish death threats, an old vicar, who later turns out to be an imposter, visits a stranger and tells him of a string of horrifying events, and a trapped woman refuses to be rescued. Amid these goings-on is the rationalist, Holmesian character Rupert Grant, whose supposedly masterful "deductions"—actually examples of abductive guesswork—about these strange happenings always turn out to be wrong.

Chesterton uses this backdrop to set up the real hero of the story, who is the alleged lunatic, Basil Grant. In the end, it is the so-called maniac— the man who sees beyond mere symptoms—who is shown to be absolutely sane. It is the apparent sanity that most people consent to that is shown to be insanity. Chesterton's assertions here challenge consensus theories of truth and echo Evelyn Underhill's quip that "sanity" may merely consist "in sharing the hallucinations of our neighbours."[213] There is always a danger that the standards by which we measure our perceptions may correspond with convenience rather than truth.[214] Chesterton presents the idea that the "word convention means literally a coming together" and that this sense of agreement is unhelpful if it is "presented to the imagination as a silent mob" that exists to mask, hide, and mystify.[215] Therefore, for Chesterton, common sense is located primarily in what is sense rather than just in what is common.

Basil Grant's seeming lunacy is really his idiosyncrasy—his ability to see truth without necessarily getting the "mere facts" right.[216] This idea is pre-empted early on in the novel:

> "Facts," murmured Basil, like one mentioning some strange, far-off animals, "how facts obscure the truth. I may be silly—in fact, I'm off my head—but I never could believe in that man— what's his name, in those capital stories?—Sherlock Holmes. Every detail points to something, certainly; but generally to the wrong thing. Facts point in all directions, it seems to me, like

212. Ibid., 6–7.
213. Underhill, *Mysticism*, 14.
214. Chesterton, *Illustrated London News*, May 14, 1932; Underhill, *Mysticism*, 14.
215. Chesterton, *Illustrated London News*, May 14, 1932.
216. Chesterton, *The Club of Queer Trades*, 32.

the thousands of twigs on a tree. It is only the life of the tree that has unity and goes up—only the green blood that springs, like a fountain, at the stars."[217]

For Chesterton, truth, which is linked to faith, it is not the mere facts. Truth is located in something that is alive; in something that brings unity. Facts may be understood either as isolated truths or as truths that exist prior to the intuition of the dramatic interpretive experience. And Chesterton argues that these are both misleading points of departure. In fact, it is possible to accurately represent all the facts whilst still missing or neglecting the truth that holds the facts together. This is perhaps why one may agree with another person on the specific description of an event in a drama, but not necessarily its signification or significance. In simple terms, therefore, the problem of the lunatic is this: insanity is established when the insistence upon mere facts subverts, obscures, or detracts from understanding rather than extending or supporting a larger understanding of the truth that contains them. With no anchor in the possibility of a larger story, truth becomes, in Nietzsche's words, nothing more than a "mobile army of metaphors" that have become worn out,[218] or, in Jean Baudrillard's terms, a simulacrum that conceals the "truth" that there is no truth.[219] Without the recognition of the relationship between faith and facts, what is left is only an abstraction or a copy of something that does not exist: a symptom of an illness that is not there, a signifier with no signified, a "liquidation of all referentials" or something meant that ultimately does not mean anything.[220] Society itself then becomes (at least in appearance), as Guy Debord argues, pure spectacle.[221] In Chesterton's terms, what is left is a world of "imitators of their imitators of their imitators endlessly repeating the very same imagery and terminology ten thousand times."[222]

Chesterton demonstrates that the issue of the right-relationship between whole (faith) and part (facts) in which truth is located is not only applicable to how facts are commonly over-emphasized, but is also applicable to how logic (the particular) and truth (the universal) are related:

> Logic and truth, as a matter of fact, have very little to do with each other. Logic is concerned merely with the fidelity and accuracy with which a certain process is performed, a process which

217. Ibid., 16.

218. Nietzsche, *The Portable Nietzsche*, 46.

219. Baudrillard, *Simulacra and Simulation*, 1.

220. Ibid., 2.

221. Debord, *The Society of the Spectacle*.

222. Chesterton, *Illustrated London News*, June 23, 1932.

can be performed with any materials, with any assumption. . . .
On the assumption that a man has two ears, it is good logic that
three men have six ears, but on the assumption that a man has
four ears, it is equally good logic that three men have twelve.
And the power of seeing how many ears the average man, as
a fact, possesses, the power of counting a gentleman's ears accurately and without mathematical confusion, is not a logical
thing, but a primary and direct experience, like a physical sense,
like a religious vision. . . . Logic has again and again been expended, and expended most brilliantly and effectively, on things
that do not exist at all. There is far more logic, more sustained
consistency of mind, in the science of heraldry than in the science of biology. . . . There is more logic in [Lewis Carrol's] *Alice
in Wonderland* than in the [British Parliament's] *Statute Book.*
. . . The relations of logic to truth depend, then, not upon its
perfection as logic, but upon certain pre-logical faculties and
certain pre-logical discoveries.[223]

After acknowledging the role of the pre-logical, Chesterton states
that "you can only find truth with logic when you have already found truth
without it."[224] Here, both "physical sense" and "religious vision" are given
as possible *a priori,* pre-factual, pre-logical conditions.[225] It is important
to maintain the relationship between the abstract and the concrete. One's
sensate experience of the physical world is cast into question only insofar
as it ignores the possibility of a "religious vision."[226] In Chesterton's estimation, if doubt is taken as a given, trust, as the bedrock of knowledge, is
taken for granted and is therefore forgotten. And if trust, as the expression
of our epistemic limitations, is taken for granted, the result is either the
absolutism of the sense-impressions of empiricists or the hyper-rationalism
of deconstructionists.

Chesterton claims that "[t]he man who cannot believe his senses [the
solipsist or "panegoist"] and the man who cannot believe anything else [the
materialist] are both insane."[227] Yet, their insanity is not necessarily a problem of argumentation, doctrine, or logic, but a problem of "the manifest
mistake of their whole lives." This stress on the "whole" of life shows that
Chesterton's conception of truth is closer to the existential model offered by
Søren Kierkegaard (1813–55) than it would be to any conception of truth as

223. Chesterton, *Daily News,* February 25, 1905.
224. Chesterton, *G. K.'s Weekly,* March 29, 1930.
225. Chesterton, *Daily News,* February 25, 1905.
226. Ibid.
227. Chesterton, *Collected Works, Volume 1,* 229.

purely propositional. Truth is about existing within what one understands and is therefore "not [simply] a matter of knowing this or that, but of being in the truth."[228] Truth is something embodied and lived—it is "a way"—rather than something adhered to merely rationally.[229] Chesterton writes that it consists primarily of an "inwardness and sincerity" rather than a list of dogmas to be adhered to, although it also does not mean discarding dogmas entirely.[230] Simply put, intellectual assent to truth is insufficient.

Lunacy is located in the purely rational or rationalized conception of truth—a failure to embrace the dramatic, interrelated nature of being. It takes faith as a loving, kenotic posture towards what is, rather than the totalistic assertion of knowledge before we can insist that our thoughts and experiences "have any relation to reality at all."[231] To deny this is to fall into a trap that Chesterton refers to as the "suicide of thought."[232] While this is a metaphor, it may be linked to Chesterton's way of understanding literal suicide—as the end point of solipsism—as "the ultimate evil."[233] It is the refusal to "take an interest in existence" or to pledge allegiance to life.[234] He argues that the "man who kills a man, kills a man," but that the "man who kills himself, kills all men; as far as he is concerned he wipes out the world."[235] The suicide of thought follows this same pattern: it is a way of thinking that shuts out the real.

A further implication of placing facts above faith is that one's conception of reality becomes terribly constricted. The lunatic may not necessarily be utterly oblivious to reality; he is not, so to speak, living in another world. However, his apprehension of the world he does live in is insubstantial. The lunatic "seeks to get the heavens into his head. And it is his head that splits."[236] Through reason, he seeks to "cross the infinite sea and so make it finite."[237] The suicide of thought, then, is not the absence of thought. Instead it is about rendering thought absolute. It is rooted in the assumption that (rational) thought can contain and tame the reality. This is a widespread problem in a great deal of modern thought after Descartes. Faith in *cogito*

---

228. Kierkegaard, *Provocations*, 53.

229. See Simpson, *Truth is a Way.*

230. Chesterton, *Collected Works, Volume 20*, 72.

231. Ibid., *Volume 1*, 230.

232. Ibid., 233.

233. Ibid., 276.

234. Ibid.

235. Ibid.

236. Ibid., 220.

237. Ibid.

conceals the fact that *being precedes thought*. Chesterton uses the phrase "as mad as a hatter" to highlight the point of this argument: the hatter is mad because he has to "measure the human head."[238] The lunatic's world is wholly defined by the limitations of the human mind. What is strictly conceivable, perhaps what is only provable or acceptable, becomes the rather shoddy measure of what is true.

The final principle of Chesterton's philosophy of common sense is that he assumes that it is better to read reality as a picture than as a pattern.[239] To assume the opposite is to "think at the wrong end."[240] Chesterton observes that a lunatic's "explanation of a thing is always complete, and often in a purely rational sense satisfactory."[241] The "insane explanation, if not conclusive, is at least unanswerable."[242] As an example, we could think of a man who comes up with a theory that everyone has a conspiracy against him. Unfortunately, the only way to contradict his theory is to point out that those very same people deny being conspirators, and that "is exactly what conspirators would do."[243] The problem here is not that the lunatic's theory does not make any sense, but that it does. As a theory caught up in the psychotic vortex of the purely literal and horrifically prosaic, it cannot break out to comprehend the world through the poetic. It cannot comprehend the world without comprehension. And so the lunatic is wrong because his theory may explain "a large number of things, but it does not explain them in a large way."[244] It is typical of the professors and intellectuals to take a "thin explanation and carry it very far. But a pattern can stretch for ever and still be a small pattern."[245] When the pattern is taken as absolute, the picture and its real meaning cannot be recognized.

Chesterton's reference to the "popular philosophical joke" about whether the chicken or the egg came first is a helpful example on what it means to allow a pattern to supersede the actual picture.[246] Ultimately, the endless "mental chain" is built upon an illusion, namely that the chicken and the egg have equal significance. In reality, they are "in different mental

238. Ibid.

239. Chesterton, *The Everlasting Man*, 244.

240. Chesterton, *Collected Works, Volume 1*, 230.

241. Ibid., 222.

242. Ibid.

243. Ibid.

244. Ibid.

245. Ibid., 225.

246. Chesterton, *What's Wrong with the World*, 18.

worlds."[247] The one is a means and the other is an end. The egg exists to pro-duce chickens, but the chicken does not necessarily exist solely to produce eggs. To enforce a pattern on the relationship between chickens and eggs is to make the mistake of divorcing a process from its "divine object."[248]

The idea of seeing a picture and not a pattern and its implications for grappling with Chesterton's process of interpretive understanding is demonstrated directly in his short story "The Song of the Broken Sword" through how many people in the story interpret the character of Arthur St. Clare. In the end, the central protagonist Father Brown begins to describe what "everybody knows," namely, that

> Arthur St. Clare was a great and successful English general. [Everybody] knows that after splendid yet careful campaigns both in India and Africa he was in command against Brazil when the great Brazilian patriot Olivier issued his ultimatum. [Everybody] knows that on that occasion St. Clare with a small force attacked Olivier with a very large one, and was captured after heroic resistance. And, [everybody] knows that after his capture, and to the abhorrence of the civilized world, St. Clare was hanged on the nearest tree. He was found swinging there . . . with his broken sword hung round his neck.[249]

At the end of this monologue, Father Brown observes that there is something missing from this story that "everybody" supposedly "knows."[250] In the story, St. Clare is reputed to be a great and successful general whose life ends because of a series of surprisingly poor decisions. This brings the reader, in tune with Chesterton's reasoning, to wonder if the reputation of this man was deserved. Father Brown explains this anomaly through a metaphor: "Where does a man hide a leaf? In a forest. But what does he do if there is no forest? He grows a forest to hide it in. . . . And if a man had to hide a dead body, he would make a field of dead bodies to hide it in."[251] His meaning is this: if there is an answer to this riddle, it is not concealed at all, but apparent in plain sight. It has been perceived as part of a pattern when it is in fact an anomaly in a picture. Therefore, the problem is not with the answer, but with the reader's inability to perceive it. It is simultaneously revealed and concealed in its visibility. St. Clare's virtues are only virtues in appearance.

247. Ibid.
248. Ibid., 19.
249. Chesterton, *Father Brown*, 154.
250. Ibid.
251. Ibid., 159.

The idea of Arthur St. Clare is somehow incongruent with the actual Arthur St. Clare. Father Brown explains that while St. Clare read the Bible, which would be a clear literary rhetorical device or symbol to demonstrate his virtue, paradoxically, this is exactly what conceals his fatal flaw: "He was a man who read his Bible. That was what was the matter with him."[252] Even in this abrasive statement, Chesterton is challenging the reader to consider the nature of isolating truth from existence and thus reducing it to a mere proposition; on its own, this may be read as a heresy, but such a reading becomes questionable in light of what follows:

> When will people understand that it is useless for a man to read his Bible unless he also reads everybody else's Bible? A printer reads a Bible for misprints. A Mormon reads his Bible, and finds polygamy; a Christian scientist reads his, and finds we have no arms and legs. St. Clare was an old Anglo-Indian Protestant soldier. . . . Of course, he found in the Old Testament anything that he wanted—lust, tyranny, treason. Oh, I dare say he was honest, as you call it. But what is the good of a man being honest in his worship of dishonesty?[253]

When referring to this same passage, Žižek argues that Chesterton is demonstrating tremendous "theological finesse" in allotting responsibility for the general's downfall, not to his betrayal of the Christian faith through "moral corruption due to the predominance of base materialist motives," but rather to something that is "inherent" in Christianity itself.[254] However, while Žižek praises Chesterton greatly, he does so without understanding the subtlety of his argument. Chesterton's argument is not for or against a particular theology, nor is it to support or oppose any particular doctrine or dogma through what he is writing here. He is suggesting something that is not only relevant to theological discourse, but that is applicable to the hermeneutic experience.

The problem with Arthur St. Clare is not with the Bible, but with his assumptions—his self-imposed limitations—as an actor in the drama of life and as a reader of this text. To suggest, as Chesterton does, that the "printer reads a Bible for misprints" or that the "Christian scientist reads his [Bible], and finds we have no arms and legs" is to intimate that the perspective of the reader has utterly overthrown the alterity of the authorial intention underpinning the text, as well as the text's actual meaning.[255] In other words,

252. Ibid., 167.
253. Ibid.
254. Žižek , In Defense Of Lost Causes, 97.
255. Chesterton, Father Brown, 167.

the reader has taken his own pattern of understanding and assumed that it accounts for everything in the picture before him. This does not give rise to the "birth of the reader," to use Roland Barthes's language, but rather to the death of the reader: the reader, in claiming totalitarian ownership of the meaning of the text, is not reading at all, in the same way that someone who wears a blindfold to an art gallery is not looking at art at all.[256]

By reading like a lunatic—that is, by allowing pattern to precede picture—one relinquishes one's right to understand what is being said. This is to say that the death of the author may be taken as that which oscillates between univocity and equivocity. Chesterton implicitly critiques this dualism in his use of the possessive pronoun: "*his* Bible."[257] The reader, when claiming the ownership of meaning without acknowledging his own prejudices, actually distances himself from the text. Such a split between reader and text misses Chesterton's view of the drama of being. Žižek actually falls into the very trap that Chesterton is trying to warn his reader against: he sees only what he wants to see by what is there, rather than what is meant by what is there. As a consequence, he fails to see at all.

Another way of saying that picture should supersede pattern is to say that intentional story should supersede fragmented and decontextualized propositions. For drama to be present and hermeneutics to be possible, meaning must be meant for something. Alison Milbank notes that to "tell a story, whether one's own or a traditional tale, is to mediate the world in its intentionality and narrative character. . . . [T]o tell a story is to affirm that there is meaning to life, and that experience is shaped and has entelechy."[258] In contrast, the ossification of the reader's reading closes the text and closes the mind of the reader; ideas of interplay, movement, and negotiated meaning are ruled out. Indeed, the problem of the lunatic as it relates to hermeneutics is ultimately that there can be no story.

Furthermore, Milbank argues that it is not surprising that "our own age has such trouble with plotmaking in novels" when "historical pastiche, novels based on real events, or postmodern bricolage" become substitutes for story.[259] The ossification of the reader's interpretation argues that interpretation exists only for its own sake, isolated from further dialogue. There can be no movement, no openness to possibility, and no character development with such an imposition: the unfolding of the story has been decided

---

256. Barthes, "The Death of the Author."

257. Chesterton, *Father Brown*, 167, emphasis added.

258. Milbank, *Chesterton and Tolkien as Theologians*, 11.

259. Ibid.

before the story has even been told or read; the nature of the performance has been determined before the actors have even walked onto the stage.[260]

To summarize, there are essentially five principles at the center of Chesterton's philosophy of common sense that naturally promotes human dignity and an honest hermeneutic. The first is that attitude and doctrine are inextricably linked, meaning that truths about the world need to be framed in such a way that they are both practical and personal. The second is the idea that reality ought to supplant illusion, while acknowledging its place. This suggests that it is generally possible to know the difference between truth and falsehood. This gives rise to the third principle of common sense, which is that good should trump evil. It is this principle that emphasizes Chesterton as a moral philosopher-poet. The fourth principle is that faith, as the bedrock of the interpretive experience, is what guides the understanding of facts. Finally, with the aim of distinguishing between reality and illusion, truth and falsehood, and good and evil, one should look at life as a picture or as a story rather than as a pattern of predictable outcomes. With these principles in place, the dignity of the common man is preserved, and a way is opened for Chesterton's defense of democracy, which is the broad idea that supports the common man and his common sense.

In Defense of Democracy

The greatest critique leveled by Chesterton against his Nietzschean friend Shaw is that he lacks "democratic sentiment."[261] Neither his humanitarianism nor his Socialism are democratic because these are always formulated from the perspective of an egotist and are therefore inherently opposed to the common man and his common sense. Chesterton levels a similar critique against Cardinal John Henry Newman (1801–90) when he says that he lacks "democratic warmth" by neglecting the concerns of the ordinary.[262] For Chesterton, the term *ordinary,* in its correct usage, implies "the acceptance of an order."[263] He writes on the assumption that "ordinary people" share the "common ground" of a "desirability of an active and imaginative life, picturesque and full of a poetical curiosity."[264] This means that "[i]f a man says that extinction is better than existence or blank existence better than variety and adventure," we can be sure that "he is not one of the ordinary people" that

260. See Chesterton, *What's Wrong with the World,* 129–30.
261. Quoted in Ker, *G. K. Chesterton,* 245.
262. Ibid., 331.
263. Quoted in Ahlquist, *Common Sense 101,* 271.
264. Chesterton, *Collected Works, Volume 1,* 212

Chesterton is addressing.[265] Moreover, "[i]f a man prefers nothing," then he can only be given "nothing."[266] By contrast, the truly ordinary man would agree that "we need [in] this life of practical romance . . . the combination of something that is strange and something that is secure. We need so to view the world as to combine an idea of wonder and an idea of welcome. We need to be happy in this wonderland without once being merely comfortable."[267]

In support of this practical romance and the kind of order that he believes is good for everybody, Chesterton affirms that "truth, in whatever form it is apprehended, should be a public possession."[268] This is arguably the impetus behind his involvement as a journalist in the "present stress of life as it is."[269] In connection with this involvement in disseminating truth to the masses, he maintains a democratic core at the heart of his defense of human dignity. He notices that because democracy may be attacked as the political expression of the common sense of the common man, it needs to be very strongly defended.[270] This means that democracy is not only something to defend as a belief, but is something to defend as the foundation of human action and cooperation.[271] Chesterton admits that he is a democrat, but to understand what this means one needs to prioritize his understanding of democracy over any contemporary definition of the word.[272]

William Oddie suggests that Chesterton's love of democracy is more akin to a religious conviction than it is to a political ideology.[273] Democracy means participating in the love and life of God, which certainly has political repercussions: "Once abolish the God, and the government becomes the God."[274] Whatever democracy may mean, it does not mean submitting to the will of an elite few. In fact, elitism is a kind of selfishness that ruins democracy.[275] Democracy is really about the fact that "man corporate, like man individual, has an indestructible right of self-defence."[276] And just as

---

265. Ibid., 212–13.

266. Ibid.

267. Ibid.

268. Quoted in Maycock, "Introduction," 14.

269. Ibid., 14–15.

270. Chesterton, *Illustrated London News*, December 3, 1932.

271. Chesterton, *Collected Works, Volume 5*, 449.

272. Chesterton, *In Defense of Sanity*, 326.

273. Oddie, *Chesterton and the Romance of Orthodoxy*, 191.

274. Chesterton, *Collected Works, Volume 20*, 57.

275. Chesterton, *Illustrated London News*, December 3, 1932.

276. Ibid.

individuals have "a right to [themselves]" so "a nation has a right to itself."[277] Consequently, democracy involves both private opinion and public political aims; still, it is rooted in the principle that politics ought to remain subordinate to domestic concerns.[278] Even in elevating domesticity, however, Chesterton's liberalism is of a kind that insists upon bridging the gap between the private and the public, just as his Catholicism is of a kind that insists upon calling the gap between sacred and the secular orders into question.[279]

Chesterton consequently praises the "enormous truth in the democracy of Christianity" that flattens all variations in material inequalities.[280] Christianity insists that "all men are equal, as all pennies are equal, because the only value in any of them is that they bear the image of the King."[281] Democracy, like religion, is capable of allowing ordinary people to feel extraordinary, but it also has the remarkable quality of making extraordinary people feel ordinary.[282] Democracy is "profoundly Christian" because it is an "attempt to get at the opinion of those who would be too modest to offer it. It is a mystical adventure; it is specially trusting of those who would be too modest to trust themselves."[283]

Chesterton maintains that there are certainly differences in class and qualification, but proposes that such differences ought not to undermine or overrule the human equality that is implied in the notion that man is the image of God. "All men are equal because God loves all equally; and nothing can compare with that equality."[284] Society ultimately fails to uphold democracy when it demeans the value of the common man.[285] Democracy, then, is not constituted by the opportunity to vote and it is certainly not about having the common man elect to be ruled by the egotism of the aristocratic classes.[286] While voting and canvassing remain part of democracy, its primary aim is to allow people to "have the opportunity to govern their own affairs."[287] To most people, this equates to suffrage; but Chesterton suggests that this is not a precise enough way of understanding democracy. In an

277. Ibid.

278. Stapleton, *Christianity, Patriotism, and Nationhood*, 97.

279. Ibid., 127.

280. Oddie, *Chesterton and the Romance of Orthodoxy*, 191.

281. Chesterton, *Charles Dickens*, 10; Ker, *G. K. Chesterton*, 165.

282. Chesterton, *Charles Dickens*, 10.

283. Chesterton, *Collected Works, Volume 1*, 325.

284. Chesterton, *Illustrated London News*, August 27 1932.

285. Chesterton, *The Defendant*, 62.

286. Stapleton, *Christianity, Patriotism, and Nationhood*, 79.

287. Ahlquist, *Common Sense 101*, 155; Ker, *G. K. Chesterton*, 223.

article that was to have a marked effect on Mahatma Gandhi (1869–1948) concerning his ideas on independent Indian rule,[288] he writes that the "test of democracy is not whether people vote, but whether the people rule. The essence of a democracy is that the national tone and spirit of the typical citizen is apparent and striking in the actions of the state."[289] Votes may be one way of achieving this effect "but votes are quite vain if they do not achieve it."[290] There is a difference between having a conquered people demand their own laws and the same people demanding the laws of the conqueror.

Thus, democracy concerns the prospect that ordinary people may actually choose what they want to vote for rather than have it chosen for them.[291] Indeed, democracy implies that politics may be carried out without the interference of politicians, especially considering the likelihood that the "best men" are unlikely to devote themselves to politics.[292] The best men, Chesterton suggests, are more likely to devote themselves, among other things, to practical things like farming pigs and raising children.[293]

By arguing that people should have the right to govern themselves, Chesterton is suggesting that the idea of a singular "Social Organism" is misguided.[294] Just because "every man is a biped, fifty men are not a centipede."[295] The mob ought to be a dynamic arena within which individuals with different styles of being and ways of seeing can interact and affect each other. The individual is great by virtue of his own sense of self-worth and not only by being a piece that fits into a larger puzzle.[296] Democracy even leaves room for the fool to aspire to wisdom, thereby uplifting the rest of the collective.[297] In short, democracy encourages the modest man to aim higher.[298] It allows this "graven image of God" to strive to own his own land and manage his own affairs within his own considered limitations.[299]

288. Chesterton, *Illustrated London News*, September 18, 1909; Ker, *G. K. Chesterton*, 249; Stapleton, *Christianity, Patriotism, and Nationhood*, 106.

289. Ker, *G. K. Chesterton*, 249.

290. Quoted in Stapleton, *Christianity, Patriotism, and Nationhood*, 106.

291. Chesterton, *A Miscellany of Men*, 13, 19.

292. Ibid., 19.

293. Ibid.

294. Chesterton, *What's Wrong with the World*, 15.

295. Ibid.

296. Ker, *G. K. Chesterton*, 165.

297. Chesterton, *Charles Dickens*, 9; Ker, *G. K. Chesterton*, 165.

298. Chesterton, *Collected Works, Volume 1*, 325; Ker, *G. K. Chesterton*, 224.

299. Chesterton, *What's Wrong with the World*, 42.

To defend his perspective on the common sense of the common man, Chesterton jokes that, when someone "says that democracy is false because most people are stupid," one of the most appropriate and obvious philosophical responses would be to "hit him smartly and with precision on the exact tip of the nose."[300] The idea that most people are stupid is the equivalent of seeing the world in terms of a particular, restrictive pattern instead of seeing it as a picture. The word *stupid* is too relative to be helpful. To say that most people are stupid is as stupid as saying that most people are tall. It is obvious that "'tall' can only mean taller than most people," thus making it "absurd to denounce the majority of mankind as below the average of mankind."[301]

In any case, the stupidity of people is not a reasonable argument for abolishing democracy. The academic aristocracy may wish that a man would do something only if he does it well,[302] but this would violate human freedom and thus also human dignity. The common man wants to write his own love letters and blow his own nose. He wants to do these things for himself "even if he does them badly."[303] Chesterton summarizes "democratic faith" as the notion that "the most terribly important things must be left to ordinary men themselves."[304] This would include things like procreating, raising children, and setting up the laws of the state.[305] The practical essence of democracy may be framed as that which sets up the ordinary as an ideal and therefore allows for the "Ideal Grocer," the "Ideal Plumber" and the "Ideal Postman."[306] Here, the reality and the ideal are seen as one and the same thing. Democracy allows man to truly be himself instead of always trying to be someone else.

There are a great many things that masquerade as democracy that are ultimately detrimental to democracy: "Modernity is not democracy; machinery is not democracy; the surrender of everything to trade and commerce is not democracy. Capitalism is not democracy; and is, by trend and savour, rather against democracy. Plutocracy by definition is not democracy."[307] Chesterton views the essence of democracy as being both simple and self-evident. It is the idea that if "ten men are wrecked together

300. Chesterton, *Alarms and Discursions,* 28.

301. Ibid.

302. Chesterton, *Collected Works, Volume 1,* 250.

303. Ibid.

304. Ibid.

305. Ibid.

306. Chesterton, *The Defendant,* 63.

307. Chesterton, *Illustrated London News,* July 16, 1932.

on an island, the community consists of those ten men, their welfare is the social object, and normally their will is the social law."[308] If one of those men wishes to plan a voyage or distill water, he may defend his choice in relation to the sovereignty of the community. He is, in short, "the servant of the community."[309] If he violates the authority and welfare of his community, his community will rightly see no reason to submit to him. The individual's enterprise must therefore be seen in relation to the rule of his community. His enterprise is not just a matter of economics and personal gain, but must be understood within a larger social context. The same may be said of Chesterton's dramatic hermeneutic: interpretation is not just about the whims of the individual, but is also about the ways that it may affect and interact with the views of a community.

It is because of the social dimension of human endeavors that Chesterton especially critiques the materialist doctrines of capitalism and communism. Whilst representing different approaches to economics, they share a focus on price instead of on value, and therefore reduce people to being merely tools of a transactional system. Thus, for example, instead of being considered as things to eat, apples are only considered as "things to sell."[310] Conceptions of the "Good" are disposed of in favor of the "Goods," and the whole world is soon reconfigured solely in terms of production and consumption.[311] Chesterton writes that in the particular case of capitalism, it is nonsensical to say that "Trade is Good" since this would be tantamount to worshipping "the means instead of the end," as well as forgetting the intrinsic value of things.[312] In keeping with his preference for concrete expression over linguistic abstraction, he suggests that we should be asking whether economics and trade support the inherent goodness of life and living. One should ask, in this case, whether economics was made for man instead of man for economics; for, in the end, nothing can be built

> upon the utterly unphilosophical philosophy of blind buying and selling; of bullying people into purchasing what they do not want; of making it badly so that they may break it and imagine they want it again; of keeping rubbish in rapid circulation like a dust-storm in a desert; and pretending that you are teaching

308. Ibid.

309. Ibid.

310. Chesterton, *In Defense of Sanity*, 263.

311. Ibid., 264.

312. Ibid.

men to hope, because you do not leave them one intelligent instant in which to despair.[313]

Because of his democratic leanings, Chesterton again emphasizes the importance of tradition, which manages to avoid this materialist reductionism.[314] Tradition is "democracy extended through time."[315] It is what takes the voice of the common man into account even if that man is no longer present to speak for himself. Chesterton notices that when a person appeals to the work of "some German historian" instead of appealing to the "tradition of the Catholic Church," he is again ruling that the perspective of the aristocracy should supersede the opinion of the man on the street.[316] This is analogous to neglecting the stories told by the sane "authority of the mob" in favor of a book written by the one person in the village who is mad.[317]

> Tradition may be defined as an extension of the franchise. Tradition means giving votes to the most obscure of all classes, our ancestors. It is the democracy of the dead. Tradition refuses to submit to the small and arrogant oligarchy of those who merely happen to be walking about. All democrats object to men being disqualified by the accident of birth; tradition objects to their being disqualified by the accident of death. Democracy tells us not to neglect a good man's opinion, even if he is our groom; tradition asks us not to neglect a good man's opinion, even if he is our father. I, at any rate, cannot separate the two ideas of democracy and tradition; it seems evident to me that they are the same idea. We will have the dead at our councils. The ancient Greeks voted by stones; these shall vote by tombstones. It is all quite regular and official, for most tombstones, like most ballot papers, are marked with a cross.[318]

For Chesterton, "the men of the past, being dead, are alive. They are realities. They are rivals. They are something successful, something definite, and something different."[319] Counter-intuitively, though, Chesterton underscores his appreciation of the marriage of democracy and tradition by suggesting that his philosophy was shaped primarily by fairy tales.[320] Fairyland,

313. Ibid., 269.

314. Chesterton, *Collected Works, Volume 1*, 251.

315. Ibid.

316. Ibid.

317. Ibid.

318. Ibid.

319. Chesterton, *Illustrated London News*, June 1, 1907.

320. Chesterton, *Collected Works, Volume 1*, 252.

for Chesterton, is "nothing, but the sunny country of common sense."[321] From fairy tales, one is able to gain a number of helpful insights and healthy principles. These stories are capable of pointing to the reality of how things actually work. Thus, for example, "Jack and the Giant Killer" exposes the pride of the tyrant and suggests that "giants should be killed because they are gigantic" and "Beauty and the Beast" teaches that love precedes lovability.[322] For Chesterton, therefore, stories are the worlds that reality is made of. Stories, with their firm adherence to reason, their affirmation of human responsibility and choice, as well as their promotion of the genuine possibility of miracles, are capable of reminding us who we are.[323] Stories promote the best of all commonsense attitudes, namely that of gratitude: the feeling of adventure that permeates an existence open to being in awe of the world.[324] Stories expose the stale complacency of an audience by suggesting that a dance of wills lies behind every action in this human drama. The following passage, which has a bearing on defamiliarization discussed later, illuminates Chesterton's view on repetitions that exist in nature and in the human story:

> We always fall into the mistake of supposing that if a thing repeats itself it must be mechanical, or what we call dead. But . . . a thing might repeat itself because it is very much alive. It might repeat itself because it was much too alive to want to leave off. You may observe this phenomenon in babies. A young child will go on throwing the same ball or singing the same words until all the adults are on the edge of insanity and murder. But the child does not act monotonously because he is mechanical. He acts monotonously because he is so full of vitality. I believe myself that the universe is monotonous like a child's game because there is behind it an unexhausted Will. And whether or not you believe this, it is certainly as rational a hypothesis as the automatical hypothesis.[325]

Like a child, Chesterton repeats this idea in *Orthodoxy*:

> All the towering materialism which dominates the modern mind rests ultimately upon one assumption; a false assumption. It is supposed that if a thing goes on repeating itself it is probably dead; a piece of clockwork. People feel that if the universe

321. Ibid.
322. Ibid., 253.
323. Ibid., 255–57, 263.
324. Ibid., 268.
325. Chesterton, *Daily News*, January 24, 1906.

was personal it would vary; if the sun were alive it would dance. This is a fallacy even in relation to known fact. For the variation in human affairs is generally brought into them, not by life, but by death; by the dying down or breaking off of their strength or desire. A man varies his movements because of some slight element of failure or fatigue. He gets into an omnibus because he is tired of walking; or he walks because he is tired of sitting still. . . . The sun rises every morning. I do not rise every morning; but the variation is due not to my activity, but to my inaction. Now, to put the matter in a popular phrase, it might be true that the sun rises regularly because he never gets tired of rising. His routine might be due, not to a lifelessness, but to a rush of life. The thing I mean can be seen, for instance, in children, when they find some game or joke that they specially enjoy. A child kicks his legs rhythmically through excess, not absence, of life. Because children have abounding vitality, because they are in spirit fierce and free, therefore they want things repeated and unchanged. They always say, "Do it again"; and the grown-up person does it again until he is nearly dead. For grown-up people are not strong enough to exult in monotony. But perhaps God is strong enough to exult in monotony. It is possible that God says every morning, "Do it again" to the sun; and every evening, "Do it again" to the moon. It may not be automatic necessity that makes all daisies alike; it may be that God makes every daisy separately, but has never got tired of making them. It may be that He has the eternal appetite of infancy; for we have sinned and grown old, and our Father is younger than we.[326]

Žižek rightly argues that, for Chesterton, "reality and magic are far from being simply opposed—the greatest magic is that of reality itself, the fact that there really is such a wonderful, rich world out there."[327] Furthermore, he writes that this insistence upon the magic of the ordinary is perpetuated in Chesterton's insistence upon what he calls the "dialectical tension between creativity and repetition."[328] In this argumentative reversal, Chesterton insists that what seems most mechanical is really the greatest indicator of personality. The absence of choice would more likely produce chaos than order.

Here, even the pattern is transformed into a picture—something mysteriously willed into being and now accessibly part of the human experience. In the end, the human drama is found within the context of a much larger

326. Chesterton, *Collected Works, Volume 1*, 263–64.

327. Žižek , *The Puppet and the* Dwarf, 40.

328. Ibid.

drama, and the pursuit of human dignity is sustained by something beyond the obvious boundaries of experience. This is the notion that permeates every defense discussed in this chapter. Chesterton recognizes that the fairy stories that he discovered as a child have a sense of purpose, and that this sense of purpose permeates the whole of human existence. Furthermore, these same fairy stories have a sense of personality at their center, the same sort of personality that Chesterton finds in all aspects of reality. He therefore concludes that just as there is always a storyteller behind the fantastical narratives of Fairyland, there must also be a storyteller behind the even more fantastical lives of ordinary human beings.[329] For him, even the commonplace affirms the supernatural, and the common indicates the sacred. And this sacredness is not limited, but, as was made evident in the discussion of the foundation of Chesterton's hermeneutic awareness, is something that permeates the whole of existence. This, however, is a truth hidden in a field of truths; hidden, that is, in plain sight. The sheer ubiquity of the sacred and the awe-inspiring is often what renders it invisible to us. And so, there is a need for us to find ways to awaken to it again. To help the reader to do this—to help the reader to see things as they are again—Chesterton turns to the tools of analogy, paradox, defamiliarization, and humor.

329. Chesterton, *Collected Works, Volume 1*, 264.

5

The Tools of Chesterton's Hermeneutic

Analogy

Thus far, I have outlined the philosophical context within which Chesterton operates. I have also suggested that the primary task of his hermeneutic is to promote and sustain human dignity. I have therefore argued that interpretation does not deal primarily with detached abstractions, but is something that is always rooted in one's actual posture towards existence. This means that one's hermeneutic will tend to gravitate to the possibility of some kind of existential relevance. It has already been shown that Chesterton's hermeneutic posture may be thought of as an ethical attitude geared towards preserving the voice and value of the ordinary man amidst the narrow-minded clamor and biases of elitist ideology.

In the present chapter, I discuss the tools of Chesterton's hermeneutic. These are the primary rhetorical and poetic considerations that drive his thinking towards reconciliation, reconstruction, reform, renewal, restoration, and revolution.[1] This focus starts with Hugh Kenner's contention that Chesterton's two strategies for engaging with reality are analogy and paradox.[2] However, to this I would add two further strategies. The first is that of defamiliarization, which is embedded in his use of analogy and paradox, and the second is the strategy of humor, which expresses the paradoxical/metaxological posture towards being that Chesterton encourages.

---

1. Chesterton, *Autobiography*, 324; Chesterton, *Collected Works, Volume 1*, 310, 315; Chesterton, *Collected Works, Volume 5*, 426; Chesterton, *The Everlasting Man*, 241.

2. Kenner, *Paradox in Chesterton*, 24–25.

As explained in more detail below, there is an idea that directs Chesterton's use of analogy, paradox, defamiliarization, and humor, namely the idea of the incarnation. I have already noted that the defense of the common man that is the task of his hermeneutic is reflected best in the ideal common man that is represented by the Jesus of the Gospels.[3] Thus, it should be understood that the incarnation is Chesterton's primary interpretive key. It is the anchor that unites the various strands that have been set forward in this and previous chapters. It is, as Ralph Wood notes, "the lens for detecting what is evil and what is good, what reflects the glory of God and what obscures it."[4] The very emphasis of this book on the marriage of theory and application, and the union of principles with concrete experience reflects this mysterious incarnational paradox, which is the "first act of the divine drama," whereby the word becomes flesh "on a dark and curtained stage sunken out of sight."[5]

To position Chesterton's use of analogy in terms of his defense of human dignity, one can begin with the first principle of Chesterton's common sense, namely that attitude and doctrine are interwoven. For this reason, his use of analogy is highly intuitive. Moreover, his entire mode of thinking is bound to the "wild" ethical idea of "decorum," which is analogical because it suggests that one ought to behave in a way that is congruent with one's being.[6] And, as emphasized in the previous chapter, being is a drama that unfolds in the company of other beings and in participating in Being. It is precisely this that makes decorum wild for Chesterton: it is the "wildness with which a man binds himself by one pattern of behavior when he might be sampling twenty million."[7]

It is that same wildness that is embedded, for instance, in a rash vow, which is a promise or even a compromise that binds one being to another, and allows one's conscious thoughts to be constrained by a larger reality.[8] For Chesterton, this larger reality is formed within the context of a Trinitarian God who is in his very nature love.[9] Love acts as a limitation, because it

3. Chesterton, *The Everlasting Man,* 185; Chesterton, *The Man Who Was Orthodox,* 120; Milbank, "The Double Glory," 177.

4. Wood, *Chesterton,* 214.

5. Chesterton, *The Everlasting Man,* 173.

6. Kenner, *Paradox in Chesterton,* 29; Chesterton, *What's Wrong with the World,* 48; Chesterton, *William Blake,* 177.

7. Chesterton, *William Blake,* 179.

8. Chesterton, *The Defendant,* 39; Chesterton, *The Everlasting Man,* 52; Chesterton, *What's Wrong with the World,* 48.

9. Chesterton, *The Everlasting Man,* 228.

"is in the nature of love to bind itself."[10] The idea that love is the foundation of being fits in with Chesterton's affirmation, as per the Athanasian Creed, of the Trinitarian nature of God.[11] If God is at all conceivable, he must be conceived of firstly as a God of love and relationship rather than a "God of colourless and remote cosmic control [like] the God of the stoics and agnostics."[12]

This means that the very act of creation is itself an act of love. Chesterton argues that love in the nature of God appears to complicate the essence of a divine deity who is as "isolated and simplified" as the God of Islam.[13] Ian Ker notes that, for Chesterton, the Trinity "seems a contradiction in terms."[14] As a statement concerning God's Being, the Trinity is one of the "great mysteries": a paradoxical belief that views God as being both one and three.[15] It is in this very paradox that the Trinity ought to be understood as a testament of the personality of God and of the fundamental relationality of Being. As such, it promotes interdependence, intimacy, and kind of infinite immediacy. Love, the central component of the romance of being, is fundamental to the character of God. It brings unity, specificity, direction, and wholeness to the dialectic of riddle and answer. Therefore, when the God of the Christian Scriptures observes that it is "not good for man to be alone," he is proposing that the expression of the community of his own Being ought to be evident to some extent in the drama of his creation. It therefore follows that "it is not well for God to be alone."[16]

Chesterton's use of analogy is also rooted in the second principle of common sense, which concerns the fact of reality. Analogy is the mode of thinking that accounts both for the complexity of reality and for the limits of language in its ability to explain reality.[17] It is that which allows for the interconnectedness of things and thus the participation between a sign and the actual thing it refers to. It also makes room for the differences between things, like the difference between the sign and the thing it refers to. In short, as Kenner notes, "analogy has to do with comparison."[18] It is the idea

---

10. Chesterton, *The Defendant*, 23.

11. Chesterton, *Collected Works, Volume 1*, 340; Chesterton, *The Everlasting Man*, 227; *Saint Thomas Aquinas, Saint Francis of Assisi*, 79.

12. Chesterton, *The Everlasting Man*, 228.

13. Ibid.

14. Ker, *G. K. Chesterton*, 119.

15. Chesterton, *Collected Works, Volume 3*, 299.

16. Chesterton, *Collected Works, Volume 1*, 340.

17. Kenner, *Paradox in Chesterton*, 27.

18. Ibid., 25.

that reality may be understood primarily by juxtaposing things to see how they affect each other. Analogy is the device by which one finds "agreement between agreement and disagreement."[19] It is the tool by which difference and sameness gain their meaning. For this reason, Chesterton argues that "[m]en tell more truth by their metaphors than by their statements" of fact.[20] For him, metaphor, as one type of analogy, can be less restrictive in its representation of truths. It is not limited to literalism, and so its inside is always larger than its outside.[21]

I have already noted that Chesterton points to the dignity of man as the measure of all things, and the ideal dignified man that he has in mind is Jesus of Nazareth.[22] As he reflects on the lives and work of two of his heroes, St. Francis and St. Thomas, he recognizes that one could praise each for different reasons. St. Francis, on the one hand, may be said to have "saved us from being Buddhists" simply by loving animals and St. Thomas, on the other hand, may be said to have "saved us from being [mere] Platonists" by taking the whole of Greek philosophy into account.[23] However, both of them, in various ways, embody a singular "truth in its simplest form": "both reaffirmed the Incarnation, by bringing God back to earth."[24] While Chesterton is writing about these two saints, he reveals his own intention to affirm "a dogma that is now often regarded as the most superstitious Super-humanism," namely "that staggering doctrine of the Incarnation" that is the center of the Christian faith.[25]

The paradox of the incarnation is explained by Robert Farrar Capon as "*true* God and *perfect* man in an *inseparable, but unconfused* union in *One Person.*"[26] Jesus is called "*true*" God as a reminder that "[h]e is all the God there is; there is no God at all that is not in him."[27] He is called "*perfect*" as a reminder that he is the drama of meaning as it was meant to be before the fall, as well as the promise of perfection at the end of things.[28] And yet, while his God-nature and his human-nature are found in the same human

---

19. Chesterton, *Autobiography*, 332.

20. Quoted in Knight, *Chesterton and Evil*, 376.

21. Chesterton, *Autobiography*, 49; Chesterton, *Saint Thomas Aquinas, Saint Francis of Assisi*, 131.

22. Chesterton, *The Everlasting Man*, 185.

23. Chesterton, *Saint Thomas Aquinas, Saint Francis of Assisi*, 28.

24. Ibid.

25. Ibid., 33–34.

26. Capon, *The Romance of the Word*, 309.

27. Ibid.

28. Ibid.

form, his divinity and his humanity ought not to be muddled. Differences need to be affirmed, not conflated. For example, to hold that Jesus thinks divine thoughts with his human mind is to destroy the paradox: the perfect man becomes a superman and is then no longer fully human. This paradox, therefore, is not a fusion of opposites, but the meeting of opposites that are held in tension.

In simple terms, the paradox of the incarnation refers to the belief "that deity or sanctity has attached to matter or entered the world of the senses."[29] It is a paradox, but also an event, which is illustrated towards the end of Chesterton's *The Surprise* when the Author, having observed the various disconnections and disharmonies that have resulted from the choices of his actors, pokes his head through the top of the scenery and speaks to the actors: "And in the devil's name, what do you think you are doing with my play? Drop it! Stop! I'm coming down."[30] While more will be said shortly about the structural significance of the incarnation for Chesterton in relation to paradox, it suffices to say for now that it is the key to understanding his use of analogy. To regard Jesus as the interpretive anchor in any discussion on the dignity of man is also to regard him as the key to any discussion of the divine. One example of this is found in the idea that St. Francis himself was a "Mirror of Christ."[31] For Chesterton, the dignity of St. Francis is found in his being compared to the figure of Christ. However, this is not to say that St. Francis loved mere abstractions. Rather, he is an example of one who "did not love humanity, but men" and also "did not love Christianity, but Christ."[32] This demonstrates the priority of the concrete over the abstract in Chesterton's reference to the incarnation.

Analogy is the cornerstone of epistemology because it allows for things to be explained, and it is also foundational to ontology because, as Kenner emphasizes, "*being is intrinsically analogical.*"[33] Analogy is also dramatic, because the world may be said to be a "network of analogies."[34] The primary point of Chesterton's use of analogy is that there is a definite sense of the coherence of life, which implies that a coherence of perception and meaning are also possible. He is acutely aware of the mysteriousness of life and therefore of the inexplicability of many things, and yet he notices that

---

29. Chesterton, *Saint Thomas Aquinas, Saint Francis of Assisi*, 38.

30. Chesterton, *The Surprise*, 63.

31. Chesterton, *Saint Thomas Aquinas, Saint Francis of Assisi*, 196.

32. Ibid., 196.

33. Kenner, *Paradox in Chesterton*, 27.

34. Ibid., 35.

there is a similarity even in the difference between the mysterious and the obvious.[35] Again, we notice difference only on the basis of similarity.

Thus, to say that there are things that are unknown is to imply that there are things that can be known, including the fact that we can know things as unknowable. Analogy concerns the way that everything holds together: "things can be different and yet [still] be things."[36] It is by his use of analogy that Chesterton affirms that the "things that differ are one" and in this way he continually thanks "All Being for the multiplicity of beings."[37] Consequently, analogy may be understood as a sacrament: it is that which inevitably points to the reconciliation of creation to God.

Giorgio Agamben writes that "analogy is opposed to the dichotomous principle dominating Western logic."[38] He goes on: "Against the drastic alternative 'A or B,' which excludes the third, analogy imposes its *tertium datur*, its stubborn 'neither A nor B.' In other words, analogy intervenes in the dichotomies of logic (particular/universal; form/content; lawfulness/exemplarity; and so on) not to take them up into a higher synthesis, but to transform them into a force field traversed by polar tensions."[39] This explanation stresses what is so evident in Chesterton's writings, namely that analogy resists reduction to mere structure. Rather, it suggests the transformation of structure into engagement with the drama. It insists upon a self-critical mechanism that self-reflexively admits that the theory is not the reality even while it participates in reality. Analogy thereby invites a deeper involvement in a larger story with all its mysteries and revelations.

Saying that man is the image of God is akin to saying that man is the analogy of God. Man is both like and unlike God. He should not be separated from God and yet he should still be distinguished from God.[40] For example, like God, man has the quality of personal presence and yet the reach of man's presence is obviously limited in a way that God's is not. It would be fair to state that since God created man for good, God is good. But it would be absurd to say that man is as good as God or that man necessarily chooses to remain good, since that would be tantamount to declaring that man and God are absolutely the same thing.[41] Just as the impression of a stamp does not necessarily indicate what the entire stamp looks like,

---

35. Chesterton, *Collected Works, Volume 1*, 79.

36. Kenner, *Paradox in Chesterton*, 26.

37. Ibid., 34.

38. Agamben, *The Signature of All Things*, 19.

39. Ibid.

40. Chesterton, *Saint Thomas Aquinas, Saint Francis of Assisi*, 36.

41. Kenner, *Paradox in Chesterton*, 27.

analogy indicates that it may not necessarily be possible to understand the purity of the goodness of God simply by looking at man, unless, perhaps, that man is Christ. Analogy suggests that it is possible for goodness to be "possessed by man and by God, but not in the same way."[42] This is to imply that the way one thinks, acts, and interprets must necessarily be congruent with the totality of one's being.[43]

Kenner explains this issue of congruency by citing Aquinas's example that "angels know as angels are" just as "men know as men are."[44] Accordingly, if man is confronted with "angelic knowledge," it may seem incongruent to say that he knows anything at all.[45] The question embedded in this assertion relates to how man can know something that transcends his own epistemological and ontological limitations. However, the trouble here is not primarily with the limitations of his language, but with the noticeable difference between his own being and the being of angels. Man can only understand and interpret as man. Moreover, each individual can only interpret as himself. This means that whatever he understands of that which is beyond himself needs to be translated via and for his own framework of being. This translatability is precisely what the tool of analogy supports. It allows for mysterious transcendence via the surprise of the immanent.

Chesterton takes this idea further when he notices that the understanding of individuals is affected by the particular mental worlds that they inhabit. To explain what he means, he refers to the story of the Tower of Babel found in Genesis 11:

> Among the cloudy and symbolic stories in the beginning of the Bible there is one about a tower built with such vertical energy as to take a hold on heaven, but ruined and resulting only in a confusion of tongues. The story might be interpreted in many ways—religiously, as meaning that spiritual insolence starts all human separations; irreligiously, as meaning that the inhuman heavens grudge man his magnificent dream; or merely satirically as suggesting that all attempts to reach a higher agreement always end in more disagreement than there was before. It might be taken by the partially intelligent Kensitite as a judgment on Latin Christians for talking Latin. It might be taken by the somewhat less intelligent Professor Harnack as a final proof that all prehistoric humanity talked German. But when all was said, the symbol would remain that a plain tower, as straight as

42. Ibid., 28.
43. Ibid., 29.
44. Ibid.
45. Ibid.

a sword, as simple as a lily, did nevertheless produce the deepest divisions that have been known among men.[46]

In the above passage, Chesterton begins with the story as he understands it, but then argues immediately that the meaning of the text, while lending itself to a particular direction of interpretation, namely how a collective task brought about actual divisions, is not absolutely self-evident when taken in light of different perspectives or prejudices. Chesterton's selection of the story is particularly interesting when considering that the real sin of Babel was found in the monomania of unity, which essentially amounted to the support of empire and oppression.[47] Against this violence, God steps down to multiply languages. Division and difference, as Chesterton concedes, are signs of love.[48]

The point of this plurality, though, is that the brute facts may not be brute facts. The text is interpreted by each reader just as various musicians may interpret the same piece of music differently. Chesterton demonstrates the truth of this via an interpretive experiment performed while being "locked up in a third-class [railway] carriage for a rather long journey" without any "books or newspapers" or even "a pencil or scrap of paper with which to write a religious epic."[49]

> There were no advertisements on the walls of the carriage, otherwise I could have plunged into a study of them, for any collection of printed words is quite enough to suggest infinite complexities of mental ingenuity. When I find myself opposite the words "Sunlight Soap" I can exhaust all the aspects of Sun Worship, Apollo, and Summer poetry before I go on to the less congenial subject of soap. But there was no printed word or picture anywhere; there was nothing, but blank wood inside the carriage and blank wet without. Now I deny most energetically that anything is, or can be, uninteresting. So I stared at the joints of the walls and seats, and began thinking hard on the fascinating subject of wood. Just as I had begun to realise why, perhaps, it was that Christ was a carpenter, rather than a bricklayer, or a baker, or anything else, I suddenly started upright, and remembered my pockets. I was carrying about with me an unknown treasury. I had a British Museum and a South

---

46. Chesterton, *Collected Works, Volume 5*, 489.

47. Smith, *The Fall of Interpretation*, 58.

48. Chesterton, *Collected Works, Volume 1*, 336; Chesterton, *Collected Works, Volume 20*, 596.

49. Chesterton, *Tremendous Trifles*, 75–76.

Kensington collection of unknown curios hung all over me in
different places. I began to take the things out.[50]

While he allows for almost any kind of imaginative hermeneutic,
and seems to especially encourage an almost wild foray into subjectivity,
Chesterton nevertheless discourages any ironclad interpretation that may
be "flatly contradicted by an obvious fact."[51] He is also clear that there is a
problem with assuming a theory to be the obvious explanation of any obvious fact.[52] The most obvious fact remains the prejudicial limitations of the
reader, who is in all likelihood only capable of seeing what he is expecting
to see.

Analogy as the bedrock of Chestertonian interpretation in its affirmation of the being of man is also the foundation for interpreting the world
in all its diversity. In one passage, Chesterton discloses his view on analogy as well as his remarkable "intuition of being" or "instinct for Being"
by noting that Aquinas's "first sense of fact is a fact."[53] In this observation,
facts themselves are understood has having a strange quality because they
are "largely in a state of change from being one thing to being another."[54]
Moreover, their being is always bound to the being of other things, meaning that being is understood in relational terms. But this dynamism does
not undo or destabilize being, nor does it render everything merely relative
or unreal. Instead, it affirms that things can only be one thing at a time,
as well as the simple idea that what is perceived must be understood as
being incomplete. This implies what is complete and unchanging, namely
God.[55] Chesterton, like Aquinas, is always defending the "independence
of dependent things" and therefore, by implication, also the dependence of
independent things.[56]

Chesterton contemplates the possibility that ultimately, by his limitations, man is able to recognize and pay tribute to the ultimate reality and the
ultimate perfection that is God. In the end, "God is more actual even than
Man; more actual even than matter; for God with all His powers at every
instant is immortally in action."[57] This statement may seem at first to be en-

---

50. Ibid., 76.

51. Chesterton, *Saint Thomas Aquinas, Saint Francis of Assisi*, 82.

52. Ibid.

53. Chesterton, *Saint Thomas Aquinas, Saint Francis of Assisi*, 154; Kenner, *Paradox in Chesterton*, 30, 36.

54. Chesterton, *Saint Thomas Aquinas, Saint Francis of Assisi*, 154.

55. Ibid., 154; *Collected Works, Volume 1*, 79.

56. Chesterton, *Saint Thomas Aquinas, Saint Francis of Assisi*, 36.

57. Ibid., 156.

forcing a middle-Platonist rupture between a human unreality and a divine reality, but this is not what Chesterton is aiming at. Rather, his intention is to point out that ultimately man is only real by virtue of his participation in the broad daylight of the perfection of God's Being.[58] Man's being is not something achieved by thinking in isolation, but something that is already part of God's drama. Being is not the result of thinking, as in the Cartesian *cogito*, but of Being. However, Chesterton seems to be intimating that the limited awareness of the individual may be a barrier to recognizing this.

Participation simply means "to take part in something."[59] The Thomist doctrine of participation, which is the doctrine that Chesterton adheres to, is "a theory for rendering intelligible a 'many' in any order in terms of a higher one."[60] I have already expressed this analogical idea by implication: Chesterton's morality is framed within a complex drama that I have argued is the foundation of his hermeneutic. The idea of participation is therefore a means for explaining what is held in common by a particular ontological order. Accordingly, one belongs to another by virtue of one's participation. Rudi Te Velde explains that "when a characteristic or perfection is possessed by a subject in only a partial or particular fashion, such a subject can be said to participate in that perfection."[61] Therefore, participation essentially involves "receiving partially from another."[62] This means that the subject cannot be said to be indistinguishable from the perfection it possesses, which in turn opens up the possibility that other subjects may participate in the same perfection.

This participation takes place in three different ways. In the first place, it applies to the "logical relations of species, genus and individual."[63] For example, to say that an individual person participates in the species called man is to say, in accordance with Chesterton's defense of the common man, that the individual shares in those things that are common to all men and yet remains distinct in his own being. He is both the same as and different from man. His own being is not identical with what is called human nature and yet he shares in human nature.[64] To say that the many participate in

---

58. Ibid., 157.

59. Te Velde, *Participation and Substantiality in Thomas Aquinas*, 11.

60. Chesterton, *Saint Thomas Aquinas, Saint Francis of Assisi*, 37; Clarke, *Explorations in Metaphysics*, 92.

61. Te Velde, *Participation and Substantiality in Thomas Aquinas*, 11.

62. Clarke, *Explorations in Metaphysics*, 93.

63. Te Velde, *Participation and Substantiality in Thomas Aquinas*, 11.

64. Ibid., 12.

the one is to say that there is a unique source.[65] Thus, mere diversity is an insufficient reason for dissimilarity. There must be a transcendent order by which diversity is interrelated. Additionally, the possibility of participation suggests that the source must be superabundant by nature.[66] In Aquinas's view, this application of participation is fundamentally logical rather than ontological, thus emphasizing the uniqueness of each individual and species.[67] It is by this logical relation that the difference between things may be underscored.

Participation also concerns the basic limitations of being, namely the idea that the participant needs to actually be capable of participating in the same kind of perfection that is possessed by the source, albeit in a partial way.[68] The second type of participation therefore "concerns the relations of matter-form and subject-accident."[69] This is to say that the "receiving principle may be said to participate in the received form."[70] Accordingly, for instance, a planted acorn as the receiving principle is only able to participate in the received form of the oak tree that it is going to become and cannot, by reasons of the limitations of its own being, participate, at least insofar as oakishness is concerned, in the form of an elm tree or a barberry shrub. Moreover, the original source is confined, insofar as participation is concerned, to the restrictions of the subject or specific instance of matter in which it is received. The corollary of this kind of participation is found in a third kind of participation, which states that the participating subject may be said to be dependent upon the source. An effect may therefore be said to participate in its cause even "when the effect is not equal to the power of its cause."[71] This idea is illustrated by the Dionysian analogy that objects may be illuminated by sunlight even though they are incapable of withstanding the full force of the sun.[72]

While Chesterton is not nearly as technical as Aquinas in his approach to analogy and participation, he holds the opinion that man participates in the perfection of God, because he was made in the image of God; and since God is a creator, it makes sense that man, as the image of God, would be one

65. Clarke, *Explorations in Metaphysics*, 94.

66. Ibid.

67. Te Velde, *Participation and Substantiality in Thomas Aquinas*, 12.

68. Clarke, *Explorations in Metaphysics*, 93.

69. Te Velde, *Participation and Substantiality in Thomas Aquinas*, 13.

70. Ibid.

71. Clarke, *Explorations in Metaphysics*, 93; Te Velde, *Participation and Substantiality in Thomas Aquinas*, 14.

72. Te Velde, *Participation and Substantiality in Thomas Aquinas*, 14.

too.[73] Thus, he attacks any mindset that would render everything only separate and therefore without unity. Chesterton's ontology, with its emphasis on analogy and participation, implies the transcendence of absolute distinctions between subject and object that are standard in positivist-empiricist hermeneutic regimes. Thus, he allows for the possibility of our being influenced and moved by what we perceive instead of merely objectifying the world. The modernist, on the contrary, renders the world in terms of isolation instead of participation and transaction instead of drama. Chesterton notices, for example, that according to this mindset property becomes an issue of money alone and sex becomes isolated from love, thereby eradicating the dramatic pleasures of domesticity and procreation. He argues that "[i]n both cases an incidental, isolated, servile and even secretive pleasure is substituted for participation in a great creative process; even in the everlasting Creation of the world."[74]

The centrality of participation in creation is metareferentially expressed in Chesterton's last novel—the play-like, dialogue-driven *The Return of Don Quixote* (1927)—through the character of Michael Herne, a reclusive librarian who is asked to play a small role in a play called "Blondel the Troubadour."[75] Herne initially declines the request, complaining that the play falls into a historical period—the Middle Ages—that he knows nothing about. However, he changes his mind after recognizing the similarities between his own field of expertise and the one the in the play. Chesterton depicts Herne as a highly astute, scholarly, eccentric lover of solitude. He is also very well read, especially in the history of the Hittites. Therefore, when he finally decides to act in the play, Herne ends up "[devouring] volume after volume about the history, philosophy, theology, ethics and economics of the four medieval centuries, in the hope of fitting himself to deliver the fifteen lines of blank verse allotted by Miss Ashley to the Second Troubadour."[76] At one point, while pondering the relationship between history and the fiction that he is about to reenact, Herne observes the following:

> "I wonder," he said, "how much there is in that term we hear so often 'Too late.' Sometimes it seems to me as if it were either quite true or quite false. Either everything is too late or nothing is too late. It seems somehow to be right on the border of illusion and reality. Every man makes mistakes; they say a man who never makes mistakes never makes anything else. But do you

73. Chesterton, *The Well and the Shallows*, 173; Ahlquist, *Common Sense 101*, 54.

74. Chesterton, *The Well and the Shallows*, 173.

75. Chesterton, *The Return of Don Quixote*, 59.

76. Ibid., 64.

think a man might make a mistake and not make anything else? Do you think he could die having missed the chance to live?"[77]

In this, Herne plants the idea in the reader's mind that one's perception of one's place in time falls between "illusion and reality" and thus opens up the possibility that history is not irrelevant to the human search for experiential meaning in the present, especially since history allows one to ponder other ways of being. Without history, even a history riddled with mistakes, one is likely to miss out on life itself. The inference here is that it is of vital importance to discover one's self within a larger story, in the borderlands between illusion and reality, to discover what it means to participate in a drama.

Herne is later recast as the Outlaw King and he performs his part in the play with great enthusiasm and sincerity. However, after the play is over, Herne refuses to get out of his medieval costume. His obstinate refusal to step out of the drama becomes symbolic of his own revelation that he "found the play [he] acted [to be] something much more real than the life [he had] led."[78] The actor, having been enveloped in his own dramatic interpretive experience, discovers that the inside of the drama is larger than the external drama that he had been living in. He therefore chooses to transport the mystical and moral vision of the Middle Ages into the lunacy of the present. In this scene, Herne is arguably Chesterton's parody of himself. He recognizes the seeming absurdity of insisting upon values and ideals long forgotten, but he also uses Herne to point out that such values and ideals can be rediscovered. Herne becomes a symbol of what it means to be transformed by a deeper participation in the drama of being.

Participation implies that human beings can share in those things that are common to men: Chesterton uses the example of two men sharing a single umbrella and then points out that if each of them has got an umbrella, "they should at least share the rain, with all its rich potentialities of wit and philosophy. 'For He maketh His sun to shine . . . .'"[79] The weather, for Chesterton, is a metaphor for our participation in a much larger drama that is the goodness and perfection of God. It helps us to recognize "human equality" because "we all have our hats under the dark blue spangled umbrella of the universe."[80] While Chesterton repeatedly highlights the divisions and distinctions between things, he always ends up emphasizing the unity of things. God may have broken the universe "into little pieces," but even

---

77. Ibid., 55.

78. Ibid., 200.

79. Chesterton, *What's Wrong with the World*, 69.

80. Ibid.

this division is the result of the very love that binds all things together.[81] Paradox is at the center of this analogy: love both divides and binds; it finds distinction and also union. This is no coincidence. Chesterton's thinking is just as paradoxical as it is analogical. After all, analogy is a means for juxtaposing things to observe how they interact. Analogy suggests a fusion of horizons, where paradox suggests that horizons may also clash.

Paradox

While analogy pertains to comparison, paradox pertains to the shock of contradiction, since "putting things side by side is a necessary preliminary to having them clash."[82] The very idea of analogy contains a paradox highlighted by Chesterton: there is similarity in difference and difference even in similarity. Just as saying that a thing is like another thing is to say that they are not the same thing, so saying that a thing is unlike another thing is to suggest that there is enough of a similarity between the two to make the difference noticeable enough to articulate.

Aidan Nichols observes that Chesterton has suffered grave misunderstandings because of his association with paradox.[83] This is because the word *paradox* is often taken to mean only a philosophical self-contradiction, as we find exemplified especially in many of Zeno's famous paradoxes. In 1901, a reviewer of Chesterton's *The Defendant* remarked that "[p]aradox ought to be used like onions to season the salad. Mr. Chesterton's salad is all onions. Paradox has been defined as 'truth standing on her head to attract attention.' Mr. Chesterton makes truth cut her throat to attract attention."[84]

However, as Nichols observes, the general attitude towards Chestertonian paradox has been positive especially when it is acknowledged as a means for highlighting a particular truth instead of being merely a stylistic device.[85] Ian Ker notes that "Chesterton justified his use of paradox, not as a literary device, but as a tool for understanding the world. Because 'there really is a strand of contradiction running through the universe,' it is impossible to avoid the use of paradox."[86] For him, paradox is fundamental to existence itself.[87] He therefore never agrees with those who assume that he

---

81. Chesterton, *Collected Works, Volume 1*, 337.

82. Kenner, *Paradox in Chesterton*, 25.

83. Nichols, *Chesterton*, 87.

84. Quoted in Ward, *G. K. Chesterton*, 136.

85. Nichols, *Chesterton*, 90.

86. Ker, *G. K. Chesterton*, 83.

87. Ibid., 101.

is merely "paradox-mongering."[88] Chesterton writes, "Mere light sophistry is the thing that I happen to despise most of all things, and it is perhaps a wholesome fact that it is the thing of which I am most generally accused."[89] In his view there is really "nothing so contemptible as a mere paradox; a mere ingenious defense of the indefensible," because it amounts to precisely the kind of "sophistry" that he loathes.[90] It is easy enough to resort to paradox in such a way; "[i]t is as easy as lying; because it is lying."[91]

Chesterton suggests that, broadly speaking, there are two kinds of paradox. He contends that they are not "the good and the bad, nor even the true and the false," but rather the "fruitful and the barren; the paradoxes which produce life an the paradoxes that merely announce death."[92] Furthermore, he says that a "paradox may be a thing unusual, menacing, even ugly—like a rhinoceros. But, as a live rhinoceros ought to produce more rhinoceri, so a live paradox ought to produce more paradoxes."[93] Even if a paradox is nonsense, it should be "suggestive" rather than "abortive."[94] This is to say that paradox should be there to invite debate and discussion. It should be a conversation starter, not a conversation stopper. In keeping with a hermeneutic surplus of meaning, it should trigger thought, not end thought. Chesterton refers to a number of paradoxes concocted by Holbrook Jackson to illustrate what he means. One paradox—"Suffer fools gladly: they may be right"—is clearly "fruitful and free" because "[y]ou can do something with the idea, it opens an avenue."[95] It allows for "the increase of charity," which is fitting since "charity is the imagination of the heart."[96] Another statement offered by Jackson—"Don't think—do"—is regarded by Chesterton as utterly barren, since it is like "Don't eat—digest."[97] It is the sort of idea that eradicates "decisive and dramatic thinking."[98]

As helpful as this distinction between fruitful and barren paradox may be for understanding the moral purpose behind Chesterton's use of paradox, Kenner's categorization of Chestertonian paradox gives more

88. Kenner, *Paradox in Chesterton*, 14.

89. Chesterton, *Collected Works, Volume 1*, 213.

90. Ibid.

91. Ibid.

92. Chesterton, *Illustrated London News*, March 11, 1911.

93. Ibid.

94. Ibid.

95. Ibid.

96. Ibid.

97. Ibid.

98. Ibid.

insight into the specific functions of paradox in his work. For Kenner, the three types of paradox include rhetorical or verbal paradox, metaphysical paradox, and aesthetic paradox.[99] Regarding the first type, Kenner contends that the "special rhetorical purpose of Chesterton is to overcome the mental inertia of human beings."[100] This mental inertia, Kenner argues, is itself a kind of paradox that needs to be uprooted or challenged, for human beings are often caught "in the strange predicament of seeing a thing and not seeing it."[101] For Chesterton, looking a thing does not necessarily imply seeing it properly.[102] Often we "do not even know what is meant by seeing a thing."[103] When the eye is too "lazy" to really see things, there is a need to wake it up.[104] Therefore, the aim of rhetorical paradox, as the name suggests, is persuasion; its focus is on artful deviations that draw attention to what is being said. It is Chesterton's way of encouraging the reader to refuse to let the eye rest.[105] Rhetorical paradox, especially when it is used as frequently as Chesterton uses it, draws attention to the medium of language itself to question how it assists or hinders understanding.

Kenner sees two kinds of verbal paradox in Chesterton.[106] The first calls the reader's own beliefs and perceptions into question by contradicting him. The second has a different target, but the same aim; it contradicts any particular fact to call the reader's perceptions into question. Its purpose is to "[arouse] readers to a realization of their own perception of the fact," making it apparent that the perception "is speculative rather than real."[107] In keeping with the idea of anamnesis already discussed, both kinds of verbal paradox aim to recall a precise sense of the rightness or wrongness of a thing. It takes what is unconscious and brings it out into the light.[108] It would be a mistake, however, to assume that Chesterton is only drawing attention to words and thoughts. As Belloc observes, Chesterton is not a mere "verbalist."[109] Brilliant though he is at playing with words, his aim is not only

---

99. Kenner, *Paradox in Chesterton*, 17–18.

100. Ibid., 43.

101. Ibid.

102. Chesterton, *Selected Works* , 13.

103. Chesterton, *Collected Works, Volume 13*, 344.

104. Chesterton, *Tremendous Trifles*, v.

105. Ibid., v–vi.

106. Kenner, *Paradox in Chesterton*, 47–48.

107. Ibid., 49.

108. Ibid., 49.

109. Belloc, *On the Place of Gilbert Chesterton*, 72.

to conquer mental complacency through momentarily disrupting a pattern of thought, but to elicit and deepen genuine insight.

This is why the second form of paradox is essential to understanding Chesterton. His aim is to introduce a new truth to the reader. "Chesterton is almost never concerned with weaving graceful patterns in the world of appearances."[110] In fact, he openly derides writing that dwells exclusively on style.[111] Clearly, the rhetorical alone is not compelling. What is needed is a genuine encounter with reality itself, and words ought to be the conciliators in this encounter.

Chesterton's arguments are therefore "always metaphysical; which is what justifies the devices."[112] As a consequence, he makes extensive use of metaphysical paradox, which points to the principle that there is "something inherently intractable in being itself; in the Thing," which amounts to saying that being is itself paradoxical.[113] Paradox, Chesterton says, "is built into the very foundations of human affairs."[114] The "immediate object" of metaphysical paradox is therefore "exegesis: its ultimate object is praise, awakened by wonder."[115] Kenner writes that paradox "springs in general from inadequacy, from the rents in linguistic and logical clothing; paradoxy might be called the science of gaps."[116] Not forgetting that Kenner's use of the word *science* here is more akin to the contemporary use of the word *discipline*, paradox, like analogy, points beyond itself to a new truth. Paradox is paradoxical: it is both a celebration of the analogical potency of language in its ability to create a new kinds of awareness about reality, as well as being an expression of the failure of language to capture reality. Something is both gained and lost in the translation of the medium of reality into the medium of language.

One example of how paradox can introduce a new truth is found at the beginning of Chesterton's essay "The Riddle of the Ivy":

> More than a month ago, when I was leaving London for a holiday, a friend walked into my flat in Battersea and found me surrounded with half-packed luggage.
>
> "You seem to be off on your travels," he said. "Where are you going?"

110. Kenner, *Paradox in Chesterton*, 58.

111. Chesterton, *The Well and the Shallows*, 23.

112. Kenner, *Paradox in Chesterton*, 46.

113. Ibid., 17.

114. Chesterton, *The Man Who Was Orthodox*, 166.

115. Kenner, *Paradox in Chesterton*, 17.

116. Ibid.

With a strap between my teeth I replied, "To Battersea."

"The wit of your remark," he said, "wholly escapes me."

"I am going to Battersea," I repeated, "to Battersea via Paris, Belfort, Heidelberg, and Frankfort. My remark contained no wit. It contained simply the truth. I am going to wander over the world until once more I find Battersea. Somewhere in the seas of sunset or of sunrise, somewhere in the ultimate archipelago of the earth, there is one little island that I wish to find: an island with low green hills and great white cliffs. Travellers tell me that it is called England (Scotch travellers tell me that it is called Britain), and there is a rumour that somewhere in the heart of it there is a beautiful place called Battersea."

"I suppose it is unnecessary to tell you," said my friend, with an air of intellectual comparison, "that this is Battersea?"

"It is quite unnecessary," I said, "and it is spiritually untrue. I cannot see any Battersea here; I cannot see any London or any England. I cannot see that door. I cannot see that chair: because a cloud of sleep and custom has come across my eyes. The only way to get back to them is to go somewhere else; and that is the real object of travel and the real pleasure of holidays. Do you suppose that I go to France in order to see France? Do you suppose that I go to see Germany in order to see Germany? I shall enjoy them both; but it is not them that I am seeking. I am seeking Battersea."[117]

In this exchange, Chesterton introduces a seeming contradiction, namely that by *leaving* Battersea he is in fact *going to* Battersea. This apparent contradiction disrupts a "cloud of sleep and custom" and thus reveals a "spiritual" truth that transcends the perceiving subject.[118] Additionally, what seems to be a straightforward statement of fact is really a drama. This idea only makes rational sense in relation to the story around the idea. This is not to say that a paradox always has to be completely reasonable or resolvable, but only that its accessibility to the reader is made possible when the context of the paradox is revealed. Therefore, the paradox acts both as a propositional truth and as that which transcends the propositional. Maisie Ward summarizes the importance of paradox in Chesterton's work as follows:

[P]aradox must be of the nature of things because of God's infinity and the limitations of the world and of man's mind. To us limited beings God can only express His idea in fragments. We

---

117. Chesterton, *Tremendous Trifles*, 162–63; See *The Everlasting Man*, 9; Chesterton, *Collected Works, Volume 1*, 212.

118. Ibid.

can bring together apparent contradictions in those fragments whereby a greater truth is suggested. If we do this in a sudden or incongruous manner we startle the unprepared and arouse the cry of paradox. But if we will not do it we shall miss a great deal of truth.[119]

Ward observes that the "cry of paradox" can be used as an excuse for neglecting a deeper engagement with what is really being said.[120] Alison Milbank supports this when noting that "paradox leads to a moment of recognition beyond the contradictions in which the truth becomes manifest."[121] John Milbank refers to paradox as an "'overwhelming glory' (*para-doxa*)" or as "an outright impossible *coincidence of opposites* that can (somehow, but we know not how) be persisted with."[122] Paradox belongs to the *metaxu* or the *zwischen*, suggesting that meaning is arrived at through an irreducible tension between apparently contradictory ideas.[123] Paradox reveals that sense of the *between* that epitomizes the human experience. In Chesterton's terms, paradox is "stereoscopic": it allows one to see two different pictures at once and yet be able to see "all the better for that."[124] This idea is reflected in Pseudo-Dionysius's claim that "there is distinction in unity and there is unity in distinction. When there are many lamps in a house there is nevertheless a single undifferentiated light and from all of them comes the one undivided brightness."[125]

The overall effect of paradox, then, is aesthetic. It agrees with the tensions within things, as alluded to by metaphysical paradox, and the tensions within language, as alluded to by rhetorical paradox, by accepting a third kind of tension "from which art takes its vitality."[126] Verbal paradox focuses on the word, while metaphysical paradox focuses on the world; aesthetic paradox finds the word in the world and the world in the word. For this reason, I equate *aesthetic paradox* with *incarnational paradox*. It is rooted in the acceptance of the union of the word and the world—the transcendent and the immanent—without losing the distinction between the two. The word is made flesh without reducing the word to flesh. By maintaining this

---

119. Ward, *G. K. Chesterton*, 137.

120. Ibid.

121. Milbank, *Chesterton and Tolkien as Theologians*, 88.

122. Milbank, "The Double Glory," 163.

123. Ibid., 163.

124. Chesterton, *Essential Writings*, 53.

125. Pseudo-Dionysius, *The Complete Works*, 61.

126. Kenner, *Paradox in Chesterton*, 18.

aesthetic tension, the multilayered, abundant natures of truth and being are retained and a sterility of perception is resisted.

Just as the incarnation is at the center of Chesterton's ethics and his use of analogy, so it is also at the center of his use of paradox. It is fitting, therefore, to take a look at this idea in more detail as it relates to Chesterton's hermeneutic. Christ, the "God-Man in the Gospels," represents the fullest expression of the paradoxical nature of humanity as a mixture between body and soul, for "a man is not a man without his body, just as he is not a man without his soul. A corpse is not a man; but also a ghost is not a man."[127] This fact is something that the "earlier school of Augustine and even of Anselm had rather neglected" or underplayed.[128] It is an idea that helps us to recognize that pure materialism and Gnosticism both fail to account for our humanity, since both place the body and the soul, as well as the body and the mind, at odds.[129] As a consequence of such a split, they also place reason and revelation at odds.[130] However, Christ not only symbolizes, but fully embodies the union of all of these things, even now, as is especially made real and present in the Eucharist: "How would Christ solve modern problems if He were on earth today? For those of my faith there is only one answer. Christ is on earth today; alive on a thousand altars."[131]

Indeed, his presence is an argument against the division of people from God. Therefore Christ also represents the analogical relationship between the human and the divine. He somehow contains the double nature of being both the image of God and God himself.[132] Christ is therefore at the center of Chesterton's stereoscopic vision. And yet, to understand the centrality of the incarnation to Chesterton's thinking, one needs to notice that he begins with the world he knows, as in *Orthodoxy*, or with the complexity of history, as he interprets it in *The Everlasting Man*. He asserts, as I have already pointed out, that it is only when one considers man only as an animal that we must deduce that he cannot be merely animal, and it is only when we consider Christ only as a man that we must deduce that he was more than a man.[133]

---

127. Chesterton, *Saint Thomas Aquinas, Saint Francis of Assisi*, 33.

128. Ibid.

129. Ibid., 35.

130. Ibid.

131. Schall, *Schall on Chesterton*, 180.

132. Nichols, *Chesterton*, 141.

133. Chesterton, *The Everlasting Man*, 17, 171; Chesterton, *Saint Thomas Aquinas, Saint Francis of Assisi*, 30.

Chesterton traces his own spiritual journey from a kind of paganism, through to his discovery of Christianity and finally considers his arrival at the person of Christ. At every point, he affirms that there is something in the paradoxes of Christianity and Christ that explains the way things actually are better than any other philosophical or rationalist system. I am not trying to present an apologia for Chesterton's Christianity. And yet it is clear here that his worldview affects his interpretive lens. Therefore, what follows is a brief discussion that traces Chesterton's thoughts around the paradoxical subject of Christianity and the even more paradoxical figure of Christ.

When Chesterton discusses the problems of relying on the patterning of reality, he points out that life is "not an illogicality; yet it is a trap for logicians."[134] Life "looks just a little more mathematical and regular than it is; its exactitude is obvious, but its inexactitude is hidden; its wildness lies in wait."[135] The human form illustrates his point well. Chesterton notices that the human body looks like a duplicate. One man is, at first glance, really "two men, he on the right exactly resembling him on the left."[136] Because man typically has two eyes, two ears, two nostrils, two arms, two legs, two kidneys and two lobes of the brain, the logician may deduce that he must therefore have two of everything. But this is untrue. Just when the logician expects that a man would have two hearts or two stomachs, he would be wrong; just where the rigid Platonist judges the theory to be superior to the reality, his theory fails. There is, in the end, an "uncanny element in everything" and "a sort of secret treason in the universe."[137] This simple example demonstrates that a theory of life needs to account for both the regularities of existence and its irregularities, and Chesterton discovers that Christianity is just that sort of theory, for "whenever we feel there is something odd in Christian theology, we shall generally find that there is something odd in [our experience of] the truth."[138]

On one occasion, he discusses the oddness of Christianity in light of his interpretation of various non-Christian and anti-Christian accounts of the faith. Again, his own point of view is deeply informed by the antagonisms that surround him. He points out that Christianity is often "attacked from all sides and for all contradictory reasons."[139] It is criticized by some for being too gloomy and pessimistic and then by others for being far too

134. Chesterton, *Collected Works, Volume 1*, 285.

135. Ibid.

136. Ibid.

137. Ibid.

138. Ibid., 286.

139. Ibid., 289.

optimistic; it is accused of overemphasizing human responsibility on the one hand and then of stressing divine providence too much on the other; it is labeled a nightmare by some and a fool's paradise by others; it is lambasted both for fighting too little and for fighting too much.[140] Chesterton concludes that "[i]f it falsified human vision it must falsify it one way or another: it could not wear both green and rose-coloured spectacles."[141] For him, the "shape of Christianity" is very odd indeed: it seems to carry "monstrous murder" and "monstrous meekness" quite comfortably together.[142] He follows his argument to its logical conclusion, intimating that in the end one may not necessarily deduce that Christianity must be true in light of the many contradictory accusations that have been leveled at it. Rather, one may conclude that if Christianity is "all wrong" then it is "very wrong indeed."[143] If "Christianity did not come from heaven" then it must have come "from hell"; and if "Jesus of Nazareth was not Christ, He must have been Antichrist."[144]

Chesterton claims that Christianity, like life, is not merely a neat, sensible middle ground that answers to the frenzied critique of secularists.[145] It is not merely a synthesis of all contradictions, but a home in which all such reasonable contradictions are allowed to co-exist. In the end, it satisfies the one who does not want "resignation," "amalgam or compromise, but both things at the top of their energy; love and wrath both burning."[146] If one does not want "dilution," but the exuberant potency of things at their "full strength," then Christianity provides a clear answer: in a contest between two "furious" truths, one ought to be able to keep them both and keep them both furious.[147] It is this "paradox of the parallel passions" that gives Christianity its clear vision.[148] It is this paradox that helps us to see things as they are. It allows St. Francis of Assisi to be more optimistic than Walt Whitman and St. Jerome to be more pessimistic than Arthur Schopenhauer. The passions are "free" to be what they are because they are "kept in their place."[149]

---

140. Ibid., 289–91.

141. Ibid., 290.

142. Ibid., 291.

143. Ibid., 294.

144. Ibid.

145. Ibid., 296.

146. Ibid., 296, 298.

147. Ibid., 299.

148. Ibid., 300.

149. Ibid.

The optimist could pour out all the praise he liked on the gay
music of the march, the golden trumpets, and the purple ban-
ners going into battle. But he must not call the fight needless.
The pessimist might draw as darkly as he chose the sickening
marches or the sanguine wounds. But he must not call the fight
hopeless. So it was with all the other moral problems, with pride,
with protest, and with compassion. By defining its main doctrine, the Church not only kept seemingly inconsistent things
side by side, but, what was more, allowed them to break out in
a sort of artistic violence otherwise possible only to anarchists.
Meekness grew more dramatic than madness. Historic Christianity rose into a high and strange *coup de théatre* of morality—
things that are to virtue what the crimes of Nero are to vice.[150]

The meaning of the paradoxes Christianity may be simply stated
through an analogy: Christianity keeps the strong colors of red and white,
"like the red and white upon the shield of St. George" while maintaining
a "healthy hatred of pink. It hates that combination of two colours which
is the feeble expedient of the philosophers. It hates that evolution of black
and white which is tantamount to a dirty grey."[151] Chesterton contends that
Christianity, as he understands it, "sees life with thousands of eyes belonging to thousands of different sorts of people, where the other is only the
individual standpoint of the stoic or an agnostic."[152] It accommodates "all
moods of man, it finds work for all kinds of men, it understands secrets of
psychology, it is aware of depths of evil, it is able to distinguish between real
and unreal marvels and miraculous exceptions."[153]

It is a posture towards reality that hopes to see things as they are,
with every wild complexity acknowledged; and it does this without re-
sorting to dualism or monism. In particular, its resistance to conflation is
most potently symbolized by the figure of Christ, who is both "very man
and very God."[154] He is the symbol of the meeting of ultimate extremes:
"[o]mnipotence and impotence, . . . divinity and infancy."[155] He represents
the rebellion of the divine against the rebellion of earth by establishing
harmony, and answers the raging defiance of man by the almost silent compliance of God.[156] The incarnation is the point at which the transcendent,

150. Ibid., 300–301.

151. Ibid., 302.

152. Chesterton, *The Everlasting Man*, 183.

153. Ibid.

154. Chesterton, *Collected Works, Volume 1*, 296.

155. Chesterton, *The Everlasting Man*, 171.

156. Ibid., 181.

supreme God takes the form of the lowliest, most socially insignificant man, as Kierkegaard offers.[157] Chesterton expresses this paradox with reference to the birth of Christ, where "the hands that made the sun and stars were too small to reach the huge heads of cattle."[158] And, as Kierkegaard concedes, it is precisely in the lavishness of this paradox that the scandalous, even offensive nature of the incarnation is exposed, leaving it to be either rejected or believed.[159]

To clarify Chesterton's reading of the incarnation, it is helpful to examine Žižek's suggestion that one may be tempted to "give Chesterton's [understanding of the incarnation] a different reading—no doubt not intended by Chesterton, but none the less closer to a weird truth."[160] The "weird truth" that Žižek extracts, à la Hegel, is that the incarnation signifies the loss of the "transcendent God"—the God who "guarantees the meaning of the universe, the God who is a hidden master pulling all strings."[161] For Žižek, "Chesterton gives us a God who abandons this transcendent position and throws himself into his own creation. This man-God fully engages with the world, even dies. We humans are left with no higher power watching over us, only the terrible burden of freedom and responsibility for the fate of divine creation, and thus for God himself."[162]

Žižek may be correct in pointing out that Chesterton presents a God who abandons his transcendent position to take up residence in his own creation; and he may be correct to assert that this act seems to negate the idea of a God who is the guarantor of all meaning. But Žižek is certainly incorrect to contend that the abandonment of transcendence must necessarily mean the negation of transcendence. Abandonment of authorial absoluteness does not necessarily mean the abandonment of authorship. The author may be felt to be absent from time to time, but rumors of his death may have been greatly exaggerated. Incarnation does not only refer to embodiment, for God does not become man and thus cease to be God. Rather, it presupposes the persistence of the transcendent even in immanence.[163]

For Chesterton, Christ does not only represent the meeting of the extremes of transcendence and immanence, but also symbolizes a unity of other things that had been divided throughout history. In particular, the

157. Kierkegaard, *Provocations*, 223.

158. Chesterton, *The Everlasting Man*, 169.

159. Kierkegaard, *Provocations*, 223.

160. Žižek , *Violence*, 156.

161. Ibid., 157.

162. Ibid.

163. Gadamer, *Truth and Method*, 418.

entire line of argument of Chesterton's *The Everlasting Man* shows that mythology, as a search for God by the imagination alone, and philosophy, as
a search for truth by reason alone, had followed a parallel path throughout history, but had never been able to unite, even though both shared the
quality of being "sad."[164] Chesterton contends that "[w]hat the fighting faith
brought into the world" to remedy this sadness "was hope."[165] He regards
the "Catholic faith" as "the reconciliation because it is the realisation both of
mythology and philosophy."[166]

> It is a story and in that sense one of a hundred stories; only it is a
> true story. It is a philosophy and in that sense one of a hundred
> philosophies; only it is a philosophy that is like life, but above
> all, it is a reconciliation because it is something that can only be
> called the philosophy of stories. That normal narrative instinct
> which produced all the fairy tales is something that is neglected
> by all the philosophies—except one. The Faith is the justification
> of that popular instinct; the finding of a philosophy for it or the
> analysis of the philosophy in it. Exactly as a man in an adventure
> story has to pass various tests to save his life, so the man in this
> philosophy has to pass several tests and save his soul. In both
> there is an idea of free will operating under conditions of design;
> in other words, there is an aim and it is the business of a man
> to aim at it; we therefore watch to see whether he will hit it.[167]

Once again, here is a hint at Chesterton's philosophy of common sense,
namely that the instinct for stories, as represented by mythology, and the
instinct for truth, as represented by philosophy, are both right. But implicit
in this love for stories and truth is the "dramatic instinct" for the reconciliation of both.[168]

For Chesterton, rationalism tends to "[starve] the story-telling instinct": it destroys adventure and romance, and results in an "indifference
and that detachment that is the death of drama."[169] It divides "loving from
fighting" and thus forgets that "the two things imply each other" for you
"cannot love a thing without wanting to fight for it" and you "cannot fight
without something to fight for."[170] In the end, "there is such a thing as a

164. Chesterton, *The Everlasting Man*, 240.

165. Ibid.

166. Ibid., 246.

167. Ibid.

168. Ibid.

169. Ibid.

170. Chesterton, *Appreciations and Criticisms*, 28.

human story; and there is such a thing as the divine story which is also a human story."[171] This is why, in Chesterton's view, there is no true Hegelian, Monist, relativist, or determinist narrative, and why the fundamental skepticism that "dissolves . . . actors into atoms" ends up being so monotonous.[172] Philosophy that has not understood "the philosophy of stories" may do well to piece together its propositions, but it has often failed to speak to the common man who simply wants to hear a good story,[173] but then, mythology has struggled and strained to take reason into account. With this in mind, Chesterton summarizes his case for the effect of the incarnation by contending that

> the sanity of the world was restored and the soul of man offered salvation by something which did indeed satisfy the two warring tendencies of the past; which had never been satisfied in full and most certainly never satisfied together. It met the mythological search for romance by being a story and the philosophical search for truth by being a true story. That is why the ideal figure had to be a historical character, as nobody had ever felt Adonis or Pan to be a historical character. But that is also why the historical character had to be the ideal figure; and even fulfil many of the functions given to these other ideal figures; why he was at once the sacrifice and the feast, why he could be shown under the emblems of the growing vine or the rising sun. The more deeply we think of the matter the more we shall conclude that, if there be indeed a God, his creation could hardly have reached any other culmination than this granting of a real romance to the world. Otherwise the two sides of the human mind could never have touched at all; and the brain of man would have remained cloven and double; one lobe of it dreaming impossible dreams and the other repeating invariable calculations. The picture-makers would have remained forever painting the portrait of nobody. The sages would have remained for ever adding up numerals that came to nothing. It was that abyss that nothing but an incarnation could cover; a divine embodiment of our dreams; and he stands above that chasm whose name is more than priest and older even than Christendom; Pontifex Maximus, the mightiest maker of a bridge.[174]

171. Chesterton, *The Everlasting Man,* 247.
172. Ibid.
173. Ibid.
174. Ibid., 248.

The incarnation informs how Chesterton reads a text. In the first place, the incarnation may be understood as always being implicitly present in the text as a sacrament. In *The Surprise,* for instance, the Author's intentions are already planted in his play even after his creations rebel against him. These intentions may have been misread by his actors and yet their misreading does not negate his intentions in the least. After all, the only way to properly misread something is to actually read it. Concerning the writings of Chesterton in practical terms, therefore, while he may not have direct access to Blake, Browning, or many of the others whose lives and work he writes about, he assumes that something of who they are and what they think is knowable in the present tense through their writings. Reading is not, in Chesterton's view, solely an issue of guesswork and certainly cannot regard the author as irrelevant.[175] Nevertheless, it is clear that reading is still concerned with reading the text instead of being a work of psychologism that attempts to fully explain the nature of the author. The mindset of the author may still be guessed, as Chesterton often does, but the primary focus remains the text itself.

Incarnation, as a hermeneutic key, may also be understood as the revelation of the Author's intentions through his very own arrival and presence in the text. This makes the Author's intentions explicit by moving away from the propositional and the abstract toward the personal and relational. As an example, while Chesterton is never properly present in his work, his "presence" is invoked through what many have written about him, as well as what he has written about himself, in such a way as to clarify his authorial position. Chesterton's supposed anti-Semitism may be taken as an example of this, since it is something that opponents of Chesterton are particularly fond of citing.[176]

To call Chesterton an anti-Semite, propositionally speaking, may be accurate only in the sense that Chesterton was sometimes critical of certain Semitic practices. But, then, Chesterton was often very critical of certain practices of the Christian church and the British Empire even while he loved both. Moreover, there is the fact that Chesterton himself points to his friendship with a number of Jewish people.[177] And Ian Ker notes that there was certainly no malice towards the Jews in Chesterton; indeed, he was always one of the first to cry out in anger against the way that the Jewish

---

175. Ibid., 200.

176. See Clark, *G. K. Chesterton,* 86–87; Stapleton, *Christianity, Patriotism, and Nationhood,* 127, 139–46.

177. Chesterton, *Autobiography,* 76–77.

people were maltreated.[178] This biographical information, together with a close reading of Chesterton's work, becomes an "incarnation" of Chesterton that clarifies the character of the man and thus clears him of being mislabeled and his work of being misunderstood in this way, as Ann Farmer has been particularly adept at arguing in far greater detail.[179] An incarnational reading insists upon a deeper engagement than what a merely disembodied collection of ideas can allow for. It begins with people and not with ideas.

Incarnation, therefore, is not something that happens in isolation from the text, but is precisely that which participates with the text. It is only a hermeneutic key if it fits in with the sacramental reality that has already been outlined in and expressed by the text. And, of course, as with any key, the issue is "not a matter of abstractions; in that sense a key is not a matter of argument. It either fits the lock or it does not."[180] The author's intention, narrative, and argument gain new force and clearer direction when he is present in his own drama. However, to say that incarnation acts as a hermeneutic key is not to suggest rendering absolute a univocal way of seeing. Meaning is not necessarily made explicit by an incarnational event. Just because there is surprise does not imply that mystery has been obliterated. The incarnation implies that both are always present. The paradox persists, as does the surplus of meaning. When all is said and done, there will still be more to say and do.

For Chesterton, the incarnation re-enchants the world. It affirms wonder and welcome, mystery and surprise, God and humanity.[181] All the dramatic possibilities of transcendence and immanence are reconciled in this event. All the heights and depths of participation become possible in this meeting of extremes. Broadly speaking, this paradox falls under the single banner of a subject that Chesterton returns to frequently, namely that of domesticity. On the one hand, domesticity refers to the realm of God and, on the other hand, to the realm of man. Chesterton always insists on the importance and interdependence of both as the cornerstone to understanding.[182] God, as the ground of being, is also the ground of common sense. And yet, it appears it takes courage to adopt the Christian view of God as incarnate. Chesterton observes that people would more "readily swallow the untested claims of this, that, or the other" or drown in a sea of rationalism and skepticism than adopt those four frightening words: "He

178. Ker, *G. K. Chesterton*, 21.

179. Farmer, *Chesterton and the Jews*.

180. Chesterton, *The Everlasting Man*, 215.

181. Chesterton, *Collected Works, Volume 1*, 213.

182. Chesterton, *Selected Works*, 974.

was made Man."[183] And yet, it is only in these terrifying words—in these words that accommodate the greatest extremes of life—that mysteries and surprises become most vivid.

As the above detour into Chesterton's theology of incarnation demonstrates, paradox does not undermine or disdain the dialectical antagonism that exists between two contradictions that must be overcome, but acknowledges that even dialectic needs a context when what needs to be understood is more complex than what can be accommodated by a synthesis of opposites. There is an inherent strain between dialectic and what escapes dialectic that paradox allows. This is why paradox is central to understanding even the dramatic structure of being: it is analogical or metaxological, and is therefore neither strictly univocal nor equivocal.[184] It is both a riddle and an answer, both a mystery and a surprise. As such, paradox refuses one-dimensional perspectives, deconstructionist equivocality, and a potentially formulaic, autoerotic dialectical mediation. As Duston Moore suggests, it seeks an "intimate middle point" that opens a space that accounts for reasonableness of different ways of being.[185]

Again, this middle point cannot result in the dilution of two opposites, but needs to accept a necessary relationship between two irreducible wholes. To take each part of a dualism on its own terms, apart from the dramatic dialogue of paradox, results in a distorted and diminished interpretive experience, as well as heresy. Orthodoxy, on the other hand, is comfortable with mystery and the paradoxes that point towards that mystery—a mystery that, in turn, more fully appreciates the human experience. Václav Havel stresses the paradoxical and the incarnational as fundamental to the human experience in this way: "Man is in fact nailed down—like Christ on the Cross—to a grid of paradoxes[;] . . . he balances between the torment of not knowing his mission and the joy of carrying it out, between nothingness and meaningfulness. And like Christ, he is in fact victorious by virtue of his defeats."[186]

Even though dialogue may be thought of as the interaction of two or more monologues, a dramatic hermeneutic assumes that no monologue is possible in complete isolation.[187] This is somewhat reflective of René Girard's idea that no human desire exists apart from the other and that,

---

183. Ibid.

184. Desmond, *Being and the Between*, 16.

185. Moore, "Plurivocal Eros," 175.

186. Quoted in Stranger, "Václav Havel."

187. See Žižek , "Dialectical Clarity Versus the Misty Conceit of Paradox," 235.

therefore, all are "interdividuals" rather than individuals.[188] Being, when considered to have a dramatic structure, cannot be monological, and language, even when used in isolation, is reliant on a larger linguistic and historical context. By refusing reduction and conflation, paradox is thus inherently dramatic. It resists a narrow anthropomorphic outlook on the drama with all its inherent conflicts by withstanding any attempt to conflate truth into an over-simplified universality or proposition. Moreover, it dismisses what William Desmond calls the "post-Heideggerian deconstructions that assault the ideals of univocity and unity for being totalistic."[189] The natural problem with such an assault on univocity is that it almost just as reductionistically may argue for a reverse-univocity or skepticism, since the absolute non-existence of unity is itself a kind of totalistic unity. Desmond suggests that metaphysical thinking is "plurivocal" and thus irreducible.[190] Anti-metaphysical thinking seems to inevitably become reductionistic or positivistic because it forms a totalizing worldview. This is why even the opposition of metaphysics is political.

Paradox, as already intimated, undermines the solipsistic indifference that forces notions to incessantly be shrugging off responsibility for the meanings that they confer. To reiterate what has been noted above, participation is at the heart of paradox. Reason and faith, for example, do not work against each other, but participate with each other. Logic and imagination are not contradictory, but complementary. This paradoxical logic of participation re-envisions elements of the whole, not as divided from each other, but as interdependent. John Milbank contends that such a paradoxical outlook "does not require to be 'completed' by a dialectical one, but would in reality be betrayed by it."[191] Paradox is necessarily concerned with ensuring that living with tensions does not necessarily mean synthesizing them. Chesterton contends for the necessity of retaining tensions instead of arriving at "premature synthesis."[192]

Again, paradox points again to the dramatic, multilayered structure of being. Being may be interpreted as a dialogical tension between mystery and revelation, the unknowable and the knowable, the riddle and the answer, the unnameable and the namable. Being is always between the transcendent and the immanent. Within its whole unity, it contains both part and whole, and yet, in Chesterton's terms, its inside is larger than its

188. Palaver, *René Girard's Mimetic Theory*, 152.

189. Desmond, *Being and the Between*, 17.

190. Ibid.

191. Milbank, "The Double Glory," 114.

192. Chesterton, *The Man Who Was Orthodox*, 131.

outside.[193] On contemplating the part it becomes bigger than the whole. To borrow again from Pseudo-Dionysius, Being is somehow beyond being and understanding is somehow beyond understanding; the understanding of a text is never confined to its own substance, but is instead connected to the interplay of a being with other beings.[194] No being can account for itself.

In essence, the dramatic structure of being is paradoxical just as existence is paradoxical. However, paradox as an indicator of the dialogical nature of being is in fact reliant on the interplay not of twos, but of threes. It is Trinitarian in its structure, because all opposites need at least a third component—a *tertium quid*—to work in harmony, namely the paradoxical agency that binds them together. Even stereoscopic sight, for instance, is reliant on the mind—a way of thinking through being—that holds the two images together in tension.

I believe that Chesterton's reliance on paradox enhances one of the broader fundamental aims of his work, namely the necessity of highlighting and exposing dogmas and prejudices, and thus, as mentioned already, of choosing a side.[195] By refusing to resolve or abandon tensions, paradox confronts the reader with what and how he knows and believes. However, Chesterton's use of paradox is only one aspect of the rhetorical arsenal that he uses to point to the conviction or hidden bigotry of the reader. And yet, no matter what his rhetorical tactics may be, his aim remains the "recovery of a clear view."[196]

The Catholic practice of Confession, therefore, is always at center of his outlook: his aim is to bring to light what may have been concealed.[197] He writes that "according to [one modern critic], it is morbid to confess your sins. I should say that the morbid thing is to conceal your sins and let them eat your heart out, which is the happy state of most people in highly civilized communities."[198]

193. Chesterton, *Autobiography,* 49; See *Saint Thomas Aquinas, Saint Francis of Assisi,* 131.

194. Pseudo-Dionysius, *The Complete Works,* 97.

195. Chesterton, *All Things Considered,* 10; Chesterton, *Collected Works, Volume 1,* 331; Chesterton, *What's Wrong with the World,* 23.

196. Milbank, *Chesterton and Tolkien as Theologians,* xiii.

197. Chesterton, *Daily News,* January 18, 1908; Chesterton, *What's Wrong with the World,* 23.

198. Chesterton, *Daily News,* January 18, 1908; Chesterton, *The Man Who Was Orthodox,* 158.

He suggests that there are "two things, and only two things, for the human mind, a dogma [or doctrine] and a prejudice."[199] He explains that the difference between these may be understood as follows:

> A doctrine is a definite point; a prejudice is a direction. That an ox may be eaten, while a man should not be eaten, is a doctrine. That as little as possible of anything should be eaten is a prejudice; which is also sometimes called an ideal. Now a direction is always far more fantastic than a plan. I would rather have the most archaic map of the road to Brighton than a general recommendation to turn to the left. Straight lines that are not parallel must meet at last; but curves may recoil forever. A pair of lovers might walk along the frontier of France and Germany, one on the one side and one on the other, so long as they were not vaguely told to keep away from each other. And this is a strictly true parable of the effect of our modern vagueness in losing and separating men as in a mist.[200]

Chesterton insists that man "is a creature who creates cataclysms"; his "whole nature and object on earth is to draw those black lines that do not exist in inorganic nature."[201]

> [Man] separates things and makes them special. Take, for the sake of an instance, the admirable and fascinating subject of meals. A cow eats all day; its hunger, I suppose, grows gradually and vaguely at the beginning, is slowly and increasingly satisfied, and then gradually again dies away. It is an evolutionist. But man is made for revolutions, or rather he makes them; he is formed for abrupt departures and great experiments. He faces the cataclysm called Lunch. It is a thing of black lines; decisive like a religion or a rebellion. It begins at some time and (except in extreme cases) ends at some time.[202]

Chesterton goes on to say that man makes "monogamy, patriotism, oaths before magistrates, monetary obligations, religion, honour, civic obedience, [and] theology, all on the same sacred principle on which he makes lunch."[203] The point is that human beings are creatures whose lines may not necessarily all look the same, but who all create lines and boundaries

---

199. Chesterton, *What's Wrong with the World*, 23.

200. Ibid.

201. Chesterton, *Daily News*, September 9, 1905.

202. Ibid.

203. Ibid.

between their ideas, ideologies and philosophies. They set up divisions between their abstractions of the concrete.[204] In fact,

> [t]he abstract is a symbol of the concrete. This may possibly seem at first sight a paradox; but it is a purely transcendental truth. We see a green tree. It is the green tree that we cannot understand; it is the green tree which we fear; it is the green tree which we worship. Then, because there are so many green trees, so many men, so many elephants, so many butterflies, so many daisies, so many animalculae, we coin a general term "Life." And then the mystic comes and says that a green tree symbolizes life. It is not so. Life symbolises a green tree. Just in so far as we get into the abstract, we get away from the reality, we get away from the mystery, we get away from the tree. . . . God made the concrete, but man made the abstract. A truthful man is a miracle, but the truth is commonplace.[205]

Chesterton contends that one should, so to speak, not only love the picture, but also acknowledge and appreciate the frame.[206] It is not enough to just have dogmas and prejudices; one has to also possess an awareness of one's own dogmas and prejudices. Chesterton even equates an unnoticed dogma or prejudice with the ultimate crime of ignorance: ignorance of being ignorant.[207] One remedy to this ignorance of ignorance is paradox, since it retains the boundaries between things. And boundaries allow one to be confronted with what one actually believes. Without such boundaries, it is almost certain that one will end up oblivious to the fog of one's own prejudices.

This emphasis on uncovering dogmas and prejudices is not an argument for absolute agreement or epistemic arrogance. Instead, it is a hope that the reader will acknowledge that he, like all people, looks "at life through different coloured spectacles," and that each person's particular philosophical stance does have confines and consequences.[208] Chesterton aims to promote the kind of hermeneutical self-awareness—an awareness of the way in which one is reading and looking—that will allow for a better understanding of one's own interpretive experience. He writes, "I count it

204. Chesterton, *The Speaker*, May 31, 1902.

205. Ibid.

206. Ibid.

207. Chesterton, *Saint Thomas Aquinas, Saint Francis of Assisi*, 103.

208. Chesterton, *Collected Works, Volume 1*, 290; Chesterton, *Saint Thomas Aquinas, Saint Francis of Assisi*, 103.

a service to contemporary thought to tell people what they do apparently think; if only to contradict it."[209]

Chesterton is always intent on exposing underlying assumptions and therefore suggests that "when you have lost your way quite hopelessly, the quickest thing is to go back along the road you know to the place from which you started."[210] However, this journey back to the "first facts" of a situation is concerned with more than mere "material facts" since "the first facts are never material facts. The invisible always comes before the visible, the immaterial before the material."[211] Gadamer echoes this when he stresses the importance of becoming aware of one's own hidden "fore-meanings and prejudices" as one engages with a text; after all, a lack of awareness in this regard places the reader at odds with the text.[212] Acknowledging such prejudices is not meant to abolish the subjectivity of the reader, but to deepen it in relation to the objective. It encourages the reader to be critical of the ways that his prejudices may prevent or contribute to his interpretive understanding. To expose assumptions and open up dialogue, Chesterton casts a strange light on the fatigue of familiarity. It is this strange light, which may be called defamiliarization, a hermeneutic tool to which I now turn.

Defamiliarization

Alison Milbank points out that for Chesterton the world is a baffling place "incapable of being enmeshed in a phrase or a formula."[213] It is the mistake of the lunatic, who is blinded by his belief in the possibility of real interpretive immediacy, to assume that it can be summed up, packaged into neat categories and reduced to the confines of human reason. It is also the mistake of the lunatic to rely entirely on his ability to grasp the answers instead of his awareness of the plenitude of questions. This is particularly well demonstrated in the novel *The Poet and the Lunatics* (1929) in which Chesterton imagines a conversation between the poet Gabriel Gale and a few men of science, who are the lunatics in the story. The dialogue begins with the poet discussing the way one ought to see flowers: "'The subject of flowers is hackneyed, but the flowers are not,' the poet was insisting. 'Tennyson was right about the flower in the crannied wall; but most people don't

---

209. Chesterton, *Illustrated London News*, August 25, 1934.
210. Chesterton, *Illustrated London News*, July 14, 1906.
211. Ibid.
212. Gadamer, *Truth and Method*, 271.
213. Milbank, *Chesterton and Tolkien as Theologians*, 92.

look at flowers in a wall, but only in a wallpaper. If you generalise them, they are dull, but if you simply see them they are always startling."[214]

"The flower is a vision because it is not only a vision," Chesterton writes elsewhere; "Or, if you will, it is a vision because it is not a dream."[215] Through Gale, Chesterton argues that the subject of flowers, in being overused or unthinkingly reproduced, cannot be regarded with much awe. Surprise thereby gets reduced to sentimentality. By regarding flowers as a mere pattern instead of as a picture, they cannot really be admired. Familiarity breeds unfamiliarity and a lack of gratitude; and unfamiliarity breeds contempt.[216] The combination of absolutizing and generalizing the subject can become a mechanical process that, as is evident in this reference to William Morris's wallpapers,[217] apparently saps the life from the subject. After all, wallpaper is meant to decorate rather than draw attention to itself; each flower on the wallpaper remains, like a leaf hidden in a forest, hidden in plain sight; each flower exists to draw attention away from itself. But recognizing each flower in nature as unique suggests a reason to be enthralled. For the human mind, the process of repetition often restricts wonder and prevents apprehending anything in the world as it is. The archetypal lunatic, as already discussed, defaults to reductionism that refuses to see what really is: "'Well, I can't see it,' said the man of science. . . . 'I'm afraid we fellows grow out of the way of seeing it like that. You see, a flower is only a growth like any other, with organs and all that; and its inside isn't any prettier or uglier than an animal's . . . .'"[218]

The lunatic here aims to make his world predictable, which results in unpredictability and surprise being diminished, ignored, or dismissed. The poet instead favors a posture towards reality that allows for the possibility or inevitability of surprise. To continue the metaphor of the flower within reference to analogical participation, one daisy in a field looks like another daisy, thus allowing for the generalization that gives the name *daisy* to both flowers.[219] However, the poet here argues that the generalization alone is not sufficient for perceiving accurately. All daisies that grow naturally are in a sense quite different; each has its own story and its own unique life while being connected to the life around it. Once again, the perception of the poet is Chesterton's ideal. The poet certainly argues for similarity and

214. Chesterton, *Selected Works*, 1239.

215. Chesterton, *Saint Thomas Aquinas, Saint Francis of Assisi*, 169.

216. Chesterton, *The Everlasting Man*, 15.

217. Chesterton, *Twelve Types*, 10.

218. Chesterton, *Selected Works*, 1239.

219. See Chesterton, *Collected Works, Volume 1*, 238.

alikeness, since one flower is like another flower, and one person may be like another person. But he also argues for difference, since, once again, to say that something is like another thing is to say that the two are not exactly the same. "Saying something is like a dog is another way of saying it is not a dog."[220] The lunatic argues for an "ugly uniformity," but the poet argues for differentiation even within similarity.[221] Chesterton demonstrates the applicability of exact propositional truth, but suggests rightly that the universality of propositional truth accounts neither for the larger story nor for the details within the larger story. The parts of the story are interconnected and interdependent, but each part of the story needs to be understood as something that participates in the whole.

The human tendency to miss the uniqueness of each flower by mechanizing the understanding of reality arises because of a kind of intellectual fatigue. As mentioned in the previous chapter, Chesterton notes that the "variation in human affairs is brought into them, not by life, but by death; by the dying down or breaking off of their strength or desire."[222] Consequently, Chesterton suggests that repetition is not a sign of fatigue, but of an appetite of "eternal infancy" that constantly returns, revises, and revolutionizes.[223] It is the eternal infant that has the strength of will and attention to be able to remain enthralled by the glory of the ordinary. Even God's repetitions in nature are theatrical encores and signs of constant vigilance.[224]

However, this appetite for repetition needs to be distinguished from the patterning and predictability that has been attributed to things by scientistic lunacy. Mere mechanization, as a process that has been set into motion like a watch or a time bomb, may well be impersonal and may rightly cause fatigue because it suggests an absence of attention. Chesterton observes that the mistake is not that the mechanisms and mechanization of engines are "too much admired, but that they are not admired enough. The sin is not that engines are mechanical, but that men are mechanical."[225] In saying this, he reminds the reader that a mechanical man cannot enjoy or be aware of even the strangely unique drama of echoes and repetitions. This is precisely the problem presented by scientific determinism, which in positing the presence of only cause and effect avoids the possibility of choice. In Chesterton's view, the determinist comes to "bind, but not to loose" so that

220. Chesterton, *The Everlasting Man*, 114.

221. Chesterton, *Illustrated London News*, October 30, 1920.

222. Chesterton, *Collected Works, Volume 1*, 263.

223. Ibid.

224. Ibid.

225. Ibid., 113.

the chain of causation becomes the "worst chain that ever fettered a human being."[226]

Chesterton, as always, remains highly critical of any attitude that "proposes turning various laws in nature into absolutes."[227] He does this because "he is aware of the way that the language of apparently pure objectivity, particularly in the sciences, is a means for dulling the senses to the marvel of perception."[228] Choice, therefore, remains imperative to the awareness that Chesterton is promoting. For example, as much as choice produces a number of disturbances and irregularities in *The Surprise*, thus frustrating the purposes of the Author, it is still essential to the overall drama.

However, the implication that every item within this drama of the real is uniquely placed is that each thing needs to be uniquely understood and noticed within its world. If life were a symphony, each note, rhythm, dynamic and instrument's significance to the unfolding of the music is noticed. In the drama of life, every setting, actor, gesture, conflict and resolution is uniquely suited for the unfolding of the story. While patterns may be evident in the unfolding drama, these patterns are ultimately an argument for a picture.[229] They insist that there is a mind behind the order of things. For Chesterton, the determinist is a person who "sees too much cause in everything" and is therefore incapable of recognizing the presence of choice.[230]

On the other hand, Chesterton sees a world that must be as deliberate as it appears to be. To encourage the reader to notice the presence of choice, he constantly attempts to disrupt perception. He uses the tools of analogy and paradox to create a process of defamiliarization, a term translated from the Russian *priem ostranenie* used by literary critic Viktor Shklovsky.[231] By presenting the familiar in a new way, he allows the reader to see a thing as if for the first time, thereby breaking the spell of habituation. Defamiliarization, in Shklovsky's view, prevents the "algebrization" or "over-automization" of language that renders it unconscious of its own meaning and function.[232] Defamiliarization allows for the disclosure of meaning that would otherwise remain hidden. In Chesterton's own terms, it resists the "worship of law."[233] And as Lawrence Crawford contends, it results in "a *restoration* of

226. Ibid., 227.

227. Reyburn, "Chesterton's Ontology," 52.

228. Ibid.

229. Chesterton, *Illustrated London News*, September 24, 1932.

230. Chesterton, *Collected Works, Volume 1*, 221.

231. Milbank, *Chesterton and Tolkien as Theologians*, xv.

232. Shklovsky, "Art as Technique," 13.

233. Chesterton, *Collected Works, Volume 1*, 246.

difference."[234] Defamiliarization allows for the revival of the "human sense of actual choice."[235] It may be viewed as that which renders the text separate and even alien from the reader to allow the reader to distinguish between things in the text. It restores the boundary line between the subject and his object of contemplation.

However, Chesterton's use of defamiliarization is not perfectly congruent with Shklovsky's theory. Shklovsky's defamiliarization, which is largely reliant on the construction of what he calls "poetic" language, is difficult to decipher and define. It may thus be likened to Jacques Derrida's *différance*.[236] Alison Milbank observes that Shklovsky lauds "avant garde obscurity" that allows the poetic to be cocooned within its own self-referentiality and thus remain untainted by the reality that it is supposed to be referring to.[237] As such, it is a *différance* that is detached from a lived-in dramatic experience. Contrary to this, Chestertonian defamiliarization is not merely concerned with the production of difference for the sake of creating an isolated or insulated chain of signifiers, but rather with a restoration of meaning and one's concrete engagement with reality. The aim is not to detach the text from its meaning, but to detach the perception of the reader from its own unconscious preconceptions in order for a new experience of meaning to be possible. It concerns the restoration of one's first astonishment at the very presence of the text.

Chesterton is acutely aware of the potential of any method or technique to produce a stale encounter with the world. This is why he argues that imagination's central function is to disrupt or revolutionize "our whole orderly system of life."[238] The prime function "of imagination is not to make strange things settled, so much as to make settled things strange; not so much to make wonders facts as to make facts wonders."[239] Imagination, as the ability to see something as something else, to see one thing through other things, does not operate on a plane outside of human experience. Rather, imagination argues for a deeper engagement with the drama of real life. As such, Chestertonian defamiliarization is similar to Berthold Brecht's notion of the *Verfremdungseffekt* or "estrangement effect," which "consists of taking an object or relationship of which one is to be made aware . . . from something ordinary, familiar, immediately accessible, into something peculiar,

234. Crawford, "Viktor Shklovskij: Différance," 211.

235. Chesterton, *Collected Works, Volume 1*, 240.

236. Crawford, "Viktor Shklovskij: Différance," 212.

237. Milbank, *Chesterton and Tolkien as Theologians*, 32.

238. Chesterton, *The Defendant*, 60.

239. Ibid.

striking and unexpected."[240] The obvious may be represented in a way that renders it incomprehensible at first, but only so that its genuine meaning may be revisited and better understood. If familiarity dulls perception, then defamiliarization is what brings about a new kind of awareness by stripping the familiar of its familiarity. It calls for the destruction of the assumption that the object of contemplation does not need an explanation.[241]

Chesterton refers to Shakespeare as one who challenges the familiar by truly understanding the nuances and complexities of the drama of life; he is able to constantly revise and re-envision what is often simply assumed to encourage a deeper engagement, not just with concepts, but with reality itself.[242] His thinking here mirrors the analogical, paradoxical concept of the great reversal expressed by Jesus at various points in the Gospels: it is the spiritually bankrupt who are blessed (Matt 5:3) and the submissive who inherit the earth (Matt 3:5); it is those of sound judgment who are most in danger of suffering from impaired judgment (Matt 9:9–12); it is the humble who are truly great (Luke 9:48; 14:11), and the last who will be first (Matt 19:30); it is those who lose their lives for the sake of Christ that find their lives (Luke 9:24), and it is those who claim to see (understand) whose blindness (ignorance) remains (Matt 13:13; John 9:41). These reversals all follow a process of defamiliarization whereby one detaches oneself from the object of attention to become fully present to it. Defamiliarization, therefore, involves a departure, followed by hospitality. And this hospitality suggests that the strangeness of a thing can give it its significance.[243]

The centrality of choice in the process of developing one's awareness is established when one recognizes that to see things as they are, we need to also see things as they are not; or, at least, we need to see things differently from the way we have become accustomed to seeing them. Moreover, choice needs to be highlighted as an act of the imagination and not just of the will. Indeed, Chesterton is particularly skeptical of the praise of mere will that is promoted by Schopenhauer and Nietzsche precisely because it is against the choice, for choice is essential to imagination. Chesterton observes that to praise the will alone is really to paralyze it and to render any object of the will irrelevant.[244] The "essence of will" is found in its particularity.[245]

240. Ibid.

241. Brecht, "Alienation Effects In Chinese Acting," 143.

242. Chesterton, *Collected Works, Volume 1*, 219.

243. Chesterton, *The Everlasting Man*, 23.

244. Chesterton, *Collected Works, Volume 1*, 243.

245. Ibid.

Chesterton's use of defamiliarization re-establishes the particularity of choice. By destabilizing the familiar, one is compelled to decide again. By asking the reader to reconfigure the context of a particular truth or idea, Chesterton encourages him to take note of its specificity. This is why, to refer to an example already mentioned, Chesterton can utter something that apart from its context is heterodox or even blasphemous—"He was a man who read his Bible. That was what was the matter with him"[246]—and then turn the idea on its head to reveal that he is arguing for a deeper orthodoxy and a deeper engagement with the actual text—in this case, the text of the Bible. However, Chesterton shows that the real blasphemy is in familiarity as over-automization. By making the familiar "blasphemy" or "untruth" unfamiliar, meaning is revealed in a new way. The untruth becomes a path on the way to encountering the truth.

Defamiliarization is also a response to the lunatic's mythification and idolization of science and rationality. When assumptions go unchecked, they become idols instead of icons; things that were meant to be looked through become things that are merely looked at. When given such a high status in culture, science and rationality gained a kind of religious significance in Chesterton's time. This undermines the entire purpose of scientific discovery:

> Physical science is like simple addition: it is either infallible or it is false. To mix science up with philosophy is only to produce a philosophy that has lost all its ideal value and a science that has lost all its practical value. I want my private physician to tell me whether this or that food will kill me. It is for my private philosopher to tell me whether I ought to be killed.[247]

This is not to recommend that science should not ever converse with philosophy or theology, but instead intimates that science should not seek to be or to supplant philosophy or theology—those discourses that are more obviously adept at considering the role of faith. It is clear to Chesterton that discourse answers to and interacts with scientific discovery, but that neither science nor faith exist to supplant the other. A scientist discovers what is there in a material sense; the philosopher is the one who ought to debate what to think about, what is there, what its value might be, and why it is there.

The demythification of science and reason calls the whole purpose of science into question, but also emphasizes the purpose of faith. Terry Eagleton notes that "[s]cience and theology are for the most part not talking

246. Chesterton, *Father Brown*, 167.
247. Chesterton, *All Things Considered*, 94.

about the same kind of things, any more than orthodontics and literary criticism are. This is one reason for the grotesque misunderstandings that arise between them."[248] The lunatic, in mythicizing science as an absolute, is unable to distinguish his faith from his reason. This is essentially what over-automization involves: it either over-emphasizes difference or it prevents one from perceiving it. This leads to a detachment of theory from reality. It renders reality disconnected or conflated by the violence of dichotomies.

Defamiliarization, as the device that allows the reader to see something as if for the first time, does not just aim to help the reader to view what is actually meant by the text. It also addresses the way that one apprehends and appropriates the meaning of a text into the drama of life. It asks the reader to be engaged in a dialogue with the text whilst simultaneously moving beyond the text, thus allowing him to consider his world in a new light. Chesterton "makes the object strange to us so that it may be reconnected by participation in a divine world."[249] Ultimately, together with his use of analogy and paradox, his use of defamiliarization provides a sacramental window on the world. Against the dualistic biases of modernity, Chesterton's participatory lens promotes a view of the material world as a sacred place. He takes an analogical, paradoxical and dialogical connection between the human and the divine to be foundational to perceiving correctly. In the end, Chesterton's way of perceiving is a hermeneutic that accepts extremes; it uncovers the divine participation with the human and the human participation with the divine.[250]

Humor

This participation, far from being a somber matter, is one of boisterous joy. Even the virtues of Christianity, compared with the virtues of the pagan, are not "sad," but "exuberant."[251] Chesterton's favorite title for himself—"jolly journalist"—is certainly fitting when we consider the overall mood of his life and work.[252] His work reflects an "essential goodness, perfect sincerity, chivalrous generosity, boundless good temper" and "a total absence of self-[importance]."[253] Intermingled with these qualities is a profound

---

248. Eagleton, *Reason, Faith, and Revolution*, 10.

249. Milbank, *Chesterton and Tolkien as Theologians*, 58.

250. Chesterton, *The Everlasting Man*, 171; Chesterton, *What's Wrong with the World*, 70.

251. Chesterton, *Collected Works, Volume 1*, 124.

252. Ward, *G. K. Chesterton*, 219.

253. Ker, *G. K. Chesterton*, 17.

unity between his "brilliant intellectual powers" and his "enormous gift of humour."[254] David Fagerberg notes that even though we are many decades away from Chesterton, he "was so clamorously happy that it is still infectious" today.[255]

Chesterton's power of levity is used very deliberately in his work as both a rhetorical strategy, and as a reflection of an ontology of plenitude. Humor, for Chesterton, is an intricate part of the human experience of truth and of understanding, which is not just something grasped and contained, but something that escapes our grasp and contains us. He defines humor simply as that which "signifies a perception of the comic or incongruous of a special sort."[256] Humor, in short, is what makes us smile or laugh. And, in smiling or laughing, we may find ourselves reconnected to our own humanity and the humanity of others. Hilarity works best in and for conditions of security—when we sense that we are safe or capable of reaching safety.[257] It may even be taken as a sign of hope.

Chesterton is frequently critical of any culture that prizes seriousness too greatly because seriousness easily slips into a morbid solemnity. He therefore contends that it is distasteful to be overly serious because it implies relational, ontological, and contextual disconnection: "If you isolate a thing, you may get the pure essence of gravity."[258] Outside the drama of being—dissociated from oneself, others, and Being itself—things become dull. This isolated seriousness may even be considered "irreligious."[259] It "is the fashion of all false religions" because taking "everything seriously" is tantamount to making "an idol of everything."[260] It transplants the individual into peripheral interests "until his limbs are as rooted as the roots of the tree or his head as fallen as the stone sunken by the roadside."[261] The point here is not that seriousness is bad in itself; seriousness is one facet of the depth and breadth of the human experience. Nevertheless, without the counterbalance or counternarrative provided by humor, seriousness will negatively affect one's hermeneutic awareness.

In fact, if over-seriousness or solemnity suggests the removal of an awareness of the multifaceted dimensions of human experience, it is

254. Ibid.

255. Fagerberg, *Chesterton is Everywhere*, 7.

256. Chesterton, "Humour."

257. Reyburn, "Laughter and the Between," 44.

258. Chesterton, *Illustrated London News*, June 9, 1906.

259. Chesterton, "On Seriousness."

260. Ibid.

261. Ibid.

certainly more of a vice than a virtue.[262] After all, it encourages a person's compliance with an easy complacency, which humor quite naturally opposes. It breeds an over-familiarity that fosters mental fatigue. This, in turn, brings about a lack of wonder and astonishment at the sheer miracle of being. Solemnity is the enemy of both gratitude and humility—two inseparable virtues in Chesterton's work. Therefore, humor, as something that has the ability to disrupt this solemnity, may rightly be considered one of the modes of Chestertonian defamiliarization.

One of the reasons that solemnity needs to be disrupted is that it presents us with a false picture of the writer's authority on a subject: "The writer of the leading article" of a magazine or newspaper, for instance, "has to write about a fact that he has known for twenty minutes as if it were a fact that he has studied for twenty years."[263] Solemnity, like pessimism, overstates itself to create an impression of mastery even when mastery is not present. Although it is not intrinsically immoral, solemnity can distort our relationship with the truth. Consequently, Chesterton argues that most people "assume that the unscrupulous parts of newspaper-writing will be the frivolous or jocular parts."[264] However, he then notes that "[t]his is against all ethical experience. Jokes are generally honest. Complete solemnity is almost always dishonest."[265] The Yellow Press, for instance, is less objectionable "when it is irresponsible" than when it is "responsible" because its irresponsibility does not make it out to be more than what it is.[266]

Humor, for Chesterton, is allied with humility in a way that undiluted seriousness or solemnity simply cannot be. In fact, for Chesterton, "[t]he secret of life" is located "in laughter and humility."[267] Conversely, pride "dries up laughter, it dries up wonder, it dries up chivalry and energy."[268] Humor also establishes a connection with common sense; that is, with our embodied and concrete participation in reality. Accordingly, "[s]o far from it being irrelevant to use silly metaphors on serious questions, it is one's duty to use silly metaphors on serious questions. It is the test of one's seriousness."[269] It is, in other words, the test of one's sincerity and one's faith. Chesterton, keeping in mind the link between solemnity and idolatry, contends that

262. Chesterton, *Collected Works, Volume 1*, 326.

263. Chesterton, *Illustrated London News*, June 9, 1906.

264. Ibid.

265. Ibid.

266. Ibid.

267. Chesterton, *Collected Works, Volume 1*, 107.

268. Ibid.

269. Chesterton, *Illustrated London News*, June 9, 1906.

a "responsible religion or theory" may be tested by the presence of levity and hilarity in discussions about it.[270] A religion or theory is trustworthy if "it can take examples from pots and pans and boots and, butter-tubs."[271] Moreover, "[i]t is the test of a good philosophy whether you can defend it grotesquely. It is the test of a good religion whether you can joke about it."[272]

Chesterton is not suggesting that truth is implicitly funny or frivolous.[273] If that were so, an alarming proportion of science, theology, and philosophy would be automatically false simply because it lacked humor. Moreover, he does not take humor to be the opposite of seriousness. If anything, humor is the obverse or counterpart of seriousness. Thus, Chesterton's aim is to highlight humor as a doorway to truth because it can create openness in an audience to alternative ways of perceiving. "Humor is expansive" and "bursts outwards" as is "attested by the common expression, 'holding one's sides.'" It "has the quality of liberty," whereas "sorrow has in it . . . a quality of confinement."[274]

The gift of a joke is it can expose an audience to fresh philosophical subtlety and a renewed appreciation for familiar things and ideas.[275] This connection between humor and seriousness is evident in the work of Shakespeare, who depicts "clowns" who are also "philosophers," "geniuses," and "demigods."[276] They are comical, but also profound; hilarious, but also serious.

While humor, humility, and truth may be married, the above hints that humor is also connected to vulnerability, which is a vital hermeneutic posture. Chesterton observes that "the heart which is there to be lightened will also be there to be hurt."[277] Humor is often a sign of defenselessness against the unabashed quiddity of existence. "[L]ike religion and morals," humor is even adept at invoking "terror" especially "when it is clad in mystery."[278] Accordingly, it ought not to symbolize an escape from the storms of life by creating a shelter of foolish optimism. It should also not represent any quick antidote to rigid pessimism. Rather, humor, at is best, is a signal of transcendence; it is a sign of the truths of the universe. Chesterton writes,

270. Ibid.

271. Ibid.

272. Ibid.

273. Ker, *G. K. Chesterton*, 110.

274. Chesterton, *Stories, Essays, and Poems*, 246.

275. Chesterton, *Illustrated London News*, March 21, 1908.

276. Chesterton, "The Humour of King Herod."

277. Chesterton, *Illustrated London News*, January 11, 1908.

278. Chesterton, *Illustrated London News*, May 5, 1906.

"Whatever is cosmic is comic[;] . . . all grotesqueness is itself ultimately related to seriousness. Unless a thing is dignified, it cannot be undignified."[279]

Here, he stresses the relationship between humor and dignity, and by doing so defamiliarizes any view of dignity that would exclude the sillier aspects of humanity. He writes, "[i]t seems to me that the problem of humour presents one primary condition and difficulty which divides it from most others. It seems to me quite clear that the process which ends in a joke necessarily begins with a certain idea of dignity."[280] This dignity contains incongruities. Human nature, Chesterton suggests, is incongruous: "Man himself is a joke in the sense of a paradox. That there is something very extraordinary about his position, and therefore presumably about his past, is the clearest sort of common sense. Alone of all creatures he is not self-sufficient, even while he is supreme."[281] "[M]an's spiritual immensity within" perpetually clashes with his "littleness and restriction without": "for it is itself a joke that a house should be larger inside than out."[282]

Moreover, man is "at once a creator moving miraculous hands and fingers and a kind of cripple. He is wrapped in artificial bandages called clothes; he is propped on artificial crutches called furniture. His mind has the same doubtful liberties and the same wild limitations."[283] Man, in short, is a between-being—both animal and angel, body and soul, flesh and spirit—and when he is confronted with the paradoxes of his own nature, he catches sight "of some secret in the very shape of the universe hidden from the universe itself."[284] He is "alone among the animals" in being "shaken with the beautiful madness called laughter."[285] He finds in the joke of his own spiritual and bodily being both "higher possibilit[ies]" and "the mystery of shame."[286]

The experience of humor is capable of connecting the human subject with his humanness. Humor arises in the clash between two poles within the self, when the congruity of man as "lord of all creation" confronts the "incongruity" of his utter dependence upon almost everything else.[287] The first shall be last; the master of everything is at the mercy of everything, and

279. Chesterton, *Illustrated London News*, June 9, 1906.

280. Chesterton, *The Man Who Was Orthodox*, 85.

281. Ibid., 84.

282. Chesterton, "Humour."

283. Chesterton, *The Everlasting Man*, 36.

284. Ibid.

285. Ibid.

286. Ibid.

287. Chesterton, *The Man Who Was Orthodox*, 84.

the lord of all is the servant of all.[288] Whatever else is perceived as comical to us points repeatedly to this dual quality of humanity. When we delight at the laughter of the hyena, the grin of a chimpanzee, or the shuffle of a penguin, it is because they mirror our humanity back to us in a strange form. The universe often appears personified to us, and it incites joy in us. If we "do not think the projection of a precipice grotesque" it is "because it is not near enough to imply any comparison with humanity at all."[289]

In the connection of humor to the unique paradoxes of human nature, Chesterton's thoughts mirror those of Henri Bergson (1859–1941), who Chesterton was familiar with.[290] Bergson writes, "the comic does not exist outside the pale of what is strictly *human*."[291] Nevertheless, while Bergson explains our laughter as the result of our being detached from the subject that amuses, Chesterton underlines the role played by our *attachment* to the subject. This is clear in his prime example of the comical:

> Why is it funny that a man should sit down suddenly in the street? There is only one possible or intelligent reason: that a man is the image of God. It is not funny that anything else should fall down; only that a man should fall down. No one sees anything funny in a tree falling down. No one sees a delicate absurdity in a stone falling down. No man stops in the road and roars with laughter at the sight of snow coming down. The fall of thunderbolts is treated with some gravity. The fall of roofs and high buildings is taken seriously. It is only when a man tumbles down that we laugh. Why do we laugh? Because it is a grave religious matter: it is the Fall of Man. Only man can be absurd: for only man can be dignified.[292]

It is our *connection* with the humanity of the tumbling man that evokes laughter. We find it funny when he sits or tumbles down because he symbolizes the fusion and clash of horizons that is at the center of the hermeneutic experience: because of him we find our conventions challenged. He is dignified, but also capable of indignity. He is civilized, but also wild and untamable. He is a man, but also a monster and a mystery.

The perception of humor results from the paradoxical combination of something agreeable and something disagreeable. Humor lives in the inoffensive offense. Without the one side of the paradox, the perception of a

288. Chesterton, *Illustrated London News*, March 21, 1908.

289. Chesterton, *The Man Who Was Orthodox*, 84.

290. See Chesterton, *Illustrated London News*, November 17, 1934.

291. Bergson, *Laughter*, 3.

292. Chesterton, *Illustrated London News*, June 9, 1906.

joke is unlikely. In a joke, the affront or offense is the thing that subverts our expectations; but it is agreeable or kind because it does not do so with malice. It is capable of maintaining man's dignity even while it exposes him as undignified. Whatever is perceived to utterly negate the dignity of man would be the opposite of a good joke. Of course, this means that personal preferences and humor thresholds will play an important part in the perception of humor. What is funny to one is not necessarily funny to another. And yet, the double-gesture of congruity and incongruity, of affirmation and negation, and of familiarity and unfamiliarity, remains essential to the structure of a joke.

Humor's theological significance, for Chesterton, is found in that "being undignified is the essence of all real happiness, whether before God or man. Hilarity involves humility; nay, it involves humiliation."[293] This means that there is even a place for vulgarity in his perception of humor. He offers that "once you have got hold of a vulgar joke you may be certain that you have got hold of a subtle and spiritual idea."[294] "Religion" is really "much nearer to riotous happiness than it is to the detached and temperate types of happiness in which gentlemen and philosophers find their peace. Religion and riot are very near, as the history of all religions proves. Riot means being a rotter; and religion means knowing you are a rotter."[295]

Chesterton believes that "[r]eligion is interested not in whether a man is happy, but whether he is still alive, whether he can still react in a normal way to new things, whether he blinds in a blinding light or laughs when he is tickled."[296] Religion is akin to a joke in that it is both coercive and liberating. We are made to laugh; we are compelled to believe.[297] We are held hostage, at gunpoint, by the joke and by truth, and it is the laughter and the truth that set us free. Both humor and religion are rooted in structures, in the idea of "institutions," and it is this that brings about enjoyment: "Most men need institutions to make them distinguish themselves; and they also need institutions to make them enjoy themselves. For, as paradoxical as it sounds, men shrink from enjoyment; they make one automatic step backwards from the brink of hilarity; because they know that it means the loss of dignity and a certain furious self-effacement."[298]

293. Chesterton, *Illustrated London News*, January 11, 1908.

294. Chesterton, *Illustrated London News*, March 21, 1908.

295. Chesterton, *Illustrated London News*, January 11, 1908.

296. Ibid.

297. Chesterton, *Illustrated London News*, January 8, 1910.

298. Ibid.

We laugh at the punch line of a joke because it explodes from within the restrictions of the familiar and yet also hints at what is beyond the familiar. We laugh at a surprise because it highlights the truth that we already knew without knowing it. A good joke returns the perceiving subject to what is central rather than to what is peripheral, which is why "[c]entripetal people are jolly" while "[c]entrifugal people are a bore."[299] This could be illustrated in any number of jokes, but I will take only two examples here, beginning with one about a man who is being given a tour around heaven by St. Peter. He is shown the different districts of heaven, where atheists, Hindus, Lutherans, Catholics, and a number of others stay. While many of the districts are without boundaries, he is astonished that the Baptist district is surrounded by a very high wall. "Why do you keep the Baptists behind this wall?" he asks St. Peter. "Keep it down, will you," St. Peter replies. "They think they're the only ones here."

The joke focuses on and therefore has the possibility of destabilizing a central aspect of human cultures: their often exaggerated prioritization of conformity, in-group biases, and sense of normativity. Another classic joke, which asks, "How many psychologists does it take to change a light bulb?" is met with the answer, "Only one, but the light bulb must really want to change." Here, the punch line exposes what is central to psychology: the active participation of the patient. There may be exceptions to the rule, but the rule remains: jokes stress ethical values, boundaries, and priorities. Even the most offensive jokes have the ability to alert us to what we really do think.

In any joke incongruity is present. However, incongruity alone is not enough to make us laugh. "Nobody laughs at what is entirely foreign; nobody laughs at a palm tree. But it is funny to see the familiar image of God disguised behind the black beard of a Frenchman or the black face of a Negro."[300] At the heart of humor is an instant of pure recognition. Through humor, we are confronted with ourselves through the otherness of others: we see ourselves, in this confrontation, as both dignified and undignified; as heroes who are are fallen; as divine and as mortal. We are glorious ruins. Even when we laugh at someone else, we remain the butt of the joke.

The religious stature of humor is especially symbolized by the incarnation, for Chesterton, which may be taken as the central joke of Christianity.[301] It is the event in which the greatest incongruity seems to be present. The Being that transcends being descends into flesh and dwells among other

299. Chesterton, *Illustrated London News*, July 10, 1909.

300. Chesterton, *Illustrated London News*, March 21, 1908.

301. Chesterton, *Illustrated London News*, January 13, 1906, Chesterton, *Illustrated London News*, January 11, 1908; Chesterton, *Illustrated London News*, January 8, 1910.

beings. And yet, the profoundest congruity is also most noticeable in this very incongruity: God is with us—his face and voice are accessible to even the lowliest of people. The greatest divide—the divide between the divine and the human—is overcome in a punch line that knocks all other punch lines flat. It is a knock-knock joke, and God himself is at the door.

The joke, then, represents reconciliation and redemption. We laugh at the joke only when we understand it from the inside, when we are reconciled with it. In hilarity, we find ourselves befriending even the negative aspects of existence. The comical is perhaps therefore an answer to the question that Chesterton proposes is the primary problem for philosophers: "How can we be both astonished at the world and at home in it?"[302] Humor, with its incongruity and its deeper reliance upon congruity, can be understood as one means by which both awe and familiarity are retained. Moreover, it is a sign of the joyful-serious philosophy that is embodied in the Christian Faith.

Humor in Chesterton's work is therefore a pivot that links a number of aspects of his hermeneutic. It indicates the transcendent, but also sets up a bridge between the transcendent and the immanent. It works paradoxically; it is a sign of the dignity of man; it creates defamiliarization, and opens a way to experience the world through the hospitality of empathic laughter. Most of all, it creates a means for encountering the new in the familiar. The presence of humor even represents, albeit partially, the promise of genuine epiphanies.

302. Chesterton, *Collected Works, Volume 1,* 212.

6

The Event of Understanding in Chesterton's Hermeneutic

Language and Mystery

Broadly speaking, Chesterton's hermeneutic seems to follow two distinct pathways. The first is the way to "immediate mystical impressions,"[1] "direct experience,"[2] "definite convictions,"[3] and "immediate meaning."[4] This way to revelation may refer to his persistent striving for a deeper sense of what is certain—a univocal or dialectical relation to being. The second is the way to recovering "the faculty of wonder, without which no man can live."[5] This is the way to mystery—a way to the equivocal, the truly astonishing, and what is impossible to mediate. If taken in isolation, these two ways present a number of hermeneutic problems. If we assume only the focus on revelation or immanence, for instance, we are likely to mistake Chesterton for being a mere uncompromising ideologue; we may end up regarding him as one who believes in the genuine possibility of an unmediated experience; that is, we may take him to be intimating a hermeneutics of pure immediacy that amounts to the end of hermeneutics. If we assume only a focus on entering into mystery, we may find Chesterton to be perpetually baffling and endlessly grasping for the impossible. If mystery

---

1. Chesterton, *The Club of Queer Trades*, 33.
2. McCleary, *The Historical Imagination of G. K. Chesterton*, 51.
3. Chesterton, *Collected Works, Volume 1*, 196.
4. Chesterton, *Charles Dickens*, 211.
5. Kelman, *Among Famous Books*, 291.

were his only anchor, he would appear to us as a mystical philosopher with no practical earthly directive and barely any significance for any engagement with hermeneutics.

Naturally, it is easier to fall into the trap of reading Chesterton only in light of the first way; that is, only in terms of what is (apparently) instantaneously discernable and comprehensible. It is this way of reading Chesterton that allows George Orwell to conclude with a fair amount of cynicism that Chesterton "chose to suppress his sensibilities and intellectual honesty in the cause of Roman Catholic propaganda."[6] Orwell continues: "Every book he wrote, every paragraph, every incident in every story, every scrap of dialogue, had to demonstrate beyond all possibility of mistake the superiority of the Catholic over the Protestant or the pagan."[7] There is much in Chesterton's work to suggest that Orwell is at least partially right. If he is totally right, though, Chesterton fails because of his own hermeneutic optimism. His respect for the Roman Catholic Church may appear somewhat out of proportion with the importance of trying to see things as they really are. This may well be tantamount to a kind of anti-polyphonic, binary monologism: "the reduction of multiple voices and consciousnessess within a text to a single version of truth imposed by the author."[8]

Orwell's critique is quite easily confirmed simply by referring to the way that Chesterton's work is appropriated in a great deal of popular discourse. It is still safe to say that today Chesterton scholarship does tend to exist "in a ghetto."[9] While we can be thankful that his *Father Brown* stories are still widely read, and that his work has been brought out of the ghetto somewhat by Slavoj Žižek's frequent references to him, it is nonetheless sad to see that the work of a man intended for a massively varied audience has become confined to a specific set of coordinates when being read and interpreted. What has been neglected, in my view, is precisely Chesterton's second hermeneutic pathway, which needs to be taken in conjunction with the first. There is still something in Chesterton that refuses to let him adopt a strict monologism and that also resists the sheer intolerance of a violent hermeneutic: it is mystery. This mystery is not a mystery over and against revelation. It is not an equivocal posture that opposes the univocal and dialectical postures. It is mystery found even in the midst of revelation—a mystery that has a paradoxical or metaxological relationship with revelation. It is, to follow William Desmond again, a recovery of the equivocal posture

---

6. Orwell, "Great is Diana of the Ephesians," 102–3.

7. Ibid.

8. Pryas, "Monlogism," 596.

9. Stapleton, *Christianity, Patriotism, and Nationhood*, 2.

towards being after traversing the dialectical. It therefore transcends the univocal, equivocal, and dialectical postures while still including them. In this chapter, I therefore aim to demonstrate that it is in the midst of this paradoxical partnership between revelation and mystery that the event of understanding occurs. This event is not one of pure comprehension, but nor is it a moment of pure incomprehension. It dwells between as both comprehension and incomprehension.

I have assumed thus far that epiphanies do occur and that certain goals, attitudes, and tools help to open the reader up to such epiphanies. But how is the advent of the epiphany to be understood in Chesterton's work? To begin to answer this question, it is helpful to return to Chesterton's understanding of the position—the situatedness—of the perceiving subject. One instance of Žižek's misquotation and misreading of Chesterton is instructive on this point. Žižek writes, "When G. K. Chesterton describes his conversion to Christianity, he claims that he 'tried to be some ten minutes in advance of the truth,'" but found that he "'was *eighteen years* behind it.' Does the same not hold even more for those who, today, desperately try to catch up with the New by way of following the latest 'post-' fashion, and are thus condemned to remain forever eighteen years behind the truly New?"[10]

Žižek's error here is forgivable considering that it is the sort of quotation error that Chesterton himself is frequently guilty of. Nevertheless, what Chesterton is actually saying is too significant to overlook. His real point is that in "[trying] to be some ten minutes in advance of the truth," he "found" that he was "eighteen *hundred* years behind it."[11] While Žižek's focus is only on a subjective experience of the fashionable, Chesterton's emphasis is on the shocking revelation of the ancient and timeless. Additionally, Chesterton suggests that his "philosophy" is not his: "God and humanity made it; and it made me," and also jokes that, while trying to come up with his own "heresy," he ended up discovering "orthodoxy."[12] For the humble subject, there is an acknowledgment that truth and meaning precede the event of understanding, even while they are only recognized in and after the event. The subject actively seeks mastery over his world only to discover that even selfhood is something that happens to and is disclosed to the self.

This again shows that the subject is located primarily within the drama as a co-participant in Being with others, from other people to "pork to pyrotechnics" in history and tradition.[13] The event of understanding is

---

10. Žižek , *In Defense Of Lost Causes*, 140.

11. Chesterton, *Collected Works, Volume 1*, 214, emphasis added.

12. Ibid., 211, 214.

13. Chesterton, *Collected Works, Volume 3*, 189.

therefore something that situates the subject—reveals the subject to the subject—within the larger drama. It is not just a moment of sudden detachment, although a sense of detachment is possible in it, but a moment of deep-rootedness. And yet this occurs without necessarily overpowering or overwhelming the subject. There is a clear protagonistic shift in the mind of the subject; there is a reorientation of the subject's stance towards the cosmos that involves the recognition that he is co-protagonist rather than the prime or sole protagonist. And yet he does not lose his subjectivity: he feels that he is leading the way, but later discovers that he was being led. In this way, Chesterton overturns any way of thinking that describes a merely active agent (the self) as taking charge over a passive object (understanding). In his view, everything is active. One may even say that everything is an actor in the drama of being. Understanding is therefore something that arises in the midst of the drama, as a new experience of what was always already present. It is this recovery of what one already possesses that is the defining characteristic of the hermeneutic event in Chesterton's work.

Žižek defines the event as "something shocking, out of joint, that appears to happen all of a sudden and interrupts the usual flow of things; something out of nowhere, without discernible causes, an appearance without solid being as its foundation."[14] However, a more Chestertonian definition of an event must challenge this appeal to groundlessness. Even as "an occurrence not grounded in sufficient [human] reasons" or as something that does not make sense when juxtaposed with the rules of a situation— and even in relation to an experience of destabilization and disorientation—the event always has a foundation in Being and exists in relation to other beings.

The pure event is, in fact, a (limited) disclosure of being (or even of Being). It may therefore be defined as a subjective, partial experience of the other (or Other), which brings about a total reframing, not just of one's understanding, but of one's very posture toward reality. In Kierkegaard's terms, it is a *subjective truth*: "an objective uncertainty held fast through personal appropriation with the most passionate inwardness."[15] It is a paradoxical occurrence, through which the subject is presented with an answer that was not anticipated in the questions that were being asked.

This paradoxical occurrence has an authority that resides outside of language even while it may speak through language. Chesterton acknowledges that "every philosophy" must rest upon the "authority or the accuracy of something" and yet the very language used to express that authority and

14. Žižek, *Event*, 2.

15. Kierkegaard, *Provocations*, 69.

accuracy is not infallible.[16] There is no "perfect scheme of verbal expression for all the internal moods and meanings of men."[17] There is no such thing as complete representation by "an arbitrary system of grunts and squeals" of the various "tones and semi-tones" of the true.[18] In fact, it is the one who fears being misrepresented who "has seen into the heart of the real nature of language."[19] Language "is not a scientific thing at all, but a wholly artistic thing, a thing invented by hunters, and killers, and such artists long before science was dreamed of. The truth is simply *that*—that the tongue is not a reliable instrument, like a stopwatch or a camera. The tongue is a most truly and unruly member, as the wise saint has called it, a thing poetic and dangerous, like music or fire."[20] Nevertheless, this does not mean that language is useless. There are still better and worse ways of saying things, just as there are better and worse ways of interpreting things.

Chesterton suggests that while the meanings of words are affected by context, and while he concedes that words can be misused as "labour-saving machinery," the real task of the communicator remains to chose words to get as close to the actual experience of understanding as possible.[21] One of Chesterton's examples is helpful for getting a sense of what he means. He offers two sentences, the first of which reads as follows: "The persuasive and even coercive powers of the citizen should enable him to make sure that the burden of longevity in the previous generation does not become disproportionate or intolerable, especially to the females."[22] The second sentence is this: "Murder your mother."[23] These two sentences mean the same thing, and yet the second is clearly closer to exposing an actual experience of understanding, even if it too carries the burden of its own imprecision.

Chesterton indicates the importance of using language in such a way as to call the reader's metaphysical prejudices into question.[24] By doing this, one stands a chance of throwing words together in such a way as to invite the reader into an openness to the intractable mystery that is discovered in the paradox of the hermeneutic event. We should be "thinking about things" rather than just being "mislead by the indirect influence of

16. Chesterton, *G. F. Watts,* 44.
17. Ibid.
18. Ibid.
19. Ibid.
20. Ibid., 45.
21. Chesterton, *Collected Works, Volume 1,* 329.
22. Chesterton, *Eugenics and Other Evils,* 12–13.
23. Ibid.
24. Chesterton, *Collected Works, Volume 1,* 329.

words."[25] The "relation of the mind to the real thing outside the mind" ought to be retained.[26] The event of understanding, then, is not predominantly a matter of articulation. It remains a matter of participation in Being and in the drama of reason. Articulation, like conscious awareness, is just one fragment of this participation.

To navigate the paradox of the hermeneutic event, I aim to play with Chesterton's interpretation of the book of Job—a text that he returned to with more frequency than many others, as if he was always expecting new insights. In his view, it is a book "better worth hearing than any modern philosophical conversation in the whole philosophical world."[27] It is a work that Edmund Burke refers to in his *A Philosophical Enquiry into the Sublime and the Beautiful* (1757) because of its ability to evoke the transcendent. He mentions one passage in particular, in which a vision is mixed in with fear and trembling, and where silence produces a voice: "*Shall mortal man be more just than God?*" (Job 4:17). There is a "terrible uncertainty" in what is being described here that reflects the uncertainty and plurivocity of the whole.[28] The book of Job is more a book of questions and provocations than of answers.

I have already noted that *The Surprise* presumes a hidden dialogue much like the one that takes place between God and Satan in the book of Job and this same intertextuality is found in some of Chesterton's other works of fiction as well. For instance, *The Man Who Was Thursday* opens with a conversation between a civilized man named Gabriel Syme and an anarchic poet named Lucian Gregory before shifting to the main drama of the story.[29] This same novel can, in fact, be read as an extended commentary on the book of Job. Mark Knight summarizes the similarities as follows:

> [F]irst, Job asks God what his purpose is, and the six detectives ask Sunday the same question; second, both God and Sunday answer in riddles; third, both Job and Syme are comforted by the riddles they hear; fourth, both God and Sunday point out the panorama of Creation to their questioners; fifth, the secret of both stories is (according to [Stephen] Medcalf) joy; sixth, both stories suggest that the protagonists suffer because they are the best of men rather than the worst of men; and finally, both *The Man Who Was Thursday: A Nightmare* and Chesterton's

25. Chesterton, *Saint Thomas Aquinas, Saint Francis of Assisi*, 167.

26. Ibid., 168.

27. Knight, *Chesterton and Evil*, 146.

28. Burke, *A Philosophical Enquiry*, 52.

29. Chesterton, *Man Who Was Thursday*, 12.

interpretation of the Book of Job link the suffering of the pro-
tagonists to the suffering of Christ.[30]

The Ball and the Cross (1910) also mirrors the opening of the book of
Job. It begins in a flying ship high above the ground with a conversation
between a lowly monk named Michael and an arrogant scientist named
Lucifer. It is only after this pretext has played out that the narrative shifts to
the drama on the ground.[31] The names of these characters cannot be overlooked. Gabriel and Michael are the names of two archangels and Lucian
and Lucifer recall the archangel who fell by standing against God—the very
same angel who appears at the start of the book of Job as the accuser and
primary antagonist in the story.

Such continuous allusions, among many other more direct references
to the book of Job, make it clear that Chesterton regards the importance of
the book of Job to be something that is only inadequately expressed when we
say that "it is the most interesting of ancient books."[32] He is not exaggerating
here. To him, it is really a book that has "eternal" significance—a significance that transcends all ages and locations. In fact, Chesterton contends
that "philosophy is either eternal or it is not philosophy."[33] And, in his view,
"all real philosophy is apocalyptic."[34] This is to say that all real philosophy
is concerned with revealing something. The book of Job also represents a
genuine attempt at a "cosmic philosophy."[35] It tries to be a philosophy that is
constructed with the entire cosmos in mind, rather than simply complying
with entirely anthropocentric aims. After all, "man can no more possess a
private religion than he can possess a private sun and moon."[36] Thus, man,
while being almost infinitely important, is still not the center of the universe.

"The first of the intellectual beauties of the Book of Job is that it is all
concerned with this desire to know the actuality; the desire to know what
is, and not merely what seems."[37] It suggests, in keeping with what I have
discussed earlier, the possibility of seeing through the created order into the
mind of the Creator. Whether or not the book of Job ultimately achieves
this will always be endlessly debatable. Nevertheless, it can at least be com-
mended for having an aim that does not simply cater to common human

30. Knight, *Chesterton and Evil,* 148.

31. Chesterton, *Ball and Cross,* 12.

32. Chesterton, *In Defense of Sanity,* 95.

33. Ibid., 96.

34. Ibid., 71.

35. Ibid., 95.

36. Ibid., 96.

37. Ibid.

egotism. In fact, it is a book that presents a number of opinions offered by a number of people without ever once suggesting that they, individually, have in fact arrived at the essence of what is really going on. There is no escape from metaxological mediation here. This is true even of the character of God in the story. Even after the last word has been spoken or penned or printed, a genuine openness to otherness remains.

The book of Job seems therefore to follow a "dialogic sense of truth," which "resists summation."[38] Again, this would be contrasted by any "monologic" sense of truth, which would strive for a neat synthesis of available information.[39] It aims, in other words, at the metaxological rather than the dialectical. The truth of the book of Job is not something that can be found in any one of its statements. Rather, it is located in its paradoxes and in the interplay between and intersubjectivity of the characters and their words. It is the presence of and reliance upon paradox that ultimately affirms the cosmic scope of its philosophy: for truth, as we have already seen, is dramatic.

The tension between mystery and revelation that we find in the book of Job is likened by Chesterton to the game of hide-and-seek, which reflects Chesterton's palimpsestic approach to reading as implying a three-tiered conception of what we are reading: what is irretrievably hidden, what is hidden, but still implied and, finally, what is actually visible. In simple terms, mystery implies the first two of these, while revelation implies the third; and yet mystery and revelation are more interwoven than the analogy of the palimpsest implies. To build on these ideas, Chesterton observes that hide-and-seek "is a popular pastime [that] assumes the truth of the text, 'Seek and ye shall find'" (Matt 7:7).[40] Therefore, any ironclad, totalistic mindset that refuses the hospitality of defamiliarization prevents genuine participation with the text. This results in the absence of both seeking and finding, and therefore the absence of both mystery and surprise.

To remedy this, mystery or mysticism supports the recovery of a clear view and a deliberate appreciation of reality that goes beyond simplistically intuited impressions into the kind of specificity that transcends purely rational explanations. In this communion with what transcends rationalities—this communication with the transrational—a level of secrecy in our partaking of the sacrament of reality is presupposed. Even where truth has nothing to do with vividness and can even tend "to look a little misty and atmospheric," it is nevertheless what brings everything else into focus.[41]

38. Newsome, *The Book of Job,* 86.

39. Ibid., 86–87.

40. Chesterton, *All Things Considered,* 65.

41. Chesterton, *Illustrated London News,* December 3, 1910.

It is mystery, as that which transcends our capacity for espistemic cer-
titude, and also as that which is endlessly knowable and unknowable, that
makes revelation possible. Only by acknowledging the place of the human
drama within the mystery of the divine drama that one is able to defend
the dignity and value of human beings. It is only meaning or dignity that is
conferred from the outside and understood from the inside that has authority. Self-generated meaning has no authentic authority and therefore does
not genuinely uphold human dignity.

Chesterton explains that there are three classes of mysteries—what
he refers to as *secrets*—that give rise to revelation. The first is a secret that
is kept to be revealed at some point. The "whole object is not to keep the
secret, but to tell it" at the opportune time.[42] This would be the kind of secret that is found in the plots of stories. In this case, mystery is in a playful
partnership with ignorance and agnosticism. Chesterton offers that "being
ignorant is the best and purest preparation for receiving the horrible revelations of the high life. Somewhat in the same way being an agnostic is
the best and purest preparation for receiving the happy revelations of St.
John."[43] He suggests—naming the coupling of mystery and revelation—that
"we Catholics are all agnostics."[44] As is his custom, he is not polarizing belief and uncertainty, since he is usually very critical of a strict agnosticism.
Instead, he is arguing that faith (in connection with Catholicism, in this
case) and ignorance (agnosticism) can be kept in tension with each other:
all belief is open to being challenged by newer insights. Considered differently, this kind of revelation is a "novelty" that "depends on ignorance."[45] It
is worth remembering Chesterton's contention that the "meek shall inherit
the earth" precisely because they have expected "nothing" and are therefore
ready to be "gloriously surprised."[46]

The second kind of mystery or secret is the one that is kept because it
is something already known to everyone.[47] The idiomatic elephant in the
room that no one wants to expose would be one example. This kind of secret
exists in another paradox since we "are asked to be silent about these things,
but we are not asked to be ignorant about them."[48] In this instance, the most

42. Chesterton, *All Things Considered*, 65.

43. Ibid.

44. Chesterton, *The Ball and the Cross*, 62.

45. Chesterton, *Illustrated London News*, September 18, 1920.

46. Chesterton, *Collected Works, Volume 1*, 69.

47. Chesterton, *All Things Considered*, 65.

48. Ibid., 66.

common thing to humanity is frequently also "most veiled by humanity."[49] The third kind of secret is the one that is kept because it is too mysterious, delicate or vague to be explained at all. This kind of secret suggests something "too good to be told."[50]

Here, ignorance, as a kind of latent awareness prior to re-membering and as a posture towards being, may be regarded as a kind of holy awe (in its positive sense) or as terror (in its negative sense). Chesterton notes that even the commonplace decision to go on a country walk is an example of this kind of secret.[51] These three classes of secrets correlate fairly well, although not exactly, with what Robert McKee calls the "three possible ways to connect the audience to a story: *mystery, suspense,* and *dramatic irony*."[52] With mystery, the audience knows less than the characters in the story. With suspense, the audience and the characters in the story have the same amount of information, leaving the sense that a revelation is on its way. And with dramatic irony, the audience knows more than the characters, and yet there is no way for the audience to inform the characters of the revelation they are about to receive. It is through these gaps in knowledge—gaps that act as the subtext of desire—that a story is propelled into surprise. And yet, in Chesterton's view on the divine drama, and as is especially evident in the book of Job, the mystery is never completely solved. Mystery remains even after revelation.

In all of the above, Chesterton points to an irreducibility that is present in the tension between mystery and revelation. Even when something is existentially familiar, for instance, it may remain epistemically fuzzy. Even if it is real, it may not necessarily be explicable in language. This allows for a constant return and remembering of what has been experienced and understood, which resists converting the perceived picture into a pattern of over-automization. Chesterton's own writing reflects this in the way that he revisits and revises subjects that he has already covered in detail. This revision is not undertaken to merely correct mistaken interpretations, although this may be a helpful byproduct of such revision. Rather, revision seeks to explore fresh ways of seeing the same thing. As I have already noted, it is not just the anomaly that has the capacity to surprise, but also the repetition. Repetition, too, leads to a confrontation with otherness; intimacy produces a kind of startling recognition of the familiar as extraordinary.[53] Chesterton

49. Ibid.

50. Chesterton, *In Defense of Sanity*, 100.

51. Chesterton, *All Things Considered*, 67.

52. McKee, *Story*, 349.

53. Chesterton, *Alarms and Discursions*, 7.

is not interested in the sort of revision that shrinks reality into a dialectical synthesis that is only a construct of a mind, as if thought were able to operate apart from the world that forms and informs it. He is interested in the kind of ocular athleticism that would allow people to see that they are part of a larger, more startling story than they have first imagined.

It is arguable that the loss of this ocular athleticism is a central a problem at the heart of the book of Job. Job is a man who, at the start of the story, lives in awe of God. He makes regular sacrifices, not only for himself, but also for his children (Job 1:1–5). And this is even noticed by God, who in conversation with Satan remarks that "there is none like [Job] in the earth, a perfect and an upright man, one that feareth God, and escheweth evil" (Job 1:8). Satan, the first skeptic in the story, is not convinced. Job's awe of God is owed, he thinks, to a "hedge" that has been placed around him (Job 1:10). God listens to Satan's complaint and accepts his challenge. He allows him to take the various safeguards around Job away, and so Job loses almost everything, including his children and his wealth. And yet, as the first chapter of the book concludes, Job retains his faith in God and therefore is said not have sinned (Job 1:21–22).

We can undoubtedly interpret the traumas of Job very literally, as actual events resulting from a duel between God and Satan. However, Chesterton warns that literalism reflects "a certain dry-throated earnestness and mental thirst," both of which are generally reflective of an "atmosphere of morbidity."[54] Literalism, as the lowest and most uninvolved level of hermeneutic engagement, rejects any surplus of meaning and therefore also silences all analogical possibilities before they have had a chance to speak. Chesterton is aware of St. Augustine's work on interpretation in his book *On Christian Doctrine*, and points out the importance of treating texts "symbolically" when appropriate.[55] There can ultimately be no definitive interpretation of a text, although we should nevertheless strive to keep our interpretation in line with what the text says. Not forgetting that Chesterton does not side with a prescriptivism either on the side of literalism or on the side of anti-literalism, then, I want to offer a slightly more parabolic reading of the traumas of Job. This is not done to belittle his traumas, but rather to highlight what Chesterton thinks of as the central problem in the human experience.

Perhaps we can read these excessive losses as emblematic of a loss of perspective: a loss of reality, truth, and vitality; or, perhaps, as a loss of context. After all, it is his *world*—the matrix of interwoven meanings

54. Chesterton, *A Miscellany of Men*, 23.

55. Chesterton, *Illustrated London News*, April 20, 1929.

symbolized by the concrete (children, possessions, health, and so on)—that is destroyed. Even if Job were not literally deprived of so much, there is a sense in which his experience represents the common human failure to take heed of what we have. As much as suffering from literal loss remains a problem, a deeper spiritual problem is evident, which is, as Chesterton suggests in his book *Magic,* that the fairytale may be stolen from us.[56] The world can be lost to us even if we do not experience this loss literally.[57] When the magic goes out of the world, a severe gloominess takes over that needs to be remedied.

This loss of the magic of the real may be linked with the loss of a positive sense of mystery. A "negative spirit" therefore overtakes one's perceptions.[58] After being inflicted with such severe suffering, not without reason, Job becomes a man possessed by self-pity. He cannot see outside of himself and beyond his own pain. And so the world is no longer viewed as a place of wonder. Instead it represents privation and destitution. Again, this may be taken as a representative expression of any tendency towards self-absorption or solipsism. And what Chesterton wants his readers to do is get away from this way of seeing, to find themselves again within a world of Being and beings. Awe and mystery are all that can cure a loss of this world.

This return to mystery, however, does not imply a need to become utterly detached from our earthly conditions. As in the example of Chesterton's remarks on the story of the Tower of Babel mentioned earlier, mystery will ultimately be understood via the concrete reality of the text. In this, we see one reason for Marshall McLuhan's reference to Chesterton as a "practical mystic."[59] It is in returning to our senses, to concrete being, that Job and the rest of us are called back to the transcendent. It is by contesting many of the impossible ideals of the imagination with a deeper kind of imagination that we encounter actual beauty, for instance; and it is this beauty that intimates the Beauty of God.[60]

Chesterton begins his "Introduction" to the book of Job by pointing out that "[t]he book of Job is among the other Old Testament books both a philosophical riddle and a historical riddle."[61] Elsewhere, in his "Defense of Nonsense," he notes that the book of Job is great because, like all "great literature," it is allegorical; its own riddles reflect the stark fact that "life

56. Chesterton, *Magic,* 27.

57. Chesterton, *Tremendous Trifles,* 162–63.

58. Chesterton, *Collected Works, Volume 1,* 47.

59. McLuhan, "G. K. Chesterton," 455.

60. Chesterton, *The Defendant,* 82–88.

61. Chesterton, *In Defense of Sanity,* 91.

is a riddle" too.[62] This foregrounding of riddles is significant, since the hermeneutic project is always one preceded and contextualized by mystery. However, mystery here cannot just refer to what is unknowable. It also refers to what is endlessly knowable. Chesterton puts the philosophical riddle aside to begin with because it seems as if he wants to first clean the lens that his reader may be using to read this ancient text: he tells us that a "few words of general explanation or warning should [first] be said about the historical aspect."[63]

This is a wise move considering that "[r]eading the book of Job has never been easy."[64] In addition to the fact that it "touches on some of the most difficult issues of human experience," it also poses a range of "interpretive problems for readers."[65] The book has many "subtle literary features" that have often been overlooked to reduce it to a template for "theodicies," even though it is more likely, as even Chesterton's commentary suggests, that it exists to deconstruct theodicies.[66] It contains a number of voices and perspectives that are impossible to merge.[67] The basic idea here, following Carol Newsome's engagement with the work of Mikhail Bakhtin, is that the text suggests an "embodied, personal quality."[68] As opposed to a strictly monological view of truth, which may easily be abstracted from its context, the book of Job requires a dialogical view of truth that stresses the irreducibility of individual voices and the importance of integral perspectives.[69] Because of its polyphonic and plurivocal form, the precise meaning of the book of Job cannot be pinned down. It presupposes the importance of an openness to truth that goes beyond the very human tendency to resort to stylized dogmas.

Even if he does not discuss such issues at length, Chesterton is aware that the book of Job is far from simple. As one always highly cognizant of his audience, though, he chooses to first home in on one of the more contemporary problems posed by the form of the book—problems that are still there for the contemporary reader. He points out the well known "[c]ontroversy" concerning the fact that the book of Job includes some fairly obvious textua

---

62. Chesterton, *The Defendant*, 8.

63. Chesterton, *In Defense of Sanity*, 91.

64. Newsome, *The Book of Job*, 3.

65. Ibid.

66. Burrell, *Deconstructing Theodicy*, 10, 13.

67. Newsome, *The Book of Job*, 22.

68. Ibid., 23.

69. Ibid.

tampering.[70] The "original scheme" undoubtedly has a few "interpolations of a considerably later date."[71] This is noticed, for instance, in the fact that God rebukes Job's friends and even addresses Job while utterly ignoring the young man Elihu; it is as if Elihu was not part of the original narrative. The literary style of the book is also not always consistent: prose and poetry are juxtaposed for reasons that are not self-evident and there are stylistic variations even within the poetry of the book.

As will always be the case when scholars step into the same territory, there are disagreements about precisely which parts have been inserted and which are part of the original. But Chesterton's research shows him that "the prose prologue and epilogue, and possibly the speech of the young man who comes in with an apology at the end" are more than likely to have been added later.[72] Still, whatever we may decide about the way that this text has been stitched together, "there is a general truth to be remembered in this connection."[73] We are most definitely dealing with something that "grew gradually" like a castle or a cathedral.[74] And while this may be perceived as a problem for the contemporary reader, it would not have bothered the original audiences of the final form of the book of Job. People of that earlier time, who were rooted in an oral culture of myth, ritual, and tradition, were almost indifferent to matters of authorship; they were certainly less interested in the "actual date and the actual author" than people caught up in the "insane individualism of modern times."[75] Chesterton jokes that even if Homer's *Illiad* may have been written by someone else who also happened to have also been called Homer, it would be of little consequence.[76] And even if "Moses was not Moses, but another person called Moses," what would it really matter?[77] Chesterton challenges the modern obsession with authorship to point out that it is really a side issue and therefore hardly relevant to the pursuit of genuine understanding. What matters most here is the wrestling match between the reader and the text, not the question of who wrote it. This much should be obvious considering that whoever wrote it, at least as far as we can tell, did not take any trouble to make their authorship an issue when they were creating the work.

70. Chesterton, *In Defense of Sanity*, 91.

71. Ibid.

72. Ibid.

73. Ibid.

74. Ibid.

75. Ibid.

76. Ibid.

77. Ibid., 92.

The central point that Chesterton wants to make on this issue is that in times of greater tribalism and more close-knit communities, it should be expected that texts would have been the fruit of the collective rather than of one individual, just as any temple would have been the product of many pairs of hands rather than of just one. Chesterton uses this observation to suggest that perhaps something is to be learned from the unified spirit of the group. The search for a cosmic philosophy is a communal one; the pursuit of truth is not something that can ever really take place in complete isolation. Several scholars would probably disagree concerning this dismissal of the issue of authorship, especially those engaging in "historical criticism,"[78] but Chesterton's reason for adhering to the principle of unity goes beyond convenience and naïvety.

Unity is not suggested as a means to uphold any wrongheaded belief in the obviousness of the meaning of the story. It turns out, in fact, that it is a matter of setting up coordinates for a helpful interpretation of the text. Unity must precede the hermeneutic event. Even if the text were completely disjointed and filled with irreconcilable differences, some kind of unity would still be assumed by the reader. Even if the text were incoherent, the reader would seek to unify his experience of the text by designating that very incoherence. Difference can only be stated on the basis of an *a priori* commitment to similarity. It seems, then, that unity not only needs to be assumed, but will be assumed, and that this very assumption is what allows a more fruitful engagement with the meaning or meanings of the text. Assuming the alternative would make the mistake of regarding the primary aim of reading to be to simply unscramble the puzzle instead of trying to figure out what is being represented by the puzzle. It is possible that unscrambling the puzzle can be helpful for better understanding what is being represented, but this does not seem to be the case here.

Therefore, even though the book of Job stands somewhat "apart from most of the books included in the canon of the Old Testament," we would be wrong to conclude that there is an "absence of unity."[79] By analogy, the fact that several people caught up in conversation disagree with each other is not proof that the conversation does not exist. Unity (conversation) is still present even when uniformity (agreement) is not.

Nevertheless, Chesterton finds more than just this general sense of unity in the book of Job. There is a consistency of aim that is remarkable considering the fact that the biblical canon contains works by multiple authors. Of course, as Chesterton notes, we my not necessarily agree on how

---

78. Newsom, *The Victorian World Picture*, 4.

79. Chesterton, *In Defense of Sanity*, 93.

such unity was ever achieved. Perhaps some spiritual guidance or "natural tradition" or clever editing process was involved. Nevertheless, unity remains.[80] Even the later additions to the book are far from arbitrary. "[L]et us remember," Chesterton writes, "that there was more unity in those times in a hundred men than there is unity now in one man. Then a city was like one man. Now one man is like a city in civil war."[81]

Chesterton maintains that even this dissonance within the book of Job fits with the "special tone and intention of the Old Testament" which consistently, albeit amidst the same spirit of debate that we find in the book of Job, comes back to this one idea—the "idea of all men being merely the instruments of a higher power."[82] This is a no doubt a fairly broad and bold statement to make and it is worth dwelling on especially within the context of mystery that Chesterton has set up. Chesterton is not dogmatically suggesting that people are just the impersonal instruments of a higher power. In fact, his persistent abhorrence of the Calvinist perspective on divine sovereignty and his equally persistent stress on the importance of defending free will help us to better understand what he means when he says this. As we move through his essay on the book of Job, he challenges this idea in such a way as to make it more of a question than it may first appear. Even this hard statement is more of a riddle than it is a solution: are people merely the instruments of God? This question, when left to resonate without a quick answer, suggests that the will of God may not be something that we can reduce to complete certainty.

Two tendencies regarding Chesterton's way of reading become evident here. The first is his resistance to taming the text. There may be a question, for instance, concerning whether the Bible may "be offered as something extraordinary or as something ordinary," but it is a matter of great importance not to resolve the question entirely.[83] We must remain open to the otherness of the text by not making our minds up too quickly. The second tendency, which is continuous with the first, is a resistance to subjecting God to our own wills and desires. Chesterton writes frequently against any temptation that we may have to control the divine or the realm of the spiritual in any way, even though our subjective experience may suggest the primacy of the "I" or ego. Even with regard to the Apostles Creed, "the word 'I' comes before even the word 'God.' The believer comes first; but he is soon dwarfed by his beliefs, swallowed in the creative whirlwind and the

80. Ibid., 92.
81. Ibid.
82. Ibid., 93.
83. Chesterton, *The Man Who Was Orthodox*, 98.

trumpets of the resurrection."[84] With regard to perceiving clearly, belief is antithetical to control; faith, as submission to what is more ultimate than the self, is opposite to certainty, not its guarantor.

Chesterton, adhering to the principle of reading the text as it is rather than as we might want it to be, is well aware of the many "atrocities and treacheries" attributed to God in the biblical canon, but we ought to be careful not to pin these down to a definitive explanation of God's character. As even what tradition refers to as the progressive revelation of the Scriptures seems to show, such occurrences are more likely to be symbolic of the sheer otherness of God and the difficulties faced by people in discerning his character, than concrete delineations of his actual will. Chesterton does not name these "atrocities and treacheries" directly, but he does point out that "judges and prophets of Israel" were particularly guilty of supporting these things. In particular, stories like those of Jael hammering a tent nail into the head of a tyrant (Judg 4) or of Samson's mass murder by suicide (Judg 16) must strike us as troubling. Surely, no one who reads the entire canon can deny that some truly awful things are recorded to have been done in the name of God and even at his bidding.

Nevertheless, Chesterton suggests that there are those who are "too Christian" to see any sense in this tyrannical view of God; they may read the stories, but they do not necessarily accept them as descriptions or prescriptions regarding what ought to be.[85] The stories may reflect God as he was understood by his people at the time, but Chesterton leaves room for the possibility that this is not what God is actually like.

Thus, Chesterton intimates that while the question of how God uses his power is at the center of the canon, the way that God comes to be understood through a series of palimpsestic negotiations evolves. This much should be obvious even in the earliest stories, where Abraham, for example, begins, as any ancient Near Eastern pilgrim influenced by a Mesopotamian culture would begin, by believing that child sacrifice is a good and godly thing and conclude by believing that it is not (Gen 22). This changing of opinions may challenge Chesterton's notion "that there was more unity in those times in a hundred men than there is unity now in one man," but we should be careful before assuming that he is setting up a way of reading that negates the vital place of negotiation and difference. Unity does not suggest the absence of progression. Unity does not prescribe univocity. Rather, unity is assumed as the bookends of a book even when fragmentation may be found on every one of its pages.

84. Quoted in Belmont, *A Year with G. K. Chesterton*, 112.
85. Chesterton, *In Defense of Sanity*, 93.

Chesterton moves on to claim that the Old Testament holds clear com-monsensical ideas that "strength is strength, that cunning is cunning, that worldly success is worldly success" and that these things will be used by the God of Job "for His own ultimate purpose" in the same way that "natural forces or physical elements" will be used to suit his aims.[86] Consequently, God "uses the strength of a hero as He uses that of a Mammoth without any particular respect for the Mammoth."[87] The "atmosphere of the Old Testa-ment" as Chesterton sees it is that "[t]he heroes of the Old Testament are not the sons of God, but the slaves of God, gigantic and terrible slaves, like the genii, who were the slaves of Aladdin."[88]

Without more careful consideration, it may seem here that Chesterton is forgetting his tendency to prioritize the picture over the pattern. How-ever, we know from Chesterton's other writings that he rejects the idea of an overbearing and domineering divinity. Moreover, we need to remember that Chesterton is talking about a God whose mysteriousness is prioritized as a hermeneutic coordinate. Therefore, even where man is recognized as the tool of the divine, there is a great deal that remains a riddle even in that recognition. After all, a tool can be used in any number of ways, or not used at all. This is presumably why Chesterton uses that word "atmosphere."[89] There is a general mood or overarching trend to be accounted for and it can be argued that the mood is one that regards the divine more in terms of authoritarianism than, for instance, in terms of servanthood. However, it is this very dialectic of authority and servanthood that is challenged by Chesterton's paradoxical vision.

The point remains that however people may have understood him, God is the goal, the end, the *telos*. Even when he is hiding behind the scenes, every action on the stage gestures towards his reality. And even when his ul-timate will and purpose are unknown, it is still certain in the minds of many Jewish and Christian people of faith that his ultimate will and purpose will be done. This central axiom operates as the goal of the biblical narrative, but this does not necessarily mean that we can be completely certain what this goal is or how it will be achieved. Thus, even when Chesterton insists upon this idea as the glue that holds the text together, he is not really adopting a rigid interpretive approach. Rather, to presume unity is precisely the same thing for him as adopting a critically optimistic posture that allows for a rich, nuanced story to be told, with all its surprises and unexpected insights.

86. Ibid., 94
87. Ibid.
88. Ibid.
89. Ibid.

There is still a clear "philosophical object," which is to better understand man's relationship with the divine.[90]

After offering that the Old Testament presents an atmosphere of divine dominance, Chesterton states that an even more "central idea of the great part of the Old Testament may be called the idea of the loneliness of God."[91] He sees God not just as the "chief character of the Old Testament," but almost as "the only character in the Old Testament. Compared with His clearness of purpose, all the other wills are heavy and automatic, like those of animals; compared with His actuality, all the sons of flesh are shadows."[92] Chesterton makes a move here in his interpretation that is notably Platonist: he puts forward the suggestion that God is more real than the apparent reality; the truly "real is always seen in some measure *through* the apparent" while "the apparent is never adequate to the task of fully containing and defining the real."[93] This fits with the definition of the hermeneutic event offered above: an event is an encounter with the transcendent through the immanent or, as in *The Surprise,* it is the discovery of the Author *behind* the drama as experienced *through* and *in* the drama. This is the very "note that is struck" in the book of Job: "With whom hath [the Almighty] taken counsel?"; "I have trodden the wine press alone, and of the peoples there was no man with me."[94]

God needs no counsel, support, or defense. His creation and his creatures are secondary and dependent upon him, while he is primary and the only one who can be said to be truly independent. And yet, he chooses to interact with his creation. He stands, like an author, completely apart from the text. Yet he still opts to interact with it, almost as a co-reader of the text, regarding "the patriarchs" as "His tools or weapons; for the Lord is a man of war."[95] Thus, Joshua may as well have been an "axe," and Moses "a measuring-rod."[96] Sampson can be likened to a "sword" in the hand of God, and Isaiah to a "trumpet."[97] Even the saints of the church provide a face to this God; they are "as it were, little statuettes of Him."[98]

---

90. Ibid.

91. Ibid.

92. Ibid.

93. Tyson, *Returning to Reality*, 9.

94. Chesterton, *In Defense of Sanity*, 94.

95. Ibid.

96. Ibid.

97. Ibid.

98. Ibid.

Chesterton places a heavy and perhaps unappealing accent here on the violence of God, but it seems to me that ultimately he sees this violence more metaphorically than literally. It represents a ferocious commitment to love and righteousness. There is a battle to be fought, but that battle ought to be fought at the level of the symbol: through ideas expressed in words and through acts of compassion and empathy. This battle, at its very root, involves negotiating the nature of God. Even if we do not like the depiction of God in the Bible, Chesterton insists on his characteristic superlativeness: "God is stronger than man" and "more secret than man."[99] "He means more" and "knows better what He is doing" than any one else does.[100] These may seem like assertions of an immediate knowledge, but in keeping with Chesterton's awareness of the imperfection of language, and almost in the manner of Pseudo-Dionysius, he keeps on appealing to what language can never do justice to: the *more,* the *beyond,* the *excessive* character of God. Additionally, "compared with Him we have something of the vagueness, the unreason, and the vagrancy of the beasts that perish."[101] In the book of Job, this idea is proposed in the following way: "It is he that sitteth above the earth, and the inhabitants thereof are as grasshoppers" (Job 39:20). Just in case the reader has not found the point, Chesterton goes on: "The book is so intent upon asserting the personality of God that it almost asserts the impersonality of man. Unless this gigantic cosmic brain has conceived a thing, that thing is insecure and void; man has not enough tenacity to ensure its continuance."[102] Again, this resonates with the encounter with the hermeneutic event: the human subject perceives himself to be the protagonist, only to discover that he is an extra in God's play.

Chesterton therefore affirms something already discussed: God is the ground of being, the transcendent source of all goodness: "Except the Lord build the house their labour is but lost that build it. Except the Lord keep the city the watchman watcheth but in vain."[103] He consequently sees this emphasis on the plans and purposes of God as something of a literary exaggeration, which in the mind of any dualist would bring about a world of negations, with God against man or God as the antithesis of creation. We know, however, that Chesterton is no dualist even when pointing out that "the Old Testament positively rejoices in the obliteration of man in comparison with the divine purpose. The Book of Job stands definitely alone

---

99. Ibid., 94–95.
100. Ibid., 95.
101. Ibid.
102. Ibid.
103. Ibid.

because the Book of Job definitely asks, 'But what is the purpose of God? Is it worth the sacrifice even of our miserable humanity?'"[104]

The ambiguity in the first question must be noted. Job does not just ask what sort of plans God has, but rather whether or not there is any point to God being there at all: "Is it worth the sacrifice even of our miserable humanity?"[105] The loss of Job's world amounts to a question about the value of anything or anyone, God included. But even if we see God as a rival to our present experiences, there must be a sense in which such rivalry would be akin to the rivalry between reality and fantasy. In the end, the rivalry is false.

Even if God is not "grander and kinder" than experience and understanding have led us to believe, Chesterton contends that it would still be better to cling to the notion that God can "use His tools" or "break his tools" as he pleases than to believe wrongly in the supremacy of our own perceptions.[106] In fact, it is in the pursuit of the truly real that we should ask what God is up to; we need to ask what he is doing with his tools and "what are they being broken for?"[107] This is the primary "philosophical riddle, the riddle of the Book of Job."[108]

Already in the above, we can see that Chesterton, striving as always for clarity against any kind of conceptual fog, has set down strong interpretive boundaries. God is certainly still a character in his reading of the book of Job, rather than being only a mystical force. He is presented as a person rather than an idea; and as such he has some very strong opinions about how things should and should not be. Chesterton opts for this clarity on the assumption that "[t]he modern habit of saying, 'This is my opinion, but I may be wrong,' is entirely irrational" and that the "modern habit of saying 'Every man has a different philosophy; this is my philosophy and its suits me'" is equally problematic.[109] Such statements are really evidence of "mere weak-mindedness."[110]

It would nonetheless be a mistake to think that Chesterton is merely opting for a dialectical clarity that is beyond reproach or debate. Rather, it may be argued that the dialectical dogmatism that has become so evident up to this point is in fact a necessary step in the process towards paradox. One cannot have a suitable clash of opposites without the opposites being

104. Ibid.
105. Ibid.
106. Ibid.
107. Ibid.
108. Ibid.
109. Ibid.
110. Ibid.

somewhat self-evident. Even if Chesterton's reading of the character of God in the book of Job appears in the beginning to be frighteningly narcissistic, towards the end of his essay God is shown to be outrageously humble. In the beginning, while Chesterton dwells on the riddles of Job, God is as certain as an axiom even if he escapes all definition. Towards the end, while Chesterton dwells on the revelation of God, this same God becomes more surprising than the wildest surprises of the universe.

However, before rushing to a definitive conclusion, Chesterton sets up his view of the book of Job in terms of the familiar Chestertonian dichotomy of optimism and pessimism. This may seem like an anachronism and yet it suggests a great truth: in matters of human discourse, people do tend to lean either one way or another. And both moods have something to teach us about the human experience, even if pessimism is ultimately the worst of the two terms from a hermeneutic perspective.[111] I have already established the importance of beginning the reading of any text with a critical optimism, and what follows affirms this. For Job's friends, while at first seeming to be optimists themselves, are in fact deeply pessimistic. They are so pessimistic, in fact, that they cannot properly listen to their friend even while he endures unimaginable catastrophes. Pessimism is a hindrance to interpretive clarity and earnestness.

Job, on the other hand, while appearing at first to be a pessimist, turns out to not really be a pessimist at all; he "does not in any sense look at life in a gloomy way. If wishing to be happy and being quite ready to be happy constitute an optimist, Job is an optimist."[112] He is not a happy optimist, obviously, but a "perplexed optimist; he is an exasperated optimist; he is an outraged and insulted optimist. He wishes the universe to justify itself, not because he wishes it to be caught out, but because he really wishes it to be justified."[113] This in essence is a claim that Job is on the side of hermeneutic clarity and genuine understanding even in the face of what is impossible to explain. Unlike the skeptic, who obliterates sense before the evidence has been presented, he expects to find meaning when he is looking for it.

A critical optimism therefore retains its hermeneutic vitality. And this optimism, which is akin to a hope in the possibility of the event of understanding, is soon followed by a reminder of Chesterton's emphasis on loyalty in matters of interpretation. Job does not approach his quest for meaning or justification before God without a firm conviction that a connection to

111. Chesterton, *Daily News*, August 16, 1901.

112. Chesterton, *In Defense of Sanity*, 96.

113. Ibid.

God, as the "name of mystery," should remain primary.[114] Accordingly, "[h]e demands an explanation from God," not "at all in the spirit in which Hampden might demand an explanation from Charles I," but rather "in the spirit in which a wife might demand an explanation from her husband whom she really respected."[115] Even though he is obviously perplexed, disappointed, and even angry at his Maker, he nonetheless complains to his Maker "because he is proud of his Maker. He even speaks of the Almighty as his enemy, but he never doubts, at the back of his mind, that his enemy has some kind of a case which he does not understand."[116] Job will toy with "blasphemy," but only because of his profound and unabashed belief in the very one that he seems to denounce; he exclaims, "'Oh, that mine adversary had written a book!' It never really occurs to him that it could possibly be a bad book."[117] Indeed, in a typical Chestertonian twist of the logic of the expected, it turns out that "blasphemy" is only possible when belief is sustained. If belief fades, if conviction dies, blasphemy fades and dies along with it.[118]

Adopting the posture of a reader of an impenetrable text that he wishes to be able to understand, Job wants God to make his intentions clear to him. He wants to interview the Author to find out if he has read his work correctly. And he does this by holding to the unshakeable opinion that the Author actually has some purpose and a desire to carry out this purpose. This is why Job "shakes the pillars of the world and strikes insanely at the heavens"; he lashes out at the stars, not in order "to silence them," but "to make them speak."[119] The text of creation and experience may be impenetrable, but they must be saying something about the Author.[120]

Job feels excluded from the truth of his own experience. His experience is one of being cast aside or even of being locked out of meaning. His mind is filled with questions without answers: "Why is light given to a man whose way is hid, and whom God hath hedged in?" (Job 3:23); "What is my strength, that I should hope? And what is mine end, that I should prolong my life? Is my strength the strength of stones? Or is my flesh of brass? Is not my help in me? And is wisdom driven quite from me?" (Job 6:11–13); "Is there not an appointed time to man upon earth? Are not his days also like the days of an hireling?" (Job 7:1); "[H]ow should man be just with God?"

---

114. Chesterton, *The Everlasting Man*, 24.
115. Chesterton, *In Defense of Sanity*, 97.
116. Ibid.
117. Ibid.
118. Chesterton, *Collected Works, Volume 1*, 44.
119. Chesterton, *In Defense of Sanity*, 97.
120. Ibid.

(Job 9:2). Such questions highlight his sincere desire for the event. But what he needs is not a detailed set of answers to each of these questions. Rather, what he needs is a sense of his own position within the drama. This sense of context, of a place within the play, of a consciousness of Being more than a consciousness of his own reason, is what he has no access to.

Keeping Job's question in mind, Chesterton offers the first genuine challenge to what has thus far seemed to be an unyielding and tyrannical view of God. And he does so by pointing out that Job's so-called comforters are in fact "pessimists."[121] They are pessimists because they hold "not that God is good, but that God is so strong that it is much more judicious to call Him good."[122] Of course, a kind of optimism does fuel this conviction, but it is, in Chesterton's view, the wrong kind of optimism. Like "evolutionists . . . they have something of the vital error of the evolutionary optimist."[123] "They will keep on saying that everything in the universe fits into everything else: as if there were anything comforting about a number of nasty things all fitting into each other."[124]

Their explanations for evil reflect three kinds of explanation that are still commonly found today. The first is idea that the evil done to Job amounts to a message that God is punishing him for something he has said or done. The second is idea is that this experience of trauma must have been provided by God as an opportunity to learn. And the third is that Job should stop complaining so bitterly and selfishly since others out there are much worse off than he is. We shall see later how God, "in the great climax of the poem," turns every explanation and argument "altogether upside down."[125] The friends of Job, like Job himself, want a unifying theory. But in a profound twist it turns out that such a theory on its own would still be insufficient for confirming the goodness of the Creator.

It seems to me that underneath this essay, Chesterton is making a subtle, but profound point: the more we regard our confrontation with mystery to be a confrontation with a terrifying and almost wicked force, the more likely we will be to set up false rules and boundaries to create a sense of safety and security. Job's friends believe in an impatient God—a God who will reprimand without giving answers—and not in a God of love; they adopt a God of pure instrumental or concurrent causality rather than of influential causality; they do not believe in a God of infinite generosity

121. Ibid.
122. Ibid.
123. Ibid.
124. Ibid.
125. Ibid.

who considers the individual needs of people. Thus, they find themselves with a constricted hermeneutic.

I have said that Chesterton begins his essay on the book of Job with a very rigid sense of who God is, but the minute he starts to engage with the moment of an almost catastrophic revelation, when God steps into the scene to utter a few words—we do not know precisely how this looks because it is fundamentally unimaginable—Chesterton's apparent rigidity melts. Elihu has been speaking, of course, but there is a point in the narrative in which it seems to occur to everyone that Elihu is speaking the very words of God. Perhaps this is a double-discourse, whereby the voice of a man and the words he speaks, appear to the listener to have the approval of another Author. Or, perhaps, Elihu has been blown clear from the story by a terrible whirlwind.

It would be an overstatement to suggest that God provides answers when he shows up. In fact, it would be utterly wrong. At the end of the poem, like the Playwright who steps into the end of *The Surprise* to announce his incarnation, "God enters (somewhat abruptly)" and "the sudden and splendid note" is struck "which makes the [book of Job] as great as it is."[126] We may have expected a series of solutions and resolutions to all the complaints leveled at him; we may have expected God to defend himself. Indeed, a "more trivial poet" may have "made God enter in some sense or other in order to answer the questions" or made God the mouthpiece of yet another human theodicy,[127] but "[b]y a touch truly to be called inspired, when God enters, it is to ask a number more questions on His own account."[128]

Ironically, it is this abrupt entrance of the divine that renders the book of Job a "drama of skepticism."[129] We may have expected God to step in, like a *deus ex machina,* to resolve all the tensions that have been put forward in this interplay of antagonisms. But instead God appears as the ultimate skeptic. "He does what all the great voices defending religion have always done. He does, for instance, what Socrates did. He turns rationalism against itself."[130]

This sustained moment of revelation represents a moment of pure awe for Job. He finds himself caught up in the sublime. One could read God's questions as the representation of the unrepresentable. God asks Job why he speaks "without knowledge" and where he was when the "foundation of

126. Ibid.
127. Ibid.
128. Ibid., 98.
129. Ibid.
130. Ibid.

the earth" was laid and then continues with a range of other questions on various other facets of the created order (Job 38–41). It is as if "all human questioners" have not asked enough questions, or simply that their questions have been of no real use because their focus has been on retaining control over the uncontrollable. They have sought to reduce the surplus of meaning to something neat and transportable.

But God steps in as if to demonstrate the proper way of asking questions, which does not amount to a simplistic demand for answers. "The poet" or poets who put down these words have therefore made God "accept a kind of controversial equality with His accusers."[131] If every aspect of dialogue in the book of Job has seemed thus far to be part of an "intellectual duel," it is clear that God's response to Job and his accusers has furthered the duel past all intellectualizations. "The everlasting adopts an enormous and sardonic humility. He is quite willing to be prosecuted. He only asks for the right which every prosecuted person possesses; He asks to be allowed to cross-examine the witness for the prosecution."[132]

Chesterton uses the metaphor of a legal trial to further his argument about the book of Job. In a sense God has seemed to be the accused. Now that he has shown up, it becomes clear that he is not the accused after all, but the judge. And so he "asks of Job . . . the question that any criminal accused by Job would be most entitled to ask. He asks Job who he is. And Job, being a man of candid intellect, takes a little time to consider, and comes to the conclusion that he does not know."[133]

This is a lovely example of Chesterton at play. There is no literal question about who Job thinks he is in the book of Job, but it does seem implicit in this episode. Job announces after God's torrent of questions that he had no idea what he was talking about, that he had not been paying attention, and that he knows that God is still God, and that this God "can do all things" (Job 42:2–5). Job is comforted and repents (Job 42:6). God's speech is the "culmination of the inquiry" and its effect is deeply felt by the story's main character.

This culmination is strikingly reflected in the moment of revelation in *The Man Who Was Thursday*, when Gabriel Syme discovers who Sunday—the supposed arch-villain in the story—really is. Sunday turns out to be a force for good rather than for evil. "I am the Sabbath," Sunday reveals, "I am the peace of God."[134] Sunday represents an ever-present reconciliation that

131. Ibid.
132. Ibid.
133. Ibid.
134. Chesterton, *The Man Who Was Thursday*, 170.

some find irreconcilable. Thus, it is shown how Syme tries to get to the root of evil, which is precisely what political moles are expected to do; and yet, the deeper he digs and the more he discovers, the more apparent it becomes that there really is no pure origin of evil. The book can act as a parable, which suggests that even taking negativity as the point of departure ultimately leads to a realization of the goodness and plenitude of being. Chesterton, in this way, preemptively addresses the negativity that drives Jacques Derrida's deconstruction by suggesting, on language, that even taking the negative insistence on difference and the absolute absence of presence results in a sense of the plenitude of meaning. If you take negativity as your departing value—and go out looking for it as Thursday does—you will find that you cannot help, but fall back into the meaningful. The book of Job, however, exposes the fact that this meaning is not automatically something we can articulate because it is found in a posture towards being, in a recognition of the secret hidden within all things. Syme grapples with this intractability towards the end of his story.

> "Listen to me," cried Syme with extraordinary emphasis. "Shall I tell you the secret of the whole world? It is that we have only known the back of the world. We see everything from behind, and it looks brutal. That is not a tree, but the back of a tree. That is not a cloud, but the back of a cloud. Cannot you see that everything is stooping and hiding a face? If we could only get round in front—."[135]

Revelation

This desire to "get round in front" is suggested by Sunday's revelation of himself, as well as by God's entrance in the latter chapters of the book of Job, which I am taking here as a symbol of the event of understanding. But what precisely is its effect? This is a question that Chesterton feels has been unanswered even when he has reached the climax of the book of Job. He therefore elects in his own "Introduction" to that book to go back to revise his interpretation. There is good sense in this strategy; for, in a sense, all true reading is rereading. Thus, he returns again to God's speech and its contents, and notes that it "represents all human sceptics routed by a higher scepticism."[136] This higher skepticism turns out to be what Chesterton would regard as the logic of mysticism. It is a skepticism that has been overextended and has therefore reversed on itself. Chesterton uses the same logic that says that if

135. Chesterton, *The Man Who Was Thursday*, 160.
136. Chesterton, *In Defense of Sanity*, 98.

you give a person enough rope they will hang themselves. Socrates follows this logic when he allows sophistry to destroy itself, and Jesus uses it to show that the Sadducees "[cannot] imagine the nature of marriage in heaven" if "they had not really imagined the nature of marriage at all."[137]

Everything in our human constructions of the world must have an end, even doubt. It is my favorite moment in Chesterton's essay on the book of Job when he proudly announces the end of pride: "In dealing with the arrogant asserter of doubt, it is not the right method to tell him to stop doubting. It is rather the right method to tell him to go on doubting, to doubt a little more, to doubt every day newer and wilder things in the universe, until at last, by some strange enlightenment, he may begin to doubt himself."[138] The truest inspiration of this speech is that it shows God responding to Job, not with answers to all the riddles, but with further riddles. He does not want to abolish mystery, but to advance it. Still, the main hermeneutic event for Job is probably not located in the words that God says, but in the fact that he reveals himself. It is this eventual disclosure of God—pure meaning experienced as pure enigma—that leaves Job "satisfied" even though all he has been presented with is "something impenetrable."[139] The event, this real absent-presence, is felt to be transformative even while it remains obscure.

One of the interpretive problems posed by the book of Job relates to the interpretive paradigms of the various questioners. The architecture of the questions asked and statements provided works according to a very specific scaffold and framework adopted by each of the characters. Simply stated, each questioner is only likely to find what they are looking for; they are only likely to find what fits with the already established paradigms that they possess. However, this problem depends upon assuming that a "pure or total structure" is the only thing at work in the hermeneutic encounter, thus "reducing whatever happens within its bounds to its own unbending logic" and thus risking the "rendering of . . . events arbitrary and interchangeable, meaningful only in so far as they exemplify its internal laws."[140] Furthermore, this would assume that "[e]vents can only instantiate the structure, not raise a hand against it."[141] Such an assumption is problematic in terms of Chesterton's ontology. A Chestertonian view of the event must account for its irreducibility and ineffability.

137. Ibid.
138. Ibid., 99.
139. Ibid.
140. Eagleton, *The Event of Literature*, 199–200.
141. Ibid.

I have already mentioned Schindler's contention that revelation, as the introduction of something new into the soul, can be understood as the recasting of an anticipation in the moment of the encounter. This means that the event itself, occurring in midst of the clash and fusion of horizons, reframes the perspective of the subject to make room for its own acceptance. It needs to be said, though, that this is comprehensible only against the background of a co-participation in Being. Without a participatory ontology, this event would scarcely be conceivable. The event arises out of a co-participation, per the Augustinian-Platonist model, in forms that are "ideas in the mind of God, which necessarily inform any particular existing thing with its intelligible essence."[142] The event is a gift, given by the Being that all beings participate in.

Alison Milbank notes that gifts involve exchange, even if the exchange is of nothing for something.[143] While it may be said that God gives and creates out of his abundance rather than out of lack, in existential terms there is no such thing as a free gift. Every gift comes at a cost or, at least, is experienced as coming at a cost. Indeed, the very notion of a gift implies that the gift benefits the receiver far more than it does the giver, even when giving is receiving. A gift is a kind of positive injustice; it is unfair that one should receive so much more than what one has earned. Chesterton is aware of negative injustices in the world, and he does not turn a blind eye to the problem of evil, but he is on the whole more perplexed by the abundant generosity of life. People are created and born without asking to be, leaving Chesterton to wonder if there is not some Being, rather than some impersonal deterministic process, to thank for the "present of birth."[144] The true nature of gift, however, is not located in any transactional process, but in the dramatic experience of the giver who gives and in the receiving of the gift—an experience that cannot be reduced to any one aspect of a process.

This is why the revelation, for Job at least, is experienced as a "darker and more desolate" impenetrability, rather than as an eradication of mystery. Even if the revelation were to include a series of explanations, the mystery is still deepened for those who experience it. The paradox is such that when the mystery is at its most mysterious, revelation becomes possible. This same idea is evident in Chesterton's *Magic* (1913), when the Stranger/Conjurer at the center of this fantastic comedy announces that his best trick—a trick so convincing that the skeptical Morris Carleon is driven mad trying

142. Tyson, *Returning to Reality*, 137.

143. Milbank, *Chesterton and Tolkien as Theologians*, 118.

144. Chesterton, *Collected Works, Volume 1*, 258.

to figure out how it works—is really no trick at all.[145] The Conjurer, whose name is not known throughout the play, exposes the illusion by admitting that it is not an illusion at all. This, it turns out, is the really unbelievable and ungraspable thing. Even Smith, the priest, is compelled to acknowledge that his own convictions are representative of a fundamental disbelief. Smith knows that there are "spirits," but somehow cannot believe it.[146] The framework of his own thoughts refuses to fit with the architecture of reality.

In the end, Morris Carleon has to be calmed and brought to sanity by being told a lie about the trick. He therefore is only able to return to an approximate sanity rather than actual sanity. He cannot accept a higher, more mysterious kind of reason.[147] Chesterton affirms the place of reason through the mouth of Father Brown: "[R]eason is always reasonable, even in the last limbo, in the lost borderland of things. I know that people charge the Church with lowering reason, but it is just the other way. Alone on earth, the Church makes reason really supreme. Alone on earth, the Church affirms that God Himself is bound by reason."[148] Indeed, it is "bad theology" to attack reason.[149]

So it is not that reason needs to be discarded in order for mystery to thrive. Rather, reason needs to be more fully embraced. It is Job's friends who set up restrictions according to which God should operate and they therefore end up presenting a false God. It is Job, on the contrary, who fully asserts the promise of reason and is thus able to open himself up to a wider revelation of God. An "assertion of reason is not reason's self-assertion; it is instead the call for an act of faith, which goes beyond reason."[150] It is faith that pulls Job towards the event of understanding.

Job is fully aware of the limits of his own reasoning, but feels that reason can still be trusted: reason—"Surely I would speak to the Almighty, and I desire to reason with God" (Job 13:3)—is grounded in faith—"Though he slay me, yet will I trust in him, but I will maintain mine own ways before him" (Job 13:15). What this means, in practical terms, is that we do not determine the limits of knowledge; Being itself does this. Reason is not a capacity that is set into motion by Job or anyone else in his or their own terms, but is something in being, as that which is given its being by God. This is to say, following Schindler again, that "reason is always of the whole.

145. Chesterton, *Magic*, 58.

146. Ibid., 60.

147. Chesterton, *Collected Works, Volume 1*, 222.

148. Chesterton, *Selected Works*, 366.

149. Ibid., 369.

150. Schindler, *The Catholicity of Reason*, 262.

On the one hand, reason has already grasped the whole of being in some respect 'before' it has grasped any particular being, and it has grasped the whole of any particular being in some respect before it grasps any of its parts."[151] There is therefore an intimacy with reality that precedes any conscious awareness of its meaning for us.

This seems to be something that Job knows or believes. He understands on some level that his grasping for an answer is a reaching out for the One who grounds being. When Zophar answers Job, for instance, he insists upon the absolute unknowability of God: "Canst thou by searching find out God?" (Job 11:7). Job, however, seems fully aware of his own limitations and yet still feels that it is possible to have contact with God. While his accusers *know,* Job *believes.* Whereas knowledge here may amount to an assertion of self, belief asserts the reliability and faithfulness of the Absolute Other. And this, as St. Paul contends, is what would have been "counted unto him for righteousness" (Rom 4:3).

For Chesterton, this gap between knowledge and belief indicates the presence of real mystery and revelation. An encounter with the divine is felt on some level to be ungraspable. And it is precisely this feeling that satisfies, albeit it in an unexpected way. Similarly, before this deluge of questions, Job is dissatisfied and, after it, he is consoled. "He has been told nothing, but he feels the terrible and tingling atmosphere of something which is too good to be told. The refusal of God to explain His design is itself a burning hint of His design. The riddles of God are more satisfying than the solutions of man."[152] This is almost as if to say that the mystery is, especially on mysterious matters, a superior response to any explanation. The presence of this mystery—and it is its experienced presence—throws light onto the whole scenario. In one fell swoop, "God rebukes alike the man who accused, and the men who defended Him; that He knocks down pessimists and optimists with the same hammer."[153] The event throws every person's coordinates into question. Thus, it is "in connection with the mechanical and supercilious comforters of Job" that we find an "inversion" to top all inversions:

> The mechanical optimist endeavours to justify the universe avowedly upon the ground that it is a rational and consecutive pattern. He points out that the fine thing about the world is that it can all be explained. That is the one point, if I may put it so, on which God in return, is explicit to the point of violence. God

---

151. Schindler, *The Catholicity of Reason,* 9.
152. Chesterton, *In Defense of Sanity,* 99.
153. Ibid.

says, in effect, that if there is one fine thing about the world, as far as men are concerned, it is that it cannot be explained.[154]

God demands that nothing less than everything is inexplicable. We may imagine this revelation as something akin to that which Aquinas experienced—an experience so rich and deep that the prince of theologians was rendered speechless.[155] The word has become flesh, and so it seems that there is no need for the flesh to be sublimated into words again. It is not that mediation ceases, as the silence of Aquinas might suggest, but that the limits of mediation become more fully embodied by the subject.

By highlighting the extraordinary "inexplicableness of everything" evident in God's speech, Chesterton arrives at the conclusion that there seems, underneath it all, to be a kind of "positive and palpable unreason."[156] For instance, the question of why rain falls in the "desert where no man is" implies that seeing things as they are will also involve recognizing what is not necessarily commonsensical.[157] In fact, Chesterton compares the epiphany of the divine to that unique, British form of humor known as "nonsense," which suggests an "escape into a world where things are not fixed horribly in an eternal appropriateness."[158] Nonsense suggests that apples can "grow on pear trees" and that "any odd man you meet may have three legs."[159] This recourse to unreason and nonsense should not be taken literally though. It is more a challenge to rationality—the human capacity to reason—than to reason itself.

Our rationality, it turns out, is often an excuse for seeing the world as perfectly predictable and reasonable when it is really nothing of the sort.[160] "[L]ife is a riddle," which is precisely what the book of Job shows.[161] The world is therefore not only "tragic, romantic, and religious," but also "nonsensical."[162] The Creator in the book of Job shows up, not to present us with the explicability of creation, but to confront us with its "undecipherable unreason."[163] "God will make man see things, if it is only against the black background of nonentity. God will make Job see a startling universe

---

154. Ibid., 99–100.

155. Chesterton, *Saint Thomas Aquinas, Saint Francis of Assisi*, 130.

156. Chesterton, *In Defense of Sanity*, 99.

157. Ibid.

158. Chesterton, *The Defendant*, 45.

159. Ibid.

160. Ibid.

161. Ibid., 47.

162. Ibid., 49.

163. Ibid.

if He can only do it by making Job see an idiotic universe. To startle man God becomes for an instant a blasphemer; one might almost say that God becomes for an instant an atheist."[164] Chesterton, as enamored by contrasts as ever, exaggerates his case here. However, he does not want the reader to miss the connection between the failure of reason and the birth of insight, awe, and wonder. In the end, "[t]he well-meaning person who, by merely studying the logical side of things, has decided that 'faith is nonsense,' does not know how truly he speaks; later it may come back to him in the form that nonsense is faith."[165]

The most startling thing about Chesterton's reading of the book of Job is the fact that he presents God as a "Maker" who is "astonished at the things He has Himself made."[166] It is this aspect of Chesterton's reading that is highlighted in particular by Žižek to suggest that the book of Job offers the first official "critique of ideology" in literary history.[167] Instead of stepping in to affirm the Lacanian big Other—the imaginary god that manifests the collective spirit and acts as a guarantor of law and order—God steps in to challenge the expected coordinates of the entire system of meaning in creation. He shows Job all kinds of "created things"—"the horse, the eagle, the raven, the wild ass, the peacock, the ostrich, the crocodile"—but in such a way that he makes them each out to be monstrous.[168] His speech becomes a "psalm or rhapsody of the sense of wonder."[169] It is not merely a careful legitimation concerning why things are the way they are. The world is "much stranger . . . than Job ever thought it was."[170] Job's primary fault, if such a judgment may be allowed, has therefore been to ask questions according to specific coordinates of understanding that were not even vaguely reflective of the reality. He was stuck inside his own perceptions and therefore could not see beyond them.

One could read the divine entrance into the story in many other ways. God may for instance be deemed something of a tyrant or perhaps even as indifferent to Job and his sufferings. His appearance may be regarded as "pure boasting, a horror show with elements of farcical spectacle—a pure argument of authority grounded in a breathtaking display of power."[171] God's

---

164. Chesterton, *In Defense of Sanity,* 100.

165. Chesterton, *The Defendant,* 49–50.

166. Chesterton, *In Defense of Sanity,* 100.

167. Žižek , *The Puppet and the Dwarf,* 125.

168. Chesterton, *In Defense of Sanity,* 100.

169. Ibid.

170. Ibid.

171. Žižek , *The Puppet and the Dwarf,* 133.

answer to Job would then be understood as fundamentally unsatisfactory, as if God is simply saying, "You see all that I can do? Can *you* do this? Who are you, then, to complain?"[172] This reading, far from showing a God who is in control, reveals a vulnerable God who acts utterly defensively. His boasting, if that is what it is, would merely be an attempt to mask his own impotence. Thus, one of the traditional ways of reading God's entrance is to see it as affirming the gap between God and man—the sheer distance between his might and man's insignificance. But this is not how Chesterton reads the story, and even Žižek suggests that opting for such a reading should be resisted.

Indeed, the book of Job does not side with any simplistic legitimation. "Job's properly ethical dignity," as Žižek sees it, "lies in the way he persistently rejects the notion that his suffering can have any meaning, either punishment for his past sins or the trial of his faith, against the three theologians who [have] bombarded him with possible meanings."[173] In the end, surprisingly, God takes Job's side rather than the side of the big Other. There is no direct answer to his suffering; words can only fail. There is only the inexplicable: it is God.

In a sense, though, it is God's inexplicability that is felt as intimacy, as a moment of identification and recognition. It is in God's sheer and brutal otherness that his proximity and love are confirmed. It is in the mystery that the sacrament is received, just as it is in the Eucharistic sacrament—the symbol of God's partaking in the suffering of man—that mystery is received.

Against any hermeneutic certainty and the myth of immediacy regarding the reading of God's entrance, Chesterton intimates in his reading that however we may try to define God, our definitions will always be wrong. Following Aquinas, we find that God is revealed as that which is "not in a class; so it is clear that he cannot be defined, or given a formula by genus and difference."[174] Moreover, God's "essence is being itself" as an "excess" that is "not to be comprehended, for he is infinite and cannot be contained in any finite being."[175] God "is called incomprehensible because he cannot be seen by us as perfectly as he is capable of being seen."[176] And, since a "thing can be named" only "to the measure that it can be known," naming God becomes a futile exercise. One who "knows God best" will find that "whatever

---

172. Ibid.

173. Žižek, *The Puppet and the Dwarf*, 125.

174. Aquinas, *Selected Philosophical Texts*, 85.

175. Ibid., 86.

176. Ibid., 87.

he thinks and says falls short of what God really is."[177] Even a view of God's entrance as horrific must therefore be read as an attempt to suggest God's astonishing otherness through familiar literary devices.

It is in facing this mystery that Chesterton comes closest to articulating something of a negative theology, which is best understood though recounting the precise way that God may be understood as being both "beyond being and thought."[178] Chesterton always starts with the remarkable thingness of things: "a thing must first be to be intelligible."[179] Being and intelligibility are forever bound: "Whatever is thought is thought most basically and generically as some being," such that being, at its most basic, is "what is there for thought"; it is "that which is available for thinking."[180] Plato's conception of being as form or idea is built upon this identification of being and intelligibility: ". . . ideas are realities,"[181] but, for Plato, whatever is apprehended seems to be slightly less real than the ideas or forms in which they participate. This is not to say that "as appearance or images, sensibles are . . . mere illusions, or nothing (as Parmenides may have believed), but neither are they being itself, the reality which appears, the universal natures apprehended by the intellect. They are rather, as Plato says, 'in between' 'that which altogether is,' i.e. intelligible reality, the forms, and 'that which altogether is not,' i.e. nothing."[182] This "between," for Plato, is the world of opinion. For us, it is the world of hermeneutics. It is how things seem to us as we negotiate their relationship with reality and unreality. This is where Chesterton would only partially agree. For him "eggs are "eggs" and not just appearances of forms.[183]

For Chesterton, the central danger of Platonism is that it places too much emphasis on the idea and not enough on things. He nevertheless regards everything as "secondary and dependent" upon "God," who is still more actual than what we can perceive.[184] Eggs may be eggs, but God is more real than the reality of those eggs. There is some larger Good that "provides that which makes the forms able to be known and the intellect able to know them," which is to say that the Good "is the enabling source of

177. Ibid., 88–89.

178. Perl, *Theophany*, 5.

179. Chesterton, *Saint Thomas Aquinas, Saint Francis of Assisi*, 135.

180. Perl, *Theophany*, 6.

181. Chesterton, *The Everlasting Man*, 125.

182. Perl, *Theophany*, 7.

183. Chesterton, *Saint Thomas Aquinas, Saint Francis of Assisi*, 135.

184. Chesterton, *Saint Thomas Aquinas, Saint Francis of Assisi*, 158; Chesterton, *In Defense of Sanity*, 94.

intelligibility and intellection"[185] If we follow Plotinus's interpretation of Plato and Pseudo-Dionysius's interpretation of both, it would then be clear that this Good—the One or God—is beyond being in a very precise sense: this Good is not *a* being even while it gives being to all things. This negative theology is therefore not so much a claim about language as it is a claim about a metaphysical truth: even negation in language (saying what God is not) risks treating God as a being among other beings, albeit greater than other beings. Thus, this negative theology makes the claim that God can never be an object of thought. He cannot be treated as a conceptual object at all.

This, if some speculation may be forgiven, is what I think Chesterton is hinting at when he refers to the event—the entrance of God—as a moment of "positive and palpable unreason."[186] God is experienced somehow as being beyond experience, known as unknown and unknowable, and this is what brings about Job's reorientation and also brings him to the epiphany of his own situatedness. Truth is concealed even in its unconcealment. This is perhaps why "[t]ruth . . . must of necessity be stranger than fiction," for we have the habit of constructing "fiction to suit ourselves."[187] This, for Chesterton, is where the "unconscious artistic accuracy" is most evident in the book of Job. The poet or poets have "contrived to let fall here and there in the metaphors, in the parenthetical imagery, sudden and splendid suggestions that the secret of God is a bright and not a sad one—semi-accidental suggestions, like light seen for an instant through the cracks of a closed door."[188] It is sometimes the darkness that illuminates. It is the mystery that reveals.

Obviously, the book of Job also portrays God as being more than a little enamored by his world, which means that he cannot help but exult over it. When he asks almost sarcastically, for instance, if Job was present when "the foundations of the world were laid . . . when the sons of God shouted for joy," it is as if there "must have [been] something to shout about."[189] In fact, there is such a trumpet blast of celebration evident in God's soliloquy that he seems to be a God who overcomes even that which is impossible to overcome. And he does this by evoking further impossibilities. There is in this "a hint of some huge Armageddon in which evil shall be at last overthrown."[190] Any corrupt utterance or belief will not have the last word, since in God all

185. Perl, *Theophany*, 8.

186. Chesterton, *In Defense of Sanity*, 100.

187. Chesterton, *Collected Works, Volume 1*, 66.

188. Chesterton, *In Defense of Sanity*, 100.

189. Ibid., 101.

190. Ibid.

things are reconciled. God smashes the optimism of optimists and the pessimism of pessimists to reveal a larger optimism, which "[breaks] through agnosticism like fiery gold round the edges of a black cloud."[191] In this, Job experiences a total reorientation towards his world. In the process, he recovers and rediscovers the very world that he seems to have lost. His fortunes and family are restored to him, if only by a lengthy and painful process of defamiliarization.

On interpreting the book of Job, Chesterton writes that "the Book of Job must be credited with many subtle effects which were in the author's soul without being, perhaps, in the author's mind. And of these by far the most important remains even yet to be stated."[192] This is a powerful expression of Chesterton's interpretive awareness: the interpretation of the text does not depend on what the author intended, and is also not something that can be confined to any one ideological perspective. This hermeneutic openness is especially important on matters like the nature of evil, the reason for suffering, and especially the very nature of God, that are inherently mysterious.

Chesterton deals with the question of "whether God invariably punishes vice with terrestrial punishment and rewards virtue with terrestrial prosperity."[193] The temptation of the storyteller and of the reader is to provide an answer that brings about too clear a set of ideological parameters.[194] If the "Jews had answered that question wrongly they might have lost all their influence in human history."[195] It would have been easy enough, for instance, to answer the question in the affirmative by saying that God is good to the good and horrible to the wicked. But such an answer would have reduced life to a set of wrongheaded coordinates: such an obvious formula for prosperity renders goodness subservient to success. In other words, the inherent goodness of being good would have been ditched. But the book of Job "saved" the Jews from the logic of prosperity. By choosing to rely upon a fundamental suspension of any clear answer, "it does not end in a way that is conventionally satisfactory. Job is not told that his misfortunes were due to his sins or a part of any plan for his improvement."[196] His sufferings have been a real experience, but they are not purposeful in any simplistic sense.

191. Ibid.
192. Ibid.
193. Ibid.
194. Ibid.
195. Ibid.
196. Ibid.

Chesterton goes back to the prologue to note again that Job was "tormented not because he was the worst of men, but because he was the best."[197]

And this, it turns out, is the paradox that may well be the most comforting. Sometimes the best man gets the worst deal. In *The Everlasting Man*, Chesterton notes that the "Book of Job avowedly only answers mystery with mystery."[198] Again, we find Job comforted, not with answers, but "with riddles."[199] When "he who doubts can only say, 'I do not understand,' it is true that he who knows can only reply or repeat 'You do not understand.'"[200] And yet, "under that rebuke there is always a sudden hope in the heart; and the sense of something that would be worth understanding."[201]

Still, "[i]t is the lesson of the whole work that man is most comforted by paradoxes."[202] The central paradox—that of a good man at the center of an immeasurable tragedy—makes Job a prelude to Christ. As mentioned above, the wounds of Christ are "prefigured in the wounds of Job."[203] By mentioning this, Chesterton affirms the mystery of suffering, not as something dealt with only abstractly by God, but as something that is carried in the body of God. It is reconciled, not by abstract reasoning, but by being absorbed by the Word made flesh. Perhaps Job's primary experience of the event of understanding is that he recognizes God, not just as some distant, detached Other, but as incarnate, as being with him in his time of anguish. The event of understanding, found in the paradoxical interplay of the mysterious and the revealed, the joy and the agony, the transcendent and the immanent, returns Job to the gift of being itself.

Chesterton leaves the end of the book of Job to the reader without extensive commentary, but it is evident that it is an ending that keeps with Chesterton's philosophy. Job finds himself admonished: he has heard rumors of God, but has now seen him (Job 42:5). God chastises Job's friends for their ludicrous theologies, and then turns his attention to his suffering servant. God "blessed the latter end of Job more than his beginning" (Job 42:12), so that Job died at the ripe old age of one hundred and forty years, "being old and full of days" (Job 42:17). Where the narrative of the book of Job began with a man in a good place, and moved towards a picture of a man who had, in effect, lost reality, it finishes with justice, abundance, and

197. Ibid.
198. Chesterton, *The Everlasting Man*, 98.
199. Ibid.
200. Ibid.
201. Ibid.
202. Chesterton, *In Defense of Sanity*, 102.
203. Ibid.

reconciliation. The end of the story is therefore a reminder of the gift of being, which is mediated to him a new way.

7

Conclusion: The Grace of Mediation

The Gift of Mediation

IT SHOULD BE CLEAR by now that getting a sense of Chesterton's hermeneutic—his unique engagement with and perception of the drama of meaning—is not so much about locating precise methodological coordinates as it is about better understanding what it means to rollick within the playground of a participatory philosophy. Seeing things as they are therefore does not concern adopting a possessive attitude towards things. Rather, it concerns a particular posture towards being that elicits wonder. This posture is not so much about seeing the world without mediation as it is about becoming aware of the mediation—the implicit horizon of understanding and explicit worldview—that is so easily concealed from us by virtue of its being "too big to be noticed."[1]

Chesterton wants to expose those "little thoughts" that "pervade the whole atmosphere in a manner only comparable to that of the most minute insects: insignificant and almost invisible, but innumerable and almost omnipresent."[2] Metaphorically speaking, his "occupation in life is catching flies."[3] It involves not just noticing that the air has been clouded by an edgeless swarm of opinions, but also finding ways to clear the air so that the sky may be properly appreciated. Still, even when Chesterton is concerned with "direct and individual impressions," his hermeneutic is not one that

1. Chesterton, *The Annotated Innocence of Father Brown*, 244; Chesterton, *Illustrated London News*, 7 December, 1907.

2. Chesterton, *Illustrated London News*, 33 October 1932.

3. Ibid.

assumes pure immediacy.[4] As I have shown particularly in the previous chapter, the event of understanding is tempered and contextualized by mystery. Additionally, the objective world is experienced subjectively—that is, through a living, breathing, thinking subject.

Chesterton's selection of interpretive hierarchies and personal preferences is a testament to his appreciation of subjectivity and the presence of mediation: Browning is chosen over Swinburne, Cobbet over Carlyle, Dickens over Zola, Europe over Asia, France over Germany, England over France, the cockney over the Nature worshipper, tramps over dukes, the commoner over the aristocrat, the thirteenth century over the twentieth century, fairy tales over educational treatises, tradition over progress, theatre over film, beer over soda water, donkeys over motor cars, courtesy over rudeness, singing in chorus over singing in concerts, optimism over pessimism, and many others.[5]

Interpretation, then, "is not so much [about] words" as it is about "the order of words."[6] It is really the "individual" impression—the personal expression of the embodied subject in relation to a text—that is paramount.[7] When writing on impartiality, for instance, Chesterton points out his own preference is that bias should be "honestly described and declared," since "being impartial" often amounts to little more than assuming that "some people suppose the whole world to be of their [own] denomination; and therefore anything that agrees with them is universal and anything that disagrees with them insane."[8] Some fail to see "bias [as] a bias."[9] An approximate "impartiality" is only possible through the recognition of one's own "partiality" and bias.[10] It is not so much about being rid of partiality as it is about being aware of its gravitational pull. It is my aim in this chapter to explore the precise nature of this awareness of partiality and bias—this individual impression—to give an account of mediation in Chesterton's work. This is to say that I aim to discuss how mediation functions for and is experienced by Chesterton.

Hermeneutic tradition is clear that it is both undesirable and impossible to argue for the absence of mediation. The world as it appears to us is constituted of relations between things that are always negotiated.

4. Quoted in Lea, *The Wild Knight of Battersea*, 50.

5. Cammaerts, *The Laughing* Prophet, 35.

6. Chesterton, *Illustrated London News*, April 18, 1936.

7. Quoted in Lea, *The Wild Knight of Battersea*, 50.

8. Chesterton, *Illustrated London News*, March 22, 1924.

9. Ibid.

10. Chesterton, *Illustrated London News*, February 14, 1914.

Chesterton contends that even the "chain of a sentence" is "only as strong as its weakest link" (by which he means the use of "conjunctions" in a sentence—those components of the sentence that are most responsible for alerting the reader to the relations between ideas).[11] He understands that substituting one word in a sentence for another is a problem for meaning, but suggests that "[altering] your conjunctions" is far more detrimental, since it is more likely to "make you mean the very opposite to what you do mean." Changing "'and,' or 'but,' or 'though'" can create a "vast amount of moral and emotional difference."[12] If you change the mediation, the message is significantly altered.

> For example, there is a great deal of difference which part of your statement you put as a confession in parenthesis or which part is the end of the original sentence. It makes a great deal of difference (emotionally speaking) whether you say, "She is your mother, but she is trying to poison you," or whether you say, "She is trying to poison you, but she is your mother." In its effect on the feelings, the one means the exact opposite of the other. You create one situation when you say, "Professor Pinker, though he is a great philosopher, drops his h's." You create quite another situation when you say, "Professor Pinker, though he drops his h's, is a great philosopher." In the former case your fine features are contorted into a cold and unpleasant sneer. In the latter case they are irradiated with a generous and manly heat which calls down thunders of applause from the public meeting which you are at the moment addressing.[13]

For Chesterton, the way that things relate to each other—how they are placed in conjunction—is of supreme importance in the interpretive experience. He therefore encourages a specific way of relating to things that amounts to finding a means to encounter things anew. Chesterton promotes a way of engaging with the world that brings the individual into the paradox of feeling both serenity and adventure, welcome and surprise.[14] To navigate the nature of Chesterton's posture towards being, it is helpful to begin by noting a distinction that he makes between utopian and paradisiacal thinking.[15] It would be an exaggeration to say that these two labels suggest only two possible hermeneutic postures. Rather, they offer a way of grouping any

11. Chesterton, *Illustrated London News*, August 3, 1907.

12. Ibid.

13. Ibid.

14. Chesterton, *Collected Works, Volume 1*, 212.

15. Chesterton, *Illustrated London News*, June 1, 1935.

number of hermeneutic postures under two broad umbrellas. After discussing these two groups, I then aim to home in on Chesterton's specific kind of paradisiacal thinking.

The first type of thinking, found in people fond of the notion of a Utopia in its modernist sense, offers that "it takes [only] two to make a quarrel."[16] It is a type of thinking that assumes that mediation is not present, not necessary, or simply not worth critically examining. As far as the utopian is concerned, mediation is either taken for granted or entirely ignored. In criticizing this way of thinking, Chesterton notes that "where there are really only two" people in an argument "they probably will quarrel."[17] There needs to be a mediator—an invisible third party—to establish the possibility of dialogue.

This idea of an invisible mediator who makes the conversation possible finds an analogy in Chesterton's story of "The Invisible Man." Throughout the story the presence of the culprit James Welkin is felt, but remains unseen. Just before receiving a letter, the central female protagonist Laura Hope tells of a strange experience: "'I heard James Welkin laugh as plainly as I hear you speak,' said the girl, steadily. 'There was nobody there, for I stood just outside the shop at the corner, and could see down both streets at once.'"[18] The characters that experience this "presence" without being privy to its nature assume that there can be only two explanations, namely that the presence is that of a ghost or spiritual energy, or that they are mad. Although the analogy has its limits, this may be taken as a symbol of two perspectives on mediation: if mediation is not understood, it is taken either as a ghost (it represents the equivocal sense of being) or as something totally absent, for madness implies a disjunction between thought and things (the univocal sense of being is thus prioritized).

Early on in this same story, Chesterton dispels the second explanation on the simplistic grounds that it is only sane people who concede the possibility that they are mad.[19] This implies that the second explanation is the most likely in the opinion of the characters. Even the rationalist detective Flambeau, addressing his friend Father Brown, considers the supernatural explanation most likely: "'Father,' said Flambeau, after a pause, 'upon my soul I believe it is more in your department than mine. No friend or foe has entered the house, but Smythe [the victim] is gone, as if stolen by the

16. Ibid.

17. Ibid.

18. Chesterton, *Father Brown*, 93.

19. Ibid., 94.

fairies."[20] However, it is the priest, Father Brown, who argues with reference to the issue of interpretive meaning that this "supernatural" explanation is equally problematic:

> Have you ever noticed this—that people never answer what you say? They answer what you mean—or what they think you mean. Suppose one lady says to another in a country house, "Is there anybody staying with you?" the lady doesn't answer "Yes; the, butler, the three footmen, the parlour-maid, and so on," though the parlour-maid may be in the room, or the butler behind her chair. She says: "There is nobody staying with us," meaning nobody of the sort you mean.[21]

Father Brown, by stressing the possibility of hermeneutic dislocation—argues that Laura Hope's claim to have been alone just after receiving a letter cannot be true.[22] It is not that she has been lying out of volition, but rather out of a lack of awareness. Father Brown continues: "A person can't be quite alone in a street a second before receiving a letter. She can't be quite alone in a street when she starts reading a letter just received. There must be somebody pretty near; he must be *mentally invisible*."[23] This mental invisibility applies to mediation itself and the various prejudices or "unconscious dogma[s]" that will go with that.[24] And Chesterton makes it his aim to expose such things: "I count it a service to contemporary thought to tell people what they do apparently think; if only to contradict it."[25]

Just then, Father Brown pulls back the conceptual curtain to reveal what was obvious and yet unseen: the postman who delivers all the letters in the story is the criminal. Similarly, Chesterton pulls back the curtain to expose our ignorance of mediation, which results in an ignorance of the world. There is always a postman—a mediator—who delivers the letter. Chesterton makes reference to his friend H. G. Wells's utopianism to demonstrate what can happen when the invisible third party is missing from the conversation with reality. He writes, "Mr. Wells . . . is not quite clear enough of the narrower scientific outlook to see that there are some things which actually ought not to be scientific."[26] As I read it, this implies that some things require more than an absolutely obvious, literal interpretation.

20. Ibid., 105.

21. Ibid., 106.

22. Ibid., 107.

23. Ibid., emphasis added.

24. Chesterton, *Illustrated London News*, March 15, 1919.

25. Chesterton, *Illustrated London News*, August 25, 1934.

26. Chesterton, *Collected Works, Volume 1*, 77.

[Wells] is still slightly affected with the great scientific fallacy; I mean the habit of beginning not with the human soul, which is the first thing a man learns about, but with some such thing as protoplasm, which is about the last. The one defect in his splendid mental equipment is that he does not sufficiently allow for the stuff or material of men. In his new Utopia he says, for instance, that a chief point of the Utopia will be a disbelief in original sin. If he had begun with the human soul—that is, if he had begun on himself—he would have found original sin almost the first thing to be believed in. He would have found, to put the matter shortly, that a permanent possibility of selfishness arises from the mere fact of having a self, and not from any accidents of education or ill-treatment.[27]

The terrible irony of this kind of Utopia is that it is pursued before human life is understood. The utopian dream of a destination is established without any prior sense of where we are or how we will transcend our current circumstances to get to our destination. Wells takes truth to be self-evident, which amounts to a "denial of the possibility of philosophy itself" and so ends up with a horrible denial of reality itself in all its wonderful diversity.[28] By focusing only on the world, as he assumes it to be, he loses the world as it really is. By removing an awareness of mediation—as that which sets up a perception of the world as a complete, albeit imperfect picture—he also removes the possibility of real difference or variety.

But, for Chesterton, "variety" is essential to our understanding of reality, and "[i]t is also, incidentally, the meaning of the doctrine of the Trinity."[29] Chesterton's reference to the doctrine of the Trinity points again to the fact that variety is grounded in a profound relational unity. And it is this relational unity that intimates a paradisiacal hermeneutic posture, in which "three is company and two is none."[30] "It takes three to make a quarrel," Chesterton writes in *The Thing* (1930); "There is needed a peacemaker."[31] In fact, "[t]he full potentialities of human fury" seem only to be reachable when "a friend of both parties tactfully intervenes."[32] Truly, "[t]he only way to end a quarrel is to get on both sides of it. We must have *not* merely a calm impartiality, but rather a sympathy with partiality, as it exists in both

27. Ibid.

28. Ibid.

29. Chesterton, *Illustrated London News*, June 1, 1935.

30. Ibid.

31. Chesterton, *Collected Works, Volume 3*, 138.

32. Ibid.

partisans."[33] We should not strive to be "impartial," but rather "partial to both sides."[34]

Against this, utopian thinking rests on an inability to recognize the need for a peacemaker. Thus it resorts either to an ontological dualism, where God and the world are utterly disconnected, or to ontological monism, with God either being all (as in pantheism) or nothing (as in nihilism). Both forms of thinking ultimately reduce the world to the purely immanent. The world becomes as "flat" as the wallpapers of William Morris.[35] This flat utopian thinking may take on various guises, but it always insists on the constructed divide between the secular and sacred orders. Its functional materialism implies that what is believed must always be smaller than our own minds and also insists that substance should take priority over relation.[36] This ultimately leads to the idea that things are not intrinsically meaningful and therefore need to account for and fend for themselves.

If this way of thinking is to be taken seriously, it must be assumed that real hierarchies of difference do not exist; every "individual is indeterminately and indiscernibly equivalent to every other individual."[37] This fact is not necessarily recognized by utopian thinking. Instead, utopian thinking assumes the hierarchies present in the mind as if they are present in the world too: it regards things as givens and the obvious as obvious. *No interpretation needed* is the cry of the utopian, who is perpetually shocked that others do not see the world the way he does.

For Chesterton, the conservative and the reactionary, like the progressive, modernist, meliorist, and social evolutionist, represent this flat utopianism by viewing the contemporary world "apart from the interior standards of the mind."[38] Conservativism, as a kind of negative utopianism, amounts to "mere resignation."[39] It assumes that "if you leave things alone you leave them as they are" when in reality "you do not. If you leave a thing alone you leave it to a torrent of change. If you leave a white post alone it will soon be a black post."[40] To keep things from degeneration, it will not do to leave them as is or conserve them. "If you particularly want" the white post to remain white "you must be always be painting it again; that is, you must always be

---

33. Chesterton, *Illustrated London News*, June 25, 1932.

34. Ibid.

35. Chesterton, *Illustrated London News*, June 1, 1935.

36. Tyson, *Returning to Reality*, 7.

37. Pabst, *Metaphysics*, xxx.

38. Chesterton, *Illustrated London News*, September 30, 1933.

39. Chesterton, *Collected Works, Volume 1*, 307.

40. Ibid., 320.

having a revolution,"[41] but where the conservative wants things to remain the same, the reactionary, who is a type of conservative, simply wants things to change.

> When I say reaction, I do not mean romance or tradition or loyalty or love of order, or any of these things even in their excess. I do not mean superstition or oppression or tyranny or slavery, or any of these things even in their milder forms. When I say reaction I mean reaction; the mere fact of reacting against something, or permitting that something to make us do something against it. It is said that in physics action and reaction are equal and opposite. It is a very good reason for keeping physics out of morals and metaphysics. The whole object of a wise man is not to react exactly as his opponents act; not to go so far in the one direction as the other man has gone in the other. He may, perhaps, after due reflection, go even farther; but he will not go exactly as far; nor will he go because the other has gone. He will not have his own movement made by another. If he does, though he ascends into heaven, it is only on one end of the seesaw, though he be swung like a club, he is only swinging like a pendulum.[42]

For Chesterton, a "[r]eactionary is one in whom weariness itself has become a form of energy. He is one in whom even boredom boils and ferments at least by its own stagnation,"[43] but the mere fact that he mirrors the changes in the world is a testimony to the fact that his ideal is always changing.[44] There is no eternal test because there is only the vague idea of a this-worldly utopia—something that will be arrived at sometime in the future (we know not how or upon which standards). "As long as the vision of heaven is always changing," Chesterton claims, "the vision of earth will be exactly the same. No ideal will remain long enough to be realised, or even partly realised."[45] You cannot "alter your environment" when you are continuously "changing your mind."[46]

Sadly, Chesterton is often taken to be a conservative because his work has most commonly been adopted by conservatives, who read him as just another utopian; that is, as just another means to support their conservative

41. Ibid.
42. Chesterton, *Collected Works, Volume 21*, 425.
43. Ibid.
44. Chesterton, *Collected Works, Volume 1*, 314.
45. Ibid., 312–13.
46. Ibid.

agenda. But Chesterton dissents: "I am not a conservative."[47] The conservative is really just "a man who wants to keep his money"; he is a man who wants to look out for his own interests.[48] The conservative utopian, who like the progressive "allows truth to be determined by time," lives entirely in his own world.[49] It is precisely this obsession with self-enclosure that makes his world a dull thing that is to be criticized, but not loved. Adam Schwartz tries to solve the problem of Chesterton's conservatism by redefining it as "radical conservatism"; after all, in his view, Chesterton desires "to uproot his current culture so as to reroot it in Christian tradition"[50] This is true, but it does not take full cognizance of the fact that Chesterton seems also to want to uproot aspects of the Christian tradition too. His revolution includes the idea of a repainting of the Christian faith through the continuous rediscovery of the "transcendence of God."[51] He even goes so far as to allow for an orthodoxy that enters the room via the back door of heresy; it is this revolutionary spirit that allows a person to find "wonder, curiosity, moral and political adventure, righteous indignation—Christendom."[52]

It is, for Chesterton, the great problem of his age and it certainly is a problem in our own. As we walk through the world, we are bombarded by or caught up in custom, convention, repetition, fatigue, and a number of other things, with the result that our perceptions of the world are dulled. "By hearing" we "hear," but do "not understand;" we "see," but do not "perceive" (Matt 13:14). Accordingly, Chesterton wants his reader to recover awe, a very real sense of the gift of being, and a feeling that the "settled things" are really "strange."[53] This recovery of strangeness is at the heart of his hermeneutic, which is less concerned with correct interpretation or exegetical nitpicking than it is an extension of a philosophical approach to life, which prioritizes the recovery of true wonder above almost anything else. Of course, his assumption is that recovering wonder is the same thing as recovering reality.

This, I think, is the primary gift of Chesterton's unique interactions with the drama of meaning: through his particular combination of imagination and reason, we are able to feel the scales of habitual perception fall from our eyes and meet all of existence as if for the first time: as blind men

---

47. Chesterton, *Illustrated London News*, July 6, 1935.

48. Chesterton, *Daily News*, September 8, 1906.

49. Chesterton, *Illustrated London News*, October 30, 1920.

50. Schwartz, *The Third Spring*, 68.

51. Chesterton, *Collected Works, Volume 1*, 340.

52. Ibid.

53. Chesterton, *The Defendant*, 60.

learning how to see. We are able, as his whole philosophy encourages, to return to a first astonishment at the sheer and unabashed quiddity of existence. This astonishment is encouraged by Chesterton's paradisiacal view of the world, which is rooted in a particular "faith."[54] "[S]ome faith in our life is required even to improve it,"[55] but "some dissatisfaction with things as they are is necessary even in order to be satisfied."[56] We need to be able to maintain some "equilibrium" between this "necessary content and necessary discontent."[57]

Still, true change comes from having a genuine sense of "value," and a clear and fixed ideal.[58] This ideal, as already intimated, is not just a state of mind for Chesterton. It is not merely an idea, but a concrete reality in which one continuously participates. When he contends, for instance, that one's "vision of heaven" needs to be permanent, he is not suggesting the mutability of heaven via subjective preferences, but rather its enduring presence. Its presence is found even in the riddle that is written in every heart—the riddle expressed in the idea "that two worlds are better than one."[59] Where any Utopia is a vision of another place and another time—a place or state of being that is perpetually deferred to some later date—paradise or heaven is a picture of the world that this world participates in even now. It is a confrontation with a reality that is "nigh at hand" and "within" (Luke 21:31; 17:21). Paradise is something that we need to wait for, but is also what we are already enveloped and grounded in. It is found through an openness to the world reflected best in the questions of the child:

> Every child has . . . certain profound questions in his soul. He finds those questions as open questions. He finds them open just as he finds his ears or his lungs or his nostrils open; and he knows by instinct that through these open questions he draws in the air and life of the universe. Why dreams are different from daylight, why dead things are different from live things, why he himself is different from others, why beauty makes us restless and even love is a spring of quarrels, why we cannot so fit into our environment as to forget it and ourselves; all of these things are felt vaguely by children on long empty afternoons; or by primitive poets writing the epics and legends of the morning of the world. And all legends, however barbaric, are filled with the

54. Chesterton, *Collected Works, Volume 1*, 307.

55. Ibid.

56. Ibid.

57. Ibid.

58. Ibid., 308, 313.

59. Chesterton, *Illustrated London News*, June 1, 1935.

wind of all this wider questioning. They all refer back to these ancient unfathomable wells which go down deeper than the reason into the very roots of the world, but contain the springs that refresh the reason and keep it active forever.[60]

Chestertonian mediation, then, is concerned with what it means to participate in this universe. Žižek's Hegelian reading of Chesterton helps to demonstrate the significance of this. He offers that "Chesterton's appraisal of the guillotine (which was used precisely to behead a king)" helps to clarify the nature of mediation and the understanding that results. Žižek quotes Chesterton, who writes,

> The guillotine has many sins, but to do it justice there is nothing evolutionary about it. The favourite evolutionary argument finds its best answer in the axe. The Evolutionist says, "Where do you draw the line?" the Revolutionist answers, "I draw it *here*: exactly between your head and body." There must at any given moment be an abstract right or wrong if any blow is to be struck; there must be something eternal if there is to be anything sudden.[61]

Žižek goes on to say that "[i]t is from here that one can understand why Badiou, *the* theorist of the Act, has to refer to Eternity: the Act is only conceivable as the intervention of Eternity into time."[62] It is from the eternal, from Paradise, that meaning is given. The event, albeit singular and contained, is always a reference to what is uncontained and uncontainable, multiple and multifaceted. In fact, as Adrian Pabst notes, following St. Augustine's contention, "true self-knowledge is the recognition that nothing can cause itself or sustain itself in being," for life itself is a gift, and true knowledge of the self and the world involves a recognition that we can participate in the utter plenitude of being and the good, because the highest being and good in God is "giving itself" ecstatically to creation in an original relation whose reverse face is the participation of reality in the Creator, who alone brings about their particular existence.[63]

As this intimates, recognition happens to be an important concept for giving a Chestertonian account of mediation. It is, in my view, the first of four overlapping facets of mediation, the others being imagination, humility, and gratitude, each of which I discuss in turn below. The Chestertonian

---

60. Chesterton, *Illustrated London News*, August 6, 1932.

61. Quoted in Žižek, *Less Than Nothing*, 427.

62. Ibid.

63. Pabst, *Metaphysics*, 106.

understanding of recognition is particularly well illustrated through an idea for a novel only partially developed by Chesterton in the 1890s, during his time working for Fisher Unwin. The working title for the novel was "The Man with Two Legs." The novel was to be a "philosophic," "allegorical comedy" that aimed to poke fun at various "modern thoughts."[64]

In Chesterton's outline of the book, we encounter a "professor, then a young man of depraved life and hopeless philosophy," who "finds the last remaining pleasure of life in the excitement of fighting duels in which he is the terror of the city."[65] The thrill of the fight, it needs to be said, is found largely in the fact that he is unbeatable. He symbolizes a kind of Nietzschean Overman, conquering whoever dares to challenge him. However, one day he meets "another duelist"—a "boy" who is "as deadly as himself," but whose philosophy is rooted in "fairy tales" rather than nihilism.[66] Here, experience meets innocence and strength meets infantile weakness. And yet, experience and strength loses to innocence and weakness.

While fighting with this "mysteriously elemental type," the professor comes face to face with "*Death*—his own possible death" and "suddenly realises a hundred simple experiments and pleasures he has neglected."[67] For instance, "he sees a tree half-way up the hill he would like to climb" and "realises the great vision of the whole world, blazing with possibilities, just as the sword is through his body. The boy leans on the sword in the sunset like an executioner who has beheaded another tyrant. But the tyrant lies on his back with his hands full of flowers, like a child asleep."[68] After this brush with death, "the professor recovers slowly: surprising all who knew him by his new studious and simple life."[69] He has experienced death and is now capable of experiencing resurrection.

In this early sketch, we already see a number of ideas that Chesterton would return to during his career. There is the duel, for instance—what I have termed a *clash of horizons* and what Chesterton elsewhere calls "one toppling and dizzy equilibrium [crashing] into another"[70]—but there is also the classic narrative that fuels almost all Chestertonian fiction: first, there is innocence, followed by existential despair, and a climax during which the primary experience of innocence is recovered. There is a movement, in

64. Chesterton, *Collected Works, Volume 14*, 769.

65. Ibid., 770.

66. Ibid.

67. Ibid.

68. Ibid.

69. Chesterton, *Collected Works, Volume 14*, 770.

70. Chesterton, *Collected Works, Volume 4*, 341.

other words, from taking things for granted to taking things as granted, as gifts. This story is one of returning to true "wisdom" which David Bentley Hart defines as "innocence at the far end of experience; it is the ability to see what most of us have forgotten how to see, but now fortified by the ability to translate some of that vision into words, however inadequate."[71]

This may appear at first to reflect the mediation of Hegel's dialectic, which comprises a reaction to something (an antithesis) that allows that something (a thesis) to emerge and be articulated in response to the antithesis. This is to emphasize that it is only after an antithesis has emerged that the thesis comes into view as a thesis—as something contestable and as a product of the antithesis. In the struggle between the thesis and antithesis, both are irrevocably altered. The synthesis that results, though, is not really a resolution of the thesis and the antithesis, but is rather the thesis that has become a site or coordinate within the antithesis.[72] Unlike this dialectic, which rests on negativity, Chesterton's "dialectic"[73]—which is really paradox—presumes, before intellection, both a positive beginning and a positive ending. Antithesis has neither the first nor the last word.

The issue of genetics and sexual reproduction, discussed by Chesterton as "heredity," offers a helpful metaphor for what paradoxical mediation entails. It begins with superabundance and plenitude—"[t]wo totally different people have become in the sense most sacred, frightful, and unanswerable, one flesh"[74]—and ends with greater superabundance and greater plenitude—a new life amidst other lives. This overwhelming excess is never fully comprehensible. In this meeting of two to create more, what results is both a revelation and a mystery. The revelation entails the recognition of the way that elements of two complex beings are expressed in the new life, as well as a recognition of elements that appear to be untraceable in that life. To summarize, Chesterton uses an analogy: "you know there is wine in the soup. You do not know how many wines there are in the soup, because you do not know how many wines there are in the world."[75] What results may be a synthesis of a kind, but it is not in any way a purely conceptual reality. It must be loved, nurtured, and admired. Its very excess pushes back the egotism of a more immanentist dialectic.

It is this wisdom of innocence—innocence on the other side of experience—that is perhaps best represented by the character of Father Brown,

71. Hart, *The Experience of God*, 13.

72. Fritzman, *Hegel*, 4.

73. Lauer, *G. K. Chesterton*, 92.

74. Chesterton, *Collected Works, Volume 4*, 338.

75. Ibid., 339.

who is as "wise as serpents" and yet still as innocent or "harmless as doves" (Matt 10:16). This wise-innocence suggests a posture towards being that I would equate to an "openness through otherness to that which is ultimate."[76] It is something that arises in desire's encounter with what is real. It is an openness through our experience of being with other beings that fosters an awareness of Being itself. This posture of openness—this porosity to Being—is what precipitates the event of understanding, although this is not to say that being closed off is a guarantee that the otherness of Being will not intrude into our awareness. After all, Being is plentiful, abundant, ecstatic, and exceeds expectations and limitations. Nevertheless, a particular kind of mindfulness can certainly facilitate an encounter with the intimate strangeness of being. And it is this kind of mindfulness that I believe Chesterton encourages.

While Chesterton's philosophy begins with a sense of the goodness of being and the goodness of God, he recognizes that the first step towards awareness involves the recognition that things having gone wrong. The sense that what is wrong is something *external* to us, something "wrong with the world," is misleadingly obvious.[77] What is less obvious, and therefore arguably more important to Chesterton, is the sense that there is something wrong *in* and *with* us. As a standard formula in philosophical hermeneutics goes, there is no such thing as a world without us, and therefore no possibility of it being "wrong" without us.

The primary thing that has gone wrong is that we tend to become entangled in ourselves and thus become cut off from the world. We easily forget the sacramental experience. The metaphor used by Chesterton for a failure to recognize the sacrament of sex, for example, is that of polygamy, which is "a lack of realisation of sex; it is like a man plucking five pears in mere absence of mind."[78] This "absence of mind" is found everywhere, though. Chesterton refers, for instance, to writers who insist on "impressing their own personalities instead of creating life for the world."[79] This leads to an "awful emptiness," since all of reality becomes nothing more an appearance behind which is really nothing but "nightmare."[80] To the one caught up in his own self-made prison or self-made conceptual psychiatric ward, "[t]he stars will be only dots in the blackness of his own brain; his mother's face will be only a sketch from his own insane pencil on the walls of his cell. But over his

76. Desmond, *Desire, Dialectic, and Otherness*, 17.

77. Chesterton, *What Is Wrong With The World*, 17, 23.

78. Chesterton, *Collected Works, Volume 1*, 261.

79. Ibid., 229.

80. Ibid.

cell shall be written with dreadful truth, 'He believes in himself.'"[81] It may be excessive when Chesterton refers to anyone who loses this sense of the primary experience of things as a lunatic or as a "panegotist" or "solipsist," but even this extreme terminology conveys a weird truth, namely that the one who is completely caught up in despair for more than an "innocent interlude" really cannot see things as they are because he cannot see past himself.[82] Mediation itself has been blocked. This is why so much modern philosophy may present an "outer ring" that is "artistic and emancipated" while it still demonstrates an inward despair that is truly frightening.[83]

The problem of living in a self-enclosed mental prison, in the midst of this perpetual despair, is illustrated by a parable that Chesterton tells about a man who discovers, after imbibing some beer and then spitting it out, that it is a poison. A doctor tells him that before he chooses to give up on his drinking, he will have to first make up his mind concerning what "[s]ubstitute" poison he will choose to replace it with.[84] After finding no way to escape the fact that he will forever be drinking poison, and after consulting with the magistrate and the public analyst, the man goes mad, claiming that "[t]here is no alternative to madness. It is inevitable. It is universal. We must make the best of it."[85] So, Chesterton concludes, "he killed the doctor and then went back and killed the magistrate and the public analyst, and is now in an asylum, as happy as the day is long."[86]

For the poor soul in this tale, the only way to navigate the poisoned world is to escape it. Therefore, at the center of the man's hermeneutic posture is a twofold declaration: first, that the world is a terrible, incomprehensible mess, and second, that there is almost certainly nothing that can be done about it. If everything is as good as dead, or as good as gone, it will be treated as such. In the process, the texts of life will become corpses to dissect, and meaning will become less about inner transformation and more about constructing sentences in very particular, predetermined ways. A philosophy of despair, which for Chesterton is tantamount to a philosophy built upon "mental breakdown," restricts meaning to the merely obvious. It sticks only to what is self-evident to the person doing the reading.[87]

81. Ibid.

82. Ibid., 364.

83. Ibid., 362.

84. Chesterton, *Collected Works, Volume 5*, 65.

85. Ibid.

86. Ibid.

87. Chesterton, *Collected Works, Volume 3*, 178.

This idea is powerfully extended by Chesterton's remark, on seeing "the lights of Broadway by night," that it would appear to be "a garden of glorious wonders . . . to any one who was lucky enough to be unable to read."[88] The trouble with coming into contact with the "Tree of Knowledge," which symbolizes experience and pride for Chesterton, is that the wonders of the world are so easily concealed or tainted by our instance that the world should be precisely as we have made it to be: the neon advertisements in the city, for instance, should be just what they appear to be and nothing more.[89] In the process of slipping into this sleep of custom, we become like the puppets in the first act of Chesterton's *The Surprise*; we become "everything except alive."[90] We may be "intelligent, complex, combative, brilliant, bursting with life," but, without wonder and the freedom to perceive things in a new light, we "are not alive."[91] We therefore need something comparable to the intervention of the Author in *The Surprise*, who sets his creations free from custom and complacency.

What is perhaps most fascinating about Chesterton's heavenly or paradisiacal hermeneutic is that he does not argue for any kind of intervention of some external supernatural force. After all, he does not believe in any real divide between a sacred order and a secular one. The fact is that his Father Brown seems almost to be dismissing the supernatural precisely to affirm it in the natural; he denies it as an alternative reality—a utopian interjection into this world—to affirm the fact that it permeates all of reality. Alison Milbank argues that Chesterton's Father Brown stories are

> object-lessons in the fantastic, because each begins in a credible world of service flats, tea-shops or seaside resorts out of season, but then proceeds to destabilize that comfortable sense of normality by a mysterious fact that seems inexplicable in rational terms: a dead body vanishes from a room and appears in a tree; an arrow from heaven shoots someone; a dagger flies; an automaton commits a murder; the sun kills its worshipper. The reader is faced with a seemingly supernatural incursion into the real and tries to find an explanation in which both normal context and supernatural fact can be accommodated.[92]

It is Father Brown who injects common sense into the apparent incongruity between the natural and the supernatural, into the dichotomy

88. Chesterton, *Collected Works, Volume 21*, 62.

89. Ibid., 63.

90. Chesterton, *The Surprise*, 43.

91. Ibid.

92. Milbank, *Chesterton and Tolkien as Theologians*, 46.

of nature and grace. Ironically, it is the believer in miracles who ends up demonstrating that no miracle has taken place.[93] Both Stephen Clark and Žižek observe that Chesterton's preference is always for the "prosaic explanation."[94] However, Chesterton's prosaic explanations are not meant to detract from the possibility of the miraculous or the mysterious in any way. Rather, they highlight the very miraculousness of the prosaic. This is exactly what Chestertonian recognition is: a sudden comprehension of the impossibly high value of the very fact that we are here, perceiving what we are perceiving. Chesterton does not seem to be all that picky about the nature of the intervention or mediation that brings about this recognition. In "The Man with Two Legs," it is violence that does the trick for the protagonist. But that Chesterton demonstrates this violence in a story rather than in action suggests that his primary medium for engaging with the world is through the imagination—the second facet of this Chestertonian account of mediation.

For Chesterton, reason and imagination are not at odds. In fact, as Andrew Davison notes, "*human reason is imaginative.*"[95] Chesterton points out that imagination does not stand over and against reason, but confirms it. There are some things that we can imagine, of course, like "a moon without a tide, or a tide without a moon," but reason does not permit us to imagine other things. "We cannot imagine two and two not making four."[96] Imagination confirms that "[f]our and 2 + 2 are not two things; they are one thing stated in two different ways."[97] Consequently, while imagination is usually understood as a capacity of seeing one thing as another, Chesterton suggests that a particularly "wild and soaring sort of imagination" is that which allows one to "see what is there."[98] Imagination may be conceived as a faculty for seeing a thing as something else, precisely to see a thing as if it is truly itself, as in the joke by Groucho Marx: "This man may look like an idiot and act like an idiot, but don't let that fool you—he really is an idiot." This reality may look like reality and act like reality, but don't be fooled: *it really is reality.*

Chesterton notices that some people tend to talk of "actual things that happened—dawn and death and so on—as if *they* were rational and

93. Ibid., 47.

94. Clark, *G. K. Chesterton*, 13; Žižek, "The Fear of Four Words," 25.

95. Davison. "Introduction," xxv.

96. Chesterton, *Illustrated London News*, March 22, 1924.

97. Ibid.

98. Chesterton, *The Everlasting Man*, 14.

inevitable."[99] They talk "as if the fact that trees bear fruit were just as *necessary* as the fact that two and one trees make three. But it is not."[100] Thus, Chesterton introduces the "test of fairyland" which allows us to imagine, within reason, things being other than what they are, no matter how unlikely: "trees not growing fruit," but instead growing "candlesticks" or "tigers hanging on by the tail."[101] Through imagination, we discover with a shock that it is not necessity that makes leaves grow on trees, but magic. Just because "one incomprehensible thing constantly follows another incomprehensible thing," it does not mean that "the two together somehow make up a comprehensible thing."[102]

Imagination allows us to see that many of the "terms used in the science books, 'law,' 'necessity,' 'order,' 'tendency,' and so on, are really unintellectual, because they assume an inner synthesis, which we do not possess."[103] The words we find in fairy tales, "'charm,' 'spell,' 'enchantment,'" make much more sense because "they express the arbitrariness of the fact and its mystery. A tree grows fruit because it is a *magic* tree. Water runs downhill because it is bewitched. The sun shines because it is bewitched."[104] We imagine that things can be otherwise until confronted with the monstrous surprise that things are. We entertain mental impossibilities to discover bodily miracles and incarnate realities. And this, it turns out, is not a "fancy derived from the fairy tales; on the contrary, all the fire of the fairy tales is derived from this"—the very world we live in.[105] Probability is present, of course. It may be very likely, as our experience tells us, that the sun will rise every morning. But its likelihood does not explain away its actual contingency. For Chesterton, therefore, imagination becomes a way to return us to the original astonishment of the child who finds that "[m]ere life is interesting enough." It helps us to return to the "higher agnosticism" called "[i]gnorance."[106]

This ignorance, of course, is related to the conjoined-twin virtues of humility and gratitude. I have mentioned these already, but it is worth revisiting them briefly to consider their place in this account of mediation. First, humility is regarded by Chesterton as the virtue that counteracts "the unpardonable wrong of casual resignation"—the kind of resignation that

99. Chesterton, *Collected Works, Volume 1*, 254.

100. Ibid.

101. Ibid.

102. Ibid., 255.

103. Ibid., 256.

104. Ibid.

105. Ibid., 257.

106. Ibid.

ends up regarding the sun as the mere "light of common day" rather, as an initial apprehension of it would show, than as something truly "fearful." [107] Humility is the beginning of enjoyment and is the thing that is "for ever re-newing the earth and the stars." [108] "Humility is the mother of giants" and of gigantesque epiphanies. [109] It is the virtue that is "perpetually putting us back in the primal darkness" where we can encounter "all light" as "lightning, startling and instantaneous." [110] Chesterton writes, "Until we understand the original dark, in which we have neither sight nor expectation, we can give no hearty and childlike praise to the splendid sensationalism of things." [111] Humility means that "[t]he man who destroys himself creates the universe. To the humble man, and to the humble man alone, the sun is really the sun; to the humble man, and to the humble man alone, the sea is really a sea. When he looks at all the faces in the street, he does not only realize that men are alive, he realizes with a dramatic pleasure that they are not dead." [112]

Humility is paradoxical because it affirms the rise of the fallen, the reclaiming of reality to the one who loses it and, in the drama of meaning, the discovery of meaning even in the face of its elusiveness or its loss. The one who loses his life finds it. Humility is coupled with gratitude because it affirms the simple, astonishing fact of being. And no sane person, in Ches-terton's view at least, should prefer nonexistence to existence, even a bad existence. The "highest form of thought" for him is "thanks." [113] "[G]ratitude is happiness doubled by wonder." [114] In fact, the "test for all happiness is gratitude." [115] "The whole object of art, of real romance—and above all, of real religion—is to prevent people from losing the humility and gratitude which are thankful for daylight and daily bread" [116]

With these four aspects in place—recognition, imagination, humility, and gratitude—it becomes possible to offer a definition of Chestertonian mediation. In its simplest sense, Chestertonian mediation, as that which facilitates our encounter with reality, is that which returns us to wonder and astonishment, and opens us up to surprise. It helps us to recover a sense of

107. Ibid., 128.

108. Ibid., 127–28.

109. Chesterton, *The Annotated Innocence of Father Brown*, 194.

110. Chesterton, *Collected Works, Volume 1*, 128.

111. Ibid.

112. Ibid.

113. Chesterton, *Collected Works, Volume 20*, 463.

114. Ibid.

115. Chesterton, *Collected Works, Volume 1*, 258.

116. Ibid.

both the absolute smallness and the infinite value of the individual. Chestertonian mediation is a matter of "proportion."[117]

The notion of proportion is, in fact, profoundly important for coming to grips with all hermeneutics, especially if we take Chesterton's lead. It is really "the preservation of proportion in the mind" that "is the only thing that keeps a man from narrow-mindedness."[118] "[P]roportion . . . is the principle of all reality"; it is the principle most important for our engagement with reality.[119] We "must keep the enormous proportions of a normal thing clear of various modifications and degrees and doubts more or less reasonable, like clouds clinging to a mountain."[120] It is proportion, a visual metaphor expressing what it means to get a grip on how we understand, that ensures that we "draw" the picture as well as we can, rather than turning it into something it is not.[121] If, for instance, "any artist will try to make a picture of the sunrise, he will find that a sunrise depends on proportion and not merely on light."[122]

The "artist will seize one moment when the sunrise is at its best" and will "fix the fading colour" and "freeze the crumbling clouds."[123] "He will call a halt to progress in the name of proportion, because at that moment it has that precise proportion which is the vision of beauty."[124] A proportion, which is not exactly "perfection" is precisely a "picture" (a mediation that seeks to be faithful to reality) and not a "pattern" (a concealment of reality behind a façade of false impressions and hidden agendas).[125] As much as proportion is the tool of the artist, it is the tool of the poet and hermeneut who seek fidelity to reality without presuming to do complete justice to it.[126] Proportion suggests "spiritual balance."[127] It is what keeps the "intellectual hunger for the truth" in check.[128]

Again, all hermeneutics is concerned with this issue of proportion. It deals with the relationship of one idea to others. It is the pursuit of

117. Chesterton, *Illustrated London News*, July 20, 1918.

118. Chesterton, *Illustrated London News*, November 12, 1932.

119. Chesterton, *The Everlasting Man*, 36.

120. Ibid., 53.

121. Chesterton, *Illustrated London News*, March 9, 1935.

122. Chesterton, *Collected Works, Volume 1*, 258.

123. Ibid.

124. Chesterton, *Illustrated London News*, May 31, 1924.

125. Chesterton, *Collected Works, Volume 5*, 74.

126. Chesterton, *Chesterton Day by Day*, 108.

127. Chesterton, "Dickens."

128. Chesterton, *Selected Works*, 930.

proportion that elects, for instance, the primacy of the love of God and man over all other commandments from the Scriptures, just as it is proportion that establishes order and hierarchy in an artistic composition. This sense of proportion does not, however, equate to a sense of prediction. Even a body in perfect proportion is likely to startle us with its asymmetry.[129] If one's hermeneutic prioritizes picture over pattern, proportion should follow suit.

For Chesterton, proportion, like the hermeneutic event, is primarily about recognizing one's own position in the world: "There is only one really dangerous way of making a mountain out of a molehill. It is the danger of a man being so excited about a molehill that he forgets he is on a mountain."[130] Meaning, as a negotiation between elements in the drama of being, will always be found in "[e]nclosures" and navigated within constraints.[131] "Bars and barriers" are not just accidental components of the drama of meaning, but are utterly essential to its existence.[132] Chesterton sets up an analogy between his hat and his religion to explain the importance of boundaries even when it comes to the world of ideas:

> I quite understand what modern people mean when they say that they like large and liberal religion. I do myself. In the same way I like a large and liberal hat. There are hats that are too tight for the human head; there are religions too tight for the human heart. My faith is full of liberties; and occasionally I even take liberties with those liberties. As for my hat, it is latitudinarian almost to the point of being formless. Still, my hat is my hat, not an umbrella or a tent or a public pavilion. My religion is my religion, a positive statement about the universe which can be asserted, understood, and denied.[133]

A philosophy of "mixtures"—a philosophy that is too formless to be explained, and utterly disproportionate—will only result in conceptual "mud," as all the unique colors of the world blend to form a veritable vision of solipsistic meaninglessness. And, for Chesterton, if the "loss of meaning" meant anything it would be "to the disadvantage of the loser, and not of the meaning."[134] The corollary holds: finding meaning is to the advantage of the one who finds it.

---

129. Chesterton, *Collected Works, Volume 1*, 285–86.
130. Chesterton, *Illustrated London News*, July 20, 1918.
131. Chesterton, *Illustrated London News*, December 15, 1928.
132. Chesterton, *Daily News*, September 7, 1907.
133. Ibid.
134. Ibid.

This is the true gift, the gift of finding one's place in the world; of discovering the "gifts" of the "ancient world" that are "so great that the world has ever since been striving in vain to repay them, if only by plagiarism": when we find our position in relation to "divine authority" and "divine aid," "we come to the unfathomable idea of grace and the gift of faith" that allows us to engage with the world. It is by this faith—faith as a failure of our own egotism—that we discover "that life is a gift of God immensely valuable and immensely valued."[135] This is something that "anybody can prove . . . by putting a pistol to the head of a pessimist."[136] The pistol to the head of the pessimist who is writing this book, though, is not a literal one. It is found in the words—in the jokes, illustrations, images, paradoxes, stories and ideas—of G. K. Chesterton.

Concluding Remarks: On Reading Chesterton Again

It is this same Chesterton, when remarking on the fine art of "reporting speeches," who claims that "[w]e should not object, perhaps, to the reporter making the speeches much shorter than they are; but we do object to his making all the speeches much worse than they are. And the method which he employs is one which is dangerously unjust."[137] He goes on:

> When a statesman or philosopher makes an important speech, there are several courses which the reporter might take without being unreasonable. Perhaps the most reasonable course of all would be not to report the speech at all. Let the world live and love, and marry and give in marriage, without that particular speech, as they did (in some desperate way) in the days when there were no newspapers. A second course would be to report a small part of it; but to get that right. A third course, far better if you can do it, is to understand the main purpose and argument of the speech, and report that in a clear and logical language of your own.[138]

This is sound advice for interpreting speeches and works just as well for interpreting Chesterton. I have tried my utmost to stick to the third course as closely as I have been able, having utterly failed to uphold his first piece of advice. Chesterton is clear that the usual way of reporting speeches

---

135. Chesterton, *The Everlasting Man*, 79; *Collected Works, Volume 3*, 95.
136. Chesterton, *Collected Works, Volume 3*, 177.
137. Chesterton, *Illustrated London News*, June 29, 1907.
138. Ibid.

is found in gravitating only to the part of the speech that is extravagant and sensational. This has often happened in the way that people have interpreted Chesterton.

To read Chesterton afresh means recognizing that he has, perhaps more than many of his literary contemporaries, been deeply neglected and often, when not neglected, simply misunderstood. This eventuality is ironic considering his impressive output and his endless attempts at explaining himself via every kind of repetition. The misunderstandings of him, I believe, are owed largely to the fact that many are too quick to apply wrong-headed labels to his work—a point echoed by a number of scholars.[139] These same scholars note that he is, for instance, characterized as a master without a masterpiece, as a metaphysical jester-philosopher whose concern was with eternal rather than temporal things, and as a political idealist who was out of step with mainstream political thought. Rather contradictorily, he has also been accused of being overly concerned with the temporal, and too caught up in mainstream politics. The implication here is that he is no longer relevant. He has been called a saint, but also a bigot, imperialist, and drunk. He has been thought of as a mere stylist and even an anti-intellectualist despite his frequent attacks on mere style and on poor thinking.

Chesterton himself warns us of the tendency to "fix some person with a definite label, and then proceed to deduce everything from the label and nothing from the person."[140] He goes on to point out that many have enthusiastically referred to him as a "mediaevalist" without bothering to notice that people believe in specific ideas rather than in generic spans of time. Even if an idea happened to come from the mediaeval period, for instance, it would not mean that the person who agrees with that idea would necessarily agree with everything that happened in that entire period in time. Taking this seriously, whatever labels we may wish to apply to Chesterton, it should be clear that any overly monolithic perspective on his life and work must automatically be regarded as dubious. Chesterton is simply, in the very best sense, "unclassifiable."[141] He demands to be treated as one who "thinks in terms of thought" rather than merely by association with any particular era or general body of ideas.[142]

A. L. Maycock keeps this in mind as he tackles Chesterton's work, but goes on to note a further difficulty in writing about him: "there is so much of him. Any sentence that one writes about him could be expanded into a

139. Clark, 3; Dale, *The Outline of Sanity*, 20–22; Wood, *G. K. Chesterton*, 3.

140. Chesterton, *Illustrated London News*, January 5, 1929.

141. Lea, *The Wild Knight of Battersea*, 52.

142. Chesterton, Illustrated London News, January 5, 1929.

paragraph; any paragraph into an essay; and any essay into a book."[143] "Writing about G. K. Chesterton is like climbing a mountain," writes F. A. Lea; "The end seems continually to be in sight, or to lie just over the next crest; always when the crest is reached another unfolds itself beyond that. And at last one is forced to leave off out of sheer fatigue and because the daylight is all but spent."[144] Also, as has already been noted, Chesterton paints his ideas in detailed pictures rather than using simplistic patterns or diagrams. Then, as Patrick Braybrooke suggests, he often appears to have chosen deliberate obscurity by siding with complexity.[145]

This list of complications makes sense especially given that Chesterton was really "the sworn enemy of specialization"[146] and was therefore always destined to be difficult to categorize.[147] If we are to take Chesterton as Chesterton, we need to understand that he is, in essence, as impossible to summarize as he is to classify. On once being told that he "[seemed] to know everything," Chesterton responded, "I know nothing ... I am a journalist."[148] "I am a journalist," Chesterton offers, "and am so vastly ignorant of many things, but because I am a journalist, I write and talk about them all."[149] He once claimed that he had no desire for the kind of immortality that the pursuit of a more serious literary career might have afforded him, but was instead only interested "in the present stress of life as it is."[150] This preoccupation with the daily, which explains Chesterton's supposed timelessness, remains crucial to understanding what it was that he was trying to achieve. Still, we need to take Chesterton's self-deprecation as lightly as he took it. On the vast range of subjects he covered, as should be evident in the ground covered here, he demonstrated a consistent and bewildering depth of wisdom and insight. He was, without any doubt, a formidable polymath.

Many have therefore tried to sum up their experience of reading Chesterton without too much restriction. Alberto Manguel, for one, remarks that when "[r]eading Chesterton, we are overwhelmed by a remarkable sense of happiness. . . . Words bounce and spark lights off one another as if a clockwork toy had suddenly come to life, clicking and whirring with common

143. Maycock, "Introduction," 79.

144. Lea, *The Wild Knight of Battersea*, 90.

145. Braybrooke, *Gilbert Keith Chesterton*, 5.

146. Kelman, *Among Famous Books*, 266

147. West, *G. K. Chesterton*, 23.

148. Ffinch, *G. K. Chesterton*, 175.

149. Quoted in Ker, *G. K. Chesterton*, 434.

150. Maycock, "Introduction," 14.

sense, that most surprising of marvels."[151] Many who read Chesterton have an experience that echoes Manguel's, although it would be unwise to assume the absolute universality of such an experience. There is undoubtedly a profound sense of delight to be discovered in and through Chesterton, but there is critique too, and also an almost apocalyptic urgency in places. There is, even if we may not want to admit it, darkness, although it is a darkness that never overwhelms.

In Chesterton's own lifetime, much was said to affirm his penchant for conveying delight. For example, Arthur Thorn, writing in 1922, says that Chesterton has done more than any writer of his age "to stimulate and preserve the primitive sense of wonder and joy in human life. . . . He knows, as well as anybody has ever known, that the life of man goes wrong simply because we are too lazy to be pleased with simple, fundamental things."[152] Chesterton's ideal, Thorn continues, is "the *real*, not merely the possible."[153] Maguel's and Thorn's readings certainly point us in a better direction than the simplistic labels applied to him by many others. Still, I must hasten to add that they do tend to neglect Chesterton's ability to address the full spectrum of the human experience, and not only its more blithe and blissful facets. If we forget this, we may be tempted to dismiss him as a sentimentalist or romantic idealist.

Maisie Ward asks what the "whole Chesterton" might be, both "as a man and as a writer" and thereafter provides a range of opinions. Chesterton is "a child . . . a Peter Pan, who refused to grow up"; a sociologist, distributist, and "theologian"; a "legend" of "English literature."[154] These other descriptions may be closer to the truth and yet they still fail to explain him. We may call Chesterton many other things—an apologist, essayist, novelist, playwright, or poet—but such generalizations still get no closer to summing up his unique contribution to the world of letters. They address questions of genre, but not of philosophy. Even the term *journalist* that he used more often to describe himself than any other label is inadequate for indicating how we ought to read him today. What one finds, as Ward notes about the various things written of Chesterton, is a "universal agreement that Chesterton is a very great man," but also "the widest disagreement as to wherein his greatness lay."[155]

---

151. Manguel, *Into the Looking-Glass Wood*, 203.

152. Thorn, "Preface," v.

153. Ibid.

154. Ward, *Return to Chesterton*, 5–6.

155. Ibid., 6.

The trouble we may have with pinning down what Chesterton was about appropriately turns out to be the trouble we find with all communication and all hermeneutics. In saying anything we will inevitably say both too little and too much. A thing is always what it is more than what is said about it. But is this really such a terrible thing? Chesterton himself proposes that there is a kind of "splendour" to be found even in "being misunderstood," for "if men misunderstand you, they are certain to fight you badly; they are certain to think you weak where you are strong and strong where you are weak. They are certain to go out against a bird with nets and against a fish with arrows."[156] He then claims that "to be misunderstood is to be incalculable. And to be incalculable is to be a god."[157] In the end, I know that in writing about Chesterton I too have risked reducing him to a set of neat descriptors and propositions, and thus have also risked presenting a tame version of his wild, coruscating and incisive intellect. I have done this, however, in the hope of having Chesterton misunderstood afresh. He must remain the master of surprises, and if we are not being surprised by him, perhaps we need to ask ourselves whether we are reading him at all.

And so I have offered this book as a philosophical tour of Chesterton's call to a "legendary life" of "splendid talents . . . in a thrilling theatre of events," of "vast remedies" sought, of defenses uttered with "dramatic pronouncements," of fervent belief "in one's own capacity and one's own cause," of the enjoyment of "clean habits and heroic health," and "personal dignity."[158] I have endeavored to provide a sense of Chesterton's unique way of seeing things by scrutinizing his way of reading words and their possible incarnation and enactment in the world. In the end, as should be clear by now, the point of this would be precisely to provide a gateway to the gift of being, which includes the gift of an interpretive instinct. For "all gates are gates of humility" and a sense of some primary joy comes from encountering the world and its disclosures as if for the first time.[159]

One last image from Chesterton's writings perfectly illustrates what he tries to achieve in all of his work. Chesterton revels at the way that Dickens manages to endow ordinary, everyday objects with "demoniac life" such that "things seem more actual than they really are."[160] For example, Dickens "mentions among the coffee-shops into which he crept in those wretched days on St. Martin's Lane, [one] 'of which I only recollect that it stood near

---

156. Chesterton, *Daily* News, September 12, 1903.

157. Ibid.

158. Chesterton, *The Man Who Was Orthodox*, 83.

159. Chesterton, *Collected Works, Volume 20*, 234.

160. Chesterton, *Charles Dickens*, 47.

the church, and that in the door there was an oval glass plate with COF-FEE ROOM painted on it, addressed towards the street." Dickens, though, encounters this inscription on the glass from the wrong side, and so reads it backwards—MOOR EEFFOC. The result is shock.

Chesterton suggests that this "wild word, 'Moor Eeffoc,' is the motto of all effective realism; it is the masterpiece of the good realistic principle—the principle that the most fantastic thing of all is often the precise fact."[161] For Chesterton, encountering a world of precise facts as if for the first time—meeting an astonishing, mysterious revelation with the understanding that "there is no way in which a man can earn a star or deserve a sunset"[162]—is exactly what it means to see things as they are.

161. Ibid., 47–48.
162. Chesterton, *Saint Thomas Aquinas, Saint Francis of Assisi*, 248.

Bibliography

Agamben, Giorgio. *The Signature of All Things: On Method.* Translated by Luca D'Isanto and Kevin Attel. New York: Zone, 2009.

Ahlquist, Dale. *Common Sense 101: Lessons from G. K. Chesterton.* San Francisco: Ignatius, 2006.

———. *G. K. Chesterton: The Apostle of Common Sense.* San Francisco: Ignatius, 2003.

Allen, R. E. "Anamnesis in Plato's *Meno* and *Phaedo.*" *The Review of Metaphysics* 13 (1959) 165–74.

Aquinas, Thomas. *Selected Philosophical Texts.* Edited and translated by T. Gilby. London: Oxford University Press, 1951.

Aristotle. *Metaphysics.* Translated by H. Lawson-Tancred. London: Penguin, 2004.

Arnold, Matthew. *Essays, Literary and Critical.* London: Dent & Sons, 1906.

Balthasar, Hans Urs von. *Theo-Drama: Theological Dramatic Theory, Volume 5: The Last Act.* Translated by G. Harrison. San Francisco: Ignatius, 1998.

———. "Transcendentality and Gestalt." *Communio* 11 (1984) 29–39.

Barthes, R. "The Death of the Author." Translated by R. Howard, 1977. http://evans-experientialism.freewebspace.com/barthes06.htm. Accessed: 29 April 2010.

Belloc, Joseph Hillaire. *The Great Heresies,* 1938. https://www.cs.cmu.edu/~spok/metabook/heresies.html.

———. *On the Place of Gilbert Chesterton in English Letters.* London: Sheed & Ward, 1940.

Bergson, Henri. *Laughter: An Essay on the Meaning of the Comic.* Translated by Cloudesley Brereton and Fred Rothwell. New York: MacMillain, 1914.

Blackstock, Alan R. *The Rhetoric of Redemption: Chesterton, Ethical Criticism, and the Common Man.* New York: Lang, 2012.

Baudrillard, Jean. *Simulacra and Simulation.* Translated by S. F. Glaser. Ann Arbor, MI: University of Michigan, 1994.

Braybrooke, Patrick. *Gilbert Keith Chesterton.* London: Chelsea, 1922.

Brecht, B. "Alienation Effects in Chinese Acting." In *Brecht on Theatre,* translated and edited by J. Willett, 91–99. New York: Hill & Wang, 1964.

Burke, Edmund. *A Philosophical Enquiry into the Sublime and the Beautiful.* Oxford: Oxford University Press, 2015.

Burrell, David. *Deconstructing Theodicy.* Grand Rapids: Brazos, 2008.

Cammaerts, Émile. *The Laughing Prophet: The Seven Virtues of G. K. Chesterton.* London: Metheuen, 1937.

Capon, Robert Farrar. *Genesis, The Movie.* Grand Rapids: Eerdmans, 2004.

———. *The Romance of the Word.* Grand Rapids: Eerdmans, 1995.

Chambers, Whittaker. *Ghosts on the Roof: Selected Essays,* edited by T. Teachout. New Brunswick: Transaction, 1996.

Chesterton, G. K. *The Annotated Innocence of Father Brown.* Edited by Martin Garner. Mineola, NY: Dover, 1998.

———. *Alarms and Discursions.* 1910. Reprint. London: Dodo, 2011.

———. *All Things Considered.* 1908. Reprint. Sioux Falls, SD: NuVision, 2009.

———. *Appreciations and Criticisms of the Works of Charles Dickens.* London: Dent and Sons, 1911.

———. *Autobiography.* 1936. Reprint. San Francisco: Ignatius, 2006.

———. *The Ball and the Cross.* 1910. Reprint. Nashville: Torode, 2010.

———. *Charles Dickens: A Critical Study.* London: Dodd & Mead, 1906.

———. *Collected Works, Volume 1: Heretics, Orthodoxy, The Blatchford Controversies.* San Francisco: Ignatius, 1986.

———. *Collected Works, Volume 3: The Catholic Church and Conversion, The Thing: Why I am a Catholic, The Well and the Shallows, The Way of the Cross, and Others.* San Francisco: Ignatius, 1990.

———. *Collected Works, Volume 4: What's Wrong with the World, The Superstition of Divorce, Eugenics and Other Evils, and Others.* San Francisco: Ignatius, 1987.

———. *Collected Works, Volume 11: Plays, Chesterton on Shaw.* San Francisco: Ignatius, 1989.

———. *Collected Works, Volume 13: Father Brown Stories.* San Francisco: Ignatius, 2010.

———. *Collected Works, Volume 14: Short Stories, Fairy Tales, Mystery Stories, Illustrations.* San Francisco: Ignatius, 2012.

———. *Collected Works, Volume 20: Christendom in Dublin, Irish Impressions, The New Jerusalem, A Short History of England.* San Francisco: Ignatius, 2001.

———. *Collected Works, Volume 21: What I Saw in America, The Resurrection of Rome, Sidelights.* San Francisco: Ignatius, 1990.

———. *Collected Works, Volume 27: The Illustrated London News 1905–1907.* Edited by Lawrence J. Clipper. San Francisco: Ignatius, 1986.

———. *Collected Works, Volume 28: The Illustrated London News 1908–1910.* Edited by Lawrence J. Clipper. San Francisco: Ignatius, 1987.

———. *Collected Works, Volume 29: The Illustrated London News 1911–1913.* Edited by Lawrence J. Clipper. San Francisco: Ignatius, 1988.

———. *Collected Works, Volume 30: The Illustrated London News 1914–1916.* Edited by Lawrence J. Clipper. San Francisco: Ignatius, 1988.

———. *Collected Works, Volume 31: The Illustrated London News 1917–1919.* Edited by Lawrence J. Clipper. San Francisco: Ignatius, 1989.

———*Collected Works, Volume 32: The Illustrated London News 1920–1922.* Edited by Lawrence J. Clipper. San Francisco: Ignatius, 1989.

———. *Collected Works, Volume 33: The Illustrated London News 1923–1935.* Edited by Lawrence J. Clipper. San Francisco: Ignatius, 1990.

———. *Collected Works, Volume 34: The Illustrated London News 1926–1928.* Edited by Lawrence J. Clipper. San Francisco: Ignatius, 1991.

———*Collected Works, Volume 35: The Illustrated London News 1929–1931.* Edited by Lawrence J. Clipper. San Francisco: Ignatius, 1991.

———. *Collected Works, Volume 36: The Illustrated London News 1932–1934.* Edited by Lawrence J. Clipper. San Francisco: Ignatius, 2011.

―――. *Collected Works, Volume 37: The Illustrated London News 1935–1936.* Edited by Lawrence J. Clipper. San Francisco: Ignatius, 2012.

―――. *The Common Man.* New York: Sheed & Ward, 1950.

―――. *The Coloured Lands.* 1938. Reprint. Edited by Maisie Ward. Mineola: Dover, 2009.

―――. *Chesterton Day by Day: The Wit and Wisdom of G. K. Chesterton.* Edited by Michael W. Perry. Seattle: Inkling, 2002.

―――. *The Defendant.* London: Brimley Johnson, 1902.

―――. *In Defense of Sanity.* Edited by Dale Alquist, Joseph Pearce, and Aidan Mackey. San Francisco: Ignatius, 2011.

―――. "Dickens: Encyclopaedia Britannica," 1929. http://www.cse.dmu.ac.uk/~mward /gkc/books/dickens_Britannica.txt.

―――. *Essential Writings.* Edited by W. Griffin. New York: Orbis, 2003.

―――. *Eugenics and Other Evils.* London: Cassell, 1922.

―――. *The Everlasting Man.* 1925. Reprint. San Francisco: Ignatius, 1993.

―――. *Father Brown: Selected Stories.* London: Collector's Library, 2003.

―――. "The French Revolution and the Irish." 1917. http://www.readbookonline.net/ readOnLine/20157/.

―――. *A Handful of Authors.* Edited by Dorothy Collins. New York: Sheed & Ward, 1953.

―――. "Humour, Encyclopedia Britannica." 1929. http://www.cse.dmu.ac.uk/~m ward/gkc/books/Humour.html.

―――. "The Humour of King Herod." 1920. http://www.cse.dmu.ac.uk/~mward/gkc/ books/The_Uses_of_Diversity.html#herod.

―――. *The Innocence of Father Brown.* New York: Dodd, Mead and Co., 1911.

―――. "Introduction." In *Essays, Literary and Critical* by Matthew Arnold, ix–xiv. London: Dent & Sons, 1906.

―――. *Irish Impressions.* New York: Lane, 1919.

―――. *The Man Who Knew Too Much.* 1922. Reprint. London: Dover, 2003.

―――. *The Man Who Was Orthodox.* Edited by A. L. Maycock. London: Dobson, 1963.

―――. *The Man Who Was Thursday.* London: Atlantic, 2008.

―――. *A Miscellany of Men.* London: Methuen, 1912.

―――. "On Seriousness." 1920. http://www.cse.dmu.ac.uk/~mward/gkc/books/The_ Uses_of_Diversity.html#seriousness.

―――. *Orthodoxy: The Annotated Edition.* Edited by C. M. Kibler. Lenoir, NC: Reformation, 2002.

―――. *Poems for All Seasons.* Edited by Stephen Medcalf. London: Pimlico, 2004.

―――. *The Return of Don Quixote.* 1927. Reprint. Looe, UK: House of Stratus, 2008.

―――. *Robert Browning.* London: MacMillan, 1903.

―――. *Robert Browning, Draft and Printer's Proofs.* British Library Manuscript Catalogue 73244 A-E.

―――. *Robert Louis Stevenson, Draft and Printer's Proofs.* British Library Manuscript Catalogue 73260 A-B.

―――. *G. F. Watts.* London: Duckworth, 1904.

―――. *Magic.* 1913. Reprint. Rockville, MD: Wildside, 2006.

―――. *Saint Thomas Aquinas, Saint Francis of Assisi.* San Francisco: Ignatius, 2002.

―――. *The Selected Works of G. K. Chesterton: Napoleon of Notting Hill, The Club of Queer Trades, The Man Who Was Thursday, The Innocence of Father Brown,*

Manalive, The Wisdom of Father Brown, The Man Who Knew Too Much, The Incredulity of Father Brown, The Poet and The Lunatics, and The Scandal of Father Brown. London: Wordsworth, 2008.

———. *Stories, Essays, and Poems*. London: Dent & Sons, 1935.

———. *The Surprise*. London: Sheed & Ward, 1952.

———. *The Soul of Wit: G. K. Chesterton on Shakespeare*. Edited by Dale Ahlquist. Mineola, NY: Dover, 2012.

———. *Tales of the Long Bow*, 1925. http://gutenberg.net.au/ebooks01/0100321h.html.

———. *Tremendous Trifles*. 1909. Reprint. Mineola, NY: Dover, 2007.

———. *Twelve Types*. 1902. Reprint. Fairford, UK: Echo Library, 2008.

———. *Varied Types*. 1908. Reprint. New York: Dodd, Mead & Co., 1915.

———. *The Victorian Age in Literature*. New York: Holt, 1913.

———. *What's Wrong with the World*. 1910. Reprint. San Francisco: Ignatius, 1994.

———. *William Blake*. London: Duckworth, 1910.

———. *A Year with G. K. Chesterton: 365 Days of Wit, Wisdom, and Wonder*. Edited by Kevin Belmonte. Nashville: Thomas Nelson, 2012.

Clark, Stephen R. L. *G. K. Chesterton: Thinking Backwards, Looking Forwards*. London: Templeton Foundation, 2006.

Clarke, W. N. *Explorations in Metaphysics*. South Bend, IN: University of Notre Dame, 1994.

Cone, Steven D. *An Ocean Vast of Blessing: A Theology of Grace*. Veritas. Eugene, OR: Cascade, 2014.

Conlon, D. J., ed. *G. K. Chesterton: A Half Century of Views*. Oxford: Oxford University Press, 1987.

Crawford, L. "Viktor Shklovskij: Différance in Defamiliarization." *Comparative Literature* 36 (1984) 209–19.

Dale, Alzina Stone. *The Outline of Sanity: A Life of G. K. Chesterton*. Grand Rapids: Eerdmans, 1982.

Davis, Creston, ed. *The Monstrosity of Christ: Paradox or Dialectic?* Cambridge: MIT, 2009.

Davison, Andrew, ed. *Imaginative Apologetics: Theology, Philosophy and the Catholic Tradition*. London: SCM, 2011.

———. "Introduction." In *Imaginative Apologetics: Theology, Philosophy and the Catholic Tradition*, edited by Andrew Davison, xxv–xxviii. London: SCM, 2011.

Debord, Guy. *Society of the Spectacle*. Translated by K. Knabb. 2002. www.bopsecrets.org/images/sos.pdf. Accessed 12 June 2012.

Desmond, William. *Being and the Between*. New York: State University of New York, 1995.

———. *Desire, Dialectic, and Otherness: An Essay on Origins*. 2nd ed. Eugene, OR: Cascade, 2013.

Dor, Joel. *Introduction to the Reading of Lacan: The Unconscious Structured Like a Language*. Edited by Judith Feher-Gurewich and Susan Fairfield. New York: Other, 1998.

Eagleton, Terry. *After Theory*. London: Penguin, 2004.

———. *The Event of Literature*. New Haven: Yale University, 2012.

———. *Reason, Faith, and Revolution*. New Haven: Yale University, 2009.

Fagerberg, David. *Chesterton Is Everywhere*. Steubenville: Emmaus Road, 2013.

Farmer, Ann. *Chesterton and the Jews: Friend, Critic, Defender.* Kettering, OH: Angelico, 2015.

Ffinch, Michael. *G. K. Chesterton: A Biography.* San Francisco: Harper & Row, 1986.

Fritzman, J. M. *Hegel.* Cambridge: Polity, 2014.

Fry, Roger. *A Roger Fry Reader.* Edited by C. Reed. Chicago: University of Chicago, 1996.

Gadamer, Hans-Georg. *Truth and Method.* Translated by Joel Weinsheimer and Joel Marshall. 1975. Reprint. London: Continuum, 2004.

Gilson, Étienne. *Being and Some Philosophers.* Toronto: Pontifical Institute of Mediaeval Studies, 1952.

Hart, David Bentley. *The Experience of God: Being, Consciousness, Bliss.* New Haven: Yale University, 2013.

Heidegger, Martin. *Being and Time.* Translated by J. MacQuarrie and E. Robbinson. New York: Harper Perennial, 1962.

Kelman, John. *Among Famous Books.* London: Hodder & Stoughton, 1912.

Kenner, W. H. *Paradox in Chesterton.* London: Sheed & Ward, 1948.

Ker, Ian. *G. K. Chesterton: A Biography.* Oxford: Oxford University, 2011.

Kipling, Rudyard. *Gunga Din and Other Favorite Poems.* New York: Dover, 1990.

Kierkegaard, Søren. *Provocations: The Spiritual Writings of Kierkegaard.* Edited by C. E. Moore. Maryknoll, NY: Orbis, 2002.

Knox, Ronald. "G. K. Chesterton: The Man and His Work." In *G. K. Chesterton: A Half Century of Views,* edited by D. J. Conlon, 46–49. Oxford: Oxford University Press, 1987.

Koren, Israel. *The Mystery of the Earth: Mysticism and Hasidism in the Thought of Martin Buber.* Haifa: University of Haifa, 2005.

Lauer, Quentin. *G. K. Chesterton: Philosopher without Portfolio.* New York: Fordham University, 1988.

Lea, F. A. *The Wild Knight of Battersea: G. K. Chesterton.* London: James Clarke, 1945.

Leibniz, G. W. *Philosophical Papers and Letters.* Translated and edited by L. E. Loemker. Dordecht: Kluwer, 1989.

Lewis, C. S. *Essay Collection: Literature, Philosophy and Short Stories.* London: Harper Collins, 2000.

———. *An Experiment in Criticism.* Cambridge: Cambridge University Press, 1961.

Lodge, Oliver. *The Substance of Faith Allied with Science: A Catechism for Parents and Teachers.* London: Methuen, 1907.

Makaryk, Irene Rima, ed. *Encyclopedia of Contemporary Literary Theory: Approaches, Scholars, Terms.* Toronto: University of Toronto, 1993.

Manguel, Alberto. *Into the Looking-Glass Wood.* London: Bloomsbury, 1998.

Marías, Julián. *History of Philosophy.* Translated by Stanely Appelbaum and Clarence T. Strowbridge. Mineola, NY: Dover, 1967.

Maritan, Jacques. *Introduction to Philosophy.* London: Continuum, 2005.

Maycock, A. L. "Introduction." In *The Man Who Was Orthodox,* by G. K. Chesterton, edited by A.L. Maycock, 13–81. London: Dobson, 1963.

McKee, Robert. *Story.* London: Methuen, 1999.

McCleary, Joseph R. *The Historical Imagination of G. K. Chesterton: Locality, Patriotism, and Nationalism.* New York: Routledge, 2009.

McLuhan, Marshall. "G. K. Chesterton: A Practical Mystic." *Dalhousie Review* 15 (1939) 455–64.

———. "Introduction." In *Paradox in Chesterton* by W. H. Kenner, xi–xxii. London: Sheed & Ward, 1948.

McLuhan, Marshall. *Understanding Media.* London: Routledge, 1964.

Medcalf, Stephen. "Introduction: The Flag of the World." In *Poems for All Purposes*, by G. K. Chesterton, edited by Stephen Medcalf, 1–15. London: Random House, 1994.

Merton, Thomas. *The Thomas Merton Reader.* Edited by Thomas P. McDonnel. New York: Image, 1996.

Milbank, Alison. *Chesterton and Tolkien as Theologians.* London: T. & T. Clark, 2009.

Milbank, John. *Beyond Secular Order: The Representation of Being and the Representation of the People.* Chichester, UK: John Wiley, 2013.

———. "The Double Glory, or Paradox Versus Dialectics." In *The Monstrosity of Christ: Paradox or Dialectic?* edited by Creston Davis, 110–233. Cambridge: MIT, 2009.

———. *Theology and Social Theory: Beyond Secular Reason.* 2nd ed. Oxford: Blackwell, 2006.

Moore, Duston. "Plurivocal Eros: A Metaxological Reading of Plato's *Symposium.*" In *Between System and Poetics: William Desmond and Philosophy after Dialectic*, edited by T. A. F. Kelly, 175–87. Aldershot, UK: Ashgate, 2007.

Newsom, David. *The Victorian World Picture.* London: Murray, 1997.

Newsome, Carol A. *The Book of Job: A Contest of Moral Imaginations.* Oxford: Oxford University Press, 2003.

Nichols, Aidan. *Chesterton, Theologian.* Manchester: Sophia Institute, 2009.

Nietzsche, Friedrich. *The Portable Nietzsche.* Translated and edited by Walter Kaufmann. New York: Viking, 1954.

———. *Twilight of the Idols.* Translated by T. Common. Mineola, NY: Dover, 2012.

Oddie, William. *Chesterton and the Romance of Orthodoxy: The Making of G.K.C., 1874–1908.* Oxford: Oxford University Press, 2008.

Oldershaw, Lucian. *England: A Nation.* London: Brimley Johnson, 1904.

Orwell, George. "Great Is Diana of the Ephesians." In *G. K. Chesterton: A Half Century of Views*, edited by D. J. Conlon, 102–3. Oxford: Oxford University Press, 1987.

Palaver, Wolfgang. *René Girard's Mimetic Theory.* Translated by Gabriel Borrud. East Lansing, MI: Michigan State University, 2013.

Pabst, Adrian. *Metaphysics: The Creation of Hierarchy.* Grand Rapids: Eerdmans, 2012.

Perl, Eric D. *Theophany: The Neoplatonic Philosophy of Dionysius the Areopagite.* Albany, NY: State University of New York, 2007.

Porter, S. E., and J. C. Robinson. *Hermeneutics: An Introduction to Interpretive Theory.* Grand Rapids: Eerdmans, 2011.

Pryas, Phyllis Margaret. "Monologism." In *Encyclopedia of Contemporary Literary Theory: Approaches, Scholars, Terms*, edited by Irene Rima Makaryk, 596. Toronto: University of Toronto, 1993.

Pseudo-Dionysius. *The Complete Works of Pseudo-Dionysius.* Translated by Colm Luibeid: New York: Paulist, 1987.

Reyburn, Duncan. "Chesterton's Ontology and the Ethics of Speculation." *Image & Text* (2011) 50–62.

———. "Chestertonian Dramatology." Doctoral Dissertation. University of Pretoria (2012).

———. "The Beautiful Madness Called Laughter: Chesterton's Theology of Laughter." *The Chesterton Review* 41 (2015) 473–84.

———. "Laughter and the Between." *Radical Orthodoxy: Theology, Philosophy, Politics* 3 (2015) 18–51.

Ricoeur, Paul. *Time and Narrative, Volume 1.* Translated by K. McLaughlin and D. Pellauer. Chicago: Chicago University Press, 1984.

Sayers, Dorothy. "Preface." In *The Surprise* by G. K. Chesterton, 1–12. London: Sheed & Ward, 1952.

Schall, James V. *Schall on Chesterton: Timely Essays on Timeless Paradoxes.* Washington, DC: The Catholic University of America, 2000.

Schindler, D. C. *The Catholicity of Reason.* Grand Rapids: Eerdmans, 2013.

Schleiermacher, Friedrich. *Hermeneutics and Criticism.* Edited by Andrew Bowie. Cambridge: Cambridge University Press, 1998.

Schopenhauer, Arthur. *Essays of Arthur Schopenhauer.* Edited by Thomas Bailey Saunders. New York: Burt, 1902.

Schwartz, Adam. *The Third Spring: G. K. Chesterton, Graham Greene, Christopher Dawson and David Jones.* Washington, DC: Catholic University of America, 2005.

Scott, William Stuart. *Marie Corelli: The Story of a Friendship.* London: Hutchinson, 1955.

Shklovsky, Viktor B. "Art As Technique." In *Russian Formalist Criticism: Four Essays.* Translated by L. T. Lemon and M. J. Reis, 3–24. Lincoln, NE: University of Nebraska, 1965.

Simpson, Christopher Ben. *Religion, Metaphysics, and the Postmodern: William Desmond and John D. Caputo.* Bloomington, IN: Indiana University Press, 2009.

———. *Truth Is a Way: Kierkegaard's Theologian Viatorum.* Veritas. Eugene, OR: Cascade, 2011.

Smith, James K. A. *The Fall of Interpretation: Philosophical Foundations for a Creational Hermeneutic.* 2nd ed. Grand Rapids: Baker Academic, 2012.

Stapleton, Julia. *Christianity, Patriotism, and Nationhood: The England of G. K. Chesterton.* Plymouth, UK: Lexington, 2009.

St. Augustine. *On Christian Doctrine; The Enchirodon.* Translated by J. F. Shaw. Edinburgh: T. & T. Clark, 1873.

Stranger, Richard L. "Václav Havel: Heir to a Spiritual Legacy." *Christian Century*, April 11, 1990, 368–70.

Te Velde, Rudi A. *Participation and Substantiality in Thomas Aquinas.* Leiden: Brill, 1995.

Thorn, Arthur F. "Preface." In *Gilbert Keith Chesterton,* by Patrick Braybrooke, v–vi. London: Chelsea, 1922.

Titterton, W. R. *G. K. Chesterton: A Portrait.* London: Ouseley, 1936.

Tyson, Paul. *Returning to Reality: Christian Platonism for Our Times.* Kalos. Eugene, OR: Cascade, 2015.

Underhill, Evelyn. *Mysticism: A Study in Nature and Development of Spiritual Consciousness.* Stilwell, KA: Digireads, 2005.

Weil, Simone. *Gravity and Grace.* Translated by Mario von der Ruhr. London: Routledge, 1952.

Westphal, Merold. *Whose Community? Which Interpretation? Philosophical Hermeneutics for the Church.* Grand Rapids: Baker Academic, 2009.

Ward, Maisie. *Gilbert Keith Chesterton.* London: Sheed & Ward, 1944.

———. *Return to Chesterton.* London: Sheed & Ward, 1952.

West, Julius. *G. K. Chesterton: A Critical Study.* London: Secker, 1915.

Wild, Robert. *The Tumbler of God: Chesterton as Mystic.* Tacoma, WA: Angelico, 2013.

Willet, J., ed. *Brecht on Theatre.* New York: Hill & Wang, 1964.

Williams, Donald T. *Mere Humanity: G. K. Chesterton, C. S. Lewis, and J. R. R. Tolkien on the Human Condition.* Nashville: B. & H., 2006.

Wood, Ralph C. *Chesterton: The Nightmare Goodness of God.* Waco, TX: Baylor, 2011.

Žižek, Slavoj, and Boris Gunjević. *God in Pain.* London: Verso, 2012.

Žižek, Slavoj. "Dialectical Clarity Versus the Misty Conceit of Paradox." In *The Monstrosity of Christ: Paradox or Dialectic?* edited by Creston Davis, 234–306. Cambridge: MIT, 2009.

———. *Event.* London: Penguin, 2014.

———. "The Fear of Four Words: A Modest Plea for the Hegelian Reading of Christianity." In *The Monstrosity of Christ: Paradox or Dialectic?* edited by Creston Davis, 24–109. Cambridge: MIT, 2009.

———. *In Defense of Lost Causes.* London: Verso, 2008.

———. *Less Than Nothing: Hegel and the Shadow of Dialectical Materialism.* London: Verso, 2012.

———. *The Puppet and the Dwarf: The Perverse Core of Christianity.* Cambridge: MIT, 2003.

———. *Tarrying with the Negative: Kant, Hegel and the Critique of Ideology.* Durham, NC: Duke University Press, 1993.

———. *Violence.* London: Profile, 2009.

Index

Made in the USA
Coppell, TX
09 February 2022

73264766R20180